Assessment and Correction in Elementary Language Arts

C. Glennon Rowell
University of Tennessee

Allyn and Bacon
Boston • London • Toronto • Sydney • Tokyo • Singapore

Series Editor: Virginia Lanigan
Series Editorial Assistant: Nicole DePalma
Production Administrator: Marjorie Payne
Editorial Production Service: Chestnut Hill Enterprises, Inc.
Cover Administrator: Linda Dickinson
Composition Buyer: Linda Cox
Manufacturing Buyer: Megan Cochran

Copyright © 1993 by Allyn and Bacon
A Division of Simon & Schuster, Inc.
160 Gould Street
Needham Heights, Massachusetts 02194

Library of Congress Cataloging-in-Publication Data

Rowell, C. Glennon
    Assessment and correction in the elementary language arts / C.
Glennon Rowell.
       p.   cm.
    Includes bibliographical references and index.
    ISBN 0–205–13998–1
    1. Language arts (Elementary)—United States—Evaluation.
I. Title.
LB1576. R76 1993
372. 6'044—dc20   92–296558
                                       CIP

Printed in the United States of America

10 9 8 7 6 5 4 3 2 1   98 97 96 95 94 93

To my wife, Glenn Dixon Rowell, and our son, Nathan, for their understanding, support, and patience during the writing of this book, and
to three former colleagues, Dr. Edwin H. Smith, Dr. Billy M. Guice, and Miss Fay Kirtland, who worked with me during my early professional years at Florida State University. No one could ask for finer mentors than these three friends.

Contents

Preface

In every classroom, there are students who need special help from the regular class-room teacher. Problems the students have are not severe enough to warrant special-ized help from a remedial teacher. It is up to the classroom teacher to make adjustments in what is taught and how it is taught to accommodate these students. *Assessment and Correction in Elementary Language Arts* was written to help teachers meet the needs of such children. However, the book also looks at ways of meeting the needs of those students who should be moving ahead to the next level of instruction in the language arts.

This book focuses on several themes that both the prospective and practicing teacher will find different from what they previously might have read about teaching the language arts. First, the theme of student-involved assessment and cor-rection is presented in an attempt to help the busy teacher streamline much of the effort that now goes into teaching. Second, the theme of teaching different compo-nents of the language arts (skills, concepts, vocabulary, and so on) in varied ways is systematically covered in the text. Third, meeting the needs of individuals in two types of groups, base groups and flex groups, is a theme covered throughout the text. And fourth, examining the research base for an assessment and corrective lan-guage arts program is discussed in each of the content chapters (for example, spelling, handwriting, reading, etc.) of the text.

Too often, involvement of students in assessment and correction of the lan-guage arts is little more than students passively taking a paper-pencil examination and the teacher marking the results. In this text, four theoretical positions on assessment and correction are examined throughout:

1. Students should be active learners, not passive observers.
2. Students should compete against themselves, not just against others.

3. Assessment and teaching should not be confused.
4. Assessment and correction of problems should be multidimensional.

In addition, four dimensions of assessment are also examined:

1. Preassessment activities (such as, proofreading) should be present in all teaching and should involve students.
2. Post-assessment activities should be systematic, streamlined, and should involve students.
3. Peer instruction and evaluation, where appropriate, should be utilized.
4. Projecting and charting each student's *progress* and *problems* should be carried out.

Frequently, all components of the language arts such as vocabulary, skills, generalizations, and concepts are taught the same way. While there is overlap in the way the various components of each language art (reading, speaking, listening, writing) should be taught, there are enough differences among them to warrant varied approaches to teaching. In this text, these differences are explored.

Another problem addressed in this text is that of having all students, regardless of achievement levels and instructional needs, learning the same lesson at the same time, day-after-day. In *Assessment and Correction in Elementary Language Arts*, a grouping plan for developmental needs of students will be examined via the employment of base groups. When students in different base groups need special and common instruction, a grouping plan identified as *flex groups* is explored.

Research believed to be most pertinent to teaching in a student-involved corrective program is examined. Such research as having students correct their own papers to get immediate feedback of their problems (especially in spelling), using sentence-combining techniques in written composition, and understanding the problems brought about because of differences in school language and home language for some students are some of the research areas to be explored.

Finally, a number of innovative practices are introduced to help the reader broaden his/her thinking of how to teach the language arts. Cooperative learning, modeling, coaching, and a number of practices are introduced in an effort to expand the array of techniques useful for teaching the language arts in a student-involved corrective program. In addition, some of the more traditional ways of teaching (for example, drill and practice) are addressed in ways that tie in with the themes of this book. Attention is also given to materials and equipment for teaching the language arts in a program that focuses on assessing/ correcting problems in language arts.

C G R

Acknowledgments

No one really writes a book alone. And so it is with this one. From students who first used the total text (in photocopy format) to principals and teachers who helped in the gathering of samples of children's papers, contributions were significant.

A large number of school personnel helped in the gathering of children's materials found in this book. Included are: Dr. Margie LeCoultre, Principal of Cedar Bluff Primary School (Knoxville, Tennessee); Mrs. Karen Milani, Principal of Alice Bell Elementary School (Knoxville) and teachers, Margaret Cruze, Tina Gillespie, Nancy Mitchell, Sylvia Pelley, Vicky Smith and the secretary of the school, Betty Hood; Dr. Ida Lou Stevens, Principal of Linden Elementary School (Oak Ridge, Tennessee) and teachers Bobbie Castor and Tracey Matthews; Dr. Sherry Morgan, Principal of Lincoln Park Elementary School (Knoxville) and teachers, Bettye Barnes, Laura Lawson, Judy Rathbone, and Sharon Yarbrough; Norma Cox, Assistant Principal of Ellen Myers Primary School (Harrogate, Tennessee) and teachers Cynthia Bolton, Iris Crawford, Judy Ellison, Alice Golden, Pam Hoskins, and Karen Tinnell; Jan Click, Principal of Sam Houston Elementary School (Maryville, Tennessee) and teachers Kathleen Hammontree and Phyllis Morelock; Dwight Price, teacher, and intern Jenifer Ohriner of Alcoa Elementary School (Alcoa, Tennessee); Bonnie Anders, teacher at Cedar Bluff Middle School (Knoxville, Tennessee); Linda Shubert, Principal of Talmadge Heflin Elementary School (Houston, Texas) and teacher Marguerite Held; and Kirk L. Bristol, Principal at West Genesse High School (Camillus, New York). Appreciation is expressed to these fine school personnel and to the many parents who agreed to let me use their children's written work and photographs.

A special thanks to Sue Carey and Dean Richard Wisniewski (College of Education, University of Tennessee) for allowing me to use pictures from the College's photograph file. Also, thanks to Esther J. Hasler of Jean-Bert Associates (Ft.

Lauderdale, Florida) and Bob Franklin of Franklin/Duncan (Ft. Lauderdale) for their assistance in helping find appropriate photographs.

To the following students enrolled in a corrective language arts course that I taught during the summer of 1991, a vote of appreciation is extended for their critical comments on the manuscript which served as the text for the class: Barbara J. Davis, Nicolett Levy, Beth McConnell, Karla Riddle, and Elliott Stroupe.

To Sandra Chambers who did a masterful job typing and setting up the tables, figures, and diagrams, thanks. And to staff personnel Diane Lovin and Martha Barnes who gave me training and guidance on using the word processor, a word of appreciation is in order. To Mark Rosanski who helped in duplication (and binding of copies for use in class), appreciation is extended. And to Karen Spitzer, secretary extraordinary, who helped the author in many ways on this project, a word of appreciation is extended.

To colleagues Drs. J. Estill Alexander, Betty Heathington, Ted Hipple, Carol Kasworm, and Tim Pettibone for advice and/or use of their professional materials, appreciation is herein expressed. Also, to Marti Richardson (Knox County, Tennessee Teacher Center) for use of selected materials, a word of appreciation is in order. And to Liz Wright and Songgian Lu for help in finding materials, appreciation is given.

And last but not least, thanks to the staff at Allyn and Bacon who helped with this text, with a special vote of appreciation is extended to Sean Wakely, Senior Editor (Education), Virginia Lanigan, Senior Editor, Nancy Forsyth, Executive Editor (Education), and Steve Gold for their help in the initiation of and/or carrying out of this project. Also, a special word of thanks goes to Myrna Breskin of Chestnut Hill Enterprises, Inc., for a first-rate job of seeing the manuscript through to completion.

1

Assessment and Correction in the Elementary Language Arts: An Introduction

Focus

Students in any given classroom differ in many ways. Interests, learning styles, and home backgrounds are three very important differences. Aptitude for learning is yet another important difference. Coping with these differences is a major challenge facing teachers.

Chapter 1 is about differences among students in schools and how teachers should deal with these differences. Chapter 1 is also about:

1. What makes up the language arts and how this curricular area is divided into four major strands (reading, writing, speaking, and listening)
2. How each strand of the language arts is divided into knowledge components (skills, concepts, vocabulary, and so on)
3. Why teachers should avoid language arts instruction in which group commonalities are given more consideration than are individual differences
4. What a student-involved assessment/correction* program is and how it is different from other approaches to working with individual differences
5. The advantages of a student-involved corrective program
6. How learning styles are different among students and why teachers should know about learning styles

*Assessment/correction will be referred to as a corrective language arts program in this book.

Many questions should be raised as you read this chapter. One is how to set up a corrective language arts program. As you read Chapter 1, write questions about assessment and correction in the language arts that need further exploration. To find answers to these questions, you may want to read materials referenced in the bibliography at the end of the chapter. You may bring your unanswered questions to your college class or in-service program for discussion. Chapter 1 is intended to help you understand the language arts and what is meant by a student-involved corrective language arts program.

7. The importance of socioeconomic and cultural differences in a student-involved corrective language arts program

8. The identification of interests that students have and how to use interests in a corrective language arts program

9. The importance of error analysis in a corrective language arts program

10. The need to know developmental levels in each phase of a corrective language arts program

11. The importance of knowing prerequisite skills/concepts and other basic components of the language arts curricula

Defining the Language Arts

It is important to have a good understanding of what is meant by language arts. Before reading further, write your definition of language arts. Then continue reading to see how closely your definition fits the one given in this book.

Language arts are elements and systems in any language that work together to help human beings using that language learn through language processing and communicate with each other. Such a definition is obviously a description of a broad spectrum, not only of school curricula, but life itself. But this is the way it is; the language arts cover a significantly wide array of related elements, systems, and processes of language.

Identifying Broad Strands of the Language Arts

For purposes of better understanding the complexity of the many facets of the language arts, four broad strands of this subject are usually identified. These strands are writing, speaking, reading, and listening. To better understand the structure of each, the four strands are often presented separately in books about the language arts. In daily use, however, they are integrated. Each strand has a myriad collection of substrands, for example, spelling and punctuation in the writing strand. What is to be learned in each substrand generally can be broken down into further units which include skills, facts, concepts, vocabularies, processes, generalizations, attitudes, and appreciations. These components are briefly explained in the section that follows.

Knowledge Components of Language Arts Substrands

The different knowledge components of the language arts should be known by language arts teachers. While these components have some similarities, they are different enough to warrant some diversity in instructional techniques.

Skills are behaviors or acts to be performed, such as writing a paragraph. Spelling a word, reciting a poem, capitalizing proper nouns, and placing a comma appropriately in a sentence are examples of some of the many language arts skills students should learn.

Facts are events and/or statements about someone, some object, or a time that an event occurred. Some examples of facts in the language arts are that Haiku is a type of Japanese poetry, the setting for E. B. White's *Charlotte's Web* is the barnyard, and the rhyming scheme of a limerick is AABBA.

Concepts are ideas. The idea or notion of a sentence is a concept in the language arts. Knowing what a *thesaurus* is, what a *road* is, and what a *desk* is are other examples of concepts. A tremendous number of concepts are included in the language arts curriculum.

Vocabularies are words or labels used to identify concepts. The word *road* printed in a book or written in a student's composition is an example of vocabulary. Students who read the word *road* and know its meaning have this word in their reading vocabulary. Students who can use the word *road* in their writing have this word in their written vocabulary. Students also have *listening* and *speaking* vocabularies.

Processes refer to those acts (often mental) that lead to knowledge/skill development in the form of output or product. In the language arts, one process is pausing to reflect on what one is writing. Another process is considering who one is writing for. Using context of a sentence to determine word meaning is yet another process. Many processes are related to broad "how to learn" operations, and are equally as important as what is actually learned (the product or output).

Generalizations refer to rules or statements that can be derived from the existence of a number of related factors about a specific area of the language arts. The rule that governs the spelling of the *long a* sound with "ay" when the sound is an ending syllable in a word as in *play, day, or stray* is an example of a generalization. The rule of adding an "s" to words such as *desk, book*, and *cat* to make these words plurals is another example of a generalization in the language arts.

Attitudes are one's disposition toward persons, content to be learned, animals, books, school assignments, and any number of factors. In the language arts, how one feels about writing a poem or about a character in *Huckleberry Finn* are attitudes.

Appreciations refer to positive attitudes or feelings. Being positive about poetry is an example of having an appreciation for poetry. In the language arts, much focus is on the development of appreciations, beginning with the development of an appreciation for language itself.

How the Language Arts Knowledge Components are Learned

When a teacher is making an assessment of weaknesses in any area of the language arts, it is important to know which knowledge component is being examined. Likewise, when corrective activities are being planned to help with an identified problem area, it is important to know what each component is and how it is best learned.

Most courses in educational psychology include descriptions of how children learn concepts, how skills are learned, and how various other knowledge components are learned. There are some commonalities in the ways that these components are learned in the language arts. All are dependent on frequent use of language in a meaningful way. However, educational psychologists point out some unique ways that one learns such knowledge components as skills and vocabulary. Skills, for example, are learned through practice and reinforcement over time, but such practice does not mean mere repetition. Feedback of the skill being learned is important. Mayer states that feedback that provides information rather than feedback that is mere reinforcement helps students revise what they are attempting to do and helps students build a plan for "generating internal feedback."[1] Skill development strategies that are based on research about learning, as well as research on teaching in general, are dependent on: clear identification of the skill to be learned; the provision of models which contain components of the skill to be learned; feedback in which the learner helps analyze how the skill is developing; and use of the skill during and after it has been learned.

Concepts are learned in a variety of ways. Often concepts are learned through the presentation of a mental image or picture of what is being learned. Association of the new with known concepts is an important step in learning concepts. Concepts and facts in sufficient number help in the learning of generalizations. When students are given concepts and facts and form a generalization, an *inductive approach* to learning is being followed. When a generalization is given to the learner, followed by examples of the generalization, a *deductive approach* to learning is being followed.

Studies have shown that the least effective strategies for learning vocabulary are those that call for few encounters with words and strategies in which stress is placed on word definition.[2] More effective strategies suggested by those who have done research in vocabulary development include having students relate new words to known words and using techniques in which experiential backgrounds of students are used to learn new vocabulary.[3]

Paying Attention to Differences among Students

In any classroom, differences among students are widespread and multidimensional. In addition to the differences of home background, aptitudes for learning, interests, and learning styles, students in any classroom differ in prior education and what was retained, interests in school-assigned tasks, and motivation to achieve.

There are great variations in students' abilities in each strand of the language arts; in each of the substrands of the four broad areas, such as spelling, a substrand of writing; and in each of the eight knowledge components presented earlier. For example, it is estimated that in a typical elementary school classroom, anywhere from five to eight reading levels may exist. A similar range exists in other language arts areas. Spelling levels vary as much as do reading levels; handwriting abilities are significantly different; and listening and speaking abilities vary widely among students in the same classroom. The differences cited are found as early as kindergarten and first grade. Henderson, in a study of 22 first-grade classrooms in Maryland, found that the range of language experience stories produced per week was 0 to 4.4. The range of words per story was 0-176. Some students were capable of writing well-constructed sentences while others could only dictate brief phrases and sentences.[4]

Teaching to Individual Differences Versus Teaching to Group Commonalities

Given widespread differences in so many areas of the language arts, instruction should be adapted to individual differences rather than geared to group commonalities, such as the same grade level or similar chronological ages. To better understand these two classifications as they exist in the language arts, eight practices are cited in Table 1-1. Each practice, as presented, falls more into one of the categories cited than into the other. Which of these practices exemplify attempts at meeting individual differences among students? Which are examples of instruction geared to group commonalities?

While each of the eight situations in Table 1-1 could be different from what the surface appearances indicate, numbers *one*, *two*, *four*, and *six* are examples of

TABLE 1–1 Individual Differences vs. Group Commonalities in Language Arts Instruction

---

1. A teacher regularly placing on the chalkboard a handwriting sample for a second grade class to copy (for purposes of letter practicing formation)

2. A teacher giving students in her classroom the same spelling word list to study

3. A third-grade teacher providing special lessons on paragraph writing for students in the class who need such instruction the most

4. A teacher selecting a topic such as "The Very Happiest Day of My Life" for fifth-grade students to write about

5. A fourth-grade teacher giving his class a test to determine the level (second, third, etc.) on which the students are spelling

6. A school system setting the second month of third grade for the point at which students are to begin cursive writing

7. A teacher placing several sixth-graders in small-group activities over a three-to-five day period to help these students improve their oral persuasion skills

8. A fourth-grade teacher using pictures to teach the concepts of *island* and *peninsula* to several students who are from disadvantaged backgrounds and need more visualization and imagery in concept/vocabulary development

---

instruction geared to group commonalities. In practice number *one* the teacher who has all second-grade students on the same handwriting lesson is not considering that some letter clusters (for example, counterclockwise circle letters *o, a, d, c, e, g, q*) present more problems for some students than these letters do for other students. The teacher who follows such a practice is acting as if all students are progressing at the same rate and ready at the same time for the next task. Problems that impede mastery of each segment of the handwriting curriculum are being ignored. A somewhat similar situation prevails in practice *two*, but for a different language arts area. In this situation, the teacher is assuming that all students in this classroom are on the same spelling level, which of course is an erroneous assumption.

In practice *four* in Table 1–1, differences in students' interests are not being utilized. While students in any classroom may be quite capable of designating the happiest day of their lives, they may not wish to write about it. If given a choice, some students may wish to write on another topic. Background experiences of the students are sometimes ignored as in the case where teachers ask students to write about "My Favorite Pet." Some students have never owned pets, and for them the topic may have less meaning than for students who have owned pets.

In practice *six* of Table 1–1, a widespread policy in schools, the assumption is being made that no student was ready for cursive writing before the second month of the third grade, even though some students no doubt have satisfactorily learned manuscript writing before that time. The assumption is also made that every student is ready for cursive handwriting by the second month of the third grade, which in fact is not the case.

In practices *three, five, seven,* and *eight* of those depicted in Table 1–1, some attention is being given to individual differences among students in the same classroom. The teacher in activity *three* has determined through either formal or informal means that a small group of third graders in this classroom needs corrective lessons on paragraph writing. Such lessons are being provided. Other students do not need such lessons, and presumably have been provided other types of instruction. In practice *five,* a first step toward adapting the spelling curriculum to meet the needs of individual learners is being taken in that spelling levels are being determined. A follow-up to this first step is to provide different word lists for students according to spelling levels (to be discussed in Chapter 4).

In practice *seven* of Table 1–1, a situation exists similar to the practice existing in number *three,* except the *speaking* strand rather than the *writing* strand of the language arts curriculum is being considered. The teacher involved in practice *seven,* probably through observation (an assessment technique to be discussed later in this book) has determined that, in small-group discussions, a few students are not very persuasive in arguing their points of view. Therefore, help is being provided for these several students.

In practice *eight* of Table 1–1, it appears that the teacher involved is aware that differences in backgrounds of students must be considered in teaching concepts and which students need additional help. The teacher also appears to know that the use of imagery is a primary way to teach concepts.

Teachers must be skilled in adapting teaching to the needs of individual students, including the most capable and the not-so-capable. Teachers must adjust instruction for students who need more concrete approaches to learning and students who do not need such help. Teachers must know how to challenge students who like what is being taught as well as those students who dislike what is being taught. And finally, teachers must know how to work with students who are highly motivated to achieve in school and students who are not motivated at all to achieve in school. In order to meet these demands, teachers must be skilled in determining the instructional needs of all students, grouping and regrouping students who have similar needs, organizing materials and equipment to meet identified needs, interacting with students to foster desired learning, monitoring progress of each student, and, where necessary, reteaching what has been taught.

While many teachers make adaptations in instruction for differences among learners at what Corno and Snow call the macroadaptation level (the programmatic level) and the microadaptation level (moment-to-moment decisions by the teacher),[5] in general the language arts are taught without systematic attention to the wide spectrum of differences among students in classrooms. For that reason, a corrective program in which each student is an active learner (as opposed to being passive) is needed.

Comparing Corrective and Other Programs for Meeting Individual Needs of Students

If a student-involved corrective language arts program focuses on individual differences of students rather than group commonalities, it is important to know how such a program differs from other programs that have been designed to meet individual differences. In particular, it is important to know how such a program is different from a remedial program, from individualized instruction, and from prescriptive teaching.

A student-involved corrective language arts program differs from a remedial program in three basic ways.* These are:

1. *A corrective program takes place within the regular classroom setting, whereas a remedial program is usually provided in a specialized, clinical-type room.*
2. *A corrective program deals with less severe problems, whereas a remedial program provides help for more severe cases (two or three grade levels lower than the grade in which the students in question are placed).*
3. *A corrective program does not require the services of a specialist to provide instruction; a remedial program does require a specialist.*[6]

Most schools do not have a separate remedial language arts program, except in the area of reading. Therefore, a corrective program within the regular classroom may be all that is provided to help overcome problems that students have in three of the four strands (*writing, listening,* and *speaking*) of the language arts.

Although there are common elements among a corrective language arts program and, in turn, individualized and prescriptive programs, there are some significant differences. In prescriptive and individualized programs that were so popular in the 1960s and 1970s, emphasis was often placed more on independent assignments than on small-group instruction. As will be advocated throughout this book, small-group instruction within the classroom will be the dominant grouping pattern for working with students. In addition, much more attention will be given to the various categories of differences among learners than typically was found in individualized and prescriptive programs. Finally, a variety of instructional activities will be advocated as opposed to an over-reliance on paper-pencil tasks, a characteristic of some individualized and prescriptive approaches to instruction.

*Differences cited are based primarily, but not entirely, on differences between corrective and remedial programs identified by the authors in reference number 6 at the end of this chapter.

Advantages of Corrective Teaching

There are several distinct advantages to a student-involved assessment/correction approach to teaching. The primary advantage is that each individual student is provided instruction in an area in which help is needed most, as opposed to learning (or being exposed to) what the total class is being taught. Strengths of diagnostic teaching, identified by Gutknecht, Johnson, and Chapman, appear to be appropriate for describing strengths of a corrective language arts program. These strengths are: (1) a provision for decisions about further measurement needs; (2) a cutting down on the lag time between diagnosis and implementation (correction of problems), a factor that is not present in a clinical model; and (3) the provision of regular feedback on the effectiveness of instructional activities.[7] When extensive student involvement in assessment and correction of the elementary language arts is added to these identified strengths, teaching effectiveness is increased significantly.

Knowing Students across Many Areas

In any instructional program, it is important to know students. However, in a corrective program, the importance of knowing students thoroughly is critical. This is difficult, given the teacher's busy hours in the school day. However, there are streamlined strategies for observing students, for finding out about their likes and dislikes, and for getting to know their special instructional needs. These will be presented throughout this book. *The theme of student involvement will be presented in such a way that the busy teacher can readily see how students can be involved in such strategies as proofreading, detecting specific errors they make in the language arts, keeping up with their own progress in the language arts, and comparing performances over time.*

Learning styles, students' interests, error analysis, cultural and socioeconomic differences, and curricular levels appropriate to students are considered in the sections of this book that follow. These five areas, as well as other important areas where differences exist, such as attitude toward learning a specific language arts strand, will be covered in the content chapters (writing, spelling, handwriting, listening, speaking, and reading) of this book.

Learning Styles and Characteristics

Learning styles refer to how one best learns. Generally, when one thinks of learning styles, reference is to how knowledge of preferred sensory modalities contribute to learning. In this area, teachers often are asked about sensory modalities, such as the effects of visual and auditory modes of learning or learning through hands-on manipulation of materials.

While knowing sensory modalities is an important aspect of learning styles, learning styles are considerably broader than this one area. How students react to their environment, how learners approach or get ready for a learning task (mental set), and thinking processes involved in learning are among the other variables that should be considered in studying learning styles.

Students of all ages and abilities have preferred ways to learn. Unfortunately, learning styles are not taken into account as they should be. Dunn and Dunn point out that even though many experienced teachers know that children learn in vastly different ways, they continue to provide ". . . identical lessons to an entire class at the same time and in the same way, eventually requiring a demonstration of mastery at the same hour."[8]

While there is much to discover about learning styles (especially regarding application of knowledge about styles), much is known that can affect the teaching of the language arts. Smith has identified cognitive factors of learning style as field-independence versus field-dependence, conceptualizing/categorizing, reflectivity versus impulsivity, and sensory modalities.

The field-independent learner perceives elements independently of background, requires less structure in learning, and is not as comfortable as the field-dependent learner in collaborative learning situations. The field-dependent person finds it easier to see the whole rather than the parts that constitute the whole. A field-dependent person needs more external structure, direction, and feedback and is not as comfortable with analytical situations as is the field-independent learner.

The learner who groups concepts according to functional similarity is categorizing using a relational-contextual pattern. The person who looks more at "external, objective physical attributes of stimuli and information" is relying on analytical-descriptive conceptualizing.

The impulsive learner projects answers immediately when they are thought of, while the reflective individual is more cautious in formation of answers. Thus, speed and accuracy of problem solving are affected.

Learners use their sensory modalities to gain and organize information. Four basic sensory modalities are kinesthetic (motoric), visual, auditory, and tactual (touch).[9]

It is important to know various learning styles to ensure, to the extent possible, that students are not placed in learning situations in which they cannot benefit. This does not mean, however, that a student with a particular preference for learning is never exposed to situations calling for learning through other modalities. The developmental aspect of learning how to learn, in which several modalities are used, must be fostered. Thus, a student who is a visual learner should be provided opportunities to learn in which this mode is used, but also have opportunities to learn through the auditory modality.

Implications for knowing learning styles can be seen by taking an in-depth look at a particular area. Witkin, who has been involved in research on field-dependence and field-independence cognitive learning styles, points out that learners who are field-dependent (global learners):

1. Are particularly sensitive and attuned to the social environment
2. Are prone to be guided by positions attributed to peer groups/authority figures
3. Are less motivated through intrinsic factors than are field-independent learners
4. Make more reference to others in speaking than do field-independent learners
5. Are prone to learn more from discovery techniques (where there is more teacher-student interaction) than are field-independent learners
6. Are more influenced by criticism than are field-independent learners.[10]

Witkin also points out that children with learning difficulties (especially in reading) tend to be field-dependent.[11] Adjustments in teaching are therefore critical, as will be explained in the following discussion of case studies 1 and 2.

If field-dependent learners, compared to field-independent learners, are more sensitive and more attuned to the social environment, more comfortable with collaborative learning, and profit more from discovery techniques, it is easy to see that they would probably fare better in Mrs. Soper's language arts class than in Mr. Ritter's language arts class in the case studies presented. On the other hand, field-independent learners may do quite well in working in more independent situationsas found in Mr. Ritter's classroom, although his structured approach to giving assignments may have some appeal to the field-dependent learner.

Since teachers do not teach students whose learning styles are the same, it is necessary that instruction consider all types of learners. Imagine a class of fifth

---

Case Study Number One

Mr. Ritter teaches language arts for approximately two hours per day, usually from 8:30–10:30 a.m. Reading is taught first, followed by spelling. These two areas together take about half of the language arts period. The remainder of the two-hour block is spent alternating days among writing, grammar, and mechanics (punctuation and capitalization) although an occasional oral language lesson is taught.

Mr. Ritter depends heavily on workbooks and skill sheets, with a minimum of classroom discussion about either the purpose of each skill-development activity or follow-up, other than grading each assignment which is done very meticulously. Students keep folders of their graded work, stapled in bunches, and take them home for parental signatures, usually at the end of each week.

Mr. Ritter chooses workbooks and skill sheets carefully, making sure that they are not too difficult for each student. Students often work on skill sheets that are very different from what others in the class are doing. Mr. Ritter typically has projected skill sheets for each student well in advance of the day the student is to do the activity.

Case Study Number Two

Mrs. Soper teaches language arts, beginning with homeroom at 8:15 and continuing through to around 10:30 a.m. A frequently-occurring activity during homeroom is to have two or three "mystery words" written in sentences on the chalkboard. Students, using context clues, work hurriedly in small groups to determine what the words mean. Alternative activities are provided, such as having students hypothesize about a mystery question (e.g., "Do you know where the term 'goose pimples' came from?").

Reading, writing, and oral composition are usually taught together; seldom as separate subjects. Grammar, mechanics, and spelling are taught more as separate subjects. Workbooks and skill sheets are used as needed, but with students frequently working in small groups with the teacher on examining skills being taught, step-by-step. In groups, students work on what Mrs. Soper calls "skill-development projects" in which such topics as the following are explored:
(1)   Construct as persuasive a paragraph as you can,
(2)   List six words that can be used to tell how a horse runs,
(3)   Tell four different ways that "stop" can be stated, and
(4)   Expand the sentence, "John ran home." as many ways as you can in six minutes.

graders where there are some students who are field-independent and some who are field-dependent, some who are more visual learners and some who favor the auditory mode of learning. Some few in the class learn best through hands-on types of activities.

The teacher of our hypothetical fifth-grade class has been exploring the students' favorite authors. The teacher decides that some students in the class may benefit more if given an opportunity to investigate independently and write a report on one of the authors selected for further study. Others, the teacher decides, may choose and benefit more from the chance to work in pairs or groups of three to five. But the teacher goes further. Some students may benefit more from doing a dialogue with a classmate as a culminating experience in the study of an author, but for some students individual oral reports may be more beneficial. Other ways of approaching the study of the life of the author might include: (1) making a timeline which depicts the author's early and adult life; (2) doing a make-believe interview with the author (another student who must know about the author in order to answer questions realistically); (3) doing a make-believe interview with a teacher who taught the author; (4) writing a newspaper article about the author's return to his/her hometown; and/or (5) building a replica of the house where the author grew up.

In these activities, there are opportunities for students to collaborate with each other (appealing more to field-dependent learners) as well as opportunities for students to work alone (appealing more to field-independent learners). There are opportunities for students to verbalize about the author, while at the same time, there are opportunities for students to depend more on the visual mode of learning. Such multiple assignments are helpful in reaching each individual student and are critical in a corrective language arts program.

Go back to Case Studies 1 and 2. What would you change in Mrs. Soper's and Mr. Ritter's classes to make the instruction provided more beneficial to all kinds of learners? How would you change Mr. Ritter's class to reach students who learn best through auditory or kinesthetic strategies? How would you change Mrs. Soper's instruction to reach students who depend more on tactual and/or kinesthetic learning modalities?

Several inventories are available to determine learning styles and learner characteristics. One is the *Learning Style Inventory* (LSI) by Dunn, Dunn, and Price in which assessment of learning style is made in twenty-four different areas. Included are such areas as determining preference for a quiet environment, determining preference for learning alone or with peers, and determining auditory, visual, tactile or kinesthetic modalities of learning.[12]

It takes about thirty minutes to administer the LSI. A computerized printout can be obtained of the results of the LSI if the school or school system subscribes to that service. Profiles give directions for making adjustments for each student's learning preferences.[13]

A second learning styles inventory is the *Learning Style Inventory: Primary* by Perrin. This inventory is based on the LSI and consists of twelve charts which help measure effects of the environment (sound, light, temperature) on learning, as well as various other factors such as sociological, emotional, and physical aspects of learning, motivation, and perception. The *Learning Style Inventory: Primary* is for students in Grades K–2. The inventory is administered through the use of questions read by the teacher and pictures that pupils are asked to observe.

Questions are asked about students' preferences for certain kinds of learning environments and different situations (for example, sitting or moving around to do schoolwork). Students are assured that the answers to their questions are neither right or wrong, just as preferring vanilla or chocolate ice cream is a matter of choice.[14]

A third learning style inventory is the *Swassing-Barbe Modality Index* (SBMI) which is a matching-to-sample test in which a stimulus item or sample is presented, and the student being examined is asked to duplicate the sample. Items consist of shapes (circles, squares, triangles, and hearts). Students not only duplicate patterns shown (when removed) but the sequence of patterns.

There are three testing periods, with each one focused on a different modality (auditory, visual, and kinesthetic). For example, when the child is tested to determine the kinesthetic modality, he/she feels the shapes but does not see them. The SBMI takes approximately 20 minutes per student to administer, and a profile of the relative modality strengths of each student tested is projected.[15]

Parents can provide feedback about their child's learning modality through use of the *Barbe Modality Checklists*. Two versions of the checklist for use with

Barbe Modality Checklist (Ages 5–8) *A Key to How Your Child Learns*

Listed below are incomplete sentences, followed by three ways of completing each. Distribute 10 points among the three phrases. Divide the 10 points according to how strongly each phrase describes your child. The phrase that describes your child best would receive more points than the phrase that least describes your child. For instance, if you believe each phrase describes your child equally well, mark a *3* in two blanks and a *4* in the one that favors your child even slightly more. If your child is completely described by one of the phrases, mark a *10* by it and *0* by the other two. Remember, you *must* use a total of ten points for each statement.

A. When playing, my child:	likes details and colorful things, peers at objects and moving things. ___	likes to talk, prefers toys that make sounds. ___	likes to move, climb, jump, use tools; prefers toys with moving parts. ___
B. During mealtime, my child	eats food that looks good first, sorts by color. ___	talks instead of eating, prolonging meals. ___	squirms in chair, may get up and down; often puts too much in mouth. ___
C. When reading, or being read to, my child:	is interested in pictures, wants to see pages. ___	is concerned with sounds, asks questions. ___	prefers turning pages, handling the book; doesn't sit for long periods. ___
D. When counting, my child:	likes to see objects being counted. ___	counts aloud, may make a song out of counting. ___	counts on fingers, likes to touch objects while counting. ___
E. When I scold my child, he or she:	looks away, cries. ___	cries or whines, explains away fault. ___	doesn't listen; avoids scolding by doing something. ___
F. In more formal learning, (coloring, workbooks), my child:	tries to stay in lines, uses many colors, wants things to fit in spaces. ___	Asks questions, talks during work. ___	works rapidly, impatient to get to next page, does not stay in lines. ___
G. In group situations, my child:	tends to be quiet, watches more than initiates. ___	raises voice, talks at the same time as others. ___	is either first or last in line; can't wait to get moving. ___
H. When angry, my child:	uses silent treatment, may become teary-eyes, will not look at me. ___	shouts, whines. ___	reacts physically, clenches fist or strikes out. ___
I. I can tell when my child is happy by:	facial expression. ___	voice quality. ___	body movement. ___
J. When looking for encouragement or reward, my child:	looks for a smile, must have me see accomplishment. ___	needs oral praise. ___	needs a hug, a pat on the back. ___
Total ___	**Visual** ___	**Auditory** ___	**Kinesthetic** ___

Barbe Modality Checklist (Ages 9 & Up) *A Key to How Your Child Learns*

Listed below are incomplete sentences, followed by three ways of completing each. Distribute 10 points among the three phrases. Divide the 10 points according to how strongly each phrase describes your child. The phrase that describes your child best would receive more points than the phrase that least describes your child. For instance, if you believe each phrase describes your child equally well, mark a *3* in two blanks and a *4* in the one that favors your child even slightly more. If your child is completely described by one of the phrases, mark a *10* by it and *0* by the other two. Remember, you *must* use a total of ten points for each statement.

A. My child's emotions can be interpreted by:	facial expression. ___	voice quality. ___	general body tone. ___
B. My child's hobbies and outside interests include:	reading, artwork; watching TV, movies. ___	listening to music, playing instruments. ___	sports, active games, handwork. ___
C. The part of school my child does best is:	reading and writing. ___	group discussion, music. ___	gym, art, lab science. ___
D. When studying, my child prefers:	working alone; underlining, highlighting books and notes. ___	working with someone else, asking and answering one another's questions. ___	working alone for short periods of time interspersed with breaks; rewriting notes. ___
E. When angry, my child:	uses silent treatment, either glares or looks away. ___	shouts, whines, turns up volume of TV or stereo. ___	reacts physically, clenches fist, stamps out of room. ___
F. When explaining something, my child:	describes in detail; sees color, size, shape. ___	tells more than I ever knew before, repeats self. ___	gives minimum information; information has to be pried out. ___
G. When examining something new, my child:	moves closer to it, looks from every angle. ___	asks questions about it. ___	handles it, turns it over, wants to feel texture, weight. ___
H. In a social group, my child:	watches others, ceases talking when several others begin. ___	talks at the same time as others; talks louder as noise increases. ___	puts hand on others, moves frequently, suggests doing something. ___
I. When excited, my child:	demands my attention, some visible reaction; sentences get choppy. ___	talks rapidly, gives little or no time for response. ___	cannot stand or sit still, uses hand and arm movements. ___
J. When looking for encouragement or reward, my child:	looks for a smile, must have me see accomplishment. ___	needs oral praise. ___	needs a hug, pat on the back. ___
Total ___	**Visual** ___	**Auditory** ___	**Kinesthetic** ___

FIGURE 1–1 Inventories for Determining Learning Styles

students are available. One version is for children, ages 5–8, while the second version is for ages 9 and up. Both versions are found in Figure 1–1.

Parents are asked to complete each of 10 sentences one of three ways by distributing 10 points across the three responses. The points are totaled and result in scores for each of three categories: visual, auditory, and kinesthetic learning modalities.[16]

Interests of Students

As stated, another area in which much variation exists in any grade level is students' interests. Some third graders are quite interested in pets, while others are more interested in sports heroes or model airplanes. Some students in the same third grade are not interested at all in writing about a family picnic, but exhibit great enthusiasm in writing about a sports event. Using such interests enhances the success of teaching, especially in a corrective language arts program.

How do teachers in a corrective language arts program learn about students' interests? First, through observation of everyday activities, teachers should note what students talk about, what they like to read, what topics they choose to write about, and what topics discussed in class create more attentive listening. A second way of determining students' interests is through surveys. Surveys can be detailed checklists or they can be open-ended, as found in Figure 1–2. This survey can be given at the beginning of the year and/or at a later time where it seems appropriate. A third way that teachers learn what students are interested in is through one-on-one conferences. When conferences are held, students are asked what they like to do in their spare time, what hobbies they have, where they would like to visit, and a number of other questions which reveal their interests.

Once interests have been identified, they can be used to meet individual needs of students in several ways. In Case Studies 3 and 4, two quite different systems are in place for not only keeping up with interests that students have but also for using words associated with interests to expand vocabulary development and for use in writing programs.

Analysis of Errors Made by Students

Marking errors made by students is an activity as readily associated with teaching as is the use of the chalkboard or the assigning of grades. If, however, errors are not examined to see if they fit a pattern or to determine, where possible, the cause of the problem, the most appropriate help will seldom be provided. The second grader's spelling paper in Figure 1–3 is an example of the importance of detecting error type. From this one paper, it appears that this student is having trouble adding *ing* to base words where changes must be made in the words, and in spelling plurals of words, except the simple adding of *s* to singular forms of words ending in the consonant *t*. (Note: In this paper, *table* and *lunch* should have been *tables* and *lunches*, respectively.) This student should not be allowed to continue spelling

Name _____ Room _____

1. In my free time, I like to _____ .
2. My father and I like _____ .
3. My mother and I like _____ .
4. I have _____ brother(s) and _____ sisters(s).
    My _____ and I like to _____ .
5. My friends and I like _____ .
    We play at _____ .
6. I like to help at home by _____ .
    But I do not like to _____ .
7. I (like-do not like) to play with toys and games.
    My favorite toys and games are _____ .
8. I (like-do not like) TV. My favorite programs are _____ .
    _____ .
9. I (like-do not like) to go to the movies. My favorite movies are _____ .
    _____ .
10. I (like-do not like) pets. My favorite pets are _____ .
    _____ .
11. I go to scouts (yes-no); church (yes-no); clubs (yes-no). My favorite clubs are _____ .
    _____ .
12. I (like-do not like) to take trips. I have visited _____ .
    _____ .
    I would like to visit _____ .
13. I (like-do not like) to collect things. My favorite collections are _____ .
    _____ .
14. I (like-do not like) to make things. I have made _____ .
    _____ .
15. I (like-do not like) to read. I read storybooks (yes-no); newspapers (yes-no);
    magazines (yes-no); comic books (yes-no). My favorites are _____ .
    _____ .
16. I do not like to read about _____ .
17. I (like-do not like) to go to the library.
18. I (like-do not like) to read at home. My parents like for me to read at home (yes-no).
19. If I could have any three things I could wish for, I would like _____ ,
    _____ , and _____ .
20. When I grow up, I think I would like to _____ .
    _____ .
    _____ .

FIGURE 1–2 Example of Interest Inventory (Alexander Interest Inventory)

From *Teaching Reading* 3/e edited by J. Estill Alexander, et al. Copyright © 1988 by Scott, Foresman and Company. Reprinted by permission of HarperCollins Publishers.

Case Study Number Three

Mr. Sawyer has each student in his fourth grade keep a card file on his/her interests. These interests are used not only as a part of lessons taught to the total class but to small groups and individuals.

Frequently, Mr. Sawyer asks the librarian to find books on various grade levels on from eight to ten topics on interests of students as reflected in the card files. The books from the library are carted into Mr. Sawyer's classroom, usually on Tuesday. Each student is permitted to check out at least one book on a topic of interest to him/her. Mr. Sawyer guides students to books on their reading levels. On Friday, reading groups (about four of them) are formed around interests and the books are discussed in a group meeting. The composition of each group is different from the reading groups functioning during the rest of the week.

Although there is plenty of room for "free talk" about the books read, Mr. Sawyer gives some specific assignments prior to Friday's group work. Students may be told on Tuesday that the two main characters in their books will be discussed in Friday group sessions. On some Tuesdays, students may be told that a major event will be discussed by each student. Sometimes designated students are told that on Friday they will be called on to review the total story in the book they read.

Mr. Sawyer also uses books checked out to his classroom in the writing program. When assignments are given early in the week, one or more of the following writing activities may be assigned, such as:

(1)   Students make up and write about a fictitious event in their books;

(2)   Students make up and describe a new character in their books;

(3)   Students write an advertisement for their books; and

(4)   Students compare the setting of their current book with one previously read.

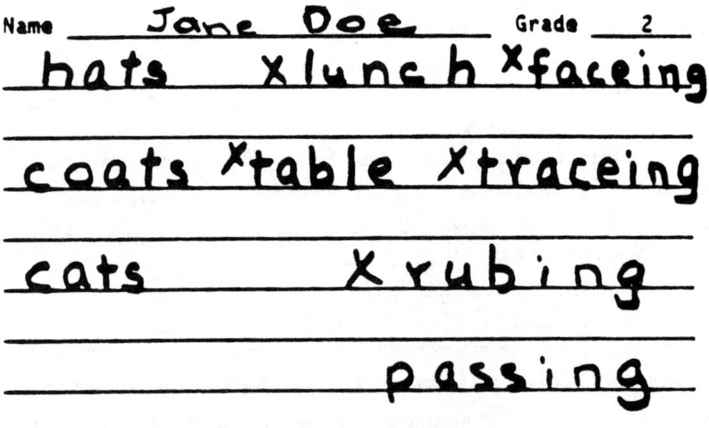

FIGURE 1–3   **Detecting Spelling Error Types**

Case Study Number Four

Miss Thomas uses interests of students to promote vocabulary development among her fourth-grade students. Miss Thomas gives an interest inventory to all students twice a year. Each student then is asked to write headings in three sections of a notebook, with each heading paralleling three highest interests given by the student on the inventory. Thus, one student may write *cowboys, baseball,* and *swimming* while another student might write *parties, watching television,* and *nurses.*

Miss Thomas then asks each student to find and write words about the topic under each heading. The words are those that can readily be identified with the headings such as *diamond* and *glove* with baseball. Students are given encouragement to find words that they have not previously known and to so indicate these in their running account of words. Resources such as magazines, pictures, library books, and the thesaurus are placed in the room for students to find words. Words found in newspapers are especially encouraged.

In addition to vocabulary, Miss Thomas regularly uses students' personalized vocabulary words in writing. Also, the words are used as supplementary spelling words.

Sometimes oral-language activities are held where groups of students with similar interests get together to discuss words that they have found that depict the most exciting event that could happen to "character" categories (cowboys, nurses, and actors on a television show), to discuss technical words that they might have found (e.g., antiseptic), or words that describe characters and/or activities depicting the students' interests.

Finally, Miss Thomas expands interests of students by having them make new headings, perhaps moving to the students next cluster of interests. Occasionally, students are asked to find words on one of their least-liked interests.

---

words that call for changes in base words before *ing* is added and making plurals from singular forms of words that end in *e* or *ch,* until appropriate help is given.

In some instances, a series of papers is needed to detect error types. In Figure 1–4, errors made by a fourth grader on any one of the five consecutive weekly test papers do not reveal the specific type of error being made, although an error pattern is suggested in the first paper. However, when examined together, it becomes more obvious that the major error type made by this student is the middle vowel sound in words that have three or more syllables (kangaroo, crocodile, beautiful, invitation). Having students record their spelling errors, to be explained in Chapter 4, is a meaningful way of getting students involved in assessing/correcting problems that they have in spelling.

For both the second grader whose errors on a single paper are depicted in Figure 1–3 or the fourth grader whose errors are recorded in Figure 1–4, the next appropriate step is to determine what the underlying problem is (for example, determining if the fourth grader is not hearing a middle syllable in some words). This may call for further assessment and then appropriate instruction. Such

Week One	Week Two	Week Three	Week Four	Week Five
(Misspelled Words)	(Misspelled Words)	(Misspelled Words)	(Misspelled Words)	(Misspelled Words)
kangroo crocidle	somone cotton	beautful women biealive	proure (for pronounce)	invition dicues (for discuss) dicustio

FIGURE 1-4   Spelling Error Types over a Prolonged Period of Time

instruction may be one-on-one, but more likely would be provided in a small group, since other students probably have similar problems.

Cultural and Socioeconomic Differences

Although knowing differences in socioeconomic backgrounds is important in any program, it is especially critical to know and work with such differences in a corrective language arts program. Several factors should be considered in getting to know students who come from disadvantaged backgrounds or from other cultures. One such factor to consider is the differences between school culture and the culture of the disadvantaged child, relating specifically to learning. Gilbert and Gay, in describing the learning styles and characteristics of lower income African-American children, point out that expectations in school are often in conflict with how these children approach learning, and that learning styles of these children are not understood by teachers. These children's learning styles are typically relational and field-dependent. In addition, African-American children benefit from working together, and these children need much more positive feedback than they usually get. Their approach to communication in the home favors oral language to a much greater degree than is found in homes of many other children. Thus, the emphasis on writing in the school culture is in conflict. Finally, African-American children's approach to learning is more multimodal and multidimensional than is learning in schools, meaning that these children's learning environment involves the physical and affective. Consequently, the school's major approach to learning, the cognitive, is in conflict.[17]

First points out that there is a significant conflict in the learning environment of schools and the learning environment of immigrant children:

. . . Many immigrant children come from communities in which the schools emphasized rote memorization. Books, pencils, and paper were rarely available, and the teacher's authority was absolute. Some have attended schools in which the only subject was political indoctrination. When they enter U.S. schools, they find that they are expected to maintain less formal relationships with the teachers, to speak out in class and voice their views, and to learn through diverse approaches, including hands-on manipulation, art, play, physical activity, and field trips.[18]

Other groups of children from lower socioeconomic backgrounds must also be considered in any school program, but especially in a corrective program. Rural children from impoverished areas such as mountainous, isolated regions of the country, need a strong emphasis on building background concepts and vocabulary to help them cope with the school culture. These children, too, need to experience many models in language arts, including both oral and written forms of standard English. In general, children from these areas need a strong emphasis on hands-on learning experiences. Concrete examples of what is being taught are highly recommended.

Teachers must understand how learning is impeded when there are differences in vocabulary and concept development of children from lower-income homes. Nothing can be taken for granted. The writer once observed a teacher trying in vain to help a third grader from an impoverished background circle either *st*, *bl*, or *sl* to indicate the consonant cluster (also called blend) for the beginning of the word that represented the picture of a *stepladder*. The word itself was not given. The child was confused because she could not hear the beginning "l" sound which is the first sound in the word *ladder*. Upon quizzing the child, the teacher discovered that the student only knew the generic concept for *ladder*. She did not know different kinds of ladders, one of which in this case, was a *stepladder*. This teacher had taken for granted that the child with whom she was working could identify different kinds of ladders.

The language arts most affected by language differences are reading and spelling. Desberg, Elliott, and Marsh, among others, have found that as dialect problems increased, achievement scores in both reading and spelling decreased.[19] Children who pronounce *fighting* and *something* by dropping the final sound in these words often spell the words without the final letter or letters (for example, *fightin* and *somethin* or *sumpn*). Students who in speech substitute *Him* for *He* as in *Him has a cold.* may transfer this to writing. Unless an understanding and skillful teacher provides corrective lessons, these problems may continue.

In a corrective language arts program, students should be taught in small-group settings for the purpose of overcoming problems where background languages interfere with learning in school. This does not mean, however, that students from disadvantaged backgrounds are placed in small groups with only students of similar backgrounds. Students learn from each other, and school should be a place where disadvantaged students hear standard English spoken, where they see in writing the standard forms that they have not seen before, and where they make transitions to these forms without having their language and other background characteristics put down. In this book, many options to grouping, such as cooperative learning groups, groups for special-needs instruction, and interests groups, among others, will be discussed as alternative ways of having students work together. In using small-group instruction, teachers maximize student involvement and participation in learning the language arts. In addition, teachers expand opportunities for knowing students more thoroughly than they otherwise would know them.

Developmental Stages

Since students in any given classroom are functioning at different developmental levels, adjustments must be made to accommodate the differences. How does a teacher in a corrective language arts program determine different levels of development? While these questions are dealt with in greater detail in Chapter 2 on grouping for corrective teaching, some basic considerations should be made at this time, relating to teachers knowing students.

Early in any school year, most teachers survey different levels of accomplishment in their classrooms. Although teachers are warned not to make hasty judgments about placing students in different levels, it is important to determine as soon as possible how students will be grouped for instruction. As long as teachers are flexible in their grouping and regrouping patterns, curricular levels can be determined in many areas of the language arts within a reasonable time. In some instances, surveys that teachers make will be formal, such as in giving spelling tests to determine on what levels students are spelling. In some instances, teachers will ask students to write a passage to help determine writing maturity. In other instances, teachers will have students write sentences that have all letters of the alphabet to help determine handwriting achievement. Students may participate in small-group discussions to determine oral-communication skills, or they may be given a listening test to determine how well they listen.

Initial surveys and study of past records at the beginning of the year are places to start determining developmental levels of students. However, initial surveys may be just a beginning. In having students write a passage to determine writing maturity, there may be a need for follow-up writing. Perhaps a passage will be assigned that is a different kind of writing (for example, expository rather than narrative) or students will be asked to write a structural element for writing, such as a paragraph. Often surveying what each student can do will take several days, even a week or so. An example of differences in writing maturity found within the same classroom is given in Figure 1–5. These fifth graders, asked to write on inanimate objects brought to life, have differing abilities in writing.

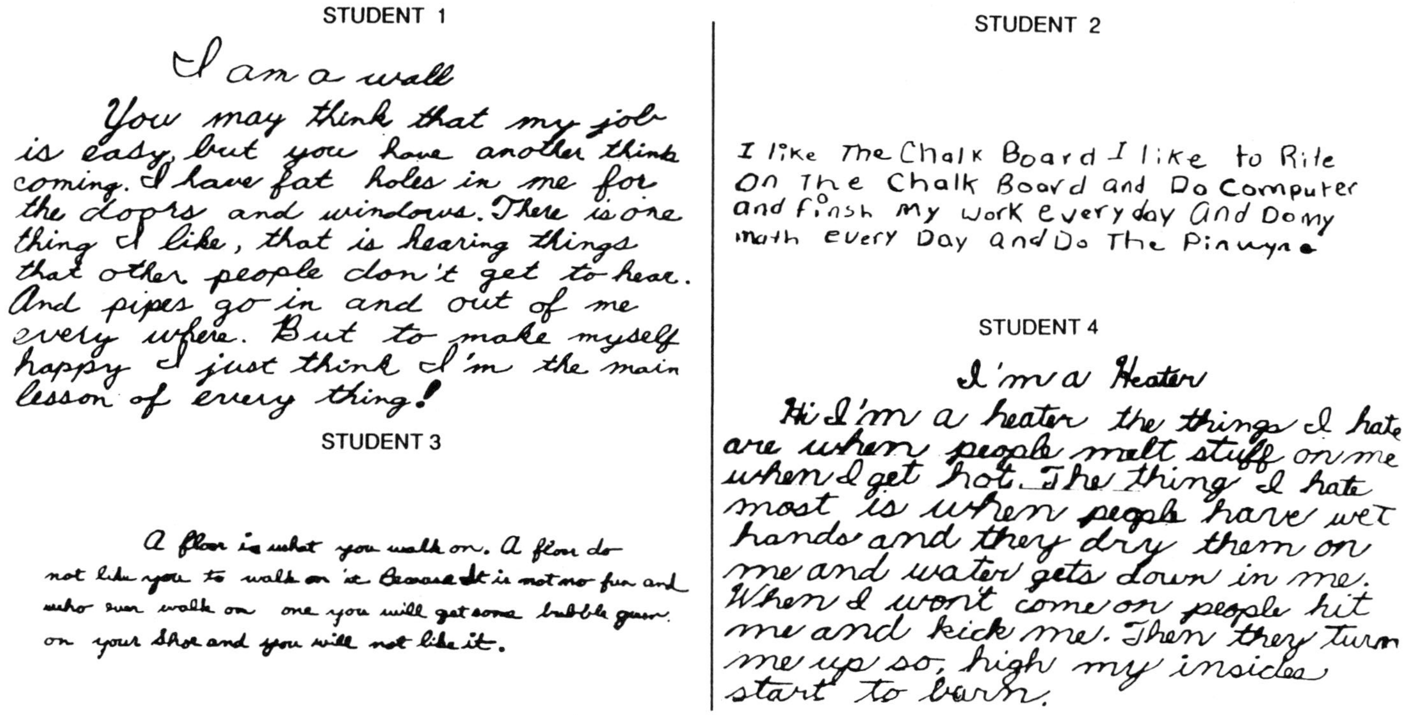

I like The Chalk Board I like to Rite On The Chalk Board and Do Computer And finsh My work Every Day And Dony Math Every Day and Do The Pianyo

I'm a heater

Hi I'm a heater the things I hate are when people mult stuff on me when I get hot. The thing I hate most is when people have wet hands and they dry them on me and water gets down in me. When I won't come on people hit me and kick me. Then they Turn me up so high my insides start to burn.

I am a wall

You may think that my job is easy, but you have another think coming. I have fat holes in me for the doors and windows. There is one thing I like, that is having things that other people don't get to have. And pipes go in and out of me every where. But to make myself happy I just think I'm the main rison of every thing!

A flor is what you walk on. A flor do not let you fall on it. Becase it is noting fun and when you walk on one you will get some bubble gum on your shos and you will not like it.

FIGURE 1-5 Differing Maturity Levels of Writing in a Classroom

Of the four papers given in Figure 1–5, students 1 and 4 appear to have similar developmental levels in so far as style of writing and imagination are concerned. However, other examples of writing may be needed to verify that these students are at similar places in their writing abilities. These two students, in all probability should be placed at a different entry point of the writing curriculum than students 2 and 3, who did not carry out the intent of the assignment. It is possible, however, that all four students whose writing is depicted in Figure 1–5, as well as other students in the same classroom, might at times be taught some lessons in writing together. They might also be in some other language arts groups together. As will be explained in detail in Chapter 2, grouping should be flexible—cutting across different developmental levels for correction of specific problems held in common by students.

Procedures for determining abilities and levels of students must be well defined and well understood by teachers. In addition, teachers must know the curriculum. Most language arts curricula are outlined in a spiral design, meaning that skills such as writing a paragraph are presented at a lower level of complexity, but later in the same year or during the following year, presented at a more complex level. Unfortunately, what often happens is that what is taught at a particular time in the year becomes locked into a specific grade level. Teachers then become reluctant to cross grade lines. Thus, a third-grade teacher may not move into an area of the curriculum with students who really are ready to move forward. In addition, teachers are too often reluctant to back students up and reteach that which has already been covered. In a corrective language arts program, these problems must be eliminated.

How Content is Organized is important in a corrective language arts program. To avoid the problem of overly rigid grade-line designations, language arts content should be arranged in broad bands. These include: (1) foundations or readiness content of an area such as handwriting; (2) formal instruction in an area which includes initial or introductory teaching of content to be taught; (3) formal instruction, intermediate level of content in an area; and (4) formal instruction, advanced content in an area. A full explanation of one curricular area, spelling, will be presented as a model in Chapter 4.

Within each of these four areas, specific skills and other components of the curriculum to be taught will be arranged in an increasingly complex arrangement, as in a spiral design, but with a high degree of flexibility built in. Thus, it is quite likely that some students in the same grade will be in the introductory level of a content area, while their classmates may be in an intermediate stage. The flexible scheme will also allow teachers to work with students who are on different grade levels in areas such as reading and spelling.

Two segments of a hypothetical writing curriculum are shown to illustrate how the curriculum is organized. The first segment comes from Level A (There are levels A, B, C, and D) in *formal writing: introductory*, and the second segment comes from level A (again, of levels A–D) of *formal writing: advanced.*

In *formal writing: introductory,* the student:
- dictates his/her own story or description of an event to the teacher or other scribe
- shows an interest in changing dictated story by adding and/or taking out words
- writes and illustrates own story

In *formal writing: advanced,* the student:
- uses *who, what, when, where,* and *how* in both narrative and expository writing
- identifies when he/she needs additional information about a topic in order to enhance writing on that topic
- uses basic resource books such as encyclopedias to gain additional information about a topic
- reads extensively on a topic in order to enhance writing on that topic

How does a curriculum organized around the design presented match up with language arts curricula in existence? This is difficult to address, given the polarization found today in the language arts. This polarization comes about because of the question of whether or not to teach what some see as an endless array of skills, sometimes called the "bottom up" approach to teaching, or to teach students in a more natural context of language use, depending on this natural use of language to lead to appropriate skill development. Some identify this as an emphasis on "meaning comes first." This has led to the term "top down" which, it is argued, leads to appropriate skill development. The whole language movement typifies this latter approach.

The debate over a "bottom up" or "top down" approach to language arts instruction will continue well into the years ahead. While the "back to the basics" movement in many states has led to the careful delineation of skills in the language arts and mathematics, the whole language movement with its broader function of language use is tending to soften skill-by-skill teaching. Yet, confusion reigns even among those who advocate whole language, as pointed out by Bergerron who, after analyzing the content of professional articles on whole language, states that whole language has been defined as a method, a philosophy, a theory, a theoretical orientation, a program, a curriculum, and even an attitude of mind.[20]

The curriculum design advocated in this book, while providing a large number of skills and other components to be learned, is not intended to be aligned with either a "bottom up" or "top down" approach to teaching the language arts. The language arts is too diverse an area to be so quickly categorized. Written composition and handwriting are good examples. Students are encouraged to be creative in written composition. Teachers are much more accepting of diversity in what and how a student writes in creative writing than in handwriting when students are learning how to form letters of the alphabet. Allowing a lot of diversity in the latter language arts area could lead to handwriting in which letters written by one student are not recognized by other students, leading to a gap in communication. John Dewey once said that, "Mankind likes to think in terms of extreme opposites. It is given to formulating its beliefs in terms of *either-ors*, between which it recognizes no intermediate possibilities . . ."[21] Whether language arts teachers have fallen into this trap over the debate of skills teaching versus whole language teaching should be considered.

The curricular design advocated in this book, given in four broad bands and clusters of skills in each, can be adapted to either a "bottom up" or a "top down" approach to teaching. If a teacher believes in the whole language or naturalistic approach to teaching the language arts, that teacher should have a good idea of what skills in a whole language activity will evolve, usually over time, from the activity. If those skills do not emerge, some additional help will be needed for the student who appears to have problems. This does not mean, however, that the teacher must abandon his/her philosophy. Such a teacher might use the curricular design suggested in this book as a reference point. For example, if students have been involved in a reading-writing activity that calls for writing persuasively, the curriculum in use could be examined to see what elements actually have been identified as persuasive or argumentative writing, such as presenting an issue, giving the writer's view, stating another's view, and so on. Through skillful questions, giving of examples, conferencing with students about their writing, and other solid interactive strategies, a teacher who believes in whole language can weave content into his/her teaching which, on the surface, might appear to be a testimony to exclusive teaching of basic skills in language arts. If, on the other hand, a teacher is of the "skills orientation" approach to teaching, the curricular design suggested in this book in which related, increasingly more difficult skills can be clustered, should prove helpful.

All teachers, regardless of what approach they take to teaching the language arts, should know the content of their discipline. Before any new skill is introduced, some thought should be given to what the students know that will help them learn the new skill. In whole language programs, activities that are more naturalistic also call for some thought to background that is needed to insure success, as well as some thought to skill development. An example in whole language can be given to explain this point. In a whole language class where stories from literature are being used to teach reading, students often are asked to retell a story in sequence rather than answer test questions about the skill of following a sequence in a story. The curricular framework identified in this book can be adapted to such an approach, with whole language teachers using the curriculum as a guide regardless of the method for determining if students know important skills.

In a language arts program, and especially one that is corrective in nature, a form of mental set or readiness for the skill or activity is developed. This is not a new idea, but one that has not systematically been implemented in the language arts. Gagné points out that prerequisites, serving as prior learning, may support the new learning by activating certain cognitive strategies (for example, attending, perceiving) and by becoming an actual part of the new learning. An example given by Gagné of prerequisite skills fulfilling this role is in the pronunciation of a printed word that has a *final e* and a *medial a* as in the word *page*. The three prerequisite skills are identifying the *final e*, identifying the *medial a*, and naming the *long a* sound.[22]

An example of the language arts skill of *syllabication* and its prerequisites, are given in Table 1–2. This design for examining the relationship of content will be given attention, not so much in an attempt to ask teachers to teach all skills and other content this way but to motivate teachers to think in terms of, *What must students in this group know in order to learn what I want them to learn.* Such a mode of thinking could indeed pay dividends in a corrective program.

Summary

1. Language arts are elements and systems within a language that aid people as they process a language and help people communicate with one another. The language arts has four basic strands, including *reading, writing, speaking,* and *listening.* Each strand has substrands such as spelling in *writing,* as well as an array of knowledge components, such as concepts, skills, generalizations, and so on.

2. When the language arts are being taught, finding weaknesses students may have, as well as correcting these weaknesses, can best be done when the various components of language arts are understood. In addition, knowing how these components are best learned adds to the effectiveness of language arts teaching. Effective teaching of all components is based on their frequent use in meaningful language situations. However, there is some variation in ways that these components are taught, and these should be known by teachers.

3. Classrooms are panoramas of differences that must be accommodated. These differences exist in specific categories, including academic abilities, background

TABLE 1–2 Prerequisites for Syllabication

New Skill: Syllabication Prerequisites

1. Detecting separate words in two-syllable compound words (e.g., *fire* and *man* in *fireman*)
2. Knowing differences between vowel and consonant sounds
3. Detecting number of vowel sounds in words
4. Understanding the concept of syllable
5. Understanding that each syllable has only one vowel sound
6. Knowing reason(s) for dividing words into syllables

experiences, interests in general, interests in learning, learning styles and character-istics, and interests in specific school assignments.

4. Too often, schools address group commonalities rather than individual dif-ferences. The same spelling word lists for all students, the same handwriting lesson for all students at the same time, and the restriction of students to the same writing topic are but three of many examples that can be given of group commonalities taking precedence over individual differences in the language arts.

5. To deal with individual differences, programmatic decisions must be made, as well as day-to-day decisions by teachers. Corrective teaching is designed to meet individual differences. Such a program helps teachers handle individual differences within a classroom, as opposed to remedial programs in which students are sent to a special classroom. Corrective teaching is done in small groups rather than being limited to independent assignments—so often a feature of earlier approaches to corrective teaching.

6. One very special feature of a student-involved corrective language arts pro-gram is knowing students. Teachers should know that there is a broad spectrum of learning styles and characteristics. Among these are field-dependent, field-indepen-dent, visual, auditory, kinesthetic, and tactual learners. In addition, there are learners who conceptualize/categorize in different ways, as well as those who are more reflective than others. Lessons planned should take into account wide differ-ences in learning modalities.

7. Error analysis is also a very important area in knowing individual learners. Teachers must look for patterns of errors rather than focus on isolated errors that students make. Students' papers are very important in this area, and a system must be established for examining a series of papers to detect error patterns.

8. Teachers must also know socioeconomic and cultural differences among students and how these impact on teaching. Children from disadvantaged back-grounds (lower income African-Americans and whites, immigrant children; chil-dren from rural, isolated, and impoverished areas; and so on) often do not have the backgrounds to cope with the school culture and its language. Adjustments must be made.

9. All students in classrooms should not be expected to perform at the same point of the curriculum in any of the language arts areas. Thus, teachers should know developmental levels and match these levels with the curricular levels of the language arts being taught. The language arts is too diverse for teachers to gravitate totally toward practices that are either all one approach to teaching or another. Teachers should be cautious about an "either-or" pitfall in teaching, always looking at the diversity of their discipline and what might be needed to teach such content. Attempting to ask what students should know before a new skill or activity is intro-duced is a principle teachers in a corrective program should follow. Knowing pre-requisite skills, concepts, and other curricular components is one way of following this principle.

Reviewing, Connecting, and Expanding What You Have Learned

Directions

In the summary section of Chapter 1, each paragraph is numbered in the left-hand margin. These have been placed there to help in class discussions on some of the ideas that follow or other ideas your college professor/in-service director might have. The activities that follow should help you better understand what you have read, expand on what you have learned, and help you put into practice some ideas advanced in this chapter.

1. (Paragraph 1) Write a definition for the language arts. Then identify the four language arts strands. Following this, select one strand and identify one or more of its substrands.

2. (Paragraph 1) Eight knowledge components in the language arts were identified. One was concepts. Can you recall other components? Perhaps in a small group, you and your classmates can together identify the eight components presented.

3. (Paragraph 2) Be able to tell in class answers to the following questions:

    a. In what one way are all eight knowledge components that you have identified taught the same way?

    b. In what ways are concepts and vocabularies learned differently?

    c. In what ways are skills and generalizations learned differently?

4. (Paragraph 3) For each category of differences presented in paragraph 3, write a one-sentence explanation of why teachers should know this area of differences among students.

5. (Paragraph 4) List from seven to ten examples of how group commonalities are given more attention than individual differences in the language arts. For each example listed, write a description of how a teacher might move from attention to group commonalities to attention to individual differences.

6. (Paragraph 5) Outline the major differences among corrective, remedial, and individualized-prescriptive teaching.

7. (Paragraph 6) Identify from five to seven different learning styles that you have learned. Write a one-paragraph definition for each learning style. Be able to argue for a rationale for teachers knowing learning styles and characteristics as a prerequisite for developing an effective corrective language arts program.

8. (Paragraph 6) Select two "quite different" students in a school where you are meeting requirements in field experiences, and do a learning styles inventory on each student. Be prepared to discuss your findings in class.

9. (Paragraph 7) Analyze written assignments of two different students in a class where you are in field experiences. Prepare a list of errors detected for each student. Be prepared to discuss the errors in class. (Optional: Without using names of your selected students, prepare an overhead transparency on detected error types to use with the class that you are taking.)

10. (Paragraph 8) Select a student from your class (if you are a teacher) or field-experience class (if you are a prospective teacher) from a low socioeconomic background. Either interview the student or do a case study. Prepare a description of the student that takes into account his/her interests, how books/learning are (are not) a part of the home environment, language patterns that appear to be different, and any other factors in this case that you consider characteristic of disadvantaged students.

11. (Paragraph 9) Plan a language arts lesson on a specific skill such as syllabication in which: (a) prerequisites are examined prior to introducing the new skill; (b) students without satisfactory mastery of the prerequisites are taught appropriate background skills and concepts; and (c) students ready for the new skill are allowed to move forward to a lesson on the new skill. One lesson with all three parts (a, b, c) may be more appropriate than three separate mini-lessons.

Endnotes

1. Richard E. Mayer, *Educational Psychology—A Cognitive Approach* (Boston: Little, Brown and Co., 1987), pp. 102–6.

2. Margaret G. McKeown et al., "Some Effects of the Nature and Frequency of Vocabulary Instruction on the Knowledge and Use of Words," *Reading Research Quarterly* 20 (1985): 522–23.

3. Dolores Durkin, *Teaching Them to Read*, 5th ed. (Boston: Allyn and Bacon, 1989), pp. 334–35.

4. Edmund H. Henderson, *Learning to Read and Spell: The Child's Knowledge of Words*: (DeKalb, Illinois: Northern Illinois University Press, 1981), p. 50.

5. Lyn Corno and Richard E. Snow, "Adapting Teaching to Individual Differences Among Learners," in *Handbook of Research on Teaching*, 3rd ed., ed. Merlin C. Wittrock, American Educational Research Association Project, (New York: Macmillan Publishing Co., 1986), p. 607.

6. Wayne Otto and Richard J. Smith, *Corrective and Remedial Teaching*, 3rd ed. (Boston: Houghton Mifflin Co., 1980), pp. 25–27.

7. Bruce A. Gutknecht, Gwen P. Johnson, and Diane L. Chapman, *Planning Effective Reading Instruction* (Dubuque, Iowa: Kendall/Hunt Publishing Co., 1987), pp. 331–32.

8. Rita S. Dunn and Kenneth J. Dunn, "Learning Styles/Teaching Styles: Should They . . . Can They . . . Be Matched?" *Educational Leadership* 36 (1979): 238.

9. Robert M. Smith, *Learning How to Learn* (Chicago: Follett Publishing Co., 1982), pp. 60–65.

10. Herman A. Witkin, "Cognitive Style in Academic Performance and in Teacher-Student Relations," in *Individuality in Learning*, ed. Samuel Messick & Associates (San Francisco: Jossey-Bass Publishers, 1976), pp. 43–68.

11. Ibid.

12. Rita Dunn, Kenneth Dunn, and Gary E. Price, *Learning Style Inventory Manual* (Lawrence, Kansas: Price Systems, 1981), pp. 2, 3.

13. Ibid., 4, 12–13.

14. Janet Perrin, *Learning Style Inventory: Primary-Manual for Administration, Interpretation, and Teaching Suggestions* (Jamaica, New York: Learning Styles Network, St. Johns University, 1983), pp. 1–4.

15. Walter B. Barbe and Raymond H. Swassing with Michael N. Milone, Jr., *Teaching Through Modality Strengths* (Columbus, Ohio: Zaner-Bloser, 1979), pp. 35–37.

16. Clinton S. Hackney and Virginia H. Lucas, *Zaner-Bloser Handwriting, A Way to Self-Expression,* Grade 3 (Columbus, Ohio: Zaner-Bloser, Inc., 1991), pp. B58, B59.

17. Shirl E. Gilbert II and Geneva Gay, "Improving the Success in School of Poor Black Children," *Phi Delta Kappan* 67 (l985): 133–37.

18. Joan M. First, "Immigrant Students in U.S. Public Schools: Challenges With Solutions," *Phi Delta Kappan* 70 (1988): 215.

19. Peter Desberg, Dale E. Elliott, and George Marsh, "American Black English and Spelling," in *Cognitive Processes in Spelling,* ed. Uta Frith (London: Academic Press, 1980), pp. 75–77.

20. Bette S. Bergerron, "What Does the Term Whole Language Mean? Constructing a Definition From the Literature," *Journal of Reading Behavior* 22 (1990): 301–29

21. John Dewey, *Experience and Education* (New York: Collier Books, 1938), p. 17.

22. Robert M. Gagné, *The Conditions of Learning,* 3rd ed. (New York: Holt, Rinehart, and Winston, 1977), pp. 267–68.

Bibliography

(Differences among Students)

Bennett, Christine I., *Comprehensive Multicultural Education,* 2nd ed. (Boston: Allyn and Bacon, 1990)

Edelsky, Carole, and Rosegrant, T. J. "Language Development for Mainstreamed Severely-Handicapped Non-Verbal Children," *Language Arts* 58 (1981): 68.

Knight, Lester N., "Reading for the Linguistically and Culturally Different Child," in *Teaching Reading,* 3rd ed., edited by J. Estill Alexander (Glenview, Illinois: Scott, Foresman/Little, Brown College Division, 1988), pp. 418-43.

Malstrom, Jean. *Understanding Language —A Primer for the Language Arts Teacher* (New York: St. Martin's Press, 1977).

Smith, Delores E. "Understanding Some Behaviors of Culturally Different Children," *International Education,* 21 (1991): 31

Smith, E. Brooks, Kenneth S. Goodman, and Robert Merideth, "Dialect Differences and School Programs," in *Language and Thinking in School,* 2nd ed. (New York: Holt, Rinehart and Winston, 1976), pp. 46–65.

Tiedt, Pamela L. and Tiedt, Iris M., *Multicultural Teaching—A Handbook of Activities, Information, and Resources,* 3rd ed. (Boston: Allyn and Bacon, 1990).

(Instructional and Diagnostic Strategies)

Burns, Paul C. and Broman, Betty L. *The Language Arts in Childhood Education,* 5th ed. (Boston: Houghton Mifflin Co., 1983).

Rakes, Thomas A. and Choate, Joyce S. *Language Arts: Detecting and Correcting Special Needs* (Boston: Allyn and Bacon, 1989).

(Learning Theory and Characteristics)

Barbe, Walter and Swassing, Raymond. *Teaching Through Modality Strengths: Concepts and Practices* (Columbus, Ohio: Zaner-Bloser, 1979).

Cornett, Claudia E. *What You Should Know About Teaching and Learning Styles* (Bloomington, Indiana: Phi Delta Kappa Educational Foundation, 1983).

(Whole Language in the Language Arts)

Altwerger, Bess; Edelsky, Carole; and Flores, Barbara M. "Whole Language: What's New?" *The Reading Teacher* 41 (1987): 144.

Edelsky, Carole. "Whose Agenda is This Anyway? A Response to McKenna, Robinson, and Miller." *Educational Researcher* 19 (1990): 7.

McKenna, Michael C.; Robinson, Richard D.; and Miller, John W. "Whole Language: A Research Agenda for the Nineties." *Educational Researcher* 19 (1990): 3.

_____ . "Whole Language and the Need for Open Inquiry: A Rejoinder to Edelsky." *Educational Researcher* 19 (1990): 12.

Slaughter, Helen B. "Indirect and Direct Teaching in a Whole Language Program," *The Reading Teacher* 42 (1988): 30.

2

Organizing for Corrective Teaching

Focus

Recall how teachers you have known helped individual students with special problems in the language arts. When several students needed extra help, what did the teacher do? Were the students left to go along with the larger group and not given extra help? Was extra help planned for a later time? How were the students grouped for this help? These are points to be addressed in Chapter 2, in which you will learn the following:

   1. How group size varies from lesson to lesson
   2. The formation of two basic kinds of groups (base groups and flexible, differentiated [flex] groups)
   3. How other grouping patterns (for example, cooperative learning groups) can be a part of a student-involved corrective language arts program
   4. How selected techniques, such as webbing (a special scheme for studying themes in literature), can be utilized in a corrective language arts program
   5. Which language arts strand (reading, speaking, listening, writing) is more easily adapted to flexible grouping schemes
   6. How a total yearly plan would look when base and flex groups are implemented
   7. How a student's weekly schedule would look when base and flex groups are used in the language arts

   In Chapter 1, differences among learners cited were in the areas of aptitude for learning, general interests of students, learning styles, students' interests in school tasks, prior training, and background experiences. These differences permeate all language arts strands and their substrands. Teachers face a tremendous task when differences in these areas are considered for a total class of 25–35 students. This task is best accomplished when there is maximum flexibility in how students are grouped for instruction. Grouping is valuable to the extent that it helps reach each individual with his/her unique problems.

As in Chapter 1, questions should be raised as you read Chapter 2. One is how to set up various kinds of groups suggested in Chapter 2. Another is the extent to which grouping procedures advocated in this book should be set up for teaching the language arts. A teacher might not be able to group students for all the language arts exactly as advocated in this book. Ask yourself questions like these, and bring them to class. They will make excellent classroom discussions.

A good way to begin thinking about organizing for and implementing a corrective language arts program is to examine some of the different situations that teachers face daily in the classroom. In Table 2–1, several kinds of teaching situations are presented. As you examine these, note different grouping patterns for carrying out the various kinds of instructional activities described.

An analysis of the group size in these situations reveals that the teachers involved worked with groups having one student, two students, five students, approximately one-third of the class, about one-half the class, and the total class. In each case, teachers assumed both direct and indirect instructional roles. Thus, in Case 1, the teacher worked directly with the one student, but indirectly with other students through monitoring of their seatwork.

In the following section, two types of grouping plans are proposed, specifically recommended for a student-involved corrective language arts program. In one plan, the focus is on placing students in groups according to different developmental levels. In the other plan, the focus is on regrouping students with common needs, regardless of developmental levels involved.

Flexible Grouping in a Corrective Language Arts Program

Grouping students for instruction has long been a concern of educators, often leading to vigorous debate. The most controversial argument has been whether to have homogeneous groups (students with similar abilities) or heterogeneous groups (students with varying abilities) for instruction. On the one hand, it has been argued that homogeneous ability groups reduce the range of abilities among the students, leading to more appropriate instruction for students whose abilities are similar. Others advocate that differences still exist among students after ability grouping, and that variations in the range of students' abilities is not only natural but facilitates students learning from each other.

TABLE 2–1   Different Grouping Patterns in the Elementary School

Case 1:   A fourth-grade student is having trouble writing a paragraph. In 5–10 minute sessions, the teacher, throughout the week, spends a total of 45 minutes helping this student, one-on one, write a simple paragraph, while other students in the class work on seatwork.

Case 2:   Five students in a fifth-grade classroom cannot write simple outlines, although they have been introduced to outlining. Two separate periods of 20 minutes each are spent by the teacher working with this small group of students. Other students do their assignments independently while the teacher works with the five students on outlining.

Case 3:   A sixth-grade teacher seldom teaches language arts to the total class. All of language arts, not just reading, is spent in small-group work (usually four groups). The teacher moves from group to group helping students. Sometimes the teacher works with all students in each small group; sometimes with individuals within each group.

Case 4:   After reading several Haiku (a special type of Japanese poetry) over several days, a language arts lesson is taught to a total group of third graders. After the major characteristics of Haiku have been covered, the class is divided into three groups to write their Haiku (each student writing his/her own Haiku). One group consists of students who the teacher thinks needs extra help on getting started with their poems.

Case 5:   Students work in pairs in a second-grade class, drilling each other on spelling words for the week. The teacher moves about, helping students with pronunciation of words and overseeing the drills.

Case 6:   Students in a fifth-grade classroom—in small groups of two or three—periodically throughout the day, use tape recorders to practice short speeches that they are going to make to the class during the following weeks. The students in their small groups tape their speeches and listen to and critique each other's speech. The teacher coordinates the activity, making sure that as many students as possible use the tape recorder when their turns come and when they can best afford to be away from other classroom activities.

Case 7:   Two large groups of third-grade students (approximately one-half the class in each) check their written compositions by using a checklist of, "Here is What a Good Composition Contains." The teacher interacts with the students to see that they are on task and understand each checkpoint on the evaluative chart being used.

Case 8:   Two first-grade students are having trouble recognizing all the letters of the alphabet. The teacher works with these two students together for a few minutes each day until they have learned to recognize all letters of the alphabet. Altogether, about one and one-half hours are spent with the students over a two-week period. While the teacher works with these two students, other students are doing seatwork.

Sometimes classes are broken down within a class, and instruction is developed for several levels of students. This grouping pattern is most often found in reading. However, such groups are frequently too rigid, with virtually no cross-grouping, and students in high and low groups sometimes get distorted concepts of their abilities.

Groups for Different Stages of Development

What is needed is a grouping plan that is considerably more flexible than what now exists. Such a plan should be one that accounts for developmental levels while at the same time, provides for regrouping to meet special needs of students. Two such models are presented in Figure 2–1

In Model 1 of Figure 2–1, the total class is presented with the same lesson initially, but then breakout groups are formed according to identified, common needs. This is basically the situation described in Case 4 of Table 2–1 where the total class is introduced to a lesson on Haiku and then broken into smaller groups. In Model 2 of Figure 2–1, developmental groups are formed already. Such formation is based on the teacher's knowledge of developmental levels of students. In this grouping pattern, students are placed in developmental levels according to the students' levels of advancement in a curricular area or the grade levels (for example, spelling grade levels) at which they perform best. In this book, these groups are referred to as base groups.

Although any classroom has different developmental levels, hasty judgments should not be made in placing students in different levels. Regrouping should also be done when needed, and flexibility should prevail. When a student is interested in a story being read by a base group other than the one in which the student is currently working, he/she should be allowed to sit in on that story. When a student catches on to what is being studied in his/her base group, the student might try another base group for a few days to see if that one is better matched to his/her level of ability. Sometimes two base groups might be so close together in an area of study that it is appropriate to merge them for a while or perhaps for the rest of the year. Sometimes two groups might work together, thus providing a group that is larger than either group. Never should base groups be as rigid as traditional reading groups have become.

Groups for Special-Needs Instruction

Another grouping pattern allows regrouping across base groups according to noted deficiencies in the same language arts area or, in some cases, noted strengths where enrichment activities would be helpful. These are flexible, differentiated groups identified in this book as flex groups. An example of a flex group would be several students working together because they have had trouble placing commas in sentences. In this kind of group, formed for one or more lessons, there may be some of

Model 1

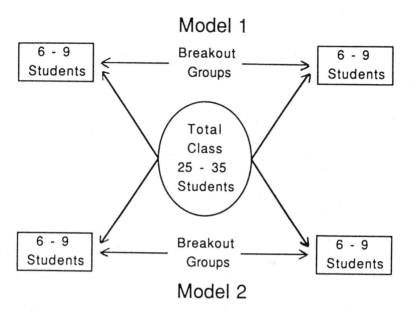

| 6 - 9 Students | ← Breakout Groups → | 6 - 9 Students |

Total Class 25 - 35 Students

| 6 - 9 Students | ← Breakout Groups → | 6 - 9 Students |

Model 2

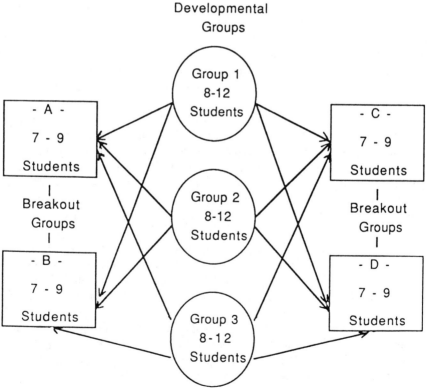

Developmental Groups

Group 1 8-12 Students

Group 2 8-12 Students

Group 3 8-12 Students

- A -
7 - 9 Students
Breakout Groups
- B -
7 - 9 Students

- C -
7 - 9 Students
Breakout Groups
- D -
7 - 9 Students

FIGURE 2–1   Two Models for Flexible Grouping

the best writers and some of the poorest writers in the classroom. Go back to the eight cases in Table 2–1 and identify the four groups that are examples of flex groups.

In Table 2–1, the student having trouble with paragraph writing (Case 1), the five students having trouble outlining (Case 2), students needing extra help getting started writing Haiku (Case 4), and the two first-grade students having trouble recognizing alphabet letters (Case 8) are all examples of flex groups. In each case, special instruction is required for some, but not all, students.

Implementation of Base and Flex Groups

How often do base and flex groups meet? This question, when answered, provides a preview of how a total language arts class would operate in a student-involved corrective program. On the average, base groups would meet two to three times per week. They might meet on Monday to: (1) take a test to determine how well the students in the group have learned what they are being taught; (2) review what had been taught the week before; and/or (3) discuss the objectives and plans for the instruction for that week. For example, one base group in a fourth-grade class might be working on a short unit on writing business letters. If the group started studying business letters on Thursday of the previous week, an assignment might have been to bring to class letters from home that *can* be shared. The students, who were encouraged to find three or four letters each, meet at a large work table in the back of the room to look at the letters for the purpose of examining the format for business letters.

After deciding the format for business letters, plans are made to write letters to nearby businesses whose owners have agreed to participate in this project. On Wednesday, students decide to whom they will write, they jot down some points they want to remember about the framework of business letters, and they decide the content for their letters. Some students may advance to the point on Wednesday where they begin writing; most, however, do not. On Thursday, the teacher works with two members of the group in a flex group (with students from other base groups) on how to use synonymous subjects to eliminate redundancy in writing (for example, substituting phrases such as "your place of business," "the establishment where you work," or "your company" for "the Pinnacle Company" [or whatever the name of the company is]). Other members of the base group are allowed to work on their letters. On Friday, the base group members either write or rewrite their business letters.

Flex groups would meet more often than two to three times per week, with the composition of each group changing more frequently than for base groups. The frequency of how often flex groups meet is dependent on how thorough the teacher is in assessing problems across the several base groups.

Spelling can be used to provide examples of several base and flex groups in operation and how the teacher might interact with the groups. On Monday, students are asked to report to their base groups according to previously determined arrangements. If there are three such groups (for example, groups identified as S, P, and E groups), students would go to their designated area in the room with materials needed for spelling. Materials needed would probably include spelling books (although some school systems are now moving to the use of word lists from other sources), spelling folders, and paper and pencils. There might also be extra lists of words, with perhaps some from subjects other than language arts. There may be lists that a school or system has developed over the years because of the troublesome nature of selected words to students in the school or system. Each base group would have its own list of words, although there would be some overlap. The different lists would, in some cases, parallel instructional levels. Once groups are in place, the teacher calls attention to what is to be done. Instructions may be listed on the chalkboard for each group, or in some cases, on a task sheet that has been prepared for that day.

Some total-class activities may exist, thus employing Model 1 of Figure 2–1. For example, the total class may be given a test to determine specific error types being made. There may be a few lessons throughout the year where the total class is brought together for instruction because too many students in each base group are doing poorly on a skill. Teachers should take advantage of situations calling for total-group instruction, but in a corrective program such instruction will not be as dominant as it now is.

Advantages of Base and Flex Groups

The advantages of base and flex groups are numerous. First, base groups enable teachers to more easily match what is being taught to the achievement levels of students. Second, base groups allow teachers to individualize instruction in a manageable way. Third, base groups provide more opportunities for teachers to interact with students. When teachers interact with students in total-group instructional situations, it is difficult to interact with more than just a few of the more aggressive, verbal, and usually brighter students. Student-student interaction, in some situations, is also best promoted through base groups.

In addition to the overall help in providing more appropriate instruction for correcting problems that students have, another advantage of flex groups is that of facilitating the match of instructional activities/materials to learning styles. If several students from various base groups are having trouble spacing between words in manuscript writing, two flex groups might be formed according to preferred learning style, such as, visual or tactile. Two separate corrective lessons should then be planned. One would have a heavy focus on visual aspects of learning to space between words; the other would have more emphasis on tactile activities in learning how to space between words. In the visually-oriented lesson, students might use a plastic overlay or grid that has vertical lines drawn to correspond to a specific sentence being written. The overlay, when placed over a student's writing, helps the student determine where problems exist, thus involving students in assessing/correcting their problems in this area.

Another advantage of flex groups is the use of students' interests in instruction. An example in writing could be the regrouping of students from different base groups who are particularly interested in horses. The students are regrouped for two or three class periods during a week of instruction. During these sessions, the students examine books on the topic from the school's media center or books brought from home. Through exploration and group discussion, students learn descriptive words for telling about horses as well as new facts about horses, such as, how horses were domesticated. This knowledge and descriptive words learned are later used in a writing assignment in base groups.

Yet another advantage of flex groups is the help provided in shoring up sagging attitudes toward a particular language arts area. If several students from different writing groups appear to be negative about poetry, one or more lessons may be planned in a flex group for these students. Poems that parallel the interests of the students in the flex group would be read. If the students are old enough, discussions could be held about specific reasons why the students do not like poetry.

Disadvantages of Base and Flex Groups

While the advantages of base and flex groups outweigh the disadvantages, nevertheless there are some disadvantages that should be mentioned. Such grouping schemes take time to organize. They are sometimes difficult to manage. They require that students be more independent in their work habits, and thus call for more training in this area. They require the use of more diversified materials and equipment than teachers may now have or use. And last, but not least, these grouping schemes require patience on the part of teachers and administrators who are implementing them.

However, even with the number of problems that might exist, the base and flex grouping scheme advocated in this book can work and be more effective than what usually exists in classrooms today. Teachers organizing base and flex groups will want to move into them slowly as will be suggested later. Teachers will also want to work together. Setting up such groups can be lonely if teachers attempt to do them alone. The support for each other and the ideas that several creative minds working together can generate will make the problems presented less threatening.

Flexible Grouping Patterns in Other Contexts

While flex groups as defined are presented to provide more flexibility in a student-involved corrective language arts program, there have been flexible grouping patterns suggested in other contexts. These patterns should also be known and used by teachers. Two other kinds of grouping patterns, peer teaching (which includes cooperative learning) and project groups, are presented in the following section of this book.

Peer Teaching/Cooperative Learning

Peer teaching involves students teaching other students. In Case 5 of Table 2–1, an example was given in which students worked in pairs in a second-grade classroom, drilling each other on the week's spelling words. At one time, reinforcement and drill activities were considered more appropriate for peer teaching than activities where new materials were to be introduced. However, with the advent of new kinds of group instruction, this has changed.

Cooperative learning involves small groups of students working together, usually to reach team goals. However, individuals have responsibilities clearly outlined and are encouraged to carry out these responsibilities. Depending on the cooperative learning strategy being used, students may teach each other, work with one student on a segment of a project assigned, and/or participate as a learner in a group situation.

Research on cooperative learning, according to Slavin, indicates that at various grade levels, this type of learning has considerable merit. The studies identified by Slavin were those done to explore the value of five well-defined strategies in cooperative learning. These strategies, briefly summarized, call for the instruction to be carefully organized with students knowing what is expected of them.[1]

Teams Games Tournaments (TGT). consists of teams of students from different races or racial groups, ability levels, and sexes (4–5 students per team). Students are given worksheets in preparation for what is identified as "instructional tournaments." Students on each team study together to get all team members ready for the tournaments, usually held once per week.

Students are placed at tournament tables (three students per table) based on past performances in the academic area being studied. Students perform academic games related to the content of practice worksheets, with each student at a table representing his/her team. Scores are kept, and tournament teams change weekly to keep the competition relatively balanced. A newsletter is prepared by the teacher announcing successful teams.[2]

Student Teams Achievement Divisions (STAD). involves the same type of heterogeneous groups formed in TGT. Students, after studying with their team members, take brief quizzes with scores then converted to team scores. The system of scoring is such that past performances are used to compare an individual student's score with reference groups similar to the student's ability and performance, not with the entire class. Each week, a procedure is employed to keep competition as equal as possible.[3]

Jigsaw. also involving small, heterogeneous groups, is usually used where a total class is organized to study a broad topic that can be clearly subdivided into smaller segments. In the language arts, a broad topic, such as "How to Write a Good Story" is an example. Segments of this topic might be "Interesting Setting,"

"Good Character Descriptions," and so on. Students are regrouped, with members in a new group assigned the same segment of content to be learned and then to be taught to original team members. A quiz follows, but results are assigned to each individual as opposed to a team score. (In Slavin"s Jigsaw II, scores are assigned to the group.) Again, segments of a broad topic to be learned and taught to other members of each student's original Jigsaw team must be very explicitly stated. In his explanation of Jigsaw, Slavin uses biography as an example of how a broad topic might be broken down into subparts, stating that this topic might be broken down into early years, schooling, and first accomplishments (of the person being studied).[4]

Small Group Teaching (SGT). consists of small groups (2–6 students per group) working on subtopics of a broader topic. The groups are further divided according to tasks to be performed, with each student pursuing his/her task. A group presentation follows that is evaluated by other students and the teacher. The focus of SGT is group inquiry, discussion, and data gathering through cooperative learning.[5]

Cooperative Integrated Reading and Composition (CIRC). is a strategy that has been specifically developed for and applied to the language arts. Three basic elements incorporated in CIRC are: (1) reading groups (8–15 students per group) in which reading levels help determine how students are grouped; (2) teams made up of two or three students within reading groups and then pairs of these teams which cut across different reading levels; and (3) basal-reader activities (or for school systems not using basals, and/or advocating whole language, other sources such as children's trade books) introduced to each original reading group by the teacher, consisting of vocabulary development, setting purposes for reading, and reviewing stories read.

Students in pairs work on numerous language arts activities together in an effort to perform well for the team on quizzes, written compositions, and book reports. Students also are involved in other team and/or paired activities such as taking spelling pretests, retelling of the story read, using the dictionary to find new words, reading/sharing stories in trade books, and participating in writers' workshops. In the latter activity, students brainstorm about a topic, listen to the teacher give instructions on form and/or techniques in writing, write, and hold peer review conferences.[6]

Why is cooperative learning important in a student-involved corrective language arts program? As pointed out in Chapter 1 lower-income African-American children benefit from working together.[7] Collaborative learning, a term designating any type of working together, incorporates all five cooperative learning strategies presented. It was also pointed out in Chapter 1 that students whose learning style is classified as field-dependent are more attuned to the social environment. Compared to students whose learning style is more field-independent, these individuals benefit from collaborative learning.[8] However, this does not mean that students from groups other than lower-income African-Americans or field-dependent learners would not benefit from the cooperative learning strategies described. Indeed, these strategies have such a variety of activities suggested that the teacher can find many activities that would appeal to others (for example, field-independent learners should greatly benefit from the individual tasks that can be a part of cooperative learning strategies).

Students in cooperative learning groups will, on numerous occasions, require special-needs instruction and can be regrouped as the occasion calls for corrective measures. When this happens, flex groups would be formed. For example, in a study of biography in Jigsaw where students want to use outlining to teach others, there may be some students who need help with their outlining skills. If so, a flex group can be formed to teach (or reteach) some basic elements of outlining. How a flex group is formed after cooperative learning groups have been organized is shown in Figure 2–2.

Heterogeneous Groups	Regrouped Learning Teams	Flex Groups For Learning Outlining*
Group 1	Team 1–Early Life of George Washington	
Group 2		
Group 3	Team 2–George Washington's Schooling	Group of Eight Students From Cooperative Learning Teams
Group 4	Team 3–First Accomplishments of Washington	
Group 5		
Group 6	Team 4–Later Accomplishments of Washington	

FIGURE 2–2   Flex Groups in the Jigsaw Cooperative Learning Strategy

*These groups are organized when the teacher recognizes that several students will use outlining for teaching others their segment of the topic.

Project Teaching

Using a project approach, students in a class would, over an extended period of time, work on one theme as a class or on a variety of themes. Although projects have more often been used in science and social studies, language arts themes lend themselves to project work. An example of one theme in the language arts that might be appropriate for project work is, "Words and Expressions That We Have Borrowed from Many Lands." During the several weeks that such a project runs, many sources would be utilized from which students search for words and expressions used in homes, school, farming, industry, entertainment, and any other designated areas. Students would be divided into small groups according to the area or phase of the project on which the students involved are working. The students would meet periodically throughout the week to plan their approach to research needed to carry out their part of the class project, how they would display or present their findings, and how they would divide up tasks.

British primary schools have made good use of project teaching, utilizing themes in three different ways. Included are schoolwide themes, one theme for an entire class, and diverse themes within classrooms.[9]

Often those who advocate the use of projects, state that the approach has more meaning than other instructional approaches. There are those who advocate that as

Project Work Helps Provide Instructional Diversity in a Corrective Language Arts Program (*Photograph by Robert Heller*).

students work through various tasks necessary for projects to be successful, skills, processes, and other components of language arts content will be learned as needed. Regardless of one's view on this position, teachers will find numerous weaknesses in language arts skills and should take opportunities to regroup students for help with identified deficiencies. If, for example, the teacher notes that several students are having trouble using an encyclopedia while studying a topic, a flex group can be formed to help those students with the skills needed. Oral language weaknesses also can be shored up when noted in project activities. If it is noted that several students need special help in making oral presentations, a flex group can easily be organized to give special instruction to these few students. Such small-group sessions not only would provide a setting for help with oral-presentation skills, but would also provide an ideal setting for the students to practice their presentations prior to giving them to the whole class.

Project teaching can be combined with activities that are frequently cited in the literature for teaching language arts. One such activity is webbing, which has been advocated for use in literature units in the elementary school. It is presented here to show a variation in project work and because it has several characteristics of student-involved corrective teaching such as differentiated instruction. Webbing is a way to divide and subdivide themes and subthemes, using a large number of trade and/or other books that are available on the topics in question. An example of webbing, given by Norton, is on "Pioneer America" in which subtopics might be pioneer values, entertainment, education of children, and environment.[10] These subtopics would then be subdivided into even more subthemes as shown in Figure 2–3. Literature units would be developed, and students would explore their subthemes by using a variety of books. The webs shown in Figure 2–3 provide an excellent system for meeting different interests of students—a difference that, as stated, must be accounted for in a student-involved corrective program.

Webbing provides many opportunities for matching learning styles with activities. Students who are *verbal* learners could be provided additional opportunities to be involved in discussions, to hear segments of stories on audio tape, to listen to presentations by their peers, and a number of other oral-language activities that they might not otherwise be provided.

Webbing, because it calls for a wide array of activities, is an excellent approach for meeting the needs of both field-dependent and field-independent learners. Activities in which students work together to investigate a variety of subtopics should have appeal to field-dependent learners. Discussions about the subthemes should provide not only opportunities to learn new information, but opportunities to work collaboratively. On the other hand, field-independent learners would be provided with ample opportunities to do independent research on a topic, design an illustration, or prepare an outline on the theme or subtheme chosen for study. Literature units developed through webbing, according to Norton, have several advantages:

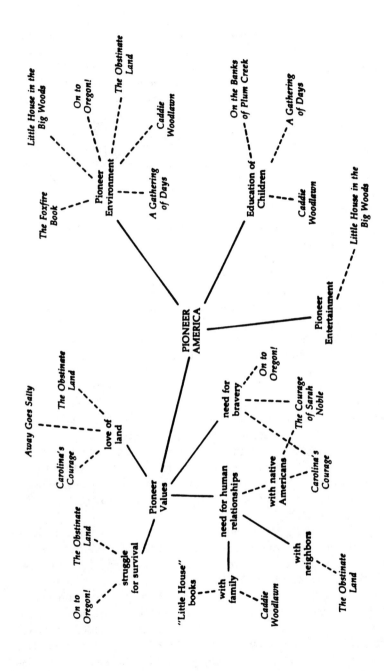

FIGURE 2–3 Flexible Grouping Through Webbing

Donna E. Norton, "Using a Webbing Process to Develop Children's Literature Units," *Language Arts* 59 (1982): 354. Copyright (1982) by the National Council of Teachers of English. Reprinted with permission.

1. *They allow teachers to differentiate instruction by providing trade books on several reading levels.*
2. *They let good and poor readers work together.*
3. *They promote integration of language arts as students plan together, discuss their topics, and present their results to an audience of their peers.*
4. *They make available interesting historical fiction and informational books that stimulate children's interests in social studies and science.*
5. *They include both fiction and nonfiction books that stimulate creativity.*[11]

Resolving Conflicts among Grouping Patterns

At this point, one could argue that the base and flex grouping schemes central to student-involved corrective teaching conflict with some of the basic tenets of cooperative learning and project groups. For example, from the beginning of their existence, base groups tend to be made up of students with similar abilities and/or developmental levels, while cooperative learning groups initially are heterogeneous. Project groups likewise tend to be more heterogeneous than do base groups. However, these are merely different groups, and add to the diversity of grouping patterns available for the teacher who would develop and implement a student-involved corrective program in the language arts.

Base and Flex Groups across the Language Arts Curriculum

Which language arts can best be adapted to a flexible grouping scheme that incorporates base and flex groups? This question will be answered in greater detail in the content chapters in this book. However, a preliminary answer is that spelling, reading, and handwriting are better adapted to the use of such groups (especially to Model 2 of Figure 2–1) than are the other language arts. Reading and spelling both can be grade-leveled, meaning that students can be tested to determine on what grade level they are reading and spelling. The handwriting curriculum is usually broken into segments according to the purpose of the handwriting content to be taught (such as, readiness for manuscript, maintenance of manuscript, and so on). Base and flex groups can easily be implemented across these curricular segments.

Written composition, listening, and speaking are not grade leveled as are reading and spelling. In addition, these language arts are not usually divided into segments according to function as is the handwriting curriculum. However, both Models 1 and 2 of Figure 2–1 can be adapted to these areas of the language arts curriculum as will be explained in the respective chapters on these topics.

Managing Base and Flex Groups Throughout the Year

At this point, a quite logical question can be asked about the number of base and flex groups that can be managed at one time and throughout the school year. Is it feasible to have base and flex groups across the total spectrum of the language arts? Base and flex groups can best be managed when the teacher does not try to set up groups for the mere existence of such groups. Grouping patterns of any kind are simply vehicles to help with instruction. When the grouping scheme alone becomes the end to achieve, rather than a means to an end, students will seldom gain what they should from the grouping scheme in use.

A cardinal rule to follow in setting up groups is one that reading teachers have been told when the question of the ideal number of reading groups comes up. The ideal number of groups is the number that fits into the timeframe and management capabilities of the teacher in charge of instruction. If there are four reading levels in a classroom and the teacher can effectively manage only three groups, provide creative instruction, and plan to meet individual needs of each student in all groups, it is better to have three groups than to go to four where any of these factors may break down. Also, too many groups in one area could mean that there are no groups in another area. The bottom line is that teachers should set up groups that they can work with and make maximum, meaningful contact with students.

In setting up base and flex groups, the teacher must be able to manage the total class, plan wisely, and teach creatively. One strategy is to start out the year with base and flex groups in perhaps two language arts areas, such as reading and spelling. Gradually, these groups can be expanded to include a third and perhaps fourth language arts area. Another strategy to follow is to combine some of the language arts when the content to be taught allows combining or integrating language arts, and when the students in a classroom can be appropriately grouped for integrated instruction. Integrating subject-matter content is an idea that has been around a long time, and flexible grouping schemes identified should enhance integration of the language arts.

A hypothetical schedule for setting up base and flex groups is shown in Table 2–2. Examine this carefully to see how year-long use of these groups might look, how to begin organizing base and flex groups, and how to integrate the language arts.

Two observations should be made about the schedule shown in Table 2–2. First, speaking and listening may be primarily taught within the context of other subjects, without base and flex groups being organized in listening/speaking for an entire year. Second, there is periodic assessment and/or reevaluation of the way students are placed in base groups. Ideally, assessment should occur frequently, but as in setting up and coordinating different groups, the teacher's time and energy must be considered. What the teacher can do, and this has been mentioned as pivotal in the kind of corrective program described in this book, is to involve students

TABLE 2–2 Yearly Plan for Implementing Base and Flex Groups

Language Arts Area	September	October–November	December–January	February–March	April-May
Reading	Three *Base Groups* Formed Several *Flex Groups* in Operation	⟶ − − ⟶	⟶ − − ⟶	*Base Groups* Reevaluated − − ⟶	Three *Base Groups* in Operation − − ⟶
Writing	Writing Needs of Students Studied	*Flex Groups* in Writing in Operation	*Base Groups* Formed Linked to Base *Groups* in Reading − − ⟶	⟶ − − ⟶	⟶ − − ⟶
Spelling	Four *Base Groups* Formed Several *Flex Groups* in Operation	⟶ − − ⟶	*Base Groups* Evaluated − − ⟶	Three *Base Groups* in Operation − − ⟶	⟶ − − ⟶
Handwriting	Three *Base Groups* Formed Several *Flex Groups* in Operation	⟶ − − ⟶	⟶ − − ⟶	*Base Groups* Reevaluated − − ⟶	Three *Base Groups* in Operation − − ⟶
Speaking*	Speaking Skills Assessed	Cooperative Learning Teams in Operation	⟹ Some Large Class Instruction	⟹ *Flex Groups* in Operation	− − ⟶
Listening*	Listening Skills Assessed	Listening Center Activities Some Large-Group Instruction	⟹ ⟹	Two *Base Groups* Formed *Flex Groups* in Operation	⟶ − − ⟶

Key: ⟶ Base Groups Continue   − − ⟶ Flex Groups Continue

⟹ Other Instructional Groups in Operation

*May be primarily taught in context of other subjects as discussed in the chapters on these language arts areas in self-assessment. Students do self-assessment in an area and report the information to teachers. Students can also make assessments of each other.

One Student's Weekly Class Schedule in a Student-Involved Corrective Language Arts Program

How might a student's language arts schedule look during a given week in a classroom where base and flex groups are operating? A hypothetical schedule has been developed for a fourth grader who is in a base group in reading, a base group in spelling, and a base group in handwriting during the early fall of the year. In this hypothetical case, the student is in a self-contained classroom and is enrolled in language arts from 8:15 a.m. to 10:30 a.m., in blocks of one hour for reading, fifteen to twenty minutes each for spelling and handwriting, and blocks of thirty-five minutes on alternating days for writing and oral language. This schedule is shown in Table 2–3.

Although the schedule shown in Table 2–3 is for one hypothetical student, it should be kept in mind that the schedule is for a small group of students. Thus, in the base groups in reading, spelling, and handwriting, there may be as many as twelve or fifteen different students involved. Some students in one base group would invariably be in the same base group in another language arts area. The same would be true for any of the flex groups organized for shoring up weaknesses in an area of the curriculum. Some of the same students will be together in some, but not all of these groups, throughout the year.

It should also be noted in Table 2–3 that grouping patterns covered in this chapter other than base and flex groups can be implemented. On Thursday, cooperative learning teams are set up for teaching students how to write more descriptively. Also, small-group work on detecting propaganda words is scheduled for speaking/listening on Wednesday. In all language arts content areas, various kinds of group work, in addition to group work found in base and flex groups, will be explored in an effort to move teachers toward a comprehensive approach to teaching language arts in a student-involved corrective program. While groups formed in project work were not identified in the week's schedule shown in Table 2–3, they easily could have been. For example, during the reading class, study of a selected theme could have been done and carried over to a second or third day as well as into the following week.

Summary

1. Teachers should be flexible in their use of grouping patterns in the classroom. Total-class instruction where all students in a classroom receive the same instruction should be provided much less frequently than it is now.

TABLE 2–3   Weekly Language Arts Instruction for One Student

Language Arts Area	Monday	Tuesday	Wednesday	Thursday	Friday
Reading	*Base Group* Story introduced and preview of what students will do in reading this week	*Flex Group* Putting more expression in voice when reading orally	*Base Group* Oral and silent reading in reading group; seatwork on noting details	*Base Group* Rereading of story; discussion of main characters in story; writing about characters as "best friends"	*Interest Group* Sharing stories about horses from books read last week; listening to story on horses
Spelling	*Base Group* Pretest on new words; discussion of word meanings; and ways they might be used during the week	*Base Group* Studying words missed, along with their meanings (with partner)	*Flex Group* Adding *ing* and *ed* to base words; Finding *ing* and *ed* words in newspapers/books	*Base Groups* Using week's spelling words in writing	*Base Group* Posttest on words for week *Flex Group* using the thesaurus to find synonyms for spelling words
Handwriting	*Base Group* Working on spacing and letter formation in cursive writing	*Flex Group* More work on spacing of letters in cursive (with emphasis on self correction)	*Base Group* Self-evaluation of five papers done in past two weeks	*Base Group* Combining outlining and handwriting lessons	No handwriting lessons today
Writing	Practice on writing better descriptions of settings and characters	Listening to students read characters as described in their written stories	No writing class today	Small-group work (cooperative learning teams) on how to write more descriptively	*Flex Group* Work with teacher and three other students on writing better transitions from paragraph to paragraph
Speaking/ Listening	No speaking/ listening lesson today	Detecting propaganda words in taped passage	Small-group work on using propaganda words	Listening appreciatively to children's classic read by teacher	Learning about effective oral book reporting

2. One basic type of grouping pattern that should be followed in a student-involved corrective language arts program is base groups. Base groups call for students on the same developmental level in a language arts area to be grouped for instruction. This pattern helps meet the needs of students as they progress from one curricular level to another level.

3. Base groups provide manageable ways to teach students in different achievement levels and to individualize instruction. Such groups also provide more opportunities for teachers to interact with students.

4. A second grouping pattern in the language arts, identified as flexible, differentiated or flex groups, allows teachers to meet individual needs of students across base groups. Common problems that have been identified are met through regrouping of students for short-term lessons.

5. Flex groups provide ways for teachers to accommodate interests, attitudes toward language arts, and learning styles of students. Flex groups also provide a meaningful context for correcting specific errors that students make in the language arts.

6. Other grouping patterns can be incorporated into a comprehensive corrective language arts program. Included are peer teaching where students teach each other in cooperative learning teams and projects where students work together (and sometimes individually) to carry out themes and subthemes. Webbing, a scheme that helps facilitate the study of themes and subthemes in trade and resource books is useful in a corrective program.

7. The basic grouping patterns advocated in this book (base and flex groups) are compatible with the use of cooperative learning teams and project groups. In combination, base and flex groups involve heterogeneous grouping patterns, while allowing students with similar abilities and/or on the same developmental levels time to work together.

8. Base and flex groups can be adapted to all language arts strands (reading, listening, writing, and speaking) and subcomponents of any of these strands (for example, handwriting and spelling). However, spelling and reading are more easily adapted to the use of base and flex groups because grade levels can be determined for these two language arts areas. The handwriting curriculum, usually divided into segments according to purpose of the content to be taught, also lends itself to easy use with base and flex groups. Written composition, listening, and oral composition are less adaptable to the grouping schemes advocated in this book, but in part, can be adapted.

9. Teachers using flexible grouping patterns must keep in mind that the way they group for instruction is a means to an end, not an end unto itself. One suggested strategy for implementing base and flex groups is to begin with a limited number of these groups and gradually work other language arts strands and substrands into the schedule.

10. The integration of the language arts should be enhanced through the use of base and flex groups, as well as through the implementation of other grouping schemes introduced in this chapter.

Reviewing, Connecting, and Expanding What You Have Learned

Directions
In the summary of Chapter 2, each numbered paragraph should be read to see if you can remember the details of the topic that the paragraph is about. The following activities are for discussion in class or for independent review of the materials covered in this chapter. In some cases, these activities will help you expand ideas that you have learned.

1. (Paragraph 1) Write a one-paragraph statement that supports the need for flexible grouping of students in the language arts.

2. (Paragraphs 2 and 3) Make a short outline on base groups. In your outline, provide such major areas as characteristics, advantages, and operating procedures for this form of grouping.

3. (Paragraphs 4 and 5) Make a short outline on flex groups. In your outline, tell the major characteristics, advantages, and operational procedures for flex groups.

4. (Paragraph 6) Develop three separate lesson plans in a language arts area. Lesson plan one should include one of the five cooperative learning strategies outlined in this chapter. Lesson plan two should include project work outlined in this chapter, but on a language arts topic. Lesson plan three should include the webbing strategy covered in Chapter 2. *Do not use any of the content (such as biography for cooperative learning) given as an example in this chapter.*

5. (Paragraph 7) List main points that you would use to defend the statement, "Base and flex groups are compatible with cooperative learning teams, project groups, and webbing."

6. (Paragraph 8) Why are the language arts areas of spelling and reading more adaptable to the use of base and flex groups than are written composition and listening? Why is handwriting more adaptable to the use of base and flex groups than is oral composition?

7. (Paragraph 9) Develop a scheme for introducing base and flex groups to a grade and school setting that you know about, such as the grade and school where you are doing or have done your practicum. Be able to discuss your scheme with others in your class.

8. (Paragraph 10) Recall some of the specific areas of the language arts where you have seen meaningful integration of language arts, such as reading and writing. Using what you recall and have learned in your reading, develop a rationale for integrating language arts in a student-involved corrective program.

Endnotes

1. Robert E. Slavin, "Cooperative Learning," *Review of Educational Research*, 50 (1980): 315–42.
2. Ibid., 319–20.
3. Ibid., 320.
4. Ibid., 320–321.
5. Ibid., 321.
6. Robert E. Slavin, Nancy A. Madden, and Robert J. Stevens, "Cooperative Learning Models for the 3 R's," *Educational Leadership* 47 (1990): 24–27.
7. Shirl E. Gilbert II and Geneva Gay, "Improving the Success in School of Poor Black Children," *Phi Delta Kappan* 67 (1985): 133–37.
8. Robert M. Smith, *Learning How to Learn*, Follett Publishing Co. (Chicago, 1982), pp. 60–65.
9. Carolyn Schluck, "Taking the Best from the English Primary School," *International Education* 15, (1986): 32–33.
10. Donna E. Norton, "Using a Webbing Process to Develop Children's Literature Units," *Language Arts* 59 (1982): 353.
11. Ibid., 348–49.

Bibliography

(Cooperative Learning)

Augustine, Dianne K., Gruber, Kristin D., and Hanson, Lynda R. "Cooperation Works!" *Educational Leadership* 47 (1990): 4.
Johnson, David W., and Johnson, Roger T. "Social Skills for Successful Group Work," *Educational Leadership* 47 (1990): 29.
Johnson, D. W., Johnson, R. T., and Holubec, E. *Cooperation in the Classroom* (Edina, Minnesota: Interaction Book Company, 1990).
Johnson, D. W., and Johnson, R. *Cooperation and Competition-Theory and Research* (Edina, Minnesota: Interaction Book Company, 1989).
Slavin, Robert E. "Cooperative Learning and the Cooperative School," *Educational Leadership* 45 (1987): 7.

(Issues in Grouping)

Wuthrick, Marjorie A. "Blue Jays Win! Crows Go Down in Defeat!" *Phi Delta Kappan* 71 (1990) 553.
Reutzel, D. Ray, and Fawson, Parker C. "Using a Literature Webbing Strategy Lesson With Predictable Books," *The Reading Teacher* 43 (1989): 208.

3

Teacher and Student
Functions in a Corrective
Language Arts Program

In Chapter 3, instructional strategies, materials, and equipment believed to be most effective for a student-involved corrective language arts program will be reviewed. A special focus will be on what roles teachers play in developing a corrective program and what unique roles students play in a corrective program.

In Chapter 3, you will learn specifically about:

1. Implementing instruction through coaching, demonstrating, modeling, and conducting effective drill and practice
2. Adapting traditional materials to a corrective program
3. Using special materials and equipment such as electronic card readers and microcomputers for corrective teaching
4. Selecting assessment and evaluative strategies that expand the paper and pencil mode frequently used to excess in schools

In this chapter, you will also learn specifically about the student's role in a corrective program in the areas of:

5. Assuming a position of an active, involved learner
6. Becoming a learner who assumes responsibility for self-assessing and self-evaluating language arts problems and progress
7. Competing against self in a specific and meaningful way
8. Practicing what is learned in the language arts on a daily basis.

As you read Chapter 3, contrast the roles of both teacher and student in a corrective program with the roles for teacher and student in a traditional language arts program. Reflect on how materials and equipment are used differently in a corrective program. Contrast strategies for assessment and evaluation in a corrective program with traditional assessment/evaluative strategies. Note also what strategies are presented for getting students more active than they often are in a traditional language arts program. Questions will come up, so bring them to class for discussion.

Utilizing a Variety of Instructional Approaches

Having a wide variety of instructional approaches plays a significant part in effecting corrective teaching. A teacher who relies too heavily on the recitation method of teaching will not be able develop a corrective language arts program. Some students need one-on-one instruction in which the teacher carefully watches as a student attempts to develop skills. Some students need to see the teacher model a skill. Some students need to manipulate objects to learn what is to be done in certain phases of the language arts. Knowing how to orchestrate these various roles becomes a primary task for teachers to perform. Several instructional approaches have already been identified in the case studies in Table 2-1. Tutoring in Case 1 where the teacher helped an individual student learn to write a paragraph is one such instructional approach. Other instructional approaches to be presented in Chapter 3 include effective demonstrations, coaching, and drill and practice.

Demonstrations

As a mode of teaching, demonstrations by teachers as well as by students not only help facilitate the learning of some content-related areas but also help develop intellectual skills of students. Learners speculate on what will happen, the method by which it will happen, and reasons why it happens.[1]

Rosenshine summarizes the research on effective demonstrations. The ten steps identified are presented in the boxed-in area that follows:

1. Present material in small steps.
2. Focus on one thought (point, direction) at a time.
3. Avoid digressions.
4. Organize and present material so that one point is mastered before the next point is given.
5. Model the skill (when appropriate).
6. Have many, varied, and specific examples.
7. Give detailed and redundant explanations for difficult points.
8. Check for student understanding on one point before proceeding to the next point.
9. Ask questions to monitor student progress.
10. Stay with the topic, repeating material until students understand.[2]

All ten research findings on demonstrations are important in any program, but they are extremely critical in a student-involved corrective language arts program. When working with students who need special help, teachers are often advised to take small, incremental steps (research item 1); to focus on one point or skill at a time (research item 2); to organize materials for mastery of what is being taught before moving on to another skill (research item 4); and to have many, varied, and specific examples (research item 6). An example of how these research findings apply to a demonstration on how to combine short, choppy sentences to make a longer, more mature sentence is shown in Table 3–1, with questions to monitor student progress given on the right.

The sentence ("The little squirrel scurried up the old oak tree.") is then written to clearly demonstrate the combined, more mature sentence. During this question and answer session, the teacher carefully notes students' responses to the questions. If some students are not able to relate *little* and *squirrel* or *old* and *tree*, these students may not be able to effectively use adjectives in writing. If students cannot write the more mature sentence ("The little squirrel scurried up the old oak tree.") or cannot see how this sentence is derived from the shorter sentences, the processes of deleting and/or rearranging words to make new sentences may be lacking and special help is needed. To broaden the approach to instruction, other examples would be given, perhaps with students making up their own short sentences and asking other students to combine them, a technique that enhances student-involvement in a corrective language arts program. As students construct and combine short sentences, the teacher can again note through observation how well students respond to this sentence-combining activity, an activity that should lead to more mature writing. Demonstrations can be done in different ways. Diagrams, pictures, and illustrated examples can be used, thus paying homage to the old adage that, "A picture is worth a thousand words." There are also personal demonstrations in

TABLE 3–1   Questions and Procedures for a Demonstration on Sentence Writing

Students are asked to read the sentences below:	Questions are raised about the three sentences:
1. The squirrel is little.	1. What happens if "little" from the first sentence is placed with the second sentence?
2. The squirrel scurried up the oak tree.	2. In what part of the second sentence would "little" be placed? Why?
3. The oak tree is old.	3. Can you combine sentence three with your revised second sentence, using only one word? What is the word and where does it go?

which an individual shows others how to perform a language arts skill, such as pronouncing a word or placing emphasis on a certain part of a sentence to get the desired meaning.

Coaching

Once generally relegated to athletics, coaching is now being expanded to its broader meaning. Adler, in the Paideia Proposal, has defined coaching as, "teaching by supervising performances to attain skills."[3] Adler also states that, "every skill is acquired by habit formation, and good habits, which skills are, result from repeated acts under the guidance of a seasoned performer who is a coach."[4] Among the various intellectual skills calling for coaching are reading, writing, speaking, and listening.[5]

Coaching, to be effective, calls for a very clear, specific understanding by the student of what the skill to be learned is, well-defined strategies for accomplishing the skill, and a very positive, supportive, caring attitude on the part of the teacher. The teacher not only demonstrates the skill to be learned, but shows how the skill is broken down, step-by-step. The teacher serves as a motivator, exhibiting enthusiasm for learning. In a student-involved corrective language arts program, coaching is important in changing negative attitudes toward learning. Students who have failed in any language arts area often resist trying again, or if these students do try, their attempts may be half-hearted ones. Over the years, such feelings are cumulative and may indeed block not only successful tries, but any tries. Thus, coaching, with a "you *can* do it," attitude is critical.

Assuming the Role of Coach

Some specific roles that the teacher can play as coach in a corrective language arts program are to:

1. Know previous successes of each student in language arts areas under study, and refer to these successes often (Example: Yes, you can make an "e." Yesterday, you made excellent "c's".)

2. Help each student set meaningful, reachable goals in the language arts, and refer to these goals as necessary. (Example: When you write about horses this time, give more facts about them than you did the last time you wrote about horses. Try to give at least three more characteristics of horses.)

3. Know how to break a language arts task down, step-by-step, and demonstrate each step for the learner. (Example: First, jot down some key ideas about the topic on which you are writing Haiku. Next, list words that help you remember the images that you want to create. Now, write your Haiku, using the words that you wrote or others that you feel are more appropriate.)

4. Help each student see progress as it is being made. (Example: Your topic sentence is a good one. Now continue with the rest of your paragraph.)

5. Help each student transfer skills, vocabulary, and other components of the language arts to the real world of reading, writing, and speaking. Continuously point out that knowing how to perform a skill is important only if it contributes to reading, writing, and speaking. (Note: This is a basic tenet of whole language teaching since the emphasis in whole language is learning necessary skills via involvement in the language arts in a naturalistic setting.)

Toward a Different Type of Drill and Practice

The need to practice what has been learned (especially skills) is an obvious part of language arts teaching. The term *drill* has become a term often used to designate practice that follows introduction of a specified skill or other content such as vocabulary. To some, however, drill means repetition of a skill until that skill is learned. Rosenshine's summary of research on seatwork (in which drill and practice most often take place) can also be used to guide drill activities. The summary includes:

1. *The need for clear instructions—explanations, questions, and feedback—and sufficient practice before the students begin their seatwork. Having to provide lengthy explanations during seatwork is troublesome for the teacher and the students.*
2. *Circulate during seatwork, actively explaining, observing, asking questions, and giving feedback.*
3. *Have short contacts with individual students (i.e., 20 seconds or less).*
4. *For difficult material, have a number of segments of instruction and seatwork during a single period.*[6]

To these suggestions can be added several others. One includes the idea of making drill and practice fit into a meaningful context. Drill does not have to be boring, simple repetition. It should be functional as in handwriting when students practice letters as they write words instead of making line-upon-line of single, isolated letters. Isolated practice leads to monotony, which in turn leads to sloppy skill development. If students are studying how to add *ing* to certain base words, a manipulative activity or a newspaper search of headlines in which *ing* has been added to base words could provide meaningful drill/reinforcement as much, if not more, than a "fill-in-the blank activity" which calls for less student involvement.

Students should also be shown that drill and practice lead to improvement in the language arts. Before and after examples of when a skill was learned should be shown on a regular basis. This idea can be as simple as students being guided to put two papers completed several weeks apart, side-by-side to discuss with the teacher what improvement has been made.

Utilizing a Variety of Materials and Equipment

Textbooks, workbooks, and equipment are, unfortunately, used too frequently at the same time and in the same way with all students in a classroom. The one exception in the language arts is reading in which there are usually three levels of a textbook series to be used in the same grade. Teachers in a student-involved corrective language arts program, to be successful, must learn to use diversified materials/equipment, including microcomputers, video equipment, and electronic card readers. These materials and equipment, along with textbooks/workbooks and programmed materials, will be covered in this section of Chapter 3.

Textbooks and Workbooks

Textbooks and workbooks constitute the primary type of materials in all schools. Furthermore, these materials will probably retain their primacy for years to come. With some adjustments, both in the purchase and use of textbooks and workbooks, the cycle of using these materials to provide the same lesson to the total class at the same time can be broken. The following recommendations are made:

1. Use several copies of textbooks/workbooks rather than a single textbook and workbook. It has been done in reading. Why not use multiple copies of textbooks/workbooks in the other language arts? School systems having access to three-to-five different state-adopted series of textbooks with their accompanying workbooks should approach adoption of books in a different way. Students would be better served if the classroom had three or more series that varied in levels of difficulty. If, for example, three developmental levels existed in an area such as spelling, which Model 2 of Figure 2-1 calls for, using more than one series enhances the chances that the three developmental levels can be matched with appropriate textbook and workbook materials. *This also enlarges the number of textbook/workbook activities, thus increasing the probability of finding activities in which students can be more involved in learning the language arts.*

2. Develop a file of worksheets arranged per skill (and other curricular components) from workbooks no longer in use. If multiple series of workbooks are in use as suggested, files of worksheets can be developed. Corrective teaching does not mean that every single page of a workbook must be covered in sequence, although there must be some attention to sequential development of skills in the language arts.

3. Develop skills packets in which students can work through several exercises that help develop a particular deficiency. In Chapter 1, it was suggested that a new skill to be learned be broken down into its prerequisite skills and concepts. Skills packets, arranged according to major skills and their prerequisites, help provide instruction geared to the special-needs of learners.

4. Laminate (cover with a plastic-like covering) worksheets that are no longer available in large quantities but are still useful for helping develop skills. Most school systems have access to laminating machines, but acetate binders can be used.

5. Develop audio guides or tapes to lessons that have been placed in work folders. Such audio guides greatly enhance learning for those students who are auditory learners.

6. Work with the school's media specialist to locate resource materials that correlate with language arts being taught. Media specialists are usually able to help locate a collection of pictures which can be used for bulletin boards, for concept and vocabulary development activities, for individual notebooks with pictures that students use, and for many other activities. Textbooks and workbooks provide skeletal materials, and the media specialist in the school can help expand what is being learned from such books. The media specialist is a key member of the instructional team in any school, but especially in a school that practices corrective teaching.

7. Examine instructional materials to determine which ones best fit the various learning styles of students being taught.

8. In whole language classes, modify skill development to fit the philosophy of this approach to teaching. Students might be asked to retell segments of stories read with skill development being noted through the way the story is told. Two examples are *sequence* and *noting details*. The skill of sequence is noted if students retell the story in the proper order; the skill of noting details is operational for students if adequate details are given in the retelling of the story. Although whole language teaching does not generally embrace the use of workbook activities that call for drill and reinforcement activities isolated from reading and writing in a naturalistic setting, occasionally, workbook activities are found which are in line with whole language teaching. An example is where a summary is provided for a longer literary passage the students have read, and students are asked to explain why the summary is (or is not) a good explanation of the larger passage.

Programmed Instructional Materials

Programmed materials can be effectively used in a corrective language arts program, but usually they are used in combination with multidimensional materials. Programmed learning materials are highly sequenced and structured, and some authorities cite such structure as one of the values of these materials. Another value of such materials is that immediate feedback is given students. Such feedback reinforces correct answers that students choose, and if the programmed materials are correctly constructed, helps the student see why errors were made.

Programmed materials are also helpful because they appeal to certain students where other materials do not. According to Carbo, Dunn, and Dunn, "Programmed instruction is ideally suited to youngsters who *prefer to work alone* and to avoid the sounds, movement, and interaction of classmates."[7] Carbo, Dunn, and Dunn also point out (1) that students who are dependent on visual learning and who need to reread materials may benefit from programmed learning materials, and (2) adaptations to programmed materials such as the adding of audio tape can be made for other learners who need auditory help.[8]

Manipulative Materials and Games

Manipulative materials and games are very helpful in a student-involved corrective language arts program. This is especially true with students who need concrete approaches to learning. Students who are more dependent on the haptical (hand-learning) modality for learning may profit more from manipulative materials than from materials in which other stimuli are used. A simple example of manipulative materials for adding sound-symbol correspondences to a word is shown in Figure 3–1.

This manipulative activity which calls into play not only haptical learning but also sight and sound modalities, makes it easier for the student to see and hear the relationships between letters and sounds. The activity can be used with pairs of students, thus involving students to a greater extent than in situations where a paper and pencil task only is used.

---

1. The letter "s" is added in the first cell in each of the diagrams below:

b. Students fold the first cell back and forth, seeing and saying the two words that can be made.

2. The letter "s" is added in both the first and last cells.

b. Students fold both cells back, seeing and saying the first word. Then the "s" in the first cell and the one in the last cell are folded back and forth and pronounced.

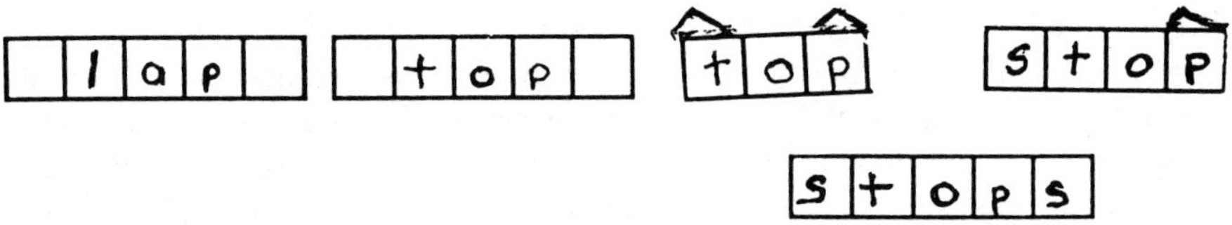

FIGURE 3–1 A Manipulative Aid for Adding Sound-Symbol Correspondence to a Word

Basic Principles for Manipulatives/Games
The following basic principles should be followed in using manipulative materials
and games in a corrective program:

1. Select or make manipulatives/games that can be used to advance specific
objectives in the language arts. The objectives selected may be generalizations,
skills, vocabulary, or any of the various components of language arts content.

2. Determine the part of the teaching cycle (introduction, reinforcement, application) where selected manipulatives and games will be used.

3. Take precautions to keep manipulatives and games from being overly time-
consuming, both in their development and use.

4. Develop and/or select manipulatives and games that are durable and can be
reorganized easily or repackaged for further use. Activities in manila envelopes are
excellent.

5. Make and/or select manipulatives and games that students can take home for
extended practice with their parents.

6. Balance the competition among students who use manipulatives/games.
Avoid having the brightest and the slowest students compete against each other,
one-on-one.

7. Plan the use of manipulatives and games in advance so that students can
independently prepare for their use (for example, prepare study guides for selected
manipulatives/games).

8. Plan manipulatives/games that can be used by an individual or two or more
students.

9. Evaluate the use of each manipulative and game to determine if the objective
being taught is being learned as intended.

Electronic Card Readers

Electronic card readers have been around for 25 years or more. Yet, their use has
never reached full potential. Perhaps the reason for this is that many teachers, faced
with the pressures of keeping up with what all students are doing, tend to gravitate
toward teaching the whole class the same lesson at the same time, rather than
working with individuals or small groups.

An electronic card reader is a machine that reads or processes a card that has a
dual, audio-track tape on it. Where a commercial company has made an imprint on
one track of a card (usually as part of a set of cards) and printed the message given
as a word, phrase, or sentence on it, the card can be used at either the introductory
or reinforcement stages of learning. The student using the machine, pushes the
correct button to hear the imprinted message as well as see the visual message
printed on the card. In addition, the student can practice repeating and hearing
his/her own voice embedded on the card, without erasing what is embedded on the
other track of the card.

Learning Through Seeing, Hearing, and Saying Takes Place With the Use of Electronic Card Readers (Photograph by Al Clemmons, courtesy of Jean-Bert Associates.)

Blank cards for use with the electronic card reader are available for teachers to make up their own sets of cards. An example of a blank card is shown in Diagram 3–1.

Some activities for use with electronic card readers follow:

1. *Sentence Combining*   Two short sentences (such as, The boy dropped his ice cream. The boy is crying.) are placed on the printed-message section of a card. Students combine the two sentences by recording their answers on the student-voice track, and then listen to the combined sentence that has been embedded on the teacher-voice track of the tape (The boy is crying because he dropped his ice cream.). Some other combinations will probably be given such as "Since the boy dropped his ice cream, he is crying." Students should be encouraged to combine the shorter sentences in more than one way, and these should be discussed in class.

2. *Using Related Words*   Card sets are made with one sentence per card that has a missing form of a word group. A direction card gives a clue word (for

DIAGRAM 3–1   A Card to be Used in an Electronic Card Reader

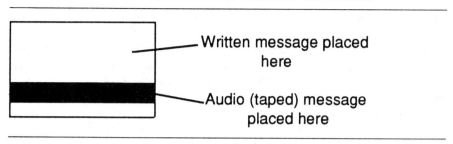

instance, a base word, *bake*) or all words to be used (*bake, baked, baking*) and tells students to complete each sentence (Card 2: The girls want to _____ a cake.). Students record the sentences, and give the correct form of the missing word on each card. Checking is done by listening to the complete sentence on the teacher-voice track.

3. *Spelling Pretests and Post-tests*   Sentences with the week's spelling words for a base group are placed on the teacher-voice track of a set of cards, one sentence per card. The word to be spelled is pronounced first, followed by the sentence. (*level*—The table top is not *level*.) Nothing is written on the printed-message part of the card, except a number that is used to identify the word being spelled. Students run the cards through the machine, and write the correct spellings of the words on their papers.

4. *Stress on Key Words or Phrases*   Sets of cards are used. A sentence is printed on each card with one word or phrase underlined, signifying that it is to be given special emphasis when read (Who did you say won the game?). Students using the card reader then check the previously recorded sentence to see how their reading differs from the teacher's recording of the sentences. Students try again if they are not satisfied with the way that they initially read the sentences.

5. *Correct Pronunciation*   Words that are mispronounced by some students (*cain't* for *can't*) are printed in sentences on sets of cards, one sentence per card (Can't you go with us to the game?). Students using this set of cards are asked to listen carefully to all words in the sentences, but especially to how the underlined words are pronounced. Each card with its sentence may be run through the card reader several times. Each student takes a turn recording the sentences and playing the teacher's recording. Before the cards are used by a second student, the teacher (or a designated student) checks the first user's recorded sentences.

Although pairs of students can work at the same time with a card reader, usually a student works alone with this machine. Some teachers leave the card reader in the corner of a room all day, and students are assigned to use various sets of cards whenever time is available.

Microcomputers

The microcomputer is one of the newest pieces of equipment for use in teaching. Software packages are rapidly increasing, and more schools are providing microcomputers for student use. Hoot identifies four major uses of computers for children: Drill and practice, tutorial exercises, simulation, and tools for a particular use such as writing a story.[9] Hoot also points out that software packages for language arts include such areas as letter recognition, alphabetization, vocabulary development, spelling, punctuation, and grammar.[10]

Some microcomputer software packages are particularly helpful in a student-involved corrective language arts program. *Whole Brain Spelling*, to be described more fully in Chapter 4, is one example. In this program, coded messages are employed to indicate the incorrectness of a word that a student has misspelled. Extra or wrong letters are crossed out in the target word, while an arrow is used to show where missing letters should go.[11]

Microcomputers can be used in a variety of ways to teach language arts (Courtesy of Apple Computer Inc.).

Videotapes and Videotaping

Videotapes and videotaping, like microcomputers, are relatively new to the educational market. Media centers are increasingly being stocked with instructional videotapes, with subjects spanning such areas as the lives of famous writers, great pieces of literature, and a variety of "how-to" tapes on various curricular topics.

Videotaping itself is of value in classrooms, especially when used for corrective purposes. In oral reporting, debate, acting out a character in a dialogue, or reading a poem, what better way is there for students to analyze their presentations than to watch videotaped playbacks? While there is not yet a large number of schools that can afford videotaping equipment, the 1990s should see more schools buying and using such equipment.

Developing Flexible Assessment/Evaluative Procedures in the Classroom

Assessing problems in the language arts and evaluating attempts to overcome the problems, while closely related, are two different processes. An example of the former is determining what problems exist in a specific area, such as spacing between words in handwriting. Evaluation refers to making a judgment about the results of one or more attempts to overcome an identified problem. A teacher may note that several students have poor spacing between words in their handwriting, implement corrective strategies, and then over a period of several days, evaluate the results of the students' work on the identified problem.

The most frequently-used procedure for assessing problems and evaluating student progress in any school subject is the use of paper and pencil tests which are usually devised by teachers. In day-to-day instruction, these tests are tied to objectives being taught or to be taught. In six- or nine-week intervals, at the end of a chapter in a textbook, at the end of a unit of instruction, and/or at the end of a week, tests are developed and given if the purposes of the tests are to measure what has been learned.

In a corrective language arts program, multidimensional forms of tests for determining errors and evaluating progress are essential. Although paper and pencil tests devised by teachers will probably continue to be important tests in a corrective language arts program, they should not be used exclusively.

What other types of assessment and evaluation procedures should be followed in a student-involved corrective language arts program? The major ones advocated in this book, and thus described, are observations, analysis of daily work in the language arts (both oral and written), oral language tests (including dictation), and standardized tests.

Observations

In the past few years, observations have increasingly become important in learning about children and their needs. The expanded interest in observation as a way to learn about children is being influenced by two factors. These are the increased attention to qualitative research where observation is a primary technique, and the recognition that how one learns the language arts is equally as important as the outcomes to be learned. In a student-involved corrective language arts program, much can be learned as teachers observe students perform specific writing tasks, interact with others during a small-group discussion, give oral book reports, react to an oral book report, and/or respond to questions asked.

In a corrective language arts program where students are placed in small groups, teachers can more easily observe students than when instruction is primarily through whole-class teaching. However, observations should not be randomly planned and carried out. They should be focused, with teachers systematically noting and recording problems observed. Follow-up lessons should then be planned to correct identified problems.

Students are also involved in the observation process. They are involved in not only their own performances but those of other students as well. Students observing a video of their own oral book report is a form of observation. In the cooperative learning activities described in Chapter 2, students who teach others are also involved in observation.

Analysis of Students' Daily Work

How do teachers develop a systematic approach for analyzing students' written and oral language arts performances? Such a system begins with the teacher knowing concepts, processes, and skills involved in the language arts to be taught. A small-group discussion can serve as an example. When students are placed in small groups to discuss a specific topic selected to help teach or improve discussion skills, the teacher should have a very clear idea of what students are to be doing to effectively perform in the discussion. In other words, what specifically is expected of students? The list of skills may be small or a small part of a larger list, but there is no guesswork on the part of the teacher in terms of what is expected of students as they participate in the small-group discussions. In Figure 3–2, a form is shown that could be used in analysis of a small-group discussion. The names of the students participating in the discussion are written at the top of the form, with clear expectations of students given.

Although codes such as + or –; Y or N, and so on, may be recorded in the appropriate cells to the right of each skill depicted in Figure 3-2, the teacher may prefer to write comments. Such comments should help in understanding not only the end result of how these skills were used in the discussion group, but also problems involved. If, for example, Andrew listens to but does not enter into the discussion taking place, a note made by the teacher would help give more specifics

Skill Area	John	Betty J.	Jim	Andrew	Sarah
1. Asks questions about the topic under discussion					
2. Enters into the discussion					
3. Knows content of topic under discussion					
4. Listens to others' comments/questions					

FIGURE 3–2   Analysis of Discussion Skills

about the lack of interaction on Andrew's part. Perhaps the topic was not of interest to Andrew. Perhaps he did not feel well that day. Perhaps Andrew is shy around the students with whom he has been grouped that day. Whatever the problem, the teacher's notes should provide information about the student's lack of participation during the discussion. In a series of small-group discussions, the teacher not only determines Andrew's skills and progress made toward their development, but makes plans to correct problems identified.

Oral-Language Testing

Asking questions and receiving answers to them is the primary way that oral language, as a testing devise, is used in schools. Much of this kind of testing is informal and is used daily. While too often this form of testing is mistakenly identified as effective group discussion, with the teacher asking questions to which only a few students respond, the use of oral language can be effective in determining language arts problems. One effective technique is dictation. It has been suggested as a tool for spelling instruction, but its use can be broader than how it is used in spelling. One example is sentence completion in which a word is left out of a dictated sentence, and students supply the missing word. The following sentences are examples of how this activity can be used.

1. The elephant, _____ to the kangaroo, is huge.
2. We were late leaving, but _____ we started.

3. Ted cannot go with us, but he is _____ a gift.
4. Birds _____ head south in the winter.
5. Jill did not say "no," but she _____ it.

Responses to these oral questions indicate whether or not the concepts and vocabulary needed to complete the sentences are understood or if certain forms of words such as adverbs *finally* and *usually* in sentences 2 and 4, respectively, can be used. In sentence 2, if students use the phrase *at last* or the word *soon*, the basic meaning of the sentence is intact. Questioning of students about other words to use could easily lead to the word *finally*, and possibly expand oral vocabulary. Likewise, in sentence 4, some students might use such words as *often, frequently*, or *always*, and discussions that follow could lead to clarification of which terms would be most appropriate and why. In sentence 5, students may use the term *inferred* instead of *implied*, thus calling for a discussion of the appropriate word for these frequently misused words.

Another use of dictation might be in punctuation where the teacher calls out a small number of sentences to be punctuated. The following five sentences are examples that can easily be dictated and punctuated by students:

1. John, my pal, is sick.
2. Sue, Beth, and Ann are sisters.
3. Jack, have you seen my dog?
4. Milk, tea, and juice are drinks.
5. We played basketball, went swimming, and went to a movie.

The five sentences are written by students as the teacher dictates each one. Before going on to the next sentence, students punctuate the sentence that they have just written. However, students may go back and check their punctuation before the teacher shows the sentences, correctly punctuated, on an overhead projector or wall chart.

Although all punctuation marks used in these sentences, as well as those omitted, are important in assessing problems of each student, targeted punctuation marks can be selected for analysis. In the five sentences given as examples, Sentences 2, 4, and 5 call for commas to be used to separate a series of words and/or phrases. While more evidence might be required than students' responses to these three sentences, failure to correctly punctuate Sentences 2, 4, and 5 provides initial indication that problems exist in the use of commas to separate a series.

In Figure 3–3, papers are shown for four students in a fourth-grade class who wrote and punctuated the five sentences. Students, upon examining the overhead transparency of correctly punctuated sentences, were asked to place a small circle where there was an error, identified for the students as a wrong or an omitted punctuation mark.

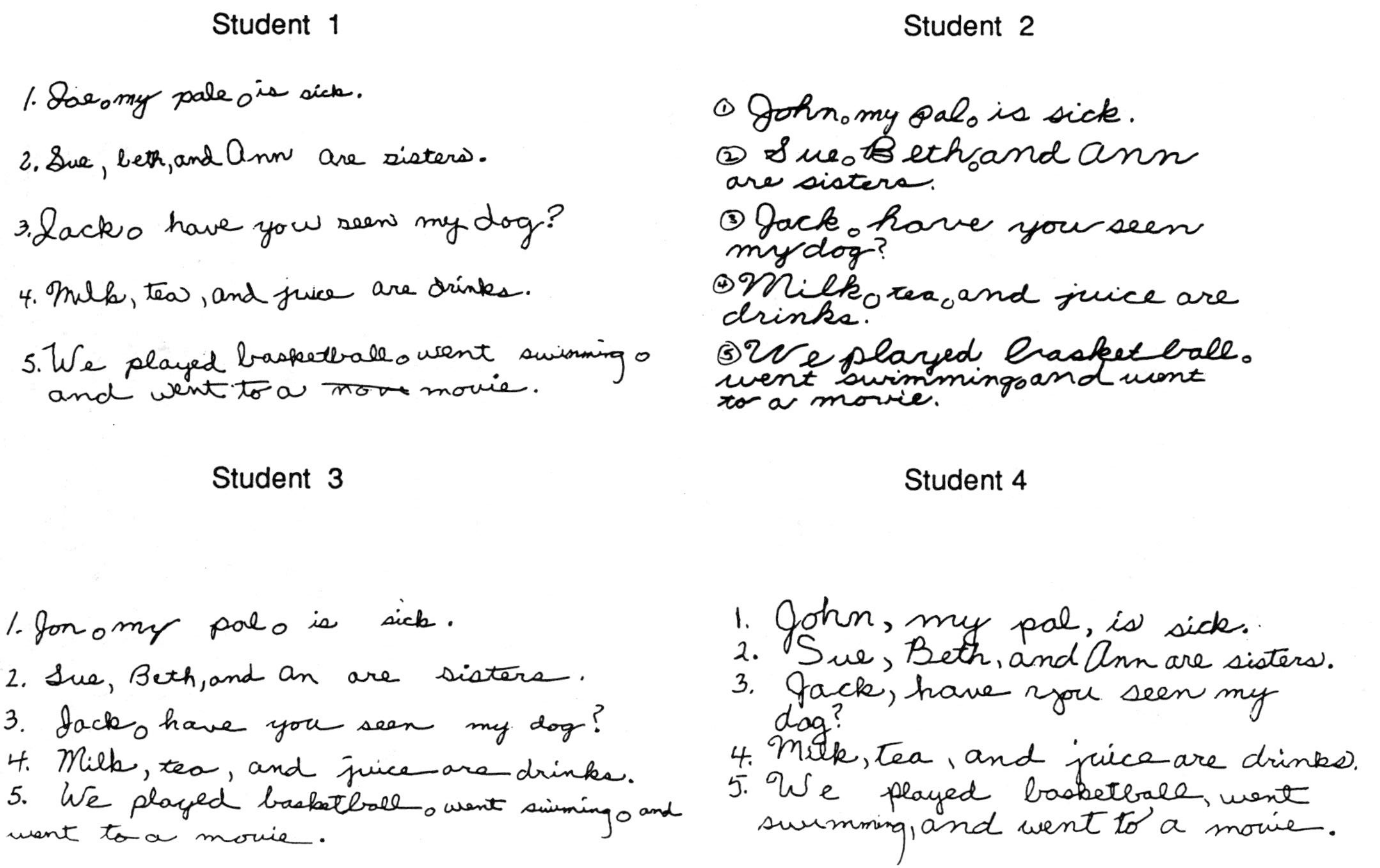

Student 1

1. Joe, my pale o is sick.
2. Sue, Beth, and Ann are sisters.
3. Jack o have you seen my dog?
4. Milk, tea, and juice are drinks.
5. We played basketball o went swimming o and went to a movie.

Student 2

① John, my pal, is sick.
② Sue, Beth, and Ann are sisters.
③ Jack, have you seen my dog?
④ Milk, tea, and juice are drinks.
⑤ We played basketball, went swimming, and went to a movie.

Student 3

1. Jon o my pal o is sick.
2. Sue, Beth, and An are sisters.
3. Jack o have you seen my dog?
4. Milk, tea, and juice are drinks.
5. We played basketball o went swimming o and went to a movie.

Student 4

1. John, my pal, is sick.
2. Sue, Beth, and Ann are sisters.
3. Jack, have you seen my dog?
4. Milk, tea, and juice are drinks.
5. We played basketball, went swimming, and went to a movie.

FIGURE 3–3 Dictated Sentence Method for Diagnosing Problems with Punctuation

In the four examples, it can be observed that Students 1 and 3 appear to have problems with use of commas to separate phrases in a series (Sentence 5), but not to separate words in a series in a sentence (Sentences 2 and 4). Student 2 appears to have problems with the use of commas to separate both words and phrases in series. Student 4 apparently has no problem with using commas to separate words and phrases given in a series. Further checking of the problems identified in the papers of Students 1, 2, 3 might be done with perhaps another set or two of dictated sentences given. The teacher might look for evidence of the problems in written work done by these students, and/or ask the students to demonstrate the rule for using commas to separate a series. If the problems are in fact verified, a flex group should be organized, with students having problems in this area regrouped for corrective assistance.

Standardized Tests

Standardized tests are tests that are usually given school-wide and/or throughout a school system for the purposes of comparing students within the school/system or with students nationwide. Most teachers are quite familiar with the procedures used for giving standardized tests and having the tests scored. Some major characteristics of standardized tests, based primarily on descriptions given by Kubiszyn and Borich, are:

1. *Specific and uniform procedures or standardized procedures are used in the development, administration, and scoring of standardized tests.*

2. *Standardized tests are developed by experts in a subject area and persons skilled in test construction.*

3. *Standardized tests, compared to teacher-made tests, are formal.*

4. *Standardized tests are norm-referenced, meaning that an individual's score on a test can be compared to how well similar students did on the same test.*

5. *Most standardized tests have been statistically treated for* validity *(the extent to which a test actually measures what it is designed to measure) and* reliability *(the consistency of measurement from one administration of the test to another).*

6. *The most predominant score used in standardized tests is the* grade equivalent score *which is reported in year and month as in a score of 4.3 (fourth year, third month). A student with a reading vocabulary score of 4.3 has done as well on this test as the average fourth grader did when the norms were developed using these materials (third month of the fourth grade). (It should be pointed out, however, that* grade equivalent scores *are easily*

> *misinterpreted. In 1981, the International Reading Association passed a resolution "strongly advocating" the abandonment of* grade equivalant *scores for reporting performances of individual groups of test takers.*[12])
>
> 7. *Most standardized tests are group tests, but some are tests to be administered to individuals.*[13]

There are several kinds of standardized tests. Included are tests of intellectual ability or aptitude tests, achievement tests, and diagnostic tests (sometimes called diagnostic achievement tests). Since the first quarter of the 1900s, intelligence tests have been used, although intelligence itself is difficult to define.[14] One definition given, which encompasses several factors typically considered to be important features of intelligence, is . . . "a complex of cognitive skills and styles of work related to effective learning and transfer . . ."[15] It should be pointed out, however, that there is much controversy surrounding the measurement of intelligence.

Achievement tests refer to those tests designed to measure how much one has learned in a particular area. Achievement tests are given in several subjects, including the language arts. Diagnostic tests are designed to pinpoint specific difficulties that a student is having in a subject or in a subset of a subject.

Teachers should be familiar with purposes and designs of standardized tests. If they are to administer such tests, they should have a good understanding of how the tests are to be administered. Most standardized tests have manuals accompanying them, and these should be carefully followed. Teachers should also know how to read test results.

Although aptitude tests have a place in a student-involved corrective language arts program, achievement tests and diagnostic tests are more useful in such a program. In Figure 3–4, skills charts are given for one often-cited achievement test, the *Iowa Tests of Basic Skills* (ITBS). As can be seen, the ITBS includes a wide variety of language arts skill areas. Among these are listening, spelling, punctuation, capitalization, reading, and usage.

An example of a diagnostic test is the *Stanford Reading Diagnostic Test*. Included among the several language arts skills for which diagnostic information can be obtained with the use of this test are auditory vocabulary, reading comprehension, and phonetic analysis. In Figure 3–5, sample questions of two types of the *Stanford Reading Diagnostic Test* are presented. Included are portions of the Phonetic Analysis and Reading Comprehension Tests for pupils in the primary grades.

If achievement tests are taken near the first of the year, how students in a class do on the various subcomponents of the tests should be considered as base groups are formed. Unfortunately, some test results are received too late in the year to be meaningful in instructional programs. If the administration of achievement tests and the resulting scores come after base groups have been formed, how these groups

	Grade	K.1-1.5	K.8-1.9	1.7-2.6	2.5-3.5	3	4	5	6	7	8–9
	Level	5	6	7	8	9	10	11	12	13	14
Test L–1:											
Spelling	Consonant Substitution			×	×	×	×	×	×	×	
	Consonant Reversals			×	×	×	×	×	×	×	
	Omission of Consonants			×	×	×	×	×	×	×	
	Addition of Unnecessary Consonants			×	×	×	×	×	×	×	
	Double Consonants			×	×	×	×	×	×	×	
	Vowel Substitution			×	×	×	×	×	×	×	
	Vowel Reversals			×	×	×	×	×	×	×	
	Omission of Vowels			×	×	×	×	×	×	×	
	Addition of Unnecessary Vowels			×	×	×	×	×	×	×	
Test L–2:											
Capitalization	Names and Titles			×	×	×	×	×	×	×	
	Dates and Holidays			×	×	×	×	×	×	×	
	Place Names			×	×	×	×	×	×	×	
	Organizations and Groups				×	×	×	×	×	×	
	Linguistic Conventions			×	×	×	×	×	×	×	
	Overcapitalization			×	×		×	×	×	×	
Test L–3:											
Punctuation	Terminal Punctuation			×	×	×	×	×	×	×	
	Comma			×	×	×	×	×	×	×	
	Other Punctuation				×	×	×	×	×	×	
	Overpunctuation				×	×	×	×	×	×	
Test L–4: Usage and Expression											
Part 1: Usage	Verbs			×	×	×	×	×	×	×	
	Pronouns			×	×	×	×	×	×	×	
	Modifiers			×	×	×	×	×	×	×	
	Context			×	×	×	×	×	×	×	
Part 2:											
Expression	Consiseness and Clarity					×	×	×	×	×	
	Appropriateness			×	×	×	×	×	×	×	
	Organization			×	×	×	×	×	×	×	
Test LI:											
Listening	Literal Meaning	×	×	×	×						
	Inferential Meaning	×	×	×	×						
	Concept Development	×	×	×	×						
	Following Directions	×	×	×	×						
	Linguistic Relationships			×	×						
	Numerical and Spatial Relationships			×	×						
	Understanding Sequence	×	×	×	×						
	Predicting Outcomes	×	×	×	×						
	Attention Span	×	×	×	×						

	Level	5	6	7	8	9	10	11	12	13	14
Test WA: Word Analysis	Letter Recognition	×	×								
	Letter-Sound Correspondence	×	×								
	Initial Sounds[1]	×	×	×	×						
	Medial Sounds[1]				×						
	Final Sounds[1]	×	×	×	×						
	Rhyming Sounds	×	×	×							
	Silent Letters			×	×						
	Substitutions, Initial[1]		×	×	×						
	Substitutions, Final[1]			×	×						
	Word Building[1]		×								
	Long Vowel Sounds				×						
	Short Vowel Sounds				×						
	Affixes and Inflections				×						
	Compound Words				×						
Test V: Vocabulary	Reading	×	×	×	×	×	×	×	×	×	×
	Language	×	×	×	×	×	×	×	×	×	×
	Work-Study	×	×	×	×	×	×	×	×	×	×
	Social Studies	×	×	×	×	×	×	×	×	×	×
	Mathematics		×	×	×	×	×	×	×	×	×
	Science	×	×	×	×	×	×	×	×	×	×
	Fine and Applied Arts	×	×	×	×	×	×	×	×	×	×
Test R: Reading	Word Recognition		×								
	Word Attack		×								
	Facts (Literal Meaning)[2]			×	×	×	×	×	×	×	×
	Inferences (Interpretive Meaning)[3]			×	×	×	×	×	×	×	×
	Generalizations (Evaluative Meaning)[4]			×	×	×	×	×	×	×	×
Test L: Language	Classification	×	×								
	Prepositions	×	×								
	Temporal Relations	×	×								
	Singular-Plural	×	×								
	Comparative-Superlative	×	×								
	Spatial-Directional Terms	×	×								
	Operational Language	×	×								

FIGURE 3–4   Skills Chart—Iowa Tests of Basic Skills (ITBS Forms G, H, J)

1. Consonant sounds, vowel sounds (in levels 7–8), consonant blends or clusters, diphthongs (in levels 7–8), and digraphs.
2. Includes understanding questions of the who, what, when, and where type, as well as those that require deducing the meaning of words or phrases from context.
3. Includes understanding cause-and-effect relationships, drawing conclusions, inferring traits and feelings, and inferring motives.
4. Involves understanding main ideas; organization; purpose and viewpoint of the author; figurative language; and the structure, mood, and style of the selection. (Copyright © 1990. Reproduced with permission of the Riverside Publishing Company.)

Test 3   Phonetic Analysis

Students are told to:

Look at the picture in the shaded box in the page. (Demonstrate). You see a picture of a cat. What letter tells the *ending* sound of "cat?"

(Students are then told why the space next to the letter "t" in the test booklet has been shaded.)

Test 5   Reading Comprehension

Students are told to:

Look at the first shaded box at the top of the page. (Demonstrate). Inside the box you see a sentence and three pictures. Read the sentence to yourself while I read it aloud: "The ball is big." One of the pictures goes with the sentence. Which picture is it?

(After pausing, the students are then guided to see why the space under the first picture is shaded.)

Students are told to:

Look at the second shaded box and read the sentence to themselves. They then are told to decide which picture goes with the sentence.

(After pausing, the students then shade in the space under the picture that they think answers the question.)

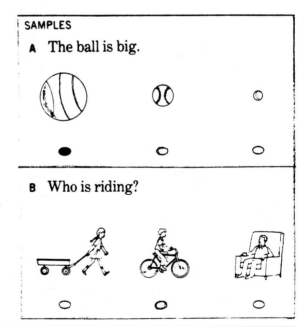

FIGURE 3–5   Two Sample Items of a Diagnostic Test (Stanford Reading Diagnostic Test)

have been organized should be reexamined in light of test results. In schools developing a corrective language arts program, there should be considerable effort on the part of the principal and teachers to have achievement tests administered early in the school year. If successful, the results of the tests can be used in the initial formation of base groups.

How students perform on standardized diagnostic tests have more meaning for the formation of flex groups than for other grouping patterns. Most schools dictate an established time of the year for giving standardized tests. Unfortunately, this limits how useful test results can be to a corrective program. Perhaps a more flexible scheduling of examinations, at least for diagnostic tests, could be worked out when a school or district implements a corrective language arts program. As is the case with standardized achievement tests, schools that adopt a corrective approach to teaching the language arts must have principals and teachers willing to make considerable efforts to identify the best times of the year when standardized diagnostic tests are to be administered.

There are other tests that are important in a corrective language arts program, and these will be given attention as appropriate in the content chapters of this book. Among these are attitude inventories, writing skills tests, specialized tests in areas such as listening and speaking, and tests to determine causes of language arts problems.

Assessment and Evaluation in a Whole Language Classroom

Teachers who advocate whole language teaching will be involved in assessing problems and evaluating student progress, but the approach used will be different than in classrooms where whole language teaching is not practiced. One variation for whole language classrooms will be the extent to which observation will be utilized. Teachers will listen and observe students more in naturalistic settings of telling and writing stories. Problems that students make will be revealed in context of the wholeness of a retold story more often than in the giving of a written test to determine problems.

Teachers in whole language classrooms should pay close attention to students' written work. Students who continue to make repeated error patterns in their writing (such as, sentences that are too long) need help. Conferences with these students in which the error pattern is pointed out or a brief note to the student prior to his/her commencing a writing project should not violate the basic tenets of whole language teaching.

Standardized tests, while not enthusiastically embraced by whole language teachers, nevertheless will probably continue to be used in most schools. Thus, teachers who implement whole language programs should join forces with other teachers to modify the use of standardized tests, including the expansion of multidimensional tests where students do more than use paper and pencil on tests.

The Student's Role in a Corrective Language Arts Program

In this section of Chapter 3, three roles that are being identified as student functions in a corrective language arts program are presented. These are: (1) The student as an active, involved learner; (2) The student as a self-assessing, self-evaluating, and self-competing learner; and (3) The student as a daily user of language arts. All three roles are greatly influenced by teacher functions, and the overlap between teacher and student roles will be seen as the following section of this book is read.

The Student as an Active, Involved Learner

Students become involved in learning the language arts when they are taught very systematically their roles as learners. For example, when a teacher is carrying out the functions of *coaching*, presented earlier in this chapter, students are taught to take pride in their work and to improve step-by-step. To assume such roles, students must learn how to focus on the goals and objectives of each lesson, a very necessary part of teaching that has been documented by research.[16] If students do not understand what is to be accomplished, they cannot be expected to help identify problems that they have in the language arts. A case in point can be given in oral language where students are working on clarity of expression, better projection of voice, and more colorful speech—three of the major characteristics of a good oral presentation. Improvement is more likely to occur when these three features are known by the student. These characteristics give more direction than when students are told, "Now try to improve on your last oral presentation."

Students are more active and involved in learning language arts when they participate in group work such as cooperative learning. Often, the student is actually engaged in teaching other students, as is the case with Jigsaw. While each student in this cooperative learning group is preparing what is to be taught to others once regrouping takes place, the objective to be learned is made quite clear.

The Student as a Self-Assessing, Self-Evaluating, and Self-Competing Learner

The writer once knew a first-year teacher who spent hours meticulously grading students' written compositions. To the young teacher's bewilderment, several students made balls out of their papers and tossed them into the wastebasket shortly after the papers were returned. These students were not involved in the process of correcting their own compositions, nor in the process of trying to improve their writing. Getting students involved in assessment of their work and in steps to correct identified problems, is equally, if not more important, than the teacher's meticulous grading of sets of compositions.

An analysis of the kind of competition that exists in schools today would reveal that there is an imbalance between group competition and self-competition, with group competition often overshadowing competition against one's past performances. If individuals and groups are not grossly mismatched, some competition among students can be beneficial. But more self-competition where students systematically make an effort to improve on past performances in each segment of the language arts, is needed in all schools.

Recording progress across a designated period of time is one procedure that students can follow to foster self-competition. In addition, self-evaluation of progress is fostered. Three characteristics of oral reporting can be used as an example. A form with the three features and what is expected within each one can be used as a checklist for students to record oral presentations over a specified timespan. If students have trouble in any one area (as in more colorful speech), a flex group can be organized to help with the identified problem.

To involve students in the recording of progress and in being more genuinely interested in learning the language arts, a new dimension of responsibility must be taught. Students must be taught, from the very early grades, that they ultimately are the ones responsible for self-improvement. Teaching this new dimension of responsibility should be deliberate, systematic, and goal-oriented. It should also be a schoolwide effort.

Almost all skill areas of language arts lend themselves to evaluation of progress over time and the development of self-competitiveness among students. In Figure 3–6, a form that can be used in handwriting is illustrative of what the author of this book calls "then and now" charts. When this form is used, samples of handwriting done several weeks apart are examined, with appropriate cells on the form completed by each student in a designated phase of the handwriting curriculum. This procedure provides students a graphic picture of not only progress made but also problems that still linger. In using this form, students would examine a set of papers that had been checked or graded by the teacher during a span of several weeks. The ground rules for students would be simple: Select four or five papers from the beginning of the designated period of time, and compare them to the same number of papers at the end of the time period. Exactness is not the focal point. The objective is for students to note improvement or the lack thereof, in specific areas such as the formation of c's and e's.

While some students in the early primary grades may not be able to make this type of comparison, skillful questions by the teacher can provide help in making some rudimentary comparisons. Thus, the foundation for students self-assessing their work in the language arts would be laid. The following questions are those a teacher might periodically ask young children about their handwriting as the children go through their handwriting folders, looking for progress that they have made:

Name _____ School _____

What to Compare	*Earlier Writing*	*Later Writing*
My c's and e's		
My i's, l's, and t's		
Neatness of my writing		
Slant of letters I make		
Space I leave between		
letters		
words		
sentences		
My margins		
My alignment		

FIGURE 3–6 **"Then and Now" Handwriting Analysis Chart**

Use + and – to indicate "good" or "not so good."

1. Did you get more happy faces on your handwriting papers early in November than you are now getting?

2. On which group of letters that you have learned to write did you get the most happy faces?

3. What were the comments on your handwriting papers that you liked the most? Which comments did you like the least?

4. Of the handwriting papers that you did in January, which ones do you like best? Which ones did you like least?

5. Of the handwriting papers that you took home last week, which one did your parents like best? Which one did your parents like least?

6. On what two papers where you practiced the same group of letters did you make the most improvement?

Using questions like these not only conditions students to begin analyzing their own language arts work, but sets the stage for self-competition. An "I can improve attitude" is very important in a student-involved corrective language arts program.

Students learn to assess and correct language arts problems when attention is called to specific errors made in the past. For example, in spelling a teacher may know that one student has problems with the middle syllable of three-syllable words. The student spells such words as *kangaroo*, *chocolate*, and *paragraph* by dropping the middle syllable (*kangroo*, *choclate*, and *pargraph*). The teacher hands the student a chart of questions prior to the checking of spelling papers. The teacher has marked the following activity and question on the chart for the student who has problems with three-syllable words:

√ **4.** Circle all words on your spelling paper with three or more syllables. Do you have enough word parts for all syllables?

In this case, the student would answer the question asked, check his/her own spelling paper, and turn in both the paper and the chart with question 4 marked. For another student whose problem is dropping ending letters of words (*somethin* for *something*), a different question on a copy of the same chart might have been marked as follows:

√ **6.** Underline the last three letters of each of your spelling words. Have you made any words too short by dropping letters like *ng*, *d*, or *t*?

Using a chart with questions marked for analysis of specific errors is related to proofreading, another technique that is helpful in getting students involved in self-assessment/evaluation. However, the chart used for analysis of errors takes the process of proofreading a step further in that the problem(s) a student might be having is specified.

Another way to get students involved in self-assessment, self-evaluation, and self-competition is to provide them with immediate feedback. Research has revealed that in situations where immediate feedback is available, students perform more effectively.[17] Unfortunately, the rush of a busy day too often prevents the giving of consistent feedback. But it does not have to be that way. Activities which call for self-checking are easy to find or to develop such as the self-checking punctuation activity shown earlier in Figure 3–3 where students punctuated dictated sentences and then checked their work via the overhead projector.

The use of models and standards is also a way to get students more involved in self-assessment and self-evaluation of their performances in the language arts. A *model* is a design to follow such as a highly descriptive sentence. A *standard* is a desired level of performance such as enunciating *all* words properly when one speaks.

Many language arts programs incorporate the use of models and standards. In handwriting, when students are learning how to form a cluster of letters with similar strokes (letters such as *i, l, t* in manuscript writing), models to follow are usually available. The component parts or strokes are typically given to enable students to copy the parts of each letter in the sequence that students are to make. When students are asked to recall how a classmate effectively used "expression in her voice" while giving an oral book report, both models and standards are being used, as is the case when a teacher weaves into his/her own speech the proper use of the contraction "aren't" after noting that several students use "ain't" in their speech. When correct slant in cursive writing is cited as a way to help make writing more legible, a model is usually available to follow. And when a teacher contrasts a poorly written paragraph with one that is well-written, a model is being used. A major task in a corrective program is to get each student to automatically search for and implement models and standards. Some suggested strategies with explanatory notes follow.

Students can be asked to create the best likeness possible of a model being followed. This usually will take several tries, but once a facsimile of the model is developed, this becomes proof to the student that he/she can come close to the model. This also activates self-competition, since the student must compare successive tries at emulating the model. An example in handwriting puts this idea in proper perspective. A primary-grade student is learning how to write a set of related manuscript letters (such as *c, e, o*). The student follows the practice book model, stroke-by-stroke. When the student thinks that he/she has made the best possible likeness of the model, the example is mounted on a small index card and taped to that student's desk for reference as practice activities continue. The model is replaced when a better example is formed by the student. As soon as possible, the letter(s) being learned are used in writing. At this point, the best representation of the target letters written in words becomes the student's model. These words, not separate letters, are then written on a small index card and taped to the student's desk.

Students are asked to do follow-up practice activities in the language arts that give attention to the characteristics of the skills previously learned. If students are writing paragraphs, several examples that have been written should be requested for use with overhead transparencies, for bulletin boards, or for acetate binders to be placed on a table that might be designated as a place where students can go to do "special writing." Group discussions about the examples of paragraphs shown on the overhead projector, either in base or flex groups (or both), should be held frequently to keep characteristics of good paragraphs highly visible. Such discussions and reviews of examples help students understand the correct forms of paragraph construction, as well as add an incentive for students who wish to have their work displayed. Motivation to improve is greatly enhanced when the teacher *coaches* each student to improve.

When students work with models and standards to follow, an individual folder should be kept to record progress and keep work samples. A model paragraph with highlighted features of effective paragraphs (well-constructed topic sentence, well-coordinated supporting sentences, effective transitional words), attached to the inside front cover of each folder can be used to remind each student of the desired characteristics of paragraph writing. As each attempt is made to write a paragraph like the model, the folder is used in several ways. Each student's attempts throughout a period of learning how to write paragraphs are numbered so that student and teacher (as coach) can see what progress has been made. The folder, in addition to containing the model paragraph and the student's attempts at following the model, might also contain other materials. Included might be a list of transitional words (therefore, but, finally) that would help the student tie sentences in paragraphs together.

Teachers and students can have "modeling" sessions in which a specified language arts skill being learned is demonstrated. (For instance, how to get students' attention at the very beginning of an oral report might be modeled in several different ways.)

The role of the teacher in modeling is critical. Hunter emphasizes that the best way to make sure that the correctness of a model is known by students is for the teacher to "demonstrate the response the student is to practice."[18] When the teacher models a skill, students actually see a skill unfolding, step-by-step. The teacher then watches carefully to see that students follow steps that have been modeled. Procedures for effective demonstrations presented earlier in this chapter, should be carefully followed as modeling takes place.

The Student as a Daily User of the Language Arts

Teachers often complain that students cannot apply what they learned during the previous week, and sometimes even the day before. Spelling is a classic example. Students who regularly make a perfect score on Friday tests often misspell some of the same words in written assignments during the following week. Students should be taught in such a way that application of what they have learned becomes automatic. How can this be done? How do students assume the role of a daily user of language arts?

When students break down a skill or examine a language arts structure such as a simple sentence, the students should be given a follow-up assignment that is focused on applying what has been learned. Rarely should there be an exception to this principle. This helps bring *analysis* and *application* together, and in the long run should lead to learning that is both more meaningful and permanent.

In a student-involved corrective program, students should be taught to look for examples of what they are learning. When the function of adjectives is being taught, students should spend time finding adjectives in writing. Newspaper advertisements and headlines are good sources for finding examples of how words are used, and old newspapers should be readily accessible. Words in ads and headlines are usually large enough to mount on a bulletin board. In some cases, students in a corrective language arts program keep examples of what they are learning in individual folders. The folder then becomes a resource for the students to use when they are writing and need examples of whatever has been learned and filed.

Summary

1. Teachers in a corrective language arts program, to be successful, must not rely on teaching strategies calling for whole-class teaching, using recitation as the dominant approach to instruction. A variety of instructional strategies must be used, including demonstrations, coaching, and drill and practice. Where possible, research findings should be followed in the implementation of instructional strategies in a corrective program.

2. A wide variety of instructional materials and equipment must be utilized if corrective teaching is to be effected. This means that traditional materials, including textbooks and workbooks, must be modified for use with small groups rather than for whole-class instruction. Both base and flex groups must be provided and a greater variety of materials and equipment should be used than is normally found in language arts programs. Electronic card readers, videotape facilities, and microcomputers should add to the variety of equipment now in use in schools. These help in the individualization of teaching the language arts, although their use does not necessarily mean that students work alone. Manipulatives and games, if appropriately developed and implemented, can also add to the variety of teaching materials necessary for corrective teaching. The greater the variety of materials and equipment, the more likely teachers are to reach individuals who have different learning styles, different interests, and different predispositions to school and to the language arts.

3. *Assessment* in the language arts refers to the identification of specific problems students might have in learning some component of the language arts. *Evaluation* refers to the noting of progress made during or after attempts have been made to correct an identified problem. In both assessment and evaluation, the teacher must not rely solely on paper and pencil tests. Other techniques and materials must be employed, including observations, analysis of each student's daily work, oral-language tests, and standardized tests.

4. In making observations a part of a corrective program, processes involved in learning must be noted, and accommodations made to correct problems. In analyzing children's papers and using oral language in the classroom, teachers must know specifically what is to be taught, relying very little on guesswork. Combining analysis of written work and use of oral language will lead to the identification of such problems as concept/vocabulary needs, misuse of punctuation, and weaknesses in the development of generalizations about language.

5. Standardized tests are useful in a student-involved corrective language arts program. However, there should be flexible use of such tests, with school personnel identifying the most appropriate time to use these tests. Three basic kinds of standardized tests are aptitude, achievement, and diagnostic tests.

6. Teachers set the stage for students to be active and involved in learning the language arts. Students must be taught their roles as learners. In a corrective language arts program, students must take pride in their work, seek to improve step-by-step, and examine ways to improve. Students must also focus on goals and objectives of what they are learning.

7. While students will continue to compete against others, more focus should be on self-competition which means competing against past performances. Keeping records of progress over time is one way of competing against past performances.

8. "Then and now" charts help students evaluate their work over a designated period of time. Questions about students' performances, when appropriately asked by the teacher, should lead to students themselves asking questions about their work. Where possible, students should be asked to watch for errors that are likely to occur in the language arts.

9. Providing immediate feedback also helps students in self-assessment, self-evaluation, and self-competition.

10. Using models and standards helps in getting students to self-assess and self-evaluate their work in the language arts. While related, standards and models are different. However, some of the same strategies work in the implementation of both.

11. Students should not be asked to analyze language arts structures without follow-up application of what they are learning. Following this principle should lead to not only more meaningful learning, but learning that in the long run is more permanent.

12. Students should be made aware of the varied use of the language arts in their environment. Newspapers and other media used daily should be helpful in making students aware of the use of the language arts.

Reviewing, Connecting, and Expanding What You Have Learned

Directions
In the preceding summary of Chapter 3, each numbered paragraph should be read carefully to see if you can remember the details of the topic that the paragraph is about. It is suggested that you reread each paragraph in the summary, and then do the activities suggested in this section of Chapter 3. In some cases, this activity may be done with a partner in your college class or in an inservice education session.

1. (Paragraph 1) Select one of the three following teaching strategies, and prepare an outline on the use of that strategy in a student-involved corrective language arts program:

    a. demonstrations
    b. coaching
    c. drill and practice

2. (Paragraph 2) Write a paragraph describing how you would be able to change traditional textbook/workbook materials from use in whole-class teaching to use in a corrective language arts program. Write a second paragraph describing how some relatively new materials and equipment can be used in a corrective language arts program.

3. (Paragraph 3) Describe two teaching situations (teachers working with students) in which the differences between *assessment* and *evaluation* are evident.

4. (Paragraph 4) If possible, observe a student in a practicum or field-experience part of your college class or, if you are currently teaching, your own class. Try to determine some specific language arts problems on which the student needs to work. Examine written work of three other students in your practicum. What problems can you identify in spelling, handwriting, and written composition?

5. (Paragraph 5) If a copy of a standardized achievement test used in the language arts is available, examine it to see what it measures. Then list some ways for using the test with base groups in a corrective program. If a copy of a standardized diagnostic test used in the language arts is available, examine it to see how you could use the test with flex groups. Make a list of ways in which you think you could use the test.

6. (Paragraph 6) Make a list of five or six ways that you can help students modify their behaviors to become more active, involved learners. If possible, work with two or three other students in your college course or inservice training session who have also made a list of ways to motivate students to be more active learners. Debate your combined lists, and select five strategies that you agree are the most important in a corrective program.

7. (Paragraph 7) Write a one-paragraph explanation of why students should be taught to compete against themselves. Give an example of self-competition in each of the following language arts areas: written composition, spelling, listening, and speaking.

8. (Paragraph 8) Explain to a designated partner in your college class or inservice session what "then and now" charts are and how they might be used in a corrective language arts program. With your designated partner, develop "then and now" charts from two different language arts areas (for instance, listening for sequence and the writing of tall tales). Prepare your charts in such a way that they can be shared with other students.

9. (Paragraph 9) Brainstorm with several of your classmates, and come up with three or four logical and streamlined ways for providing immediate feedback to students in a corrective language arts program. If you have had some practicum experiences or are an experienced teacher, be sure to recall how feedback was given to students you observed being taught or that you taught yourself.

10. (Paragraph 10) Observe a teacher or a classmate teaching a language arts lesson. Note how the teacher uses *models* and *standards* to involve students in self-assessment of language arts problems and self-evaluation of progress made. Write a critique of what you observed.

11. (Paragraphs 11 and 12) Examine a language arts textbook. Take a section of the book (such as a unit on sentence writing) and identify the activities as *analytical* or *applied* or a combination of both. Evaluate the balance between the two types of activities. Be able to discuss in your class how you would be able to take a suggested activity from the book and provide more balance between the *analytical* and *applied.*

12. (Paragraphs 11 and 12) If you are in a practicum for your college class and/or teaching your own language arts class, list as many ways as you can for getting your students to find everyday uses of what you are teaching.

Endnotes

1. John Jarolimek and Clifford D. Foster, *Teaching and Learning in the Elementary School*, 2nd ed. (New York: Macmillan Publishing Co., 1981), pp. 122–123.
2. Barak Rosenshine, "Teaching Functions in Instructional Programs," *The Elementary School Journal* 83 (1983): 339.
3. Mortimer J. Adler, *Paideia Problems and Possibilities* (New York: Macmillan Publishing Co., 1983), p. 17.
4. Ibid.
5. Ibid., p. 18.
6. Rosenshine, Ibid., 348.
7. Marie Carbo, Rita Dunn, and Kenneth Dunn, *Teaching Students to Read Through Their Individual Learning Styles* (Englewood Cliffs, New Jersey: A Reston Book—Prentice-Hall, 1986), pp. 180–81.
8. Ibid., p. 181.
9. James L. Hoot, *Computers in Early Childhood Education—Issues and Practices* (Englewood Cliffs, New Jersey: Prentice-Hall, 1986), pp. 2–3.
10. Ibid., p. 70.
11. Susan Campanini et al., *Whole Brain Spelling: A Child's Garden of Words*, 2nd ed. (Champaign, Illinois: Sublogic Communications, 1982).
12. Roger Farr and Robert F. Carey, *Reading—What Can be Measured?*, 2nd ed. (Newark, Delaware: International Reading Association, 1986), p. 154.
13. Tom Kubiszyn and Gary Borich, *Educational Testing and Measurement*, 2nd ed. (Glenview, Illinois: Scott, Foresman and Company, 1987), pp. 23, 327–56.
14. Ibid., pp. 357–63.
15. Lyn Corno and Richard E. Snow, "Adapting Teaching to Individual Differences Among Learners," in *Handbook of Research on Teaching*, 3rd ed., ed. Merlin C. Wittrock, American Educational Research Association Project (New York: Macmillan Publishing Co., 1986), p. 616.
16. David C. Berliner, "The Half-Full Glass: A Review of Research on Teaching," in *Using What We Know About Teaching*, ed. Philip L. Hosford (Alexandria, Virginia: Association for Supervision and Curriculum Development, 1984), pp. 63, 66.
17. Ibid., p. 71.
18. Madeline C. Hunter, *Improved Instruction*, (El Segundo, California: TIP Publications, 1976), p. 59.

Bibliography

(Assessment/Evaluative Strategies)

Burns, Paul C. *Assessment and Correction of Language Arts Difficulties* (Columbus, Ohio: Charles E. Merrill Publishing Co., 1980).
Marcus, Marie. *Diagnostic Teaching of the Language Arts* (New York: John Wiley & Sons, 1977).

(Instructional Strategies)

Petty, Walter C., Petty, Dorothy C., and Salzer, Richard T. *Experiences in Language—Tools and Techniques for Language Arts Methods*, 5th ed. (Boston: Allyn and Bacon, 1989).

Tiedt, Iris M. *The Language Arts Handbook* (Englewood Cliffs, New Jersey: Prentice-Hall, 1983).

(Microcomputers in Education)

Chandler, David. *Young Learners and the Microcomputer*. (Milton Keynes, England: Open University Press, 1984).

Grady, M. Tim. "Long-Range Planning for Computer Use," *Educational Leadership* 40 (1983) 16.

White, Mary Alice. "Synthesis of Research on Electronic Learning," *Educational Leadership* 40 (1983) 13.

4

A Corrective Approach
to Spelling Instruction

Focus

Take a few minutes to recall how spelling instruction was taught when you were a student. Do you recall taking a pretest and a final test each week? Do you recall if your test papers were corrected by you, a partner, or your teachers? Do you remember spelling rules or generalizations that you had to learn (for example, *i* before *e* except after . . . , and so on)?

Some practices in spelling are sound in that they are backed by research. Other practices in spelling are not as sound. Chapter 4 begins with a description of research findings that are basic to a spelling program, with particular emphasis to those research-based practices that are most critical to a student-involved corrective program. Other major topics to be addressed in Chapter 4 include:

1. Arranging the spelling curriculum to break the locked-in designation of content for a specific grade, a major impediment to the establishment of a corrective program
2. Determining prerequisites for new skills to be introduced in spelling
3. Determining students' spelling levels
4. Setting up base and flex groups in a spelling program
5. Designing assessment and corrective activities for students in both base and flex groups

As you read Chapter 4, recall what you have learned in this book about differences among students and how these differences should be accommodated in spelling instruction. You will learn about some suggested ways of presenting a group of words for spelling instruction. Ask yourself if what you are reading is appropriate for both the visual and the auditory learner. You will learn about the use of manipulatives/games in a spelling program. What group of learners do these appeal to, and how should manipulatives/games be used? How about students working together to study spelling words? What are the advantages of having the "best" and the "slowest" spellers in the same group? Some of these questions will be answered as you read. Others will come up for discussion in your class. Do not hesitate to write questions, and ask them as appropriate.

Research of Significance to a Student-Involved Corrective Spelling Program

Over the years, spelling has become a regular part of the language arts curriculum. Frequently, there is a spelling book that is separate from other books for the language arts, and often there is a spelling workbook. Almost always there is a separate instructional period for spelling. And usually, there is an overly-routinized approach to instruction. Too often, students in the same classroom have identical word lists for spelling, take the same pretest (and at the same time), take an identical final or posttest (again, at the same time), and march lockstep through the same instructional activities, day-after-day. An optional approach to such practices is a corrective approach that meets the spelling needs of each individual in the classroom.

Where should teachers start such a program? To begin with, teachers in a corrective program, like teachers in all spelling programs, should know what practices in spelling are backed by research. Such practices can be identified, since spelling is one of the most researched of the language arts. Nine basic practices are presented, all focused on building background for implementing a corrective spelling program.

Practice Number 1: Deciding Which Words Should be Taught and in What Grade They Should be Taught

Word lists for individual lessons in spelling textbooks are not casual lists in that several important decisions have been made about their use for a lesson. A decision had to be made first about the words as a small part of the large number of words selected for the series. Second, a decision had to be made to place the words at the grade level where they were placed. Third, a decision had to be made to group the words on the list for an individual lesson.

Selecting Words to Spell

As students move from the lower to the upper elementary school grades, they will be introduced to many spelling words, altogether totaling as many as 3,000 different words. There is general agreement today that a decisive factor to be considered in selecting words is to choose those that students use in their writing, since the basic purpose for learning to spell is to help foster good writing skills.

One of the most significant studies dealing with selection of words for a total spelling curriculum is one done many years ago by H. D. Rinsland. In his study, Rinsland surveyed 1,500 schools from different social and economic areas of the United States.[1] It was revealed that 100 words constituted about 60 percent of all words used in children's writing. As the number of most-frequently used words increased to 250 words, 500 words, and so on, the percentage of usage increased. Thus, the 2,000 most-frequently used words constituted 95 percent of the words that children used in their writing.[2] In Word List 4–1 at the end of this chapter, the 1,000 most frequently used words are given by frequency list. This list should closely parallel lists of the first 1,000 words found in most spelling series, since the Rinsland list is frequently cited as a base list.

Placement of Selected Words at the Appropriate Grade Level

Research has been less decisive in determining at what grade level to place words than in selecting a large corpus of words. Emmett Betts' comprehensive studies of spelling textbooks revealed that those who write textbooks seldom agreed on the grade level at which words should be used. Some authorities have argued that students' needs to spell words render the development of formal lists at particular grade levels a somewhat hopeless task.[3] Nevertheless, for formal spelling, words must be placed for study at various grade levels, although a given group of students should not be compelled to study only those words assigned to the grade level of the students. While the authors of spelling texts have considered a number of factors (for example, general interests of students) in placing words at different grade levels, the teacher in a corrective language arts program must be flexible enough to adapt words identified for a given grade level to meet specific needs of the students being taught. If words do not lend themselves for writing on the interests that students have or if they are too difficult for students in a class, it is doubtful that the spelling program will be successful.

Grouping of Words for Separate Spelling Lessons

In recent years, there has been a movement toward grouping of words for instruction according to sound-symbol relationships. Sound-symbol relationships, in linguistic terms, are called *phoneme-grapheme** correspondences. Among the several

---

*Phonemes are significant speech sounds, meaning that if they are changed (for example, cat changed to hat or cat to cap), a new word with a different meaning is formed. When phonemes are referred to in narrative form, they are usually indicated with slash marks: /h/ is

studies on sound-symbol patterns is the *Stanford Spelling Project*, sponsored by the U.S. Office of Education and conducted by Paul Hanna and others. Using the computer, over 17,000 words were analyzed to determine phoneme-grapheme correspondences.[4] It was revealed that the spelling of the English language is more predictable than previously believed. Some phonemes such as the short vowel sounds (as, *short a* in *at, cat*) and consonant sounds (as, /b/ in *big*; /d/ in *mad*) were spelled more than 95 percent of the time with the graphemes found in these words <*a*>, <*b*>, <*d*>, regardless of what position the phonemes occurred in the words. Considering position for some phonemes, other spellings were quite predictable such as <*a*> for the *long a* phoneme found in a non-ending syllable as in *table* which is spelled <*a*> 81 percent of the time.[5]

Whether a textbook is used or local spelling lists have been developed, teachers should be aware of schemes used for grouping words to teach and reinforce specific patterns. For example, a second-grade teacher who is using a locally-produced word list is working with a small group of students and comes across the word *made*. On the same list is a word that patterns the same way. This word is *make*. Emphasizing this pattern and having students recall other words with the pattern (CVCe) could help in the learning of other words with this pattern. This is especially critical in a corrective program where some students may not easily discover the sound-symbol, word-building,* or other patterns on their own.

There are two basic approaches to looking at the relationships between sounds (phonemes) and their representative symbols (graphemes), and for purposes of grouping for instruction, teachers should know these patterns. One approach is the *sound-symbol*, while the other is the *symbol-sound* approach.

Sound-Symbol Approach. Attention in this approach is first focused on hearing the target sound and then noting how it is spelled. An example would be to have students listen for the *long a* sound in *able* or *day* and then note how the sound is spelled. In the first word, the target sound is spelled with a single letter *a* (The grapheme is <a>.). In *day*, the *long a* is spelled *ay* (The grapheme is <ay>.).

Symbol-Sound Approach. More attention is initially focused in this approach on visual aspects of the word. The visual arrangement or pattern formed by the sequence of letters, such as words like *had, pan, and sad* is given attention initially. In these three words, the letter arrangement or *symbol-sound* pattern is the

---

the first of three phonemes in the word hat. Graphemes refer to symbols used to represent phonemes. In hat, the first phoneme /h/ is represented by the grapheme h. When writing about graphemes, brackets < > are usually used. Thus, <h> means that one is referring to the grapheme used to represent the phoneme /h/. Graphemes may be single letters as is <h> or more than one letter as in the word tough where <ou> and <gh> represent two different phonemes.

*Word-building or morphological patterns refer to relationships governing how a new word is created by adding parts to it, as in how making is formed by adding ing to make.

CVC or consonant-vowel-consonant pattern. In most cases, this pattern dictates a short vowel sound.

Example of a Sound-Symbol Approach. An example of the sound-symbol approach is shown in Figure 4–1, an individual lesson from *HBJ Spelling, Level 2*. A tenth word is included in the lesson to introduce the concept of an exception to the use of *a-e* to spell another sound. This word is *have* in which the vowel sound is

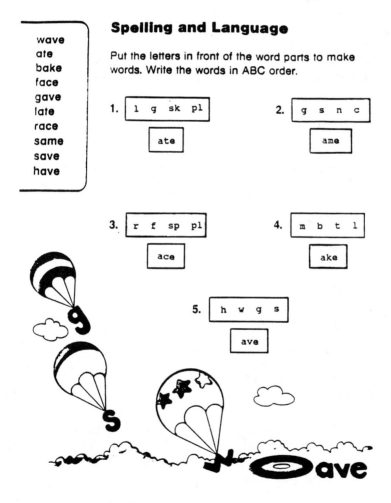

FIGURE 4–1 Grouping Spelling Words Using Sound-Symbol Correspondences

short a.[6] The authors of the HBJ series could have chosen to focus on the CVCe pattern (*symbol-sound* approach) which, in most cases, dictates the *long a* sound.

Students who have trouble with *symbol-sound* or letter arrangement may not have trouble with the other approach, *sound-symbol*. A student whose learning style is more visual than auditory may be able to more readily see the CVCe pattern where the focus is first on the visual arrangement of the letters as opposed to the *sound-symbol* approach where more emphasis is initially on auditory processing (using auditory clues or processes to unlock the language).

Spelling textbooks and locally-developed word lists should focus on other types of linguistic patterns, one which was identified in the footnote on word building earlier in this chapter. All such patterns must be thoroughly known by teachers in corrective programs, with particular emphasis on difficulties that arise when students from diverse backgrounds and different learning styles are taught to spell.

Practice Number 2: Presentation of Words in a List or in Context Form

There has been controversy about presenting words in a list, sometimes called a direct approach, and presenting words in context, sometimes called an indirect or sentence method of presentation. According to Allred, the list method has usually been favored in most of the early studies that focused on these two different ways to make initial presentations of words in spelling.[7] According to Mickler, however, questions in these earlier studies have been raised related to students not seeing the words when they were dictated in sentences (context presentation) and not focusing enough on the spelling of the words. Introducing the words in lists and using the words in context might be a more effective combination.[8]

Practice Number 3: Teaching Spelling Generalizations

Should spelling generalizations be taught? If so, which ones? These questions have been asked for a long time. Based on conclusions from research, and especially a study by Thomas G. Foran, Allred says that the following should be considered in teaching spelling rules:

1.   Only a few rules should be taught. Those taught should have no or few exceptions.
2.   Some rules should be taught, for children will generalize what they have learned, and such generalizing should be directed as far as the spelling of English words permits.
3.   Only one rule should be taught at a time.
4.   A rule should be taught only when there is need of it.
5.   The teaching of the rule should be integrated with the arrangements or grouping of the words in the textbook.

6. Rules should be taught inductively rather than deductively (to be discussed later).

7. There should be ample reviews of the rules both in the grades in which they have been learned and in the following grades.

8. Tests of knowledge of the rule should insist not so much upon logical precision as on comprehension and ability to use the rule.[9]

Using these practices when spelling generalizations are taught should simplify teaching, a condition that is particularly important for students who have trouble with spelling. Teaching a limited number of rules (Number 1), teaching only one rule at a time (Number 3), integrating the teaching of a rule and the way words are grouped in the textbook (Number 5), and having ample reviews of rules taught (Number 7) are especially critical principles in a corrective spelling program.

Practice Number 4: Teaching Spelling Generalizations Inductively

As presented in Practice Number Three, students learn inductively when they are presented with enough information to form a generalization rather than being told the generalization initially (which would be more of a deductive approach). In reviewing the research in spelling instruction, Mickler states that:

> *The results of reported studies appear to support the use of inductive teaching strategies for teaching spelling generalizations. This method further appears to be particularly valuable in producing long-term retention and a transfer of knowledge to unknown words.*[10]

Two conditions required for inductive teaching of patterns and generalizations are: (1) information or data of sufficient quantity to enable students to discover or generalize what is being taught; and (2) motivation of students to critically examine the data. Word lists can be prepared in advance to present students with appropriate data, such as lists of words in which /k/ is the last sound as in *sick, book, block, sack, black,* and *quick* to teach that /k/ preceded by a short vowel sound results in spelling /k/ with <ck>. Word lists can also be derived from students' experiences by giving conditions, such as *think of all words that you can in which the last sound heard is /k/*. Words elicited from the students are placed on the chalkboard and the generalization is then pulled from the data.

Practice Number 5: The Role of Tests in Spelling Instruction

Although there are some changes underway in spelling programs where the emphasis is on an integrated curriculum, typical practices in teaching of spelling are: (1) the giving of pretests at the beginning of the week; (2) having students concentrate more on the words that they missed; (3) doing several activities to learn spellings and meanings of the words; and (4) having a final test during the last part of the week. The practices identified (1-4), known as the *test-study-test* approach to spelling instruction, differ from a frequently-contrasted approach to spelling instruction, the *study-test* approach. In the latter approach, students study all words first and then are tested on how well they can spell them.

There is considerable support for the *test-study-test* approach to spelling, going back over forty years. Loomer and Strege cite reviews of studies such as M. G. Blanchard's and G. A. Fitzgerald's in stating that the *test-study-test* approach is more appropriate.[11]

While teachers in most corrective programs should follow the *test-study-test* approach to spelling instruction, there may be some situations where testing in advance is not wise. The student who habitually misspells three-fourths of the words given out might fare better studying a very limited number of words, followed by a test. The emphasis would be on building confidence in spelling. Students who have problems with patterns may be able to spell some words in a pattern, but not be able to generalize to other words. It may be necessary to let those words remain in a list to be studied. For example, spelling /j/ with the grapheme <dge> in words like *hedge* and *budge* would more likely be facilitated by reference to easier words on a list such as *edge* and *fudge*.

Practice Number 6: How Students' Spelling Test Papers Should be Corrected

Studies have been made on the effect of students correcting their own test papers. After reviewing several studies, Fitzsimmons and Loomer state that the *corrected-test* method is one of the most important factors "leading to spelling achievement."[12] Loomer and Strege stress the importance of schools developing a clear perception of the *corrected-test* procedure, adding that this self-correcting technique helps each student in the following ways:

1. It provides him/her with an immediate opportunity to see what words cause him/her difficulty.
2. It allows him/her to see the part of the word that caused him/her difficulty.
3. He/she can immediately set about to correct any errors that he/she may have made.
4. The procedure calls the student's attention to how critical his/her own perceptions concerning self improvement are to the learning process.[13]

Correcting one's own spelling test papers is an excellent example of self-assessment and self-evaluation, earlier noted as important student roles in a corrective program. Students see exactly what spelling problems they are having and, with the teacher's guidance, correct the problems. For some, the act of seeing and correcting their problems becomes a motivational factor.

Practice Number 7: How Much Instructional Time Should be Spent on Spelling

The amount of time to spend on spelling instruction during the school week was first explored in the 1890s by J. M. Rice, who found that instruction in excess of 75 minutes per week had little effect on spelling achievement. Since then, other studies have been done which support Rice's original study. Regardless of the exact amount of time, excessive instruction in spelling is not necessary. Allred points to motivation and interest as key factors, stating that, "The task of learning to spell resembles that of reading the dictionary: the subject might be of interest, but the plot changes too often . . . "[14]

While in general, an average of fifteen minutes per day will be enough time for instruction in spelling, a corrective program calls for some flexibility in time spent per lesson as the need arises. A few techniques, such as those calling for manipulative materials, might take more time than those calling basically for oral and/or visual learning. Involving students in self assessment/tracking of their own progress might also take extra time, and especially as systems for doing so are being initiated.

Practice Number 8: Learning to Spell as a Conceptual Process

Historically, learning how to spell was seen as a process of memorizing and arranging letters in words in proper sequence. This was based, in large part, on the belief that English spelling was irregular or unpredictable.[15] This belief has been dispelled by the *Stanford Spelling Project*, described earlier, and other studies. Linguistic analyses (Noam Chomsky and Morris Halle; Richard Venezky) that go beyond letter-sound relationships, as well as research on how children learn to spell (Charles Reed, James Beers, and Edmund Henderson) have, according to Templeton, significantly shifted the focus from spelling as a process of *memorizing* to spelling as a process of *conceptualizing*.[16]

These two processes are shown on the continuum in Figure 4–2. Those identified in the continuum as "conceptualizing" should become established procedures in any spelling program, but especially in a student-involved corrective program where students who need special help may have a difficult time memorizing.

Practice Number 9: The Value of Peer Tutoring in the Teaching of Spelling

Peer tutoring in spelling, although not extensively researched, has nevertheless been found to be of value. Mickler states that studies indicate peer tutoring to be of value via increased communication among students and better attitudes toward spelling. Students help each other with record keeping systems, graphing strategies (showing progress), and administration of pretests.[17]

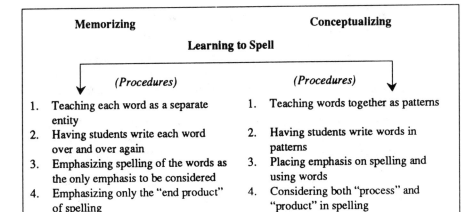

FIGURE 4–2 Two Processes for Learning to Spell

*Morphophonemic refers to the tendency in the English language for many words to retain all or part of their spelling, even though the form and pronunciation of words change as in *photograph* to *photography* and *preside* to *president*.

Recent research on cooperative learning appears to justify peer tutoring for spelling instruction. Augustine, Gruber, and Hanson make the following recommendations for using cooperative learning with spelling:

1. Have students form heterogeneous triads with one high, one average, and one low scoring speller in each group. Triads work together to study spelling throughout the year.

2. Monday—Students, sitting together in their teams, take the pretest together. They self-correct their pretests and note which words are difficult to spell.

3. Tuesday—Teams choose spelling games and activities for spelling words. An example might be the Jigsaw strategy presented in Chapter 2 in which the word list is divided among team members. Each team member devises a strategy for teaching his/her segment of the words to others in the group.

4. Wednesday—To prepare for the spelling test, teams coach each other for five minutes. The practice test is taken individually. Teams reconvene to compare test papers, to tutor team members who misspelled words, and to "celebrate accurate papers."

5. Thursday—If all team members have accurate test papers from the previous day, free time is provided. However, any misspelled words result in the entire team tutoring student(s) who misspelled words.

6. Friday—Students who misspelled any words on the practice test are "coached" for five minutes. Similar procedures are followed on the spelling test given on this day that were followed for the practice test, with each student taking the test individually and the teams reconvening to examine papers.[18]

Developing and Following a Spelling Curriculum for Corrective Teaching

As described earlier, students who are to be taught in a corrective program should not be locked into a prescribed grade-level curriculum. While grade-level words may be designated (but without locking students into a level simply because they are in that grade), students in a corrective spelling program should be moving through various skills, generalizations, and other parts of the curriculum at a pace that they, as members of base and flex groups, need at a particular time. The curriculum recommended for a corrective spelling program in Table 4–1 is arranged in ascending levels of complexity, starting with *Building Background for Spelling*, moving into *Spelling: Introductory Level*, then into *Formal Spelling: Intermediate Level*, and finally into the *Formal Spelling: Advanced Level*. Under each category, a suggested order of teaching is recommended, beginning with Level A and advancing to the highest level (B, C, D) given in that category. However, such an order is not totally linear, meaning that some areas across the levels within a category may be taught together as will be explained later.

Adapting Spelling Textbooks and/or Locally-Developed Word Lists to a Corrective Spelling Curriculum

How do teachers adapt the spelling textbook or locally-developed word lists to the type of curriculum designed in this book? First, it is important to abandon the "one textbook/one workbook or any singular type of materials" approach to teaching spelling. Through support from appropriate personnel in a school/system, supplementary spelling materials are easy to accumulate. Second, a system for classifying supplementary materials must be set up. The materials can easily be organized into the four broad categories identified in the outlined spelling curriculum. Third, the materials can be packaged for easy use. If workbooks no longer in use by a school/system are part of the accumulated materials, the workbooks can easily be torn apart and selected skill sheets either laminated or placed in acetate binders for use more than once. Students can be taught not to write directly on skill sheets. (See "Textbooks and Workbooks" for review.)

TABLE 4–1   A Spelling Curriculum for a Corrective Program (Elementary Grades)

Developing a Background for Formal Spelling Instruction

Level A   The Student:
1.   shows interest in words on experience charts.
2.   recognizes boundaries (beginnings/endings) of words on experience charts.
3.   recognizes own name when written by the teacher.
4.   shows interest in labeling/naming his/her drawings.
5.   is interested in scribbling.
6.   recognizes simple, reoccurring words on charts/chalkboard.
7.   recognizes that letters in words are written in sequence.
8.   identifies separate letters in words.
9.   recognizes that some words begin with upper-case and some with lower-case letters.
10.   dictates sentences and stories to the teacher or volunteer.

Level B   The Student:
11.   names letters of the alphabet in order presented (both lower- and upper-case).
12.   matches upper-case letters with their lower-case counterparts.
13.   names sequence of letters in simple words.
14.   groups words that begin with the same letters.
15.   groups words that have the same middle letters.
16.   groups words that have the same ending letters.
17.   matches rhyming words.

Level C   The Student:
18.   recognizes likenesses and differences in sounds at beginning of words.
19.   recognizes likenesses and differences in medial sounds of words (three-letter words).
20.   recognizes likenesses and differences in ending sounds of words.
21.   recognizes the same sound in different positions of words.
22.   associates sound/symbol relationships in frequently-occurring words.
23.   recognizes all letters of the alphabet.
24.   uses basic speech sounds by naming easily-recognized pictures.
25.   writes own first and last names.
26.   arranges letter cutouts of alphabet in proper order.
27.   uses singular-plural forms of words in dictated stories.
28.   matches words that tell plural and singular nouns *(dog-dogs cat-cats)* with appropriate pictures.

Level D   The Student:
29.   makes four basic strokes (horizontal, vertical, diagonal, and circular) lines in manuscript.
30.   repeats alphabet from memory.
31.   arranges letter cutouts to spell simple words, relying on memory to sequence letters.
32.   writes simplest of letters in manuscript.
33.   writes simple words, using a model.
34.   writes simple words from memory.
35.   copies simple stories the teacher has written for class or individual.
36.   writes all letters of the alphabet, using a model (both upper- and lower-case).
37.   writes words independently.
38.   writes all letters of the alphabet (both upper- and lower-case) from memory.
39.   reads at about second-grade level.
(When a student has satisfactorily progressed this far, he/she is ready for *Formal Spelling: Introductory.)*

Formal Spelling: Introductory

Level A The Student:

1. recognizes words that make up compound words.
2. recognizes concept of syllable.
3. writes graphemes < c >, < m >, < d >, < b >, < s >, < l >, < + >, < p >, < n >, < e >, < i >, < o >, < g >, < f >, < r >, < a >, for sounds represented in such words as *cat, man, bed, got, nap,* and *sit.* Note: Sounds and their representative symbols are introduced in order that they appear in common words students know.
4. changes simple CVC words (*cat* to *cap, did* to *rid, map* to *tap,* and *bat* to *bad*).
5. writes common spellings of short vowel sounds; /i/ as in *in;* /e/ as in *egg;* /o/ as in *not;* /a/ as in *at;* /u/ as in *but.*
6. seeks help in spelling when needed.
7. recognizes that some sounds are spelled more than one way.
8. recognizes that words are not always spelled the way they sound (e.g., *said*).
9. recognizes CV pattern and how to change words in this pattern (e.g., *so* to *go*).
10. recognizes VC pattern and how to change words in this pattern (e.g., *an* to *am*).
11. uses simple resource charts/books to learn how to spell unknown words.
12. writes words when they are called out.
13. checks own papers after spelling words are given out.
14. writes words from memory to form simple sentences.
15. expresses interest in spelling correctly and in spelling lessons.
16. tells simple story or description of an event.
17. writes stories or descriptions of event.
18. recognizes that some sounds are spelled with more than one letter (e.g., *tell*).
19. writes graphemes < ay >, < a >,< a-e >, for *long a* sound; < i >, < i-e > for *long i* sound; < e >,< ee > for *long e* sound; < o-e > for *long o* sound; and < u >, < u-e > for *long u* sound.
20. recognizes CVCe pattern in words such as *like, cake,* and *ride.*
21. makes new words by substituting sounds/ symbols in CVCe words.
22. follows sequence of study steps* in learning how to spell new words.
23. writes stories independently.
24. uses proofreading steps to check spelling.**
25. spells initial consonant clusters *st, sp, bl, pl,* and *sm* in context of known words.
26. spells final consonant clusters in easily recognized words.
27. spells consonant digraphs *wh* and *th.*

*Study steps vary from spelling series to series. A typical set of steps follows: (a) Look at the word (to be learned), (b) Say the word, (c) Cover the word, (d) Write the word, (e) Check the spelling of the word.

**Proofreading schemes also vary. See Table 4–5 for an example of a proofreading scheme.

Level C The Student:

28. spells new words by adding suffixes *ly, er* and *est.*
29. spells new words by adding prefixes *un* and *dis.*
30. uses prefixes and suffixes in writing.
31. spells contractions *can't* and *won't* in writing.
32. changes verbs to their "ing" form three ways (as in *go-going; make-making;* and *stop-stopping*).
33. uses "ing" words in writing.
34. uses homophones in writing. (e.g., *fair, fare*)
35. writes words with variant spellings of consonant sounds: /t/, /d/, /m/, /n/, /l/, /r/, /s/, /k/, and /p/.
36. writes words with variant spellings of short vowel sounds.
37. writes words with variant spellings of long vowel sounds.

Continued

TABLE 4-1 *Continued*

---

38. recognizes and spells CVCC pattern as in *hand, lump,* and *mend.*
39. substitutes sound/symbols in CVCC pattern to form new words.

Level D The Student:
40. substitutes words in writing for purposes of expanding, clarifying, and rewriting ideas.
41. uses source books to find more appropriate words than those commonly used in writing.
42. verifies spellings of words used in writing by using the dictionary.
43. in writing, uses multiple meanings of words such as *run, saw,* and *cold.*
44. spells words with /y/, /z/, and /ng/.
45. spells words with < th > for two different sounds as in *than* and *thank.*
46. spells words with *sn, gr,* and *br* consonant clusters.
47. spells words with /i/ spelled < y > as in *party.*
48. changes words from nouns to adjectives by adding < y > as *salt* to *salty, air* to *airy.*
49. spells words with < oo > as in *good.*
50. spells words with /aw/ written < a >, < au >, and < o >.
51. writes abbreviations Mr., Mrs., and Ms.

(When a student has satisfactorily progressed this far, he/she is ready for *Formal Spelling: Intermediate.*)

Formal Spelling: Intermediate

Level A The Student:
1. uses words in writing that have suffixes *ful* and *ness.*
2. writes with the same base word repeated (e.g., *hand* y, *hand* kerchief, *hand* shake).
3. changes verbs ending in *m, n,* and *t* to their *ing* forms.
4. knows morphemes* with multiple meanings such as *er.*
5. knows how to use prefix *re* in writing.
6. writes abbreviations for days of the week and months of the year.
7. spells possessives 's and s'.

*Morphemes are structural units that have meaning either alone or when placed with another morpheme. The *er* morpheme is an example of the latter. It is a *bound* morpheme. A word like teach in teacher has meaning by itself and is called a *free* morpheme.

Level B The Student:
8. uses dictionary to verify spellings and pronunciations of plurals.
9. knows how to verify meanings of words.
10. spells initial consonant clusters *thr* and *str.*
11. spells final consonant clusters *st* and *sp.*
12. spells < sh >, < ch > and < ng > for sounds they represent.
13. spells schwa ǝ sound in initial and medial positions.
14. uses position of sounds in words to determine spelling of those sounds such as /a/ in *able;* /a/ in *stay.*
15. writes variant spellings of long vowel sounds such as < uy > in *buy;* < ie > in *grief.*
16. writes variant spellings of short vowel sounds such *as* < ai > in *plaid;* < ea > in *deaf.*
17. writes stories with expanded vocabulary/creative expressions.

Level C The Student:
18. uses mnemonic devises to spell hard-to-remember words (e.g., "prince of a pal" for principal).
19. expands knowledge of CVC, CVCe, and CVCC patterns.
20. expands spelling ability by submitting sounds/symbols for CVC, CVCe, and CVCC patterns.
21. spells "demon" or hard-to-spell words.

22. expands use of study steps in spelling new words.
23. uses proofreading and other systems for checking spelling.
24. expands use of source books in writing.
25. looks for and catalogs spelling-error types (middle syllable, word ending, transposition, and other error types).
26. writes *ies* form of plurals.

Level D   The Student:
27. expands use of prefixes to include *mis* and *in*.
28. expands use of suffixes to include *ed, less,* and *able*.
29. uses dictionary to verify prefixes and suffixes.
30. uses dictionary to verify plural forms of words.
31. uses prefixes and suffixes added to the same base word as in *disagreeable*.
32. spells past tense of words using *d, ed,* and *t* .
33. spells abbreviations of states in region of his/her part of the country.
34. spells abbreviations for parts of speech.
35. spells abbreviations for words that denote time (hr., mo., yr., p.m., and a.m.).
36. spells abbreviations for frequently-used mathematics terms (ft., yd., sq., dz.,).

(When a student has satisfactorily progressed this far, he/she is ready for *Formal Spelling: Advanced.*)

Formal Spelling: Advanced

Level A   The Student:
1. expands ability to spell consonant and vowel sounds.
2. expands use of basic spelling patterns CVCe, CCVC, and CVCC to make new words.
3. demonstrates facility to write major prefixes and suffixes in words.
4. demonstrates facility to write all parts of speech correctly.
5. demonstrates facility to write independently with correct use of major abbreviations.
6. expands spelling of demon, tricky words.
7. continues use of proofreading and study steps.
8. expands use of plural spellings, correctly writing unusual singular-plural combinations (e.g., ox-oxen; leaf-leaves).
9. expands use of dictionary to check for unusual spellings of plurals.
10. spells *ible* suffix.

Level B   The Student:
11. spells unusual past tense forms of verbs *(bit, bled, bought, built)*.
12. expands knowledge of spellings for abbreviations (such as professional titles) and uses dictionary to verify them.
13. writes contractions *I've* and *I'd*.
14. writes correct form of possessive for plural, compound, and noun phrases.

Setting Up a Flexible Grouping Plan for Spelling Instruction

Within each classroom, there should be several spelling groups which vary according to grade levels. The curriculum for each group, including word lists, should match the spelling level of the group. When this occurs, developmental levels of students and specific problems individuals have in spelling are best served. The base and flex grouping scheme previously discussed is ideally suited to flexible grouping in spelling.

Setting up Base Groups in Spelling

Base groups, organized to meet developmental needs of students, function somewhat like current reading groups but with much more flexibility. Thus, regrouping of students from different base groups for help on noted spelling deficiencies would lead to more effective special-needs instruction. Such groups of students would become flex groups, organized for a relatively small number of lessons to correct a specific deficiency.

Base Groups Organized by Curricular Levels

In the spelling curriculum in Table 4–1, base groups through Level D of *Developing a Background for Spelling Instruction* would be organized according to formal and informal readiness-type tests. As students perform various activities for this area of the curriculum, teacher observation plays a significant role in the formation of small groups of students who are developmentally at the same level in

Small-Group Work is Important in a Corrective Spelling Program (*Photograph by Robert Heller*).

spelling. It is important at this stage for a systematic tracking system to be in place. An example of a system for use with Level C, skill areas 18–22 (sound-symbol relationships) follows in Figure 4–3. At the top of the chart, students' names from a base group are placed. On the left-hand side of the chart, the related skill areas to be taught are listed.

In Figure 4–3, note that there is room to add "other skills." Since the learning of language arts skills is not always linear, there may be an opportunity to teach or reinforce a skill area not planned to be taught at the time a targeted skill is to be taught. An example might be given for skill area 18 in Table 4–1. A word such as *cat* might be used to call attention to the beginning /k/ and how it is the same as the beginning sound in *can*. Since *cat* is the singular form of a noun, some reference, perhaps through students bringing it up, may very well be made about *cat* and the

Skill Areas	Sue	Stan	Ellen	Joy	Toby
18. recognizes likenesses and differences in sounds at the beginning of words.					
19. recognizes likenesses and differences in medial sounds of words (three-letter words at first).					
20. recognizes likenesses and differences in ending sounds of words.					
21. recognizes the same sounds in different positions of words					
22. associates sound-symbol relationships in frequently-occurring words.					
other skills.					

FIGURE 4–3 A Tracking System for Skill Areas 18–22, Level C (Background for Spelling)

plural form, *cats*. Thus, skill area number 28, "uses singular-plural forms of words," may be taught along with skills 18–22. The teaching of this additional skill may be cursory, with more details given later, or if already taught, the skill may be reinforced. Teachers often have to take a detour of the exact lesson that has been planned, and an open category such as "other skills" on tracking charts helps systematize the teaching/evaluation of what is taught or has been taught in the language arts.

Cells on the chart in Figure 4–3 should be large enough to permit notes on progress made. To illustrate the use of such a chart, a hypothetical situation involving Toby can be given. If Toby has trouble recognizing differences between phonemes /n/ and /m/ in initial position of words, this information would be recorded. At the same time, other initial consonant sounds may cause no confusion for Toby, and this, too, is recorded.

Base Groups Organized by Spelling Levels

Once a group of students has advanced to the *Formal Spelling: Introductory Level* and words are given out each week, the teacher should begin making plans to form base groups according to spelling levels of the students. However, only those students who have shown satisfactory progress in the total spectrum of readiness skills would be at this point. In a readiness program for students in first grade, it is doubtful that all students will be ready to begin the formal spelling of weekly word lists at the same time. Gradually, other small groups will reach the stage where they will be ready to begin spelling of word lists.

During the first three-to-four weeks of formal spelling lessons where words are given out, students become acquainted with the routine of taking a pretest, correcting their own papers, examining misspelled words, and taking posttests. It is critical that a foundation be established for getting students to take responsibility for carefully analyzing/correcting their own spelling test papers. It is also important that students begin seeing the relationship between their weekly work in spelling class and the use of spelling in everyday writing, with attention also focused on analysis/correction of spelling in writing in other areas.

As the teacher begins to note differences in how the students who are studying word lists spell, it is time to determine variations in spelling levels. One procedure for finding such levels has been advocated by Burrows, Monson, and Stauffer. This four-step procedure can be used as is for finding levels of older students where spelling levels have not been determined, but should be modified slightly for much younger children. The procedure follows:

1. Select a sample of words from spelling books at each level of the series in use (20–25 words per sampled list). Randomly select the words (such as every tenth word).

2. Have students take a test on each list of twenty-five words, beginning with the lowest level. (Tests should probably be given over a span of several days.)

3. Note which students make less than 70 percent on the test. They do not take the test on the next level. The level at which they first fall below 70 percent is their designated spelling level.

4. Continue testing those students who make 70 percent or higher. Eventually, all students will be appropriately placed. In most classrooms there will be approximately four groups.[19]

The degree to which the words randomly selected are appropriate for placing students on their grade level depends on the degree to which an appropriate scale was used to determine grade-level difficulty. In Table 4–2, a spelling-levels test appears that was developed by randomly selecting words from the 500 most frequently-used words on the Rinsland List (Word List 4–1, part 1) and for part of the sixth-grade list, the second 500 most-frequently used words (Part 2 of Word List 4–1). Level of difficulty was determined by using the *New Iowa Spelling Scale,* a

TABLE 4–2   Spelling-Levels Tests

2nd Grade	3rd Grade	4th Grade	5th Grade	6th Grade
1. all	1. an	1. afternoon	1. across	1. built
2. am	2. as	2. almost	2. again	2. carried
3. and	3. bed	3. any	3. another	3. caught
4. at	4. call	4. best	4. asked	4. company
5. ball	5. candy	5. brown	5. aunt	5. couldn't
6. be	6. dear	6. class	6. began	6. different
7. big	7. dogs	7. cut	7. birthday	7. during
8. book	8. door	8. ever	8. bought	8. else
9. boy	9. eat	9. fine	9. catch	9. enough
10. can	10. far	10. found	10. country	10. friends
11. come	11. feet	11. games	11. didn't	11. gifts
12. do	12. five	12. grades	12. dinner	12. guess
13. dog	13. girl	13. hope	13. girls	13. grew
14. go	14. happy	14. king	14. goes	14. music
15. good	15. hill	15. letter	15. haven't	15. pencil
16. into	16. ice	16. lots	16. heard	16. pictures
17. look	17. likes	17. miss	17. house	17. quite
18. no	18. man	18. must	18. I'll	18. rabbits
19. on	19. men	19. never	19. it's	19. Saturday
20. one	20. mother	20. off	20. jumped	20. since
21. so	21. room	21. our	21. please	21. skates
22. to	22. six	22. part	22. right	22. stayed
23. will	23. then	23. reading	23. used	23. their
24. yes	24. tree	24. ride	24. watch	24. Thursday
25. you	25. want	25. sat	25. wrote	25. until

scale that can be used to determine what percentage of students at each of grade levels 2–8 can spell some 5,000 high-frequency words.[20] When 60 percent* of the students at a grade level could first spell the word selected, the word appeared as one appropriate for students at that level. Thus, *letter* appears on the fourth-grade list since this is the lowest grade at which 60 percent or more of the students could spell that word.[21] Using the procedure described earlier, this word list can be used to determine spelling levels as an alternative to teachers developing their own lists.

A System for Using Differentiated Word Lists for Students in Base Groups

Once base groups have been formed, it is essential that a system be established for providing weekly spelling words for students in each group. The following suggestions are made for both the provision and monitoring of separate word lists for each base group:

- Use different levels of a spelling series within the same classroom. Thus, in a third-grade class, students spelling on levels other than the third-grade level would use books on their levels. This is a tricky feat to accomplish, since students on the lowest grade levels are sensitive about their placement. This is especially true when these students consistently remain in the lowest groups. However, using the system of flex groups, where students are mixed across base groups, will help offset the feeling of being behind for those who are in a book below the grade of other students. Also, word lists from different levels of spelling textbooks can easily be written on paper when all base groups take a pretest or posttest together. For systems with their own word lists, there should be different levels of words for students to progress through at their own pace, although certain common words across the disciplines may be found on each group's list.
- Use mimeographed word lists as part of each student's spelling folder. Some teachers already do this, especially where the school system has its own word lists. These lists are organized in such a way that a segment (8–14 words) is easily adapted to weekly study.
- Provide assignments that students can do together but with separate word lists. Pretests can easily be given at the same time, incorporating several different groups having their own word lists. The teacher calls out a list of words, but gives a code to signal which group of students should spell each word (S, P, E; tigers, lions, leopards), or the teacher might hold up a right hand, left hand, or no hand to designate who should spell a word. Other activities can be done

*This percentage was chosen since students surveyed in the development of the *New Iowa Spelling Scale* were given tests early in the year. A figure of 60 percent would probably mean that later in the year, the percentage of students able to spell selected words would be higher.

together, but with base groups using their group's words. Students can look for words in their books that pattern the same way as do the words on their separate lists. Students can also use their word lists in numerous ways throughout the rest of the school day. These include use in the writing curriculum, in oral-language activities, and other curricular areas. Groups of students can also take a test placed on audio tape at a listening center.

Setting up Flex Groups in Spelling

In Chapter 2, flex groups were defined as clusters of students from across base groups who need help in a common area. These students may be on different developmental levels, but a common problem calls for special-needs instruction. Whether the problem area is distinguishing between *long* and *short vowel* sounds or adding *ing* as indicated for the student whose paper was identified in Figure 1–3, students are regrouped as a flex group for special-needs instruction.

Flex Groups Organized Through Spelling-Error Analysis

One major approach to working with flex groups in spelling is through analysis of spelling error types. Teachers should have a very good command of spelling errors and, of equal importance, their probable causes. As Hodges states:

> *Growth in spelling ability develops in conjunction with observing and checking one's attempts and in correcting those attempts to correspond to standard orthography. Simply correcting errors is not sufficient, however. Analyzing the errors to determine the* causes *for them provides knowledge that can be used in spelling other words. An ability to distinguish correct spellings from incorrect ones and to correct both the mistakes and their causes is a critical part of spelling ability. . . .* [22]

Types of spelling errors, along with projected causes for these errors have appeared in several language arts publications.[23] There is much agreement on both the error types and their probable causes. In Table 4–3, the most-frequently identified error types and their probable causes are identified. These errors and their probable causes should be thoroughly known by teachers in a student-involved corrective spelling program. As teachers learn more about spelling problems of students being taught, spelling errors and probable causes other than those in Table 4–3 can be identified and corrected.

A Systematic Approach to the Tracking of Spelling-Error Types

Since students should be involved in analyzing/correcting their own errors, there must be a streamlined system established for involving each student in the recording/tracking of spelling errors. It is therefore essential that an appropriate form be used and kept in individual spelling folders. A suggested form is shown in

TABLE 4–3   Spelling Errors and Their Causes

Error Type	Examples	Probable Cause
1. Poor handwriting	*stop* for *stop*	Lag in handwriting development or carelessness
2. Transposition or reversal	*iorn* for *iron*	Inadequate attention to letter sequence
3. Omission of word ending	*somethin* for *something*	Incorrect pronunciation or poor articulation
4. Word substitution	*there* for *their*	Misunderstanding about how each word is used
5. Carelessness	*airt* for *art*	Poor attitude towards spelling; poor work habits; rushed work
6. Overphonetic error	*sed* for *said*	Overgeneralization about English spelling patterns
7. Omission of middle syllable	*principal* for *principal*	Failure to hear the middle syllable
8. Omission of letter parts	*through* for *thorough*	Poor visual discrimination; inattention to detail
9. Confusion of words similar in sound	*on* for *own*	Failure to hear differences in pronunciation of the two words
10. Word endings substituted	*everybode* for *everybody*	Lack of knowledge about optional spellings
11. Wrong grapheme substituted	*birfday* for *birthday*	Failure to hear all sounds in a word; inattention to detail
12. Omission of part of grapheme	*bit* for *bite*	Lack of knowledge about grapheme parts
13. Adding extra part of grapheme	*alleways* for *always*	Inattention to detail; overgeneralization
14. Adding *ing* to verbs incorrectly	*stoping* for *stopping*	Misunderstanding of rules governing adding of *ing*
15. Making plural forms of nouns incorrectly	*churchs* for *churches*	Misapplied rules for forming plurals

Figure 4–4. This form has a place for students to record their misspelled words, exactly as they are misspelled. To the right of each misspelled word, the correct spelling is written so that students can see the errors made, a practice earlier cited as a sound, research-based practice.[24] The fourth grader's paper, depicted in Figure 1–4, is shown in Figure 4–4 as it would look when the procedure and form described herein is implemented over an eight-week period. The form helps teachers more easily identify troublesome error types, thus leading to the formation of flex groups.

A Prerequisites Skills Approach to Forming Flex Groups

Another approach to forming flex groups is through use of tests on prerequisite skills, concepts, and other components of the spelling curriculum, an idea advanced in Chapter 1. When students move into a new skill area, the teacher should determine the extent to which prerequisites have been learned by the students. Identified weaknesses provide the grouping pattern for flex groups. In the case of syllabication, presented in Table 1–2, several of the prerequisites might not have been learned by students. Therefore, these students would be placed in a flex group and be taught prerequisites for learning syllabication.

Some of the prerequisites for learning new skills in spelling are shown in Table 4–4. These components are from the spelling curriculum in Table 4–1, but

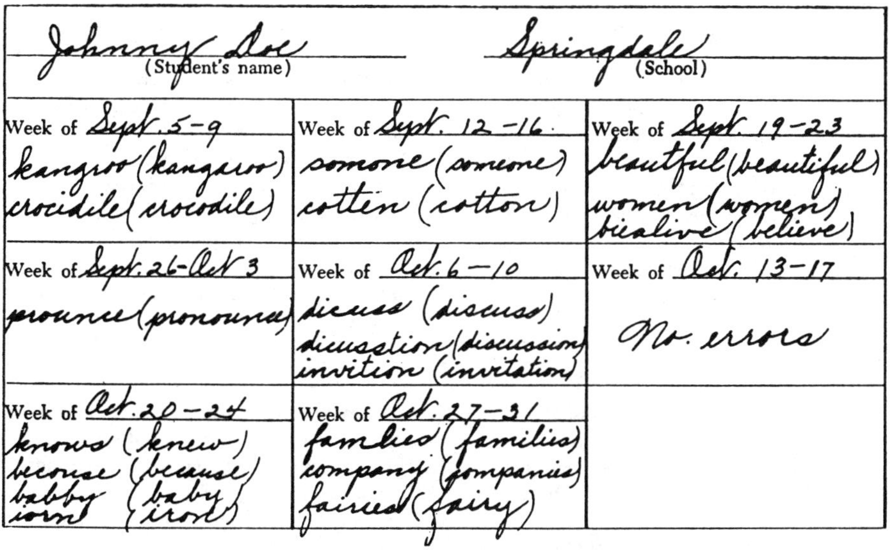

Johnny Doe (Student's name) Springdale (School)

Week of Sept. 5–9 kangroo (kangaroo) crocidile (crocodile)	Week of Sept. 12–16 somone (someone) cotten (cotton)	Week of Sept. 19–23 beautful (beautiful) women (women) bicalive (believe)
Week of Sept. 26–Oct 3 prounce (pronounce)	Week of Oct. 6–10 dicuss (discuss) dicussion (discussion) invition (invitation)	Week of Oct. 13–17 No errors
Week of Oct. 20–24 knows (knew) becouse (because) babby (baby) iorn (iron)	Week of Oct. 27–31 famlies (families) company (companies) fairied (fairy)	

FIGURE 4–4 Recording Spelling Errors Over a Prolonged Period

C. Glennon Rowell, "Don't Throw Away Those Spelling Test Papers . . . Yet!" *Elementary English* 52 (1975) 254. Copyright (1975) by the National Council of Teachers of English. Reprinted with permission.

other components of the curriculum can be similarly set up. While some teachers may elect not to use the prerequisites approach to the development of flex groups, there should always be some attention to prerequisites needed for learning new skills in language arts.

Informal, easy-to-use checkups shown in Figure 4–5, can help determine if prerequisites have been learned. Arranged on index cards and perhaps laminated, these checkups can be used with individuals or with small groups.

TABLE 4–4 Prerequisites for Selected Skills in a Spelling Program

(1)	(4)
New Skill: Alphabetizing 1. Recognizing letters of the alphabet 2. Sequencing letters of the alphabet 3. Knowing reasons for alphabetizing 4. Recognizing letters when ordered in words 5. Understanding concept of ordering words by using second and third letters in words	New Skill: Recognizing the multiple meaning of the morpheme *er* 1. Detecting word parts in affixed words 2. Recognizing words/understanding meanings of words with *er* added to base words (e.g., *teacher, higher*) 3. Recognizing transition in meaning and use of words changed to different forms (e.g., *teach* to *teacher; high* to *higher*) 4. Understanding the concept of *suffix*
(2)	**(5)**
New Skill: Writing variant spellings (*ey, eigh, ea*) *of the long a sound* 1. Differentiating between *long a* and other basic speech sounds 2. Understanding that sounds in words are represented by symbols 3. Understanding that different symbols are used to represent the same speech sound 4. Knowing common ways (<a>, <ai>, <a-e>, <ay>) to represents the long a sound	New Skill: Adding *ing* to *base* words ending in *n, m, b, p, d,* and *t* 1. Understanding the concept of *base* words 2. Recognizing letters that usually represent consonant sounds 3. Recognizing consonants *n, m, b, p, d,* and *t* 4. Detecting word parts in affixed words 5. Writing *ing* endings of words when no changes are made in base words (e.g., *fishing, leaping*) 6. Differentiating between long and short vowel sounds
(3)	**(6)**
New Skill: Adding prefixes *un* and *dis* to words 1. Detecting word parts in affixed word 2. Understanding the concept of base words 3. Understanding the concept of *prefix* 4. Knowing the meaning of not 5. Recognizing the difference in meaning between word pairs where prefixes have been added such as *happy, unhappy; like, dislike*	New Skill: Writing possessives of words showing common ownership (e.g., Ann and Bill's house) 1. Recognizing and using concept of ownership in speech 2. Spelling/writing common forms ('s, s') for showing ownership 3. Spelling/writing possessive form for plural nouns (e.g., boys') 4. Understanding concept of common ownership 5. Understanding concept of separate ownership where two nouns are used

A Mastery-Test Approach for Forming Flex Groups

A third approach to forming flex groups is to group students according to noted deficiencies on mastery tests. This approach probably is more suited to older students who are given a series of tests on words that are to be mastered prior to the students moving on to middle or junior high school. Words such as the Rinsland's 1,000 words of highest usage (Word List 4–1, parts 1 and 2) and additional lists might be given out at intervals during the year. Students who miss more than a designated percentage as set by the teacher or the school, are grouped for special

---

1. Look at the seven words as you pronounce them (teacher may pronounce them). Circle each word that has two words in it.

a.	book	d.	mailman	g.	most
b.	fireman	e.	daylight	h.	candy
c.	light	f.	off	i.	words

2. In each word below, circle the place where you hear a vowel sound. Underline where you hear the consonant sounds.

a.	am	if	at	be	by
b.	bad	big	had	and	end
c.	went	week	road	ago	into

3. To the right of each word below, write the number of vowel sounds you hear in each word.

Words	Number of Vowel Sounds	Words	Number of Vowel Sounds
a. can	_____	e. road	_____
b. best	_____	f. after	_____
c. letter	_____	g. teacher	_____
d. city	_____	h. grandmother	_____

4. Words have parts called *syllables*. Each syllable has only one vowel sound. Tell how many syllables each word below has by counting the vowel sounds that you hear.

Words	Number of Syllables	Words	Number of Syllables
a. along	_____	e. fishing	_____
b. bird	_____	f. looked	_____
c. looking	_____	g. flowers	_____
d. grandmother	_____	h. tomorrow	_____

5. Words are divided into syllables to help with the pronunciation of words. Also, in writing, words are divided at the end of a line when there is not enough room to finish a word that you have started. In the examples below, which use is in place?

   a. The old dog was sad. She was look
      -ing for her home.
   b. Say "yesterday" for me. Say "yes-ter-day."

FIGURE 4–5 Sample Prerequisite Skills Tests (Syllabication)

instruction on words missed. These students continue in flex groups until they can spell the required percentage of words.

Flexibility: A Criterion for Base and Flex Groups

It should be reiterated that when base and flex groups are put into operation in a spelling program, students must be continuously evaluated to determine if they are grouped appropriately. Flex groups will have more variations in how students are grouped than will base groups, but the latter should by no means be made up of the same students all year. Teachers should frequently check to determine if placements in base groups are to remain the same, a practice that, as stated earlier, happens too infrequently in reading groups.

Appropriate Activities in a Corrective Spelling Program

A student-involved corrective spelling program should have a preventive focus in which students try to avoid problems in spelling. Having students correct their own test papers in spelling and record spelling errors should be reminders to students to check a particular problem that they have been having, such as a transposition or reversal error. Other reminders are provided in the section of this book that follows. All include a focus on getting students to check their work prior to submitting completed assignments, identified in the Preface of this book as a critical dimension of assessment. The five items that follow relate to this dimension and to other procedures focusing on the involvement of students in assessment of problems in spelling.

Self-Assessment Activities

1. Codes-in Margin System. This system, to be presented more fully in Chapter 5, "Writing," includes codes for students to use in examining their written work checked by the teacher. Instead of the teacher red-marking the body of the papers, codes are used on the line where an error occurs in the margin of each page of a composition. One code is for spelling.

2. Proofreading. A proofreading system is one which helps students develop the habit of systematically checking their papers before they turn them in to the teacher. In spelling, research indicates that there are positive effects when students are taught a proofreading system, and the system is enforced. One suggested proofreading system follows in Table 4–5.

3. Spelling-Error Reminder Cards. This system includes cards to remind students of types of spelling errors that have been particularly troublesome in the

TABLE 4–5 A Proofreading System

a. Examine all letter formations, but especially those that are made in a similar way (e.g., *g* and *q*, *d* and *b*, *e* and *i*).

b. Recheck the sequence of letters in each word spelled.

c. Recheck to see that all added word parts are correctly made (e.g., adding *ing* to *make* to form *making*).

d. Make sure that the correct form of each word has been written (e.g., *helped* instead of *help*).

e. Make sure that all words to be capitalized begin with an upper-case letter.

past. Students who are having problems with any of the types of errors presented in Table 4–3 are provided "reminder cards" while they are writing a composition or taking a spelling test. It is probably more economical to have five or six "reminders" on a single, laminated card with places to check the error type for which students are having trouble. An example of a spelling-error reminder card is presented in Figure 4–6.

Directions: Answer the item(s) checked by placing an "x" under either "yes" or "no." Do this before handing in your paper, and clip the card to your paper.

Yes   *No*

1. Look at the last two or three letters of each of your spelling words. Are the endings of all words correctly made (e.g., *something* not *somethin*)?

2. Look at all words on your list with three or more syllables. Have you spelled all parts of each word (e.g., *principal* not *princpal*)?

3. Look at all words that have "t's" and "i's" in them. Are all "t's" crossed and all "i's" dotted?

4. Have you remembered to write all letters in each word in the proper order that they should appear (e.g., *iron* instead of *iorn*)?

5. Have you remembered that not all words are spelled the way they sound (e.g., *said* not *sed*)?

FIGURE 4–6 Spelling-Error Reminder Card

4. Prediction/Analysis of Correct Spelling. This is a system, recommended by Mickler, as a *metacognitive* approach to analyzing one's spelling. In this approach, students work with partners in the following ways:

Example

a. One student gives out spelling to the other, using each word in a sentence.

1. enough
2. graph
3. tough
4. roughly
5. couldn't
6. didn't

b. The student writing the words places each one in a column, with several spaces to the side of each word.

1. *enough*
2. *graf*
3. *tough*
4. *ruffly*
5. *could't*
6. *didn't*

c. A "#" is placed to the left of a word if the meaning of the word was known prior to the sentence being given out. If not, an "X" is placed to the left of the word.

1. # *enough*
2. X *graf*
3. # *tough*
4. X *ruffly*
5. # *couldt*
6. # *didn't*

d. Numbers 1, 2, 3, and 4 are placed to the left of the codes used above (# or X) to indicate one of the following:

1. 2# *enough*
2. 1X *graf*
3. 2# *tough*
4. 3X *ruffly*
5. 4# *couldt*
6. 2# *didn't*

The student spelling the words:
1. is absolutely sure the word is spelled *correctly*.
2. thinks the word is spelled *correctly* but is not sure.
3. thinks the word is spelled *incorrectly* but is not sure.
4. is absolutely sure the word is spelled *incorrectly*.

e. The student then checks his/her spellings, comparing the spelled words with the words given out.

1. 2# *enough*
2. 1X *graf*
3. 2# *tough*
4. 3X *ruffly*
5. 4# *Could't*
6. 2# *didn't*

f. All correctly-spelled words are circled; all misspelled words are written, corrected to the right of the word. Words in which students correctly predict the spelling or misspelling are "boxed" in.

1. 2# [*enough*]
2. 1X *graf* *graph*
3. 2# [*tough*]
4. 3X [*ruffly*] *roughly*
5. 4# [*Could't*] *Couldn't*
6. 2# (*didn't*)

[*enough*]

g. The student must explain to a classmate or the teacher why each word spelled incorrectly was misspelled and how, in the future, correcting the misspelling will prevent future problems with the word.[25]

While this system may at first appear time-consuming, once students learn the codes, the system becomes easier. According to the author of this system, it makes students think about words they are to spell which is too often left out in spelling programs emphasizing rote learning.*

*Personal conversation with Dr. Jan Mickler who developed and has implemented this system.

5. Facility with Spelling. There are various systems designed to determine how well students know spelling patterns. The following involves students in analysis of any number of phoneme-grapheme patterns.

a. *Transformation Activity* (modified) Gattegno's *Teaching Words in Color* has several transformation activities that are useful in helping determine (and develop) skill and flexibility in spelling. Transformations are made in a number of ways, as follows:

1. Substitution—substituting a sound/symbol to a word as in changing *cup* to *cap* or *tap* to *rap*
2. Addition—adding a sound/symbol to a word as in changing *pat* to *pats* or *can* to *scan*
3. Insertion—inserting a sound/symbol within a word, as in changing *sip* to *slip* or *sat* to *slat*
4. Reversal—reversing sounds/symbols in words as in changing *pat* to *tap* or *mad* to *dam*
5. Rearrangement—rearranging the letters but not in exact reverse order such as changing *pat* to *apt* [26]

One variation that can be introduced to this activity is to use codes to indicate which transformation is to be used. Codes such as *s* for substitution, *a* for addition, *i* for insertion, *r* for reversal, and *re* for rearrangement signal which transformation is to be made.

One activity that is especially helpful is the placing of a word in the center of several radiating arrows. Each arrow has a code (*s, a, i, r, re*) on it which indicates the transformation to be made. Students make as many transformations as they can. Students may add lines with arrows, thus indicating just how well they can manipulate the pattern being studied. An example follows:

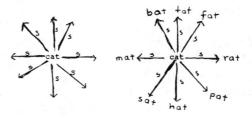

In this simple CVC word, students first change the initial sound/symbol. A second activity may call for changes in medial sounds/symbols, while yet a third activity might call for changes in final sounds/symbols. Although not suggested by Gattegno, this activity is easily modified for use on the microcomputer. It requires a minimal amount of graphics. Students merely keep adding radiating lines as they think of (or see) ways to change the pattern.

After the basic transformations have been introduced, students show how one would move from a word like *pat* to *not*, using only one transformation at a time and without making subtractions (reducing the number of sounds/symbols).[27] This change might look like: pat $\xrightarrow{S}$ pot $\xrightarrow{S}$ not. A more complex change might have been to go from *pat* to *plot* which calls for mixed kinds of transformations as follows: pat $\xrightarrow{S}$ pot $\xrightarrow{S}$ lot $\xrightarrow{a}$ plot. There are usually a number of ways that students can make transformations. The activity is one where students like to put their responses on the chalkboard. It also lends itself to small-group activity.

b. Another approach to assessment of pattern facility is to list words on the left side of a vertical line and ask students to write on the right other words that pattern the same way. Two examples of the CVCe pattern follow:

made | make, mate, cape, fake, wake, take, gate
kite | bite, bike, nice, hike, like, site, mice

   In this activity, small groups can compete. The groups are given a word and asked to make a string of other words that pattern the same way. A time limit such as five minutes is given, with the winner being the group with the longest string of words.

c. Another approach to determining pattern facility is to place several words having a targeted spelling (for example, each word having a different spelling of the *long a* sound) at the top of a column. Either from their own knowledge or a word list that has a large number of words with *long a* in them, students place words in the appropriate column. A modification of this activity can be made, again using the microcomputer. Words that have the *long a* sound are programmed in alphabetical order, followed by columns with target words that have the *long a* sound spelled differently (make, wait, table, play). Students regroup the words. Instead of target words with the *long a* sound, the actual ways the sounds are spelled in these words can be used, as *a-e, ai, a,* and *ay* in these examples.

d. *Whole Brain Spelling* This is a videotaped program that, as briefly mentioned earlier, has some diagnostic-corrective features. The goals of the program, according to those who designed it are to: (1) develop visual imaging skills; (2) offer 200 ten-word lists for practice by beginning spellers; and (3) diagnose and indicate areas for self-correction.[28] Word lists in *Whole Brain Spelling* are arranged by increasing levels of difficulty. A word from a list being spelled is displayed in a box. The student using the program is asked to make a mental picture of the word. Then, using the space bar on the microcomputer, the word is erased. The student is asked to see the word in the "mind's eye." The space bar is used to display the word again, with the instructions for the student to check the mental image made. Pressing return on the microcomputer, the student goes to a new word.

One corrective feature of *Whole Brain Spelling* is focused in the responses given by the student using the program. If a wrong letter is given in a word such as the giving of an *a* for the middle letter in *for*, the letter *a* is highlighted, indicating that is where the error is. If a letter is omitted as when *room* is spelled *rom*, a caret ($_\wedge$) is inserted at the place where a letter is omitted (ro$_\wedge$m). There are several other features that are helpful in learning to spell words, including letter by letter spelling of a word (*s u c c e e d*), and showing how the *case* of certain words is changed such as in *succeed* to *success*.[29]

e. The electronic card reader can be used in a number of ways to assess problems in spelling. Earlier, the card reader was recommended for use in pretests and posttests in spelling. Hasler's suggestion of using cards where symbols (letters) are left out, first for vowel sounds and then for some consonant sounds, as shown in Diagram 4–1, could be helpful for determining which phoneme-grapheme correspondences are causing difficulty for students. In this activity, three cards are needed for each word. The cards are numbered so that they are a set to be used together. Although letters are omitted on the graphics part of the cards, all letters are recorded on the teacher-voice track of the tape. Students listen to the word spelled and then spell the word on the student-voice track of the card. Some tracing of the letters is also recommended.[30] The grouping of words calling for a specific phoneme-grapheme correspondence would also help determine facility with graphemes for the target phonemes as in cards which have m   king, t   king, and b   king or   iger ,   uesday, and   all printed on them.

Self-Evaluative Activities for a Spelling Program
Activities that focus less on assessment of errors in spelling and prevention of problems before they occur should also be teamed with activities in which students look at the overall evaluation of progress made in spelling. Such activities follow in the next section of this book. Having students "step back" and look at the progress being made in spelling is helpful to the success of a corrective spelling program, especially where the teacher as "coach" knows how to motivate students to improve.

1. Then-and-Now Charts for Spelling. This system, presented in Chapter 3, helps students compare segments of their current work with earlier work done in the same language arts area. In spelling where this system is used, students are asked to take a series of spelling papers (four to eight) from an earlier period in the

DIAGRAM 4–1 Using an Electronic Card Reader to Examine Sound-Symbol Facility

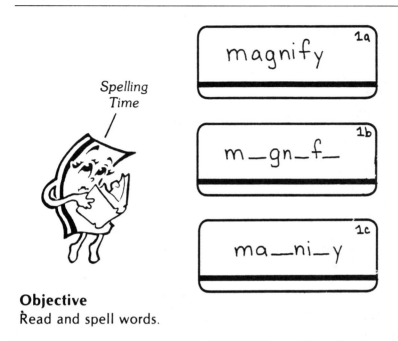

Spelling
Time

Objective
Read and spell words.

Esther J. Hasler, *Learning With Magnetic Card Activities* (Palm Beach Gardens, Florida: Jean-Bert Associates), p.20. Copyright © 1989. Used with permission.

year and the same number of papers from a later period in the year. If the spelling-error chart recommended in Figure 4–4 is used, this could substitute for the reexamination of papers since spelling errors have already been recorded. Using an appropriate form, students write the number of errors made during both the earlier and later time periods. To the right, a statement can be made about the difference as perceived by the student. An example of this form as it would be used in spelling follows in Figure 4–7:

2. Spelling Line-up. Using this system, students are encouraged to record their total spelling problems in numerical terms, without particular attention to the kinds of errors being made. Each student develops an individual chart inside his/her writing (or spelling) folder. The column is divided into four or five smaller columns, representing biweekly intervals if preferred. Each student keeps a running account of the number of spelling mistakes identified for each interval marked by columns. The objective is to reduce the numbers as shown for October: October Spelling Errors (by week): 13 \ 10 \ 8 \ 6

What to Compare	Early Spelling Papers	Later Spelling Papers	Your Comments
1. CVCe spellings			
2. Adding "ing" to verbs			
3. Spelling the middle syllable in three-syllable words			
4. Reversal errors			
5. Adding appropriate plural endings to singular forms of words			

FIGURE 4–7   **"Then and Now" Spelling Comparison Charts**

While the number of spelling mistakes is related to the amount of writing done weekly, and counting all mistakes could be tedious, this activity can be modified to have students take a random (but equal) number of papers per week during each interval designated.

Another modification of this system is to indicate to the left of each column the subject (writing, social studies, science, and so on) where errors are to be recorded. In this way, a pattern develops which helps each student evaluate how well he/she is doing in spelling across all curricular areas.

3. Evaluation of Spelling Progress in Cooperative Learning Groups. In addition to the evaluative strategies that are obviously built in to activities where cooperative learning teams are formed, cooperative learning groups can keep collective charts of spelling mistakes made by the teams on spelling test papers. The objective is to keep track of spelling mistakes of the team in order to evaluate progress made.

Corrective Activities in Spelling
The focus of the following activities is more on correcting errors in spelling than on preventing/assessing problems or evaluating progress.

1. Pattern-Word Error Follow-up. In this system, the student who misspells a word that patterns a specific way writes the correct spelling of the missed word and then finds and writes other words with the same pattern as shown in Figure 4–8.

2. Contrasting Spelling Patterns. Contrasting word pairs is helpful to students, since both sound and symbol contrasts are made. For example, seeing and

Initial Spelling	Corrected Spelling	Other Words With Same Pattern
1. *glew* x	*glue*	*true, blue, clue, flue*
2. *tramp*		
3. *raydio* x	*radio*	*baby, lady, cradle, table, crazy, paper*
4. *spring*		
5. *alter*		
6. *rouand* x	*round*	*sound, found, mound, pound, ground, hound*
7. *stamp*		
8. *stall*		
9. *grip*		
10. *temperature*		

FIGURE 4–8 Pattern-Word Follow-up

C. Glennon Rowell, "Don't Throw Away Those Spelling Test Papers . . . Yet!" *Elementary English* 52 (1975): 256. Copyright (1975) by the National Council of Teachers of English. Reprinted with permission.

hearing the relationships between words like *fed-feed* and *bet-beet* assist students in learning the short vowel–long vowel contrastive patterns in these and similar pairs.

a. One way to organize the teaching of these patterns is to place two contrasting pairs in a box, thus providing a model for students to see and pronounce. A list of words to be contrasted would then follow under the box as shown in the activity that follows:

fed-feed
bet-beet

wed-
red-
ten-
met-
pep-

Students complete the pairs by writing words that are appropriate. The words to be completed could have been the flip-side of the pattern (as those listed in the column on the left), or they could have been mixed.

Other pairs of words can be taught with the same activity, but with different patterns. Some examples are *can-cane, mad-made, bid-bide, bat-bait,* and *pad-paid.*

b. Another approach to this activity is one involving manipulative aids, an instructional technique advocated for use with certain children who learn best through haptics and/or kinesthetic learning.

Students are given a manila envelope (7 $\frac{1}{2}$ " by 10 $\frac{1}{2}$ ") with directions printed on the example shown:

Directions
  1. *Look* at the words in the box. ──────➤
  2. *Say* the words.
  3. *Spread* the words inside the envelope on your desk.
  4. *Group* the words in pairs as done in the box in the right-hand corner above.
  5. *Write* the words and say them.

| fed-feed |
| bet-beet |
| wed-weed |

The words in the envelope would be printed on 1" by 2" cards, one word per card. The words selected would be those that could be paired such as *met-meet, red-reed, ten-teen, pep-peep, step-steep,* and *bled-bleed.*

c. Another variation of *contrasting patterns* involves filling in a missing part of a circle, needed to complete the same pattern as other words that can be paired in the circle. Some examples follow:

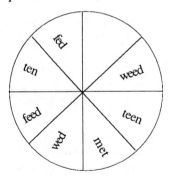 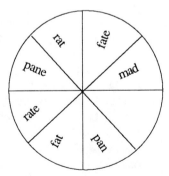

All of the patterns in these circles are short vowel to long vowel transitions made by single and double letter contrasts. In sets one and two that follow, other spelling patterns for short-vowel to long-vowel transitions are made. In sets three and four, other patterns are shown.

Set 1	Set 2	Set 3	Set 4
ran-rain	bat-bait	sip-slip	top-stop
pan-pain	pad-paid	pot-plot	tub-stub
bran-brain	lad-laid	pod-plod	lap-slap
man-main	mad-maid	pan-plan	lip-slip

3. Word-Building Activities. Systems can be implemented for teaching students word-building patterns. Two examples follow:

a. *Spelling Squares for Making Ing Words*[31]   Students are given directions to spell the word left out in each square below by using the paired patterns as models. Then students are to write a statement about what they have done. It may be appropriate at this stage to have students write the generalizations, although more examples might be needed.

kid kidding bid bidding rid	bat batting bet betting hit	bob bobbing fib fibbing rob

b. *Envelope Activity for Spelling Ing Words*   This activity involves the use of manipulatives which follow the basic guidelines for making and using manipulatives/games outlined in Chapter 3. Using manila envelopes, size $7\frac{1}{2}$ " by $10\frac{1}{2}$ ", directions are printed on the outside of the envelope as shown:

Directions
1. *Study* the words in the box. ⟶

   fish-fishing
   tell-telling
   hunt-hunting

2. *Say* the words.
3. *Put* the words and word parts inside the envelope together. They make bigger words, just like the bigger words were made in the box above.
4. On a piece of paper, *write* each bigger word that you make.
5. *Write* a statement that tells when you should add *ing* to words like the smaller words in the box above.[32]

About twelve base words are placed inside the envelope, along with a separate *ing* word part for *each* word. Variations of this activity can be made to accommodate other ways of adding *ing* to base words. Direction 3 is changed, as well as the examples given in the small box on the outside of the envelope. For adding *ing* to words ending in *final e*, direction 3 and examples for the small box on the envelope follow:

3. *Put* the word and word parts together by covering the *final e* like this:

| ride | | ing | | rid|ing |

Examples for the small box: ride-riding
hike-hiking
bake-baking

For doubling of consonants, the directions follow:

3. Put the word and word parts in the envelope together as follows:

| bat | | tt | | ing | | ba| tt |ing |

In this case, however, there are two word parts (*tt, ing*; *dd, ing*; *mm, ing*, etc.,);

Examples for the small box: bat-batting
rid-ridding
hum-humming[33]

This activity, too, is easily adapted to the microcomputer. Each of the three boxes with patterns in them is programmed on a disk to form three columns on the screen of the microcomputer. The base words for each envelope are placed on the disk in random order, but in such a way that they appear toward the bottom of the screen. Students use the middle of the screen to add *ing* to each base word, but under the box with the words that pattern the same way. Thus, *looking* would be typed in under the box having *fish-fishing*, *tell-telling*, and *hunt-hunting*.

There are numerous corrective activities that help attack problems in spelling. Several of the entries in the bibliography of this chapter contain appropriate activities. Teachers should continuously build files of such activities and use them as appropriate. Through the years, a file will grow and the task of finding suitable activities becomes easier as well as more manageable.

Summary

1. A student-involved corrective spelling program begins with an understanding of the most significant research that has been done in spelling. Included in such research are the following: Research on:

   a. Which words should be taught, where in the grades they should be taught, and how they should be grouped to be taught
   b. The presentation of words in lists, as opposed to presentation of words in context
   c. The teaching of spelling generalizations (overall conclusions from research)
   d. The inductive teaching of spelling generalizations
   e. The *test-study-test* approach to spelling instruction
   f. The *corrected-test* procedure in spelling
   g. Allocation of time for direct spelling instruction
   h. Spelling as a conceptual process
   i. The value of peer tutoring in a spelling program

2. Research on *selecting* a large group (over 3,000) words for a total spelling program has been directed toward the most-frequently used words in writing—the language arts strand to which spelling instruction should be directed. Research on *placing* words at specific grade levels has been controversial, with authors of various spelling programs not agreeing on what grade level to place words. *Grouping* words for specific lessons each week has, in the last few years, been focused on similar linguistic features such as graphemic representations of selected sounds and structural elements that students should know. Some attention should be given to arrangement of letters in words and the effect patterns (CVC, CVCe, and so on) have on sounds and the way the sounds are spelled.

3. Research tends to indicate that spelling words should initially be presented in list form, followed by use of the words in context. The former approach has been identified as a direct approach and helps in the identification of linguistic relationships of words.

4. Spelling generalizations or rules should be focused on the selection of those generalizations that have few exceptions and thus are useful. Large numbers of generalizations should be avoided. Current spelling programs have expanded the concept of generalizations to include frequently-occurring patterns such as phoneme-grapheme correspondences.

5. Generalizations/patterns should be taught inductively, which means presenting examples of data for the generalization being studied and leading students to discover the generalization or pattern. Long-term retention and transfer of knowledge prevails when generalizations are taught inductively.

6. Two basic approaches to spelling instruction throughout the week have prevailed over the years. One is the *study-test* approach where students study the words first and are then tested on them. The other is the *test-study-test* approach where students take a pretest and then concentrate on studying those words missed prior to a final or posttest on these words at the end of the week. In most situations, the latter approach is the preferred approach.

7. Research indicates that students should correct their own spelling test papers. Called the *corrected-test* method, the self-correcting scheme permits students to immediately see their spelling problems and correct specific errors.

8. Instructional time beyond 75 minutes per week pays few dividends in a spelling program, although some learners may need more time than others. Spelling instruction thus should be highly organized and focused on motivating students to spell correctly rather than on long periods of instruction.

9. Spelling instruction, once considered to be a memory-oriented task, is now considered to be a conceptually-oriented task, meaning that students should be involved in examining and thinking about linguistic patterns and relationships. Also, students should be involved in using words in meaningful writing activities and learning various processes in spelling.

10. Peer tutoring, where students help each other with pretests, record-keeping, and analysis of progress in spelling, is helpful in a spelling program. Likewise, help on spelling given each other in cooperative learning groups pays dividends. Thus, students should have opportunities to work together in a spelling program.

11. The spelling curriculum should revolve around lists of words to be used in writing, but should be organized in broad areas of content complexity, as opposed to locked-in grade levels. These elements should be organized in such a way that during the earliest school years, students are gradually introduced to both: (1) the concepts of writing (composing), word boundaries, symbols in words as representatives of sounds, rudimentary elements of writing and letter formation; and (2) the recognition of how words are alike/different with changes occurring when certain elements are added (as pluralization) and/or substituted. Students are then introduced to formal spelling lessons on a weekly basis and begin a systematic study of phoneme-grapheme correspondences, letter arrangement patterns, proofreading, writing independently, and attention to word-building skills. The spelling curriculum increases in complexity as students move to the intermediate and then the advanced stages of formal spelling. Attention increasingly is given to variant spellings of phonemes, word building, and the use of the dictionary and thesaurus as tools for spelling and writing. Spelling-error types, contractions, and abbreviations are given more attention as students move through the curriculum.

12. Base groups in spelling are made up of students who are on the same or about the same spelling levels and who therefore are studying similar groups of words, skills, and generalizations. Such groups meet from two to three times per week on the average.

13. Flex groups are clusters of students from across base groups who need special help in certain areas of the spelling curriculum. The composition of such groups generally varies from lesson to lesson. Three primary approaches to setting up flex groups are assessment of spelling-error types, assessment and evaluation of prerequisite learnings for a new skill area being introduced, and the use of mastery tests.

14. Activities in a corrective language arts program should be, in so far as possible, organized into systems that can be used to help establish spelling accuracy. Appropriate assessment, evaluative, and corrective activities should be available for teachers to meaningfully engage students as they work toward the goal of becoming competent spellers. Many activities are preventive in nature, in that students are encouraged to check their papers before submitting them to the teacher. A number of spelling activities can be done on the microcomputer, a tool that is increasingly being used to teach language arts.

Reviewing, Connecting, and Expanding What You Have Learned

Directions
In the preceding summary section, each paragraph is numbered. These are placed there for easy reference in discussions that will take place in your college classroom or in-service session. Do the activities that follow in reference to the summary or main body of this chapter. You may be asked by your college professor or in-service director to do some of these activities in small groups.

1. (Paragraph 1) For each of the nine areas listed, (a-i), describe why the research finding is important to a student-involved corrective spelling program.
2. (Paragraph 2) After reading paragraph 2 in the summary, examine the two lessons given here and answer the questions (a, b, c, d) that follow:

Lesson 1 Words to Study This Week	Lesson 2 Words to Study This Week
hen sat men rat fed	hen sat men rat fed
met ran bed man pen	met ran bed man pen
red pet pan ton fin	red pet pan ton fin

1. Circle the words in which you hear the *short e* sound.

2. Now find the words below in which you also hear the *short e* sound when you say these words.

dead   thread   hat
head   sad   bread

1. These words follow a similar letter-arrangement pattern. The pattern is CVC or consonant-vowel-consonant. Now look at the words below. Which ones are CVC words?

hate   can   pan
hat   cane   pane
ham   tape   rug

3. Look at the way the *short e* sound is spelled in the words below. The spellings of this sound have been circled.

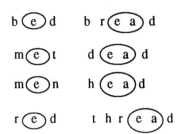

4. Write all words from your weekly list that have a *short e* sound and *circle the spellings of this sound.* Use the space below.

5. Complete the following: Two ways to spell the *short e* sound are _____ and _____.

Write the CVC words in the box below:

2. Study all CVC words in your weekly list. Listen carefully to the vowel sound in each word. Is the vowel sound short or long? Tell what the vowel sound is.

3. In the space below, make a rule that helps one spell most words that have the CVC pattern.

4. Do you know some words that *do not* fit the rule above? If so, write them in the space below.

---

a. Why might Lesson 2 have more appeal to visual learners than to auditory learners?

b. What characteristics of field-independent learners would especially match the activities in Lessons 1 and 2?

c. Why is it important for teachers to know the two major ways that phoneme-grapheme relationships are presented in Lessons 1 and 2?

d. List prerequisites as discussed in Chapters 1 and 4 for the major skills introduced in Lessons 1 and 2.

3. (Paragraph 3) Explain the value of the *list approach* to grouping of spelling words (presented in Lessons 1 and 2 of Activity Number 2).

4. (Paragraphs 4 and 5) Explain why step 3 in Lesson 2 in Activity Number 2 is an inductive approach to teaching a spelling generalization or pattern.

5. (Paragraph 6) As stated, in most situations the *test-study-test* approach to teaching spelling is the preferred approach. Identify those situations in a corrective spelling program where this approach is particularly critical. When might the *study-test* approach be more effective?

6. (Paragraph 7) Outline and/or diagram how you would involve students in a corrective spelling program in the *corrected-test* method for assessing and evaluating weekly spelling test results.

7. (Paragraph 8) Identify learning styles and organizational patterns that conceivably might take more time than 75 minutes per week for spelling instruction.
8. (Paragraphs 9 and 10) In what ways can students work in a peer-tutoring situation to foster conceptually-oriented (as opposed to memory-oriented) spelling instruction?
9. (Paragraph 11) Explain why the spelling curriculum—organized according to four levels of content complexity—is oriented more toward corrective teaching than is a grade-level content arrangement.
10. (Paragraphs 12, 13, and 14) Outline procedures for setting up and carrying out base and flex groups in a spelling program.
11. (Paragraph 14) Identify at least one activity presented in Chapter 4 for each of the following kinds of activities: assessment, evaluative, and corrective.

Endnotes

1. H. D. Rinsland, *A Basic Writing Vocabulary of Elementary School Children* (New York: Macmillan Publishing Co., 1945), pp. 6–7.

2. Mark Perkins, "A Graded Basic Writing Vocabulary Program" (Unpublished), University of Tennessee, Knoxville, Tennessee, 1984, pp. 1–3.

3. Paul S. Anderson and Patrick J. Groff, *Resource Materials for Teachers of Spelling* (Minneapolis: Burgess Publishing Co., 1968), pp. 11–13.

4. Richard E. Hodges, *The Case for Teaching Sound-to-Letter Correspondences in Spelling—A Report on the Stanford Spelling Project* (Boston: Houghton Mifflin Co., 1986), p. 1.

5. Paul R. Hanna, Richard E. Hodges, and Jean S. Hanna, *Spelling: Structure and Strategies* (Boston: Houghton Mifflin Co., 1971), pp. 82–84.

6. Richard Madden and Thorston Carolson, *HBJ Spelling, Teacher's Edition, Level 2* (Atlanta: Harcourt Brace Jovanovich, 1983). pp. 94–96.

7. Ruel A. Allred, *Spelling—The Application of Research Findings* (Washington, D.C.: National Education Association, 1977), pp. 21–22.

8. Martha Jan Mickler, "A Study of Teacher Application and Knowledge of the Components of a Researched-Based Model of Spelling Instruction," (Tallahassee, Florida: Doctoral dissertation, Florida State University, 1986), pp. 38–39.

9. Allred, *Spelling*, pp. 26–27.

10. Mickler, "A Study of Teacher Application," p. 74.

11. Bradley M. Loomer and Maxine G. Strege, *Guide to Spelling Research and Practice* (San Diego: Coronado Publishers, 1983), p. 11.

12. Robert J. Fitzsimmons and Bradley M. Loomer, *Spelling Research and Practice* (Iowa City, Iowa: University of Iowa and Iowa State Department of Public Instruction, 1977), pp. 10–12.

13. Loomer and Strege, *Guide*, p. 8.

14. Allred, *Spelling*, pp. 32–33.

15. Shane Templeton, "Synthesis of Research on the Learning and Teaching of Spelling," *Educational Leadership* 44 (1986): 73–74.

16. Ibid., 75–77.

17. Mickler, "A Study of Teacher Application," pp. 95–97.

18. Dianne K. Augustine, Kristin D. Gruber, and Lynda R. Hanson, "Cooperation Works!," *Educational Leadership* 47 (1990): 6.

19. Alvina T. Burrows, Dianne L. Monson, and Russell G. Stauffer, *New Horizons in the Language Arts* (New York: Harper & Row, 1972), pp. 245–248.

20. Harry A. Greene, *The New Iowa Spelling Scale* (Iowa City, Iowa: State University of Iowa, 1954), pp. 26.

21. Ibid., p. 100.

22. Richard C. Hodges, "The Language Base of Spelling," *Research in the Language Arts*, eds. Victor Froese and Stanley B. Straw (Baltimore: University Park Press, 1981), p. 222.

23. Paul C. Burns, *Assessment and Correction of Language Arts Difficulties* (Columbus, Ohio: Charles E. Merrill Publishing Co., 1980), pp. 184–203. Charles E. Merrill Books, "How to Correct Spelling Errors: A Teacher's Diagnostic Spelling Chart," *Education Today, Spelling Bulletin*, No. 54, "n.d." p. 2. Wayne Otto and Richard J. Smith, *Corrective and Remedial Teaching* (Boston: Houghton Mifflin Co., 1980), pp. 350–351.

24. C. Glennon Rowell, "Don't Throw Away Those Spelling Test Papers . . . Yet!" *Elementary English* 52 (1975): 253–255.

25. Jan Mickler, "A Metacognitive Approach to Spelling Instruction," *Spelling Progress Quarterly* 3 (1987): 7–9.

26. C. Gattegno, *Teaching Reading With Words in Color* (New York: Xerox Corporation, 1967), pp. 90–91.

27. Ibid., pp. 91–92.

28. Susan Campanini, et. al., *Whole Brain Spelling: A Child's Garden of Words*, 2nd ed. (Champaign, Illinois: Sublogic Communications, 1982), Directions Frame of Program.

29. Ibid.

30. Esther J. Hasler, *Learning With Magnetic Card Activities* (Palm Beach Gardens, Florida: Jean-Bert Associates, 1989), p. 20.

31. C. Glennon Rowell, "The Inductive Teaching of Spelling Patterns and Generalizations: Some Suggested Strategies," *Spelling Progress Quarterly* 2 (Fall/Winter 1985–86): 6.

32. Ibid.

33. Ibid.

Bibliography

(Diagnostic-Corrective Techniques)

Boyd, Gertrude A. and Talbert, E. Gene. *Spelling in the Elementary School* (Columbus, Ohio: Charles E. Merrill Publishing Co., 1971).

Davis, James Christopher. "Developing a Classroom System of Error Analysis," *English Journal* 7 (1988): 64–65.

Gable, Robert A., Hendrickson, Jo M., and Meeks, Jane Warren. "Assessing Spelling Errors of Special Needs Students," *The Reading Teacher* 42 (1988): 112-17.

Manning, Maryann Murphy and Manning, Gary L. *Improving Spelling in the Middle Grades* (Washington, D. C.: National Education Association, 1986).

Marino, Jacqueline L. "Spelling Errors: From Analysis to Instruction," *Language Arts* 58 (1981): 567–72.

(Theory and Research)

Allred, Ruel A. *Spelling Trends, Content, and Methods—What Research Says to the Teacher* (Washington, D. C.: National Education Association, 1984).

Beers, Carol Strickland and Beers, James Wheelock. "Three Assumptions About Learning to Spell," *Language Arts* 58 (1981): 573–80.

Dunkeld, Colin and Hatch, Lynda. "Building Spelling Confidence," *Elementary English* 52 (1975): 225–29.

Culyer, Gail Blake. "A Synthesized Approach to Selecting Spelling Words and Generalizations." (Tallahassee, Florida: Doctoral dissertation, Florida State University, 1974).

Frith, Uta, ed. *Cognitive Processes in Spelling* (London: Academic Press, 1980).

Gentry, J. Richard. "Guidelines for Evaluating a Spelling Series: A Look at the Research Base," *Spelling Progress Quarterly.* 4 (1988): 1–3.

Schlagal, Robert Clark. "A Qualitative Inventory of Word Knowledge: A Developmental Study of Spelling, Grades One Through Six." (Charlottesville, Virginia: Doctoral dissertation, University of Virginia, 1982).

WORD LIST 4–1   Most-Frequently-Used Words: 500, 250, 100. Highest Frequency from Rinsland's Study

a*	aunt	bought	clean	dog*	fell	getting**
about**	away**	box	close**	dogs	few**	girl*
across		boy*	clothes	doing	finally	girls**
after**	baby*	boys**	cold**	doll*	find**	give**
afternoon	back**	bring**	come*	done	fine**	glad**
again**	bad	brother**	comes	don't**	fire	go*
ago	ball*	brought	coming**	door**	first**	goes
air	be*	brown	corn	down*	fish	going*
all*	bear	built	could**	dress	fishing	gone
almost	beautiful	but*	couldn't		five**	good*
along**	because**	buy	country**	each**	floor	got*
also**	bed**	by**	cousins	early	flowers	grade**
always**	been**		cow	eat*	food	grandmother
am*	before**	call	cows	eggs	for*	great**
an**	began	called**	cut	eight	found	green
and*	being	came**		end	four	ground
animals	best**	camp	daddy**	enough	friend**	guess
another**	better**	can*	dark	ever	friends	
answer	big*	candy	day**	every**	from**	had*
any**	bird	can't	days**	eyes	front	hair
anything	birds	car**	dear**		full	half
apples	birthday	care	decided	fall	fun**	hand
are*	black**	cat**	did*	family	funny	happy**
around**	blue	catch	didn't**	far		hard
as**	boat	caught	died	farm	game	has*
ask	book**	children**	different	fast	games	hat
asked**	books	Christmas*	dinner	father**	gave**	have*
at*	born	city	do*	feed	get**	haven't
ate	both	class	does	feet	gets	having

Continued

WORD LIST 4–1 *Continued*

he*	large**	music	presents	sister**	thing**	war
head	last**	must**	pretty*	six	things**	warm
hear	later	my*	put*	sled	think**	was*
heard**	leaves			sleep	this**	watch
help	left	name*	quite	smell	those	water**
her*	let**	named		snow**	thought**	way**
here*	letter**	near	rabbit	so*	three**	we*
high	life	never**	rain	some*	through**	week**
hill	light	new**	ran**	something**	till	weeks
him*	like*	next**	read**	sometimes	time*	well**
his*	liked	nice**	reading	soon**	times	went*
hit	likes	night**	ready	sorry	to*	were**
home*	little*	no**	received	spring	today**	what*
hope**	live**	not*	red*	start	together	when*
horse	lived	now*	rest	started**	told**	where**
horses	long**		ride	stay	too*	which**
hot	look*	o'clock	riding	stayed	took**	while**
house*	looked**	of*	right**	still	top	white**
houses	looking	off**	river	stopped	town**	who**
how*	lost	oh	road	store	toys	why
hundred	lot**	old	room**	story	train	will*
hunting	lots	on*	run*	street	tree*	window
	love**	once**		such	trees	winter
		one*	said*	summer**	tried	wish**
I*	made*	only**	same	sun	trip	with*
ice	make*	open	Santa	Sunday	truly	won't
if**	making	or**	Claus**	supper	try	wood
I'll	man*	other**	sat	sure**	turned	woods
I'm*	many**	our*	Saturday	swimming	two*	work**
in*	may	out*	saw			world
into**	me*	over*	say**	table	uncle	would*
is*	meat		school*	take*	under	write**
it*	men**	pair	second	teacher**	until**	writing
it's	might	paper	see*	tell**	up*	wrote
its	miles	part	seen	ten	upon	
	milk**	party	send	than**	us**	yard
jumped	Miss	people**	sent	thank	use	year**
just*	miss	pet	set	Thanksgiving	used	years**
	money	picture	seven	that*		yellow
keep	more**	pictures	she*	the*	vacation	yes
killed	morning**	place**	shoes	their**	very**	yesterday
kind	most**	play*	should**	them*	visit	yet
king	mother*	played**	show	then*		you*
knew	Mr.	playing	sick	there*	walk	your*
know*	Mrs.	please**	side	these**	want*	yours
land	much**	poor	since	they*	wanted**	

Key: All words on list = 500 most frequently used words

All words with single (*) and double (**) asterisks = 250 most frequently used words

All words with single (*) asterisk only = 100 most frequently used words

WORD LIST 4–2   Second 500 Highest Most-Frequently-Used Words From Rinsland's Study

able	breakfast	course	everything	grandfather	jump	marry
above	bridge	covered	except	grandma		met
address	bright	cried		grass	kept	middle
afraid	broke	cross	face	gray	kill	mile
against	broken	cry	fair	grew	kitchen	mind
age	brothers	dad	farmer	grow	kitten	mine
airplane	build	dance	fat	gun	known	minutes
all right	building	dead	Feb.			Monday
alone	buildings	December	feel	ha	lady	month
already	business	decided	feeling	Halloween	lake	months
although'	busy	deep	felt	hands	largest	mountain
animals	butter	deer	fence	happened	late	mountains
apple		desert	field	hardly	laughed	mouth
April	cake	desk	fifth	hay	laws	move
arithmetic	cannot	discovered	fight	health	lay	moved
arm	cap	dishes	filled	heavy	learn	myself
army	captain	doctor	finished	held	learned	
arrived	card	doesn't	flag	hello	leave	names
asleep	carried	dollars	flew	helped	leg	nearly
awful	carry	dolls	flower	hen	legs	need
awhile	cars	doors	fly	himself	lesson	nest
	cats	draw	foot	history	lessons	news
bag	cattle	dressed	football	hold	let's	nine
band	cave	drink	forest	hole	letters	noise
bank	cents	drive	forget	homes	library	noon
barn	chair	dry	forgot	hospital	lights	north
baseball	chicken	during	fourth	hour	line	nose
basket	chickens		free	hours	lines	nothing
bears	chief	earth	Friday	hunt	lives	number
became	child	Easter	frightened	hurry	living	nuts
become	Christmas	easy	fruit	hurt	looks	
behind	Eve	eating	fur		lovely	ocean
believe	church	eats		ice cream	low	office
bell	cloth	education	garden	important	lunch	often
bet	club	egg	gas	inches		oil
between	coal	electric	geography	Indian	machine	ones
bicycle	coat	elephant	ghost	Indians	mail	opened
bill	color	else	gifts	inside	makes	orange
bit	colored	English	given	instead	mamma	oranges
board	colors	enjoy	gives	iron	March	others
boats	company	enjoyed	giving	island	married	outside
body	cook	even	glass	isn't	maybe	own
bottom	corner	evening	gold	I've	mean	
boxes	cotton	everybody	good-bye		means	paint
bread	countries	everyone	government	job	meet	painted

Continued

WORD LIST 4–2 *Continued*

papa	P.S.	scared	soft	sugar	threw	wasn't
papers	pull	schools	sold	suit	throw	ways
parents	pulled	sea	someone	suppose	Thursday	wear
park	pupils	seemed	sometime	surely	tired	weather
parts		self	son	surprise	tomorrow	we'll
pass	rabbits	several	song	sweet	tonight	we're
passed	race	shall	south	swim	toward	west
pay		sheep	spelling		toy	wet
pen	radio	ship	spend	tail	travel	wheat
pencil	raise	ships	squirrel	taken	tricks	whole
person	rat	shoot	stairs	takes	truck	wife
pick	reached	short	stand	taking	trying	wild
picked	real	shot	standing	talk	turkey	wind
picnic	really	showed	stairs	talking	turn	windows
piece	remember	silk	state	tall	twelve	without
pieces	rich	sincerely	states	tea	twenty	woke
pig	ring	sing	station	teach		woman
pink	robin	singing	stick	teacher's	usually	women
places	rock	sisters	stockings	teachers		won
plan	rocks	sit	stone	team	valentine	word
plant	rode	sitting	stood	teeth	village	words
plants	rooms	sixth	stop	telling		worked
plays	rope	skates	stones	tells	wagon	working
plenty	round	skating	stove	test	wait	wouldn't
pony	rubber	skin	straight	that's	waiting	written
potatoes	running	sky	streets	thinking	walked	
power	runs	sleigh	string	third	walking	young
present		slide	strong	thirty	wall	
president	sand	smoke	study	though	wants	
program	says	soap	studying	thousand	wash	

5

A Corrective Approach to
Writing Instruction

Focus

In recent years, much has been written about the neglect of writing in the curriculum. Fortunately, writing programs are increasing in schools. How corrective teaching can be applied to writing instruction is the focus of Chapter 5 in this book. The chapter begins with a discussion of what writing is and with a review of some of the most important research in written composition. Attention will be given to how both developmental (base) and flexible (flex) grouping patterns can be adapted to a writing program. Other major points to be covered in this chapter include the identification of different kinds of writing, how a corrective writing curriculum should be organized, writing as both a process and a product, major errors that students make in writing, assessment/evaluation of writing, the use of the microcomputer in a corrective writing program, and corrective activities for a writing program.

Defining Writing

Writing is the formation of a coherent message, such as a letter, directions, a poem, or more complex form of writing such as an essay or term paper. Whatever the form of writing, the act of composing or putting together elements used in writing is made operative. Petty says that " . . . Composing is inherent in using language. Each sentence is a composition. Thus, every child, indeed every individual, does have ability in composition. Not everyone's composing ability is equal, of course . . . "[1]

As you read Chapter 5, recall writing activities in which you participated when you were in school. Were these activities done with a few students or with all the class? How frequently did you write? How was your writing graded? Did you rewrite a story or other assignment often? What errors in writing did the teacher point out to you? These are important questions today. They relate to a student-involved corrective writing program. Read to see how you can develop this type of program

---

Writing should be thought of in terms of not only *what* one writes or produces, but also *how* one writes. During the past fifteen years, much has been written about writing in terms of what goes into the act of writing—a shift of great significance from the days when writing was defined more in terms of the final outcome of a child's effort to compose.

In the traditional sense, writing is of two kinds. One kind, which often dominated the curriculum was *functional writing*, referring to any kind of writing that one does primarily to communicate with others. Emphasis on good, clear business letters, friendly letters, written directions, style, writing one's view of an issue . . . all fit under the umbrella of *functional writing*.

The other kind of writing is *creative writing*, in which the emphasis is not so much on communicating with others (although that can be an aim of this kind of writing) as it is on expressing one's feelings or one's emotions in a unique way. In a sense, the audience for the two types of writing is the primary difference, with one being "others" and one being "self." There is some overlap in that some elements of writing, such as good paragraphs, may equally serve both types of writing.

A comprehensive writing program attends to both functional and creative writing. Beginning in the lower grades and extending through secondary school, an intensive program should exist in which students spend hours learning the many facets of both functional and creative writing. Programs in which there is an emphasis on word study, word manipulations, sentence building/generating/ expanding, benefit both functional and creative writing.

A stimulating environment is important to both functional and creative writing. Having meaningful assignments is important, for no more deadly approach to writing exists than having students write about events which to them are boring, void of meaning, or too mechanical.

Research of Significance to a Corrective Writing Program

While research on writing is not as extensive and definitive as is the research in spelling, some studies have been done that are of significance to a student-involved corrective writing program. These include:

1. Giving more attention to writing as a process rather than looking only at the end product to be produced
2. Viewing writing as a recursive process, rather than as a linear process
3. Using sentence-combining techniques for promoting growth in writing
4. Distinguishing between maturity and immaturity in writing
5. Knowing the place of grammar instruction in writing programs
6. Using models and modeling in writing
7. Connecting reading and writing processes and subprocesses
8. Giving appropriate feedback in writing
9. Establishing environmental conditions which promote effective writing

While there are obvious overlaps among these nine areas, each one is discussed separately for purposes of emphasis and for showing the connections to and implications for a student-involved corrective program in writing.

Practice Number 1: Giving More Attention to Writing as a Process

During the last few years there has been an increase in the attention given to *how* children write, although the research that does exist on writing as a process, "is somewhat meager and consists primarily of case studies."[2] Separate studies by J. Van Bruggen, J. Emig, C. Stallard, and D. Graves and D. Murray led to the identification of a number of processes in written composition.[3] Among these are pausing before writing segments of a composition, planning, reviewing segments of what has been written, and revising drafts.[4] A number of subprocesses are found in these larger processes, such as redrafting of compositions following discussions by the teacher and/or other students.[5]

Teachers in a corrective writing program should be knowledgeable of writing processes in order to encourage behaviors associated with effective writing. Students can be taught to stop their writing at strategic points (major segments), review what they have written, and to contemplate where to go next. And students can be taught to expand their ideas, better describe characters in their writing, and to make better transitions in various parts of their writing. Many processes can be taught.

Practice Number 2: Viewing Writing as a Recursive Process

For many years, writing was seen as a linear, or straight-line process, but today the process is seen as "recursive." Humes points out that of several linear models used over the years, the stages of *prewriting, writing,* and *postwriting,* in one form or another, have been important.[6] Humes states that:

Such theories characterize writing as a linear activity, yet current re-
search indicates that linear models are inaccurate because they actually
describe growth of the written product, not the "inner process of the per-
son producing the product." The process itself does not move in a straight
line from planning to writing to revising. All planning is not done when
ideas are written on paper; all writing is not finished before writers review
and revise. Writers move back and forth among these processes. . . .[7]

Hillocks states that, "Twenty years of research, including both the composing process and teaching methods, reveal that writing involves stop-review-start-again processes that teachers need to recognize in their assignments."[8] The teacher, in recognizing the recursive nature of writing, poses questions throughout writing, promoting students to be reflective thinkers and helping them generate ideas. At every stage of writing, students are encouraged to ask questions about their own writing.

Practice Number 3: Using Sentence-Combining Techniques for Promoting Growth in Writing

Sentence-combining refers to the process of combining two or more simple sentences, thus making a more mature sentence. An example of a sentence-combining strategy was presented in Table 3–1. It is presented again in Table 5–1 to be used as an example of sentence combining. The focus of sentence combining, as in Table 5–1, is to use any number of processes called transformations (deletion of words, addition of words, and rearrangement of words) to develop a more mature

TABLE 5–1 Transformations in Sentence Combining

Students are asked to read the sentences below:	Questions are raised about the three sentences:
1. The squirrel is little.	1. What happens if "little" from the first sentence is placed with the second sentence?
2. The squirrel scurried up the oak tree.	2. In what part of the second sentence would "little" be placed? Why?
3. The oak tree is old.	3. Can you combine sentence three with your revised second sentence, using only one word? What is the word and where does it go?

More Complex Sentence: The little squirrel scurried up the old oak tree.

sentence. Although many students will independently learn how to perform these transformations and be able to combine sentences, for some students, direct teaching of the processes will be necessary. The emphasis should be on making new sentences, not in-depth analysis of sentence parts or procedures. Take time to see what transformations have been made in forming the more complex sentence, "The little squirrel scurried up the old oak tree." In noting transformations (deletions, rearrangements), students should learn how new sentences are made as well as how to make similar sentences of their own. Hillocks traces the work of K. Hunt who did pioneer work in the measurement of syntactic maturity in sentence construction (to be discussed later) and F. O'Hare who demonstrated that direct instruction in sentence combining results in the production of more mature, complex structures and increased quality of writing.[9] The importance of sentence combining is also cited by M. Scardamalia and C. Bereiter who suggest that sentence combining may " . . . provide students with control over an organized repertoire of syntactic structures, control that allows them to pick and choose among a variety of alternative syntactic structures . . . "[10]

Teachers should model how transformations unfold. They see what is happening. As explanations are made about combining short, choppy sentences, the accompanying verbalization helps students (especially those who are dependent on the verbal mode of learning).

Study the fourth grader's composition on "The Zugba Dance" in Figure 5–1 to see where you think this student might need help in sentence combining.

Practice Number 4: Distinguishing Between Maturity and Immaturity in Writing

In a number of studies, differences between mature and immature writers are noted. Studies can also be cited which illustrate differences at various stages or ages of development, although as Mosenthal indicates, defining writing competence is made difficult by the absence of research-based paradigms for writing.[11] Nevertheless, separate summaries cited by Krashen,[12] Hillocks,[13] and Humes[14] suggest a number of known differences between good writers and poor writers or mature and immature writers.

Research done between 1971 and 1981 by J. Emig, L. Flower, L. Flower and J. Hayes, L. Odell, S. Perl, S. Pianko, N. Sommers, and C. Stallard, indicates that there are striking differences in the physical and mental strategies that good and poor writers use as they write.[15] These are shown in Table 5–2.

Some generalized features indicated by the behavioral differences between skilled and unskilled writers are that good writers: (1) show more care for how their written compositions turn out; (2) give more thought to what they are doing and how their writing will be perceived by others; and (3) are more reflective. Developing these behaviors in all students should be goals for teachers in a corrective writing program which focuses on student-involvement.

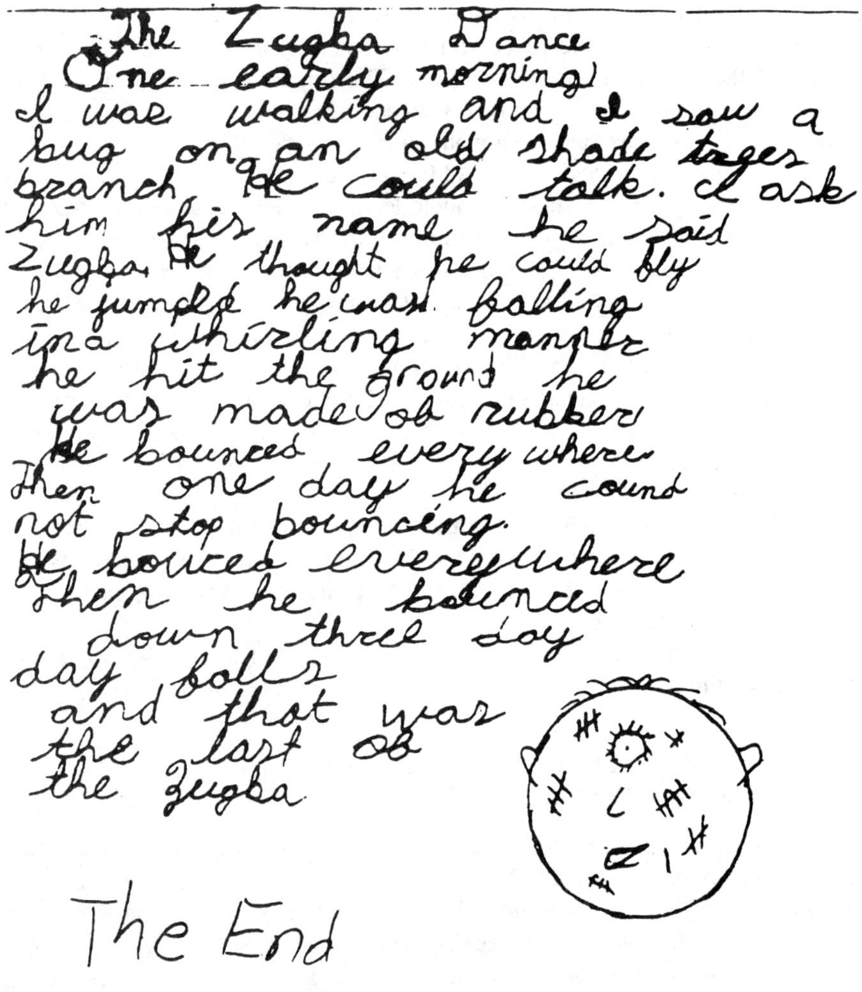

The Zugba Dance
One early morning I was walking and I saw a bug on an old shade trees branch. He could talk. I ask him his name he said Zugba. He thought he could fly he jumped he was falling in a whirling manner he hit the ground he was made of rubber he bounced every where. Then one day he could not stop bouncing. He bounced everywhere Then he bounced down three day day ball and that was the last of the Zugba.

The End

FIGURE 5–1 A Fourth Grader's Written Composition

Exercises should be planned to help students think about their readers and what they need to know. How students want to influence their readers and different techniques and goals (to persuade, to inform, and so on) should be a part of a writing program.

Practice Number 5: Knowing the Place of Grammar Instruction in Writing Programs

Numerous studies have been done on the effect that the teaching of traditional grammar (naming parts of speech, classifying different kinds of sentences, and so

TABLE 5–2 Behavioral Differences Between Skilled and Unskilled Writers

Skilled/Successful Writers	Unskilled/Unsuccessful Writers
• Conceive the writing problem in its complexity, including issues of audience, purpose, context.	• Conceive the writing problem narrowly, primarily in terms of topic.
• Shape writing to the needs of the audience.	• Have little concept of audience.
• Are committed to the writing.	• Care little about the writing.
• Are less easily satisfied with first drafts. Think of revision as finding the line of argument. Revise extensively at the level of structure and content.	• Are more easily satisfied with first drafts. Think of revision as changing words or as crossing out and throwing away. Revise only at the level of single words or sentences.
• Are able to pay selective attention to various aspects of the writing task, depending on the stage of the writing process.	• Often try to do everything perfectly on the first draft. Get stuck on single word choices or on punctuation, even at early stages, when good writers ignore punctuation and concentrate on getting ideas down.

Barbara Fassler Walvoord and Hoke L. Smith, "Coaching the Process of Writing," *Teaching Writing in All Disciplines*, C. Williams Griffin, ed. (San Francisco: Jossey-Bass, Inc. 1982), p. 7. Copyright © (1982) by Jossey-Bass, Inc. Reprinted with permission.

on) has on writing ability. Bushman, in a comprehensive survey of grammar research, goes back to studies in the early 1900s (F. Hoyt, 1906; J. Boraas, 1917; and W. Asker, 1923), and points out that despite the recent publishing of grammar textbooks and English teachers' proclamations that grammar study improves writing, findings do not support the value of grammar to writing.[16]

In one summary of the research on grammar (H. Meckel, 1963), the transfer value of teaching traditional grammar was questioned. The reviewer stated that if there was any value in grammar instruction to writing improvement, it would have to be in the editorial stage of writing where the effects of grammar study have not had enough emphasis.[17] In R. Harris' longitudinal study in England, it was pointed out that students who had formal study of grammar knew more about grammar but did less well in writing than students whose grammar instruction was limited to correction of errors as they came up in writing.[18] In W. Elley et al's study in New Zealand, students were taught over a four-year period. No-grammar instruction was compared to two kinds of grammar instruction—generative* and traditional

*Generative grammar, sometimes called transformational-generative grammar, focuses on transforming a kernel sentence (Boys sing.) into a more detailed, elaborate sentence (After winning their games, the boys sing loudly.).

grammar. No significant differences were found in writing quality and subscores for mechanics of writing.[19] It has also been pointed out that formal grammar instruction may have a harmful effect in that such instruction usually is substituted for instruction in written composition.[20]

Fraser and Hodson are critical of some of the most-frequently cited research illustrating the lack of transfer that grammar instruction has on the teaching of writing. In doing so, they offer some sound advice about teaching grammar. Some of the major points are:

1. Grammar should be studied inductively "in extended language-in-use" context (children's own writing).

2. A didactic, prescriptive, isolated skill-drill approach to grammar instruction can be defeating and should be avoided.

3. Grammar study should not be a substitute for writing.

4. Teach grammar in relation to a writing or reading task.

5. Teach grammar when children can handle formal systems of abstract reasoning—when students can conceptualize (identified as usually in early adolescence).

6. View grammar as a supplement to "the main diet of reading and writing."

7. Draw grammar instruction from established (traditional) and modern-day (transformational-generative) grammars.[21]

In a corrective writing program, these points are critical. Students who are having problems in language arts will not be helped by a comprehensive, highly analytical study of what could be an almost endless array of bits and pieces of information about the English language. Students should be learning about the fundamentals of writing via involvement in writing, rather than learning about isolated elements of language structure.

Practice Number 6: Using Models and Modeling in Writing Instruction

Hillocks traces using of model compositions in writing to the classical academies of Greece and Rome when students were taught rhetorical principles to be incorporated in orations.[22] Hillocks references N. Stein and T. Trabasso in stating that,

> *... This belief in antiquity is not far removed from what modern-day cognitive psychologists have shown about discourse processing—for example, that our processing and production of stories are guided by bare-bones outlines or schemata of the essential elements of stories.[23]*

Hillocks, however, does point out that the use of models is more focused on "... identifying, naming, and perhaps evaluating the parts or features of models," and that procedures for producing models should be encouraged.[24]

Scardamalia and Bereiter identify various structures that are now being used in research for framing written discourse, including such structures as story grammars, discourse schema, script, superstructure, and framers. Scardamalia and Bereiter further point out that " . . . a major requirement for competence in writing is learning the essential form of various literary types—narrative, exposition, argument, and the like."[25]

Story grammars, diagrams that enable students to see the structure of a story, often help break a story down into parts such as characters, plot, and setting. The story parts are then graphically illustrated in some meaningful way such as a set of illustrations arranged in the sequence the story unfolds, columns to be filled in under a heading, or diagrams resembling flow charts. These and other skeletal structures should, however, be used for the purpose for which they are intended, not as a substitute for writing itself.

Tierney, Readence, and Dishner trace the use of story grammars (and story maps) back to Gates (1947) who "advocated the importance of story in the reader's comprehension of narrative."[26] Story grammars, according to Smith and Bean, are evolving from cognitive psychology and " . . . provide a map of major categories and their relationships that form the overall structure typical of most children's stories."[27]

Practice Number 7: Connecting Reading and Writing Processes

Historically, reading and writing have been recognized as having somewhat different functions, with reading classified as a *receptive* or "taking in" language arts and writing seen as an *expressive* or "giving out" language arts. Today, similarities in processes in reading and writing are being recognized. For example, in both of these language arts, students must interact with ideas and experiences from their backgrounds. For reading and writing to be most effective, students must be more mentally active and less passive. Birnbaum captures the relationship between reading and writing by stating that:

> *. . . Investigators in both fields* (reading and writing) *have repeatedly characterized the more proficient as more reflective in their engagements with written language than their less proficient peers. Both better readers and better writers seem to take control of the written language, formulating better questions and solutions about the unfolding text and continually monitoring their success or failure in constructing meaning in or from print.*[28]

Birnbaum also points out that because better writers and better readers are more adept at thinking about and extracting from their experiences, they use schemata more efficiently for working with both form and content of discourse.[29]

In addition to research on the identification of similarities in processes involved in reading and writing, there has been research on how they relate to each other in a broader sense. In W. Loban's longitudinal studies, it was found that in the upper-elementary grades, a high correlation existed between reading scores and ratings of writing quality. As students moved up to ninth grade, these relationships became more pronounced.[30] Good writers tend to do more leisure-time reading than poor writers do, there is an increase in the use of compound and complex sentences in writing as reading comprehension increases, there are high relationships between indices of quality composition and measures of vocabulary, and there are positive and significant relationships between T-unit* length and comprehension in reading.[31] Stotsky points out that " . . . it is possible that reading experience may be as critical a factor in developing writing ability as writing instruction itself."[32]

Krashen states that voluntary reading for pleasure contributes to the development of writing ability, increased reading generally is more effective in producing gains in writing than in increasing frequency of writing, and reading and study of literature has more effect on helping students write than does the study of grammar.[33] Eckhoff points out that children may learn various features of language such as sentence structure and punctuation as they read. In her study, Eckhoff compared different basal readers and the writing completed by students using the readers. The basals were different in that in one series a more "literary prose style" of writing was used by the authors, while in the other series, a more simplistic sentence pattern was used. Students' writing reflected sentence structure similar to that found in their respective basals. Students reading from the basals that had more complex literary prose style tended to write more complex sentences.[34] Trade books advocated in whole language classes should help expand literary prose styles of writers. Indeed, this may prove to be the single, most important value to be derived from the whole language movement.

In a corrective writing program, teachers must find ways of getting students to read more, to think more about what they read, and to write about what they read and think about. Teachers must use books extensively as resources in the writing program, relying heavily on students' interests. When group projects such as cooperative learning groups are formed for reading as explained in Chapter 2, the writing of stories can easily be tied in with each team's work.

---

*A T-unit, defined by Kellogg Hunt, is a way of measuring syntactic maturity in writing. It is defined as a single main or independent clause, plus any subordinate or dependent clause and other structures attached to the main clause. Thus, the sentence "After winning their games, the boys sing loudly." has one T-unit in it. The place of the T-unit as a way of assessing writing will be presented later in this chapter.

Reading is Important to the Developement of Writing Skills (*Photograph by Robert Heller*).

Practice Number 8: Giving Appropriate Feedback in Writing

In writing, appropriate feedback helps students clarify their ideas, expand what they have written, and restructure their writing to more effectively get their intended messages across. Krashen states that feedback should be given during, not exclusively after, the writing process. Holding conferences with students about their writing has been found to be an effective way to provide feedback.[35] Conferences should be held with individual students on a regular basis where specific factors about the individual's writing are discussed. Included among these factors should be continuous review of past writing and the development of plans to improve.

Teachers are warned to proceed with caution when giving comments about students' writing. Lickteig cites D. Graves' research/beliefs in stating that teachers should view children's compositions as "unfinished pieces." Lickteig also cites D. Graves' warning that teachers should focus more on content/ideas of what has been written than on the mechanics. In addition, knowing the interests of students helps in making comments about the content.[36] The teacher, as coach, encourages and teaches students.

Practice Number 9: Establishing Environmental Conditions that Promote Effective Writing

An environment that promotes effective writing is one in which consideration is given to both the physical surroundings and interactions among people in the environment. Of six broad areas identified by Lickteig as areas in which research has provided directions for the teaching of writing, three closely relate to or are about the environment. Feedback given by the teacher and overall teacher attitude have been identified (Practice Number 8). Two other areas are summarized as follows:

- Supportive learning environment—Primary among factors needed for a learning environment is a warm and supportive atmosphere. Also important is animation which is herein defined as "a variety of realia, pictures, books, materials, and audio-visuals . . . " An informal classroom helps promote writing as does providing choice on what to write.[37]
- Cultivation of a sense of community—Teachers who develop a kind of community setting/attitude are more successful in developing student expression (citing Graves). A sense of community has "generative" power and relieves tensions among students. A workshop approach where children work in small groups and read their stories to each other is helpful as is a teacher who moves among students during the writing process, encouraging, and being available to help students.[38]

The Writing Curriculum

The broad-bands curricular design described in Chapter 1 and given in detail for spelling (Table 4–1) is appropriate for a corrective writing program. Such a curriculum helps prevent teachers from falling into the trap of a locked-in grade level curriculum so frequently found in today's schools.

In the first stage of writing (developing a background for formal writing instruction), there is an emphasis on getting students interested in listening to stories read and recognizing story form. There is a sense of enjoyment and discovery about writing, words, and sentences. There is also an emphasis in using the senses to more fully understand and explain objects, situations, and events. In the second stage (formal writing: introductory), a sense of exploration continues, as many kinds of writing are introduced, as well as mechanics (punctuation and capitalization) used in writing. Students learn about paragraphs, write different kinds of poetry, and begin to write for different audiences. Students begin to see how sentences can be expanded and transformed. On a very basic level, students begin to look at different parts of stories, including characterization, setting, and plot.

In stage three (formal writing: intermediate), students continue to become more involved with creating written forms such as tall tales, friendly and business letters, argumentative and expository writing, and with how to use quoted materials in writing. Sentence expansion and transformations continue to be given attention. In the fourth stage (formal writing: advanced), the focus is on more detailed types of writing, such as class papers, writing of notes from documents and discussions in class, and short stories. Students go more into depth on doing different kinds of writing (narrative, descriptive, argumentative, and expository) than in previous levels.

Organizing for Writing Instruction

Base groups where students work with others on the same developmental levels and flex groups for special-needs instruction are ideal grouping arrangements for writing instruction. However, such grouping patterns must be carefully set up and remain flexible, with changes being made when necessary.

Informal Assessment for Forming Base Groups in Writing

There are several ways to organize students in a writing class according to the level of development that students in the class are on, although finding writing levels is not as precise a procedure as is finding reading or spelling levels. The first four suggestions are informal.

Specific Elements of the Writing Curriculum for Forming Base Groups

Students should be tracked from the easiest to the more developed segment of the writing curriculum that a school follows. Progress through the curriculum during the previous year can be used to determine initial base-group placement. Informal tests of segments of the curriculum can also be developed to help in the placement of students in base groups. For example, students who have been taught various kinds of writing (such as, narrative, descriptive) would be asked to write a brief composition demonstrating that they have retained basic elements of this type of writing from prior instruction. In addition, the use of portfolios, to be discussed later, can be tied in with year-to-year progress and aid in the placement of students in base groups at the beginning of the year.

If the broad-bands curriculum advocated is followed, informal tests might be developed for the school or school system to determine where students should be placed at the beginning of the year. Thus, some students would be in one broad level (such as formal writing: intermediate), while others might be in a lower band.

Daily Writing Assignments

During the first two or three weeks of a school year, several short writing assignments can be given in an effort to determine how well students can write and what immediate and future plans are necessary for the writing program for the year. Students should be encouraged to do their best, but should be told that the writing is being done to see how much they have learned about the kind of writing being assessed.

Several topics should be given for each of about eight or ten relatively brief writing assignments. Students should be allowed to choose from the topics, but there should also be opportunities for students to develop their own topic, as long as the topic parallels the kind of writing being assessed (for instance, persuasive writing where students might prefer to make up their own topic as opposed to topics such as "Why You Will Like Our Town").

After each series of assignments on a particular type of writing, the samples are grouped into three to five categories, using a continuum for that type of writing. The following continuums for different kinds of writing may be used:

First Assignments (Descriptive Writing)
Very Descriptive _____ Not Very Descriptive

Second Assignments (Expository Writing)
Very Well Explained _____ Not Very Well Explained

Third Assignments (Argumentative Writing)
Very Persuasive _____ Not Very Persuasive

Fourth Assignments (Narrative Writing)
Very Imaginative _____ Not Very Imaginative

Observing Students' Behaviors During Writing

Over a three-to-four-week period, students should be observed as they write. Notes should be made on such behaviors of each student as: planning for writing, pausing to think what/how to write, rewriting, and sharing of writing. While these behaviors are not exhaustive, there is a limit to how many behaviors can be observed, given the fact that the teacher is attempting to learn as much about each child's writing behaviors as possible in a relatively short period of time. Teachers who wish to record behaviors of students might be wise to train one or two volunteers. Volunteers from the ranks of carefully-selected parents could provide much-needed assistance. Another approach is to focus on a few students during one or more observations. A grid such as the one in Figure 5-2 should be of help in recording writing behaviors.

Based on observed behaviors, there may, at first be just two broad base groups. One group might be made up of students who appear to spend serious time and show great concern when they write. Another group may be those students who appear to treat writing as merely another assignment to be done. With the latter group, teachers would have to spend extraordinary time planning writing experiences around interests of the students, coaching students to change their attitude toward writing, and developing activities around learning styles/characteristics of the students in the group. Conferencing on the part of the teacher would be intensified.

_____

(Student's Name)

(Directions: To the right of each behavior, make a note about how the student reacts to the situation specified.)

Behaviors

1. Responding to Assigned
    Writing Tasks   _____

2. Planning for Writing   _____

3. Pausing to Think About
    (Reflect on) Writing   _____

4. Showing Awareness of
    Audience for Whom
    Writing is Intended   _____

5. Looking for Resources to
    Aid Writing   _____

6. Rewriting Composition   _____

7. Sharing of Writing   _____

8. Showing Pride in Prose
    Writing   _____

9. Showing Interest in
    Writing in All Disciplines   _____

10. Reflecting Interest in
    Writing Poetry   _____

11. Exhibiting Interest in
    Reading What Others
    Have Written   _____

FIGURE 5–2   A Checklist for Noting Behavior Exhibited Toward Writing

Combining Analysis of Writing Samples and Observations

Writing samples and exhibited behaviors of students can be used with conferencing to group students in base groups. Papers for two students who were identified as having less imagination and did not carry out the assignment given in writing were presented earlier in Figure 1–5. Their papers are reproduced in Figure 5–3. If a file of five or six papers are collected over a two-to-three-week period, and the pattern remains somewhat the same, observations/conferences could be helpful in determining why these students are not carrying out assigned writing tasks. If students say that they are not interested in writing about topics available, teachers can easily make adjustments in topics from which the students might choose, including some topics suggested by the students themselves. If the teacher observes or determines in a conference that the students have trouble getting started, some special "starter hints" might be made available for the students to use, including the first line of topics or a writing form. For example, students might be given the following first liners for stories about objects common to a classroom:

1. As a floor, I hurt the most when my boards squeak.
2. As a chalkboard, I am often as dry as a desert.
3. The first year that I was used, I was a bright and shiny new book.
4. The library book table's legs began to groan.
5. "My bowl needs cleaning," cried the little yellow goldfish.

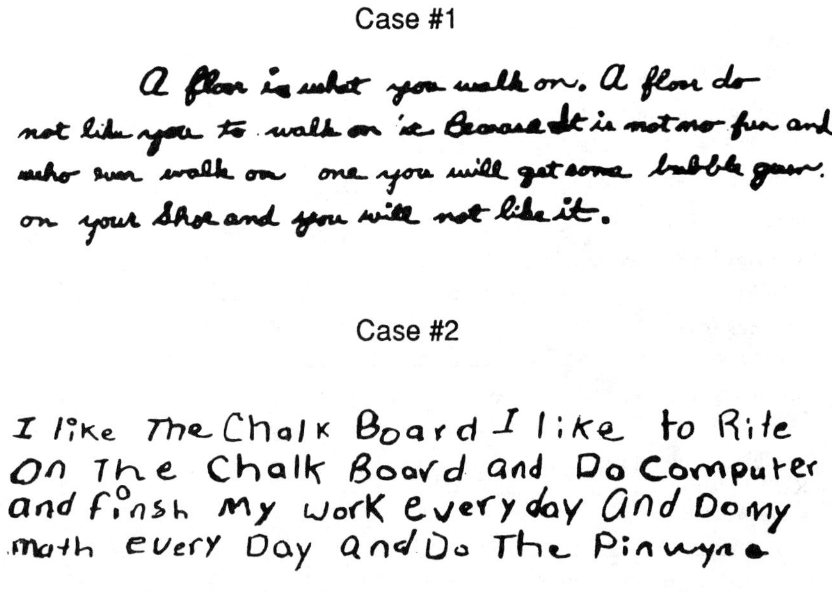

Case #1

a floor is what you walk on. a flor do not like you to walk on it because it is not no fun and who ever walk on one you will get some bubble gum. on your Shoe and you will not like it.

Case #2

I like The Chalk Board I like to Rite On The Chalk Board and Do Computer and finsh My work every day and Do my math every Day and Do The Pinwyna.

FIGURE 5–3 Writing Samples Where Improvement is Needed

While students might use these to begin their stories, the starter lines could be adapted to objects the students might prefer to write about. Thus, in number 1, the ceiling, the air conditioner, or the windows in a classroom could be substituted for floor, with students supplying appropriate substitutions for others words in the sentence.

If observation of behaviors during writing or conferencing leads to the discovery that a student simply does not know enough facts about the topic chosen, the student might be guided to find some basic facts about a topic. Reference books can be used to learn more facts.

A continuum similar to those described earlier in this chapter and the checklist of observed behaviors in Figure 5–2 can easily be used together. If a student's writing falls on the negative end of a continuum, more intensive observation might be done in an effort to determine what behaviors are creating the writing problems identified.

Formal Assessment for Forming Base Groups in Writing

Formal measures for evaluating writing have been devised, including a number of scales, although the extent to which writing scales have been used for grouping students is not well defined in the literature. Some of these scales are described, followed by some possible ways to use them in placing students in base groups.

Using Holistic Writing Scales to Determine Writing Levels of Students

One type of scale advocated is *holistic* in which the focus is on the entire or whole composition, as opposed to counted elements (such as, vocabulary count, clause length, kinds of clauses in sentences) within the composition. Cooper's definition of *holistic* evaluation is both an explanation of the merits of this type of evaluation and a description of the breadth of this approach.

> *Holistic evaluation of writing is a guided procedure for sorting or ranking written pieces. The rater takes a piece of writing and either (1) matches it with another piece in a graded series or (2) scores it for the prominence of certain features important to that kind of writing or (3) assigns it a letter or number grade. The placing, scoring, or grading occurs quickly, impressionistically, after the rater has practiced the procedure with other raters. The rater does not make corrections or revisions in the paper. Holistic evaluation is usually guided by a holistic scoring guide which describes each feature and identifies high, middle, and low quality levels for each feature.*[39]

Cooper identifies seven examples of holistic scales, including essay, analytic, dichotomous, feature analysis, primary trait, general impression, and center of gravity. While these approaches have similar features, there are some significant differences. For example, the analytic and dichotomous scales both look at important features in writing such as the worthiness of the ideas presented and questions about organization. On the dichotomous scale, answers are expressed with "yes" and "no" answers. The essay scale's interesting feature is the attempt made to match a composition according to a series of compositions which span the continuum of "exemplary" to "inadequate."[40]

Focused Holistic Evaluation

Greenhalgh and Townsend describe what they identify as "focused holistic scoring" in which the total composition and designated criteria from four sources are taken into consideration during the scoring of a piece of writing. These sources include major rhetorical demands such as persuasive, informative, and expressive writing; specific rhetorical demands which ask the student to pay attention to a detail such as "one place they would like to visit"; developmental capabilities of students; and constraints of the evaluative situation (such as the setting).[41]

In focused holistic writing, points 0–4 are awarded according to how well each criterion is met. An example of an assigned task is given:

> ***Directions*** In the picture are some things that you can use to make a swing. Look at the picture. How would you make a swing? What would you do first? Then, what other things would you do? You can choose to use all of the things or only some of them. On the next page, write about how you would use some or all of those things to build a swing. Write so that other students your age can read your paper and understand how to build a swing.[42]

In this assignment, students are being examined on the use of narration in writing, told to write for an audience, and provided visual cues (the picture) in order to help develop scoring criteria, from a "common source of information."[43] Criteria for judging papers are very adequately explained for each score, 0–4, with 4 being the highest score a student can make. For example, when a score of 2 is given, all or part of the following factors would exist:

1. *A response in which the steps in the process of building a swing are presented in a very skeletal, bare fashion. There is little or no elaboration and detail given, requiring the reader to infer a great deal.*
2. *A process that may not be related in a straightforward sequence but may reflect some skipping about that leaves the reader confused.*
3. *A sequence in which there may be major gaps; the omitted steps cause the reader to wonder, perhaps, how the tire was actually suspended from the tree.*

4. *An explanation that may contain major inconsistencies; for example, four pieces of rope were measured and cut but only two were used.*
5. *A sample that may contain extraneous information that actually detracts from the effectiveness of the explanation. The writer may wander about and include too much additional information that causes the reader to lose sight of the swing-building process and wonder instead where the writer is going.[44]*

A paper rated 4 would include some or all of these factors:

1. *A response in which the writer clearly organizes and elaborates on the major steps involved so that the reader has no difficulty in following the sequence of activity.*
2. *An explanation that goes beyond the basic procedure and elaborates on such aspects as testing the swing in some fashion to be certain it is sturdy enough or sanding and painting it to make it more attractive.*
3. *A response containing information or elaboration that goes beyond actual swing construction, but this material tends to enhance the presentation rather than be neutral or negative in effect.*
4. *A response that includes an introductory comment ("I am going to tell you how to build a swing.") and/or a concluding comment ("and that's how I would make a swing."). Such comments also indicate that the writer is aware of an audience that wants to know how a swing can be constructed.[45]*

Two examples of students' writing, one rated a "2" and the other a "4" are shown in Figure 5–4. It is relatively easy to see the differences between these compositions and to detect how the evaluative criteria cited were used to rate each one.

Greenhalgh and Townsend recommend the use of the focused holistic evaluative procedure for determining growth in various kinds of writing throughout the year. Students would be asked to write assigned compositions early and then later in the year. The procedure would also help in the evaluation of a writing program.[46] It could also be used to help place students in the appropriate base group.

Setting up Flex Groups in Writing

Once base groups are formed, teachers will note that some students in the various groups have the same or similar problems in writing. For example, a problem that several students may have is in paragraph construction or writing persuasively. Problems may exist across base groups in the area of capitalization and

Score: 2

HOW TO MAKE A SWING

> Once when I was little I always wanted to build a swing. So one day I took all my allowance and went to the store. and bought a hammer, nails, boards, rope, a tire and a ladder. When I got home I went to my back yard and put the ladder against the tree. and climb up. When I got to the branch I nailed down the boards and tided the rope around the boards and climb down and had the tire on.

Score: 4

HOW TO MAKE A SWING

> First find a very strong branch on a tree. Then find some very strong rope, in your house. or garage. Then find a ladder tall enough to reach the branch. Then put a small hole in the branch. Make sure it's big enough for the rope. Don't make it too big either. Then put the rope through the hole. Tie a knot in the rope. Then find another rope and do the same thing that you did with the first rope. Then find an old tire. Wash it off if you need to. Dry it off with an old towel or let it dry off by itself. Tie one rope on one side of the tire and the other one on the other side. Then hop on in and swing!
> The End

FIGURE 5–4   Examples of Children's Writing Scored With a Focused Holistic Writing Scale

Carol Greenhalgh and Donna Townsend, "Evaluating Students' Writing Holistically- An Alternative Approach," *Language Arts* 58 (1981); 819, 821. Copyright (1981) by the National Council of Teachers of English. Reprinted with permission.

punctuation. Whatever the problem, there are numerous times when special-needs instruction should be planned, and flex groups should be made operable. There are several ways to form flex groups, in writing and these are described.

Measuring Syntactic Maturity

There has been some attention to how students' syntax or sentence structure develops as students grow toward maturity in writing. One of the most frequently mentioned procedures is the use of the T-unit, briefly discussed earlier in this chapter. A more thorough discussion of this technique and of clause structure in general helps understand children's growth toward more mature syntax.

Hunt, who developed the T-unit procedure, identifies longer sentences, growth in vocabulary, and more words written on a topic as three features of more mature writing. However, Hunt points out that as students' writing matures, there is a larger proportion of subordinate clauses used in sentences.[47] An example given is that of two main (independent) clauses in a sentence of a fourth grader: *There was a lady next door and the lady was a singer.* Hunt states that an older student would probably not use the word *lady* twice in the sentence but instead would combine the two main clauses. One way might be to use a relative adjective clause as in *There was a lady next door who was a singer.*[48] Some examples of differences in the syntactic maturity of writing at the fourth, eighth, and skilled adult levels, given by Hunt, are presented in Figure 5–5. In these examples, six basic facts around a common theme were given to those who were to write a composition.

These examples can be used to illustrate differences in maturity levels of writing by individuals, including characteristics such as: Younger children tend to write using shorter T-units. (For example, in sentence 1 of the fourth-grade student's writing, there are two T-units. Sentence 2 also has two T-units. In each case they

---

Fourth Grade
Aluminum is a metal and it is abundant. It has many uses and it comes from bauxite. Bauxite is an ore and looks like clay.

Eighth Grade
Aluminum is an abundant metal, has many uses, and comes from bauxite. Bauxite is an ore that looks like clay.

Skilled Adult Level
Aluminum, an abundant metal with many uses comes from bauxite, a clay-like ore.

FIGURE 5–5 Syntactic Maturity of Writing at Fourth Grade, Eighth Grade, and Skilled Adult Levels

Kellogg W. Hunt, "Early Blooming and Late Blooming Syntactic Structures," in *Evaluating Writing: Describing, Measuring, Judging,* Edited by Charles R. Cooper and Lee Odell. (Urbana, Illinois, 1977) p. 95. Copyright (1977) by the National Council of Teachers of English. Reprinted with permission.

are quite short.) Younger students tend to connect sentences with conjunctions as has the fourth grader in the example given in Figure 5–5; and T-units become progressively longer as writing becomes more mature. Thus, the average T-unit length of the fourth-grader's writing in Figure 5–5 is five words (25÷5). The average length of the eighth-grader's writing is ten words (20÷2). The one T-unit in the skilled adult's writing is thirteen words, reflecting considerably greater writing facility than that of either the fourth or eighth grader.[49]

In using the T-unit as an index of maturity in writing, Burns recommends five steps given by R. Jung in analyzing a student's paper:

1. *Divide all the sentences of a pupil's composition into T-units.*
2. *Divide the total number of words in the composition by the total number of T-units. This will reveal the average length of the pupil's T-units, a very important measure for evaluating composition maturity.*
3. *Analyze each sentence in the composition in terms of the number of T-units, number of words per T-unit, ways in which subordination and coordination are indicated, means for the development of characterization, nominals, adverbials, and any other measures which affect T-unit length.*
4. *Prepare a summary outline based on the analysis of sentences, including T-unit measures, features of the pupil's syntax, methods utilized for developing characterizations, plot structure, analysis, and story interpretation.*
5. *Write an evaluation based on the data obtained in steps one to four.[50]*

A story written by a seventh grader in which the number of T-units and number of words per sentence are indicated is shown in Figure 5–6. The sentences in the composition have been numbered to help in analysis of the composition. Diagram 5–1 is useful for recording the variables used in calculating sentence maturity using the T-unit. Since teachers are busy, students can number sentences on compositions in which T-unit analysis will be done.

Go back to the three samples of writing in Figure 5–5 and determine if the seventh grader's writing in Figure 5–6 is more like the writing of the fourth grader, the eighth grader, or the skilled adult. Are there any particular problems in writing that the seventh grader has that requires special-needs instruction? Now compare the seventh-grader's composition in Figure 5–5 with the fourth-grader's composition, "The Zugba Dancer" in Figure 5–1. In what ways are they different?

How can syntactic maturity be used in settings where special-needs instruction is provided in flex groups? Burns states that analysis of students' writing using R. Jung's procedures can sensitize teachers to each student's use of linguistic features

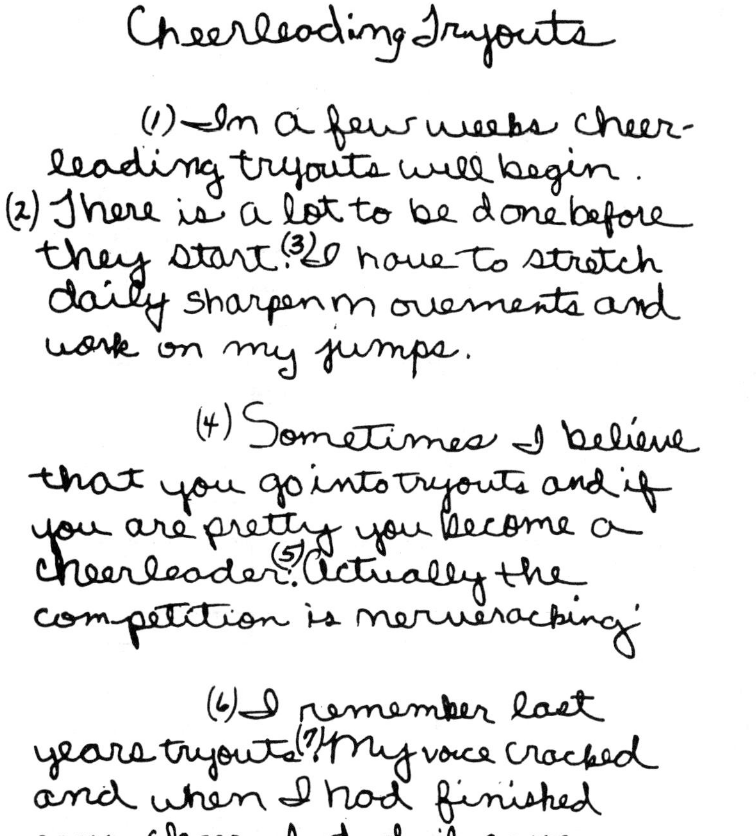

Cheerleading Tryouts

(1) In a few weeks cheer-
leading tryouts will begin.
(2) There is a lot to be done before
they start. (3) I have to stretch
daily sharpen movements and
work on my jumps.

(4) Sometimes I believe
that you go into tryouts and if
you are pretty you become a
cheerleader. (5) Actually the
competition is nervewracking.

(6) I remember last
years tryouts. (7) My voice cracked
and when I had finished
my cheer I didn't even
remember doing it. (8) I hope
that I am not that nervous
this year. (9) I don't think I will
be, because I have already had
an extra years experione.

FIGURE 5–6 Seventh Grade Student's Composition on "Cheerleading Tryouts"

in writing and focus attention on specifics in writing rather than providing general impressions.[51] The writer contends that the use of T-units can give teachers a picture of both the developmental level and the level where special-needs instruction is needed. The eighth grader whose T-units are more like those of a

DIAGRAM 5–1 Analysis of Syntactical Maturity

Student _Jane Doe_

Composition _Cheerleading Tryouts_ Date _9-15-93_

Sentence Number	No. of T-units	Number of Words per Sentence
1	1	8
2	1	10
3	1	12
4	1	17
5	1	5
6	1	5
7	2	16
8	1	10
9	2	15
		98
Total 9	Total 11	Average Length per T-unit **8.91** words

fourth grader can be taught to combine sentences in a number of ways. The students who do not yet compound adjectives (My horse is *beautiful* and *graceful*.) when other students in the classroom can do this might be taught how to combine adjectives in a flex group.

Codes-in-Margin System

A system developed by the writer that involves students in assessing their errors in such areas as punctuation, capitalization, and spelling is called a "Codes-in-Margin" system, briefly introduced for spelling in Chapter 4. Codes known by teacher and students are placed in the body of the composition by the teacher. In cases where two or more errors occur, the codes are placed in sequence of their occurrence on the line, and students learn to look for the errors in the order of occurrence.

Codes developed by one teacher and advocated by that teacher's total school system appears in Figure 5–7. An example of a draft of one student's composition in which the "Codes-in-Margins" system is used follows in Figure 5–8.

Codes in Margin

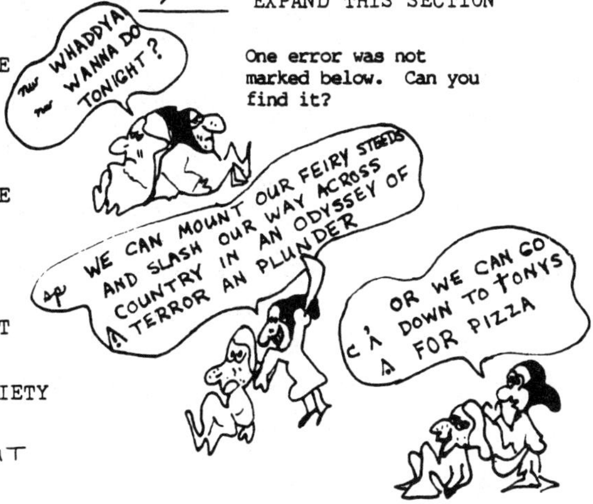

FIGURE 5–7   **A Codes-in-Margin System for Checking Problems in Writing**

Knox County, Tennessee Public Schools, *Writing Guide*, 1985, p. 18. Bonnie Anders, Cedar Bluff Middle School. Reprinted with permission.

This system makes it easy to determine which students need help in the same area of writing. Checklists similar to Figure 4–3 are used, where students' names and kinds of errors are written on the appropriate axis of a grid. Flex groups are then formed by noting who continues to make the same errors.

Codes-for-Positive-Features-Margin System

A system for paying special attention to desirable features in writing can be implemented, using "positive codes" for desirable features in writing. These codes are also placed in margins of written compositions, perhaps boxed in or underlined to differentiate from codes that stand for errors made. In Diagram 5–2, suggested "Codes-for-Positive-Features" are shown. Students may work in pairs or in small groups to find where the positive features have been marked in their papers. Later,

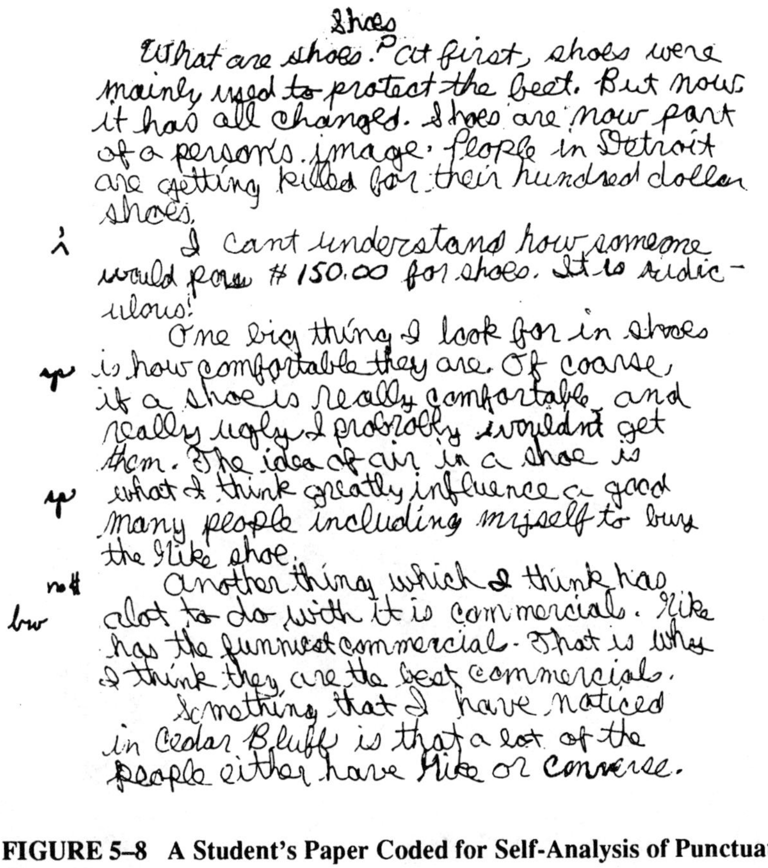

Shoes

What are shoes? at first, shoes were mainly used to protect the feet. But now it has all changed. Shoes are now part of a person's image. People in Detroit are getting killed for their hundred dollar shoes.

i I cant understand how someone would pay #150.00 for shoes. It is ridic-ulous!

One big thing I look for in shoes sp is how comfortable they are. Of coarse, if a shoe is really comfortable and really ugly I probably wouldnt get them. The idea of air in a shoe is sp what I think greatly influence a good many people including myself to buy the Nike shoe.

no¶ bw Another thing which I think has alot to do with it is commercials. Nike has the funniest commercial. That is why I think they are the best commercials.

Something that I have noticed in Cedar Bluff is that a lot of the people either have Nike or Converse.

FIGURE 5–8 A Student's Paper Coded for Self-Analysis of Punctuation and Other Errors

a transparency might be made of examples that are particularly good, thus giving students a chance to see models worth replicating.

The Jigsaw cooperative learning strategy presented in Chapter 2, can be combined with the "positive features" strategy. Each student in a group is assigned a feature to teach to the other students. After each group has learned the feature to be taught to others, the students regroup to teach their original team members the feature that they have learned.

Students whose writings seldom reflect positive features can be grouped as a flex group for special-needs instruction. For example, over a period of time, students may seldom receive the code for "a very well described setting" shown in Diagram 5–2. Thus, special instruction on how to write more descriptive settings could follow. Students can help teachers with grouping by using Diagram 5–2 to record how many codes were listed in a series of papers during a given six weeks or so of instruction.

A Prerequisite-Skills Approach to Forming Flex Groups
As in spelling, various skills in writing can be broken down into their prerequisite subskills, concepts, or other components. Paragraph construction can be used to illustrate this idea. Where the prerequisites are not known by some of the students to be taught paragraph construction, a subgroup or flex group would be formed to teach the prerequisites. Prerequisites for paragraph construction, based primarily on

DIAGRAM 5–2 Codes-for-Positive-Features-Margin System

	Codes	Positive Feature
1.	GDS	Good description of setting
2.	IL	Imaginative language
3.	GSV	Good substitution of verbs
4.	IP	Interesting plot
5.	GCD	Good character description
6.	IB	Interesting beginning

what commonly are considered to be the basic elements of paragraph writing, would include such elements as understanding the concept of sentence, constructing/writing a sentence, using conventions of capitalization and punctuation for marking a sentence, writing a topic sentence, and writing supporting sentences.

For writing, teachers can easily develop a bank of major skills with their prerequisites. As in spelling, test banks of a major skill's prerequisites can also be developed.

Setting Up a Portfolio for Writing

Teachers today are being encouraged to examine children's writing and place representative samples (and have children place samples) in portfolios. Selecting such samples gives a more complete picture of abilities in and problems with writing than examination of any one piece of writing.

To set up a portfolio for each student and to implement portfolio assessment, it is necessary to follow several specific procedures. First, a definite time period such as a six-week block of time should be designated for gathering samples. Sample selection should have a definite relationship to a specific phase of the writing curriculum, and students should know when samples are to be collected.

A second procedure should be the designation of the type of writing to be in each portfolio. If, for example, both *descriptive* and *expository* writing are extensively taught during a semester when portfolio assessment is to take place, it should be stated clearly that both types of writing are to be included in the portfolio. This message might be placed on a card or sheet of paper and attached to the inside front cover of a manila folder that will be used to hold writing samples.

A third procedure to be followed is to determine what checklists or other assessment instruments to include in a portfolio. While such checklists should be limited in number (leaving more room for samples of writing), some checklists can be helpful. The self-assessment of writing instrument shown in Table 5–3 is one that might be helpful in that it involves students in a basic tenet of corrective teaching.

A fourth procedure to be established in portfolio assessment is the development of a system for systematic review of samples of each student's writing in his/her portfolio. The system should include coaching, following the basic procedures outlined in Chapter 3.

A fifth procedure to follow in portfolio assessment is the organization and grouping of students for instruction, including the use of writing samples for placing students in base and flex groups. This follow-up to sample collection lets students know that there is a definite rationale for collecting samples of their work. In addition, samples in each student's portfolio can be effectively used to hold conferences with parents.

A sixth procedure for using portfolios in writing is the incorporation of samples from areas of the curriculum other than the language arts. When students write reports in social studies or science, the criteria learned for report writing in the language arts class should be carried out in the social studies/science report. Samples of writing in these areas should be periodically placed in students' portfolios.

TABLE 5–3 Self-Assessment of a Student's Writing

Story_____   Name_____

1. How do you feel about what you have just written? Circle one. Why do you feel this way? (Use space below where you have circled to say why *if you want to do so*.)

Not too Excited	*Somewhat Excited*	*Very Excited*

2. Compare this story with one you wrote last time. Write a sentence or two about the differences. (Be brief.)

3. What do you like best about your main character and the setting? (Be brief.)

[You may not want to go to number 4 below if you are real, real happy with what you have written.]

4. Are there any ways that you want to change your story? Jot these down, but be brief. Write "none" if there are no changes.

Story Beginning	*Characters*	*Sequence of Events*	*Use of Words*	*Setting*	*Story Ending*

The Computer in the Writing Program

Of all the language arts, the microcomputer is changing the approach to teaching writing the most. As Glynn et al. state, "Computers have revolutionized writing. They have done so by providing environments that support the cognitive processes that underlie good writing."[52] Fischer and Fischer state that, "Microcomputers allow English teachers to introduce their students to a much more powerful extension of human composing than was ever provided by pencil, paper, dictaphone or typewriter."[53]

Fischer and Fischer, admitting that writers do not engage in the writing process in a linear fashion, nevertheless point out some useful ways that the microcomputer is helpful to writing during prewriting, drafting, revising, proofreading, evaluating, and publishing. These are summarized as follows:

1. (Prewriting) *Students record what they have brainstormed, they list, sequence, and/or cluster their ideas. Students can organize their writing and get the teacher and peers to react to their ideas.*[54]

2. (Drafting) *Through an examination of ideas recorded/organized during prewriting, students can develop further structures and relationships. The microcomputer provides more legibility and allows students to make more careful appraisal than would be the case with the " . . . typical draft, with its smudges, cross-outs, marginal notes, etc. . . . "*[55]

3. (Revising) *Students can rearrange words, phrases, clauses, sentences, paragraphs, or larger sections of a composition. Students are free to pay more attention to the more important aspects of writing: " . . . For the first time in the history of writing instruction, it is feasible and indeed likely that student writers will engage in the sort of extensive revision heretofore only practiced by professional writers."*[56]

4. (Proofreading) *Students can form "peer editing groups" and use either hard copy printouts or the monitor's image to examine mechanical correctness, appropriateness of form and style, or any other errors that might be found in writing. Students will no longer avoid rewriting and making corrections as once they did with paper and pencil writing assignments.*[57]

5. (Evaluating) *Students can be engaged in formative or summative evaluation.* Students can make judgments against criteria established for a particular writing or the evaluation " . . . may*

> *be the informal, genuine, spontaneous reaction of readers to part
> or all of a composition. . . . "* [58]

6. (Publishing) *Students can use both printers and electronic
   mailing to share their writing with peers, parents, or any other
   audiences desired. The microcomputer makes not only the
   printing of student writing easier but also helps in retrieval of
   writing that has been done in the past. Students may use their
   own disks as if they were notebooks.* [59]

The microcomputer can be used to help students understand and practice different forms of writing. Using story frames that have emerged in importance in both reading and writing, the teacher may use the *memory-file* system of a word processor to provide necessary practice with whatever form is being learned. Fowler's story frames to aid primary students' comprehension skills can be adapted to writing and the microcomputer. Two such frames follow:

Important Idea or Plot*

In this story the problem starts when _____ .

After that, _____ . Next, _____ .

Then, _____ .

The problem is finally solved when _____ .

The story ends _____ . [60]

Setting†

This story takes place_____ .

I know this because the author uses the words "_____ .

_____ ."

Other clues that show when the story takes place_____

_____ . [61]

---

*Formative evaluation refers to evaluation that takes place as a program, such as writing, is being planned or developed. Evaluations might be made to change phases of the program that at the point in time need adjustment. Summative evaluation refers to decisions about the program sometimes after adjustments were made during program planning or development. The two types of evaluation are not always mutually exclusive.

†Reprinted with permission of Gerald L. Fowler and the International Reading Association.

Other forms identified by Fowler are "Story Summary With One Character Included," "Character Analysis," and "Character Comparisons,"[62] When frames are used in reading, a familiar story is used with students completing the blanks. In pairs or groups, students might discuss a story written by a classmate and complete the frame for the story selected. Suggestions might follow for improving the story. For example, where words are too general and do not clearly identify the setting, alternate, more specific words may be suggested.

Frames can also be used to help students see the major characteristics of different modes of discourse and obtain practice in writing each mode. An example can be given for *expository writing* in which different strategies are taught. Cause and effect, a strategy in *expository writing*, is an example. Using the *memory file* of the microcomputer, several frames such as the following could be developed for independent or small-group use with students.

The Storm

The rain pelted the trees for _____

_____ . Soon the winds _____

_____ . It was a furious _____

_____ . All of a sudden a big tree _____

_____ . It fell across

_____ . It was a long

time before _____ .

Students might rename the paragraph, compare different answers given to complete the frame, review the criteria introduced by the teacher for using cause and effect, revise their own or their group's completed frame after reviewing criteria for using cause and effect, and/or reverse the cause and effect in the frame. Ultimately, without using frames, students would be asked to use the microcomputer to develop their own cause and effect paragraphs or stories. Other strategies for expository writing, including *definition, example, metaphor*, and *comparison and contrast*[63] could similarly be taught.

Using the basic procedures for *argumentative writing*, the same type of frame can be developed for the *memory file* of the microcomputer. Frames can easily be developed to incorporate the characteristics on presentation of an issue, expression of the writer's views on the issue, presentation of another's point of view, and restatement of the writer's point of view.[64] An example follows:

An Argument With Our Neighbor

Last week, we had an _____ with _____ , our neighbor.

It was about _____ .

We felt that _____ .

However, _____ argued that _____

_____ .

After we discussed the problem for _____ , we still felt that

_____ .

Framed paragraphs suggested by Hennings and Grant can also be placed on the microcomputer to help students better understand how paragraphs are constructed, including the sequencing of sentences within paragraphs. An example of a framed paragraph follows:

Title*

Last week I went to the _____ .

I saw _____ . When

_____ . Then _____

_____ . At last

_____ . I thought

_____ .

Hennings and Grant state that paragraph frames help provide a logical scheme for expressing one's thought as opposed to stifling thought. They also suggest that group oral experiences precede individual use of the frames.[65]

Organizing paragraphs according to position of topic sentences can also be conveniently taught with the aid of the *memory file* of a microcomputer. The same paragraph is placed three times on a microcomputer, with the incompleted part being the first sentence for the first paragraph, a middle sentence for the second

*Reprinted by permission of the publisher from Hennings, Dorothy Grant, and Grant, Barbara M., *Written Expression in the Language Arts, Ideas and Skills.* 2nd Ed. (New York: Teachers College Press © 1981 by Teachers College Press, Columbia University. All rights reserved.), paragraph from page 158.

paragraph, and the last sentence for the third paragraph. Students are to type in the topic sentence (given initially) in each of the three paragraphs. Later, students are asked to make up their own paragraphs, including appropriate topic sentences that can be initial, middle, or final sentences. If students cannot give the same topic sentence for each of the three paragraphs, they can construct and type in three different sentences, one sentence for each position where topic sentences can go. Examples of a paragraph for each position follow:

Topic Sentence: Joseph soon solved the mystery of his missing dog, Corky.

Paragraph 1 _____

Joseph found an ad in the paper that said a red Pomeranian had wandered to the house belonging to the Smith family. He called the person whose name had been given in the ad. By noontime, Joseph was on his way to pick up Corky.

Paragraph 2.   Joseph was tireless in his search for his red Pomeranian, Corky. The little dog had been lost all week. On Sunday morning, however, Joseph found an ad in the paper that said a red Pomeranian had been found. Joseph called the number of the person listed in the ad. _____

_____ .

Paragraph 3.   Joseph's little red Pomeranian, Corky, had been lost almost a week. One day, Joseph saw an ad in the paper that read, "Small red Pomeranian pup found. Call 549– 3339." _____

_____ .

The woman who put the ad in the paper said that the little dog had been in her neighborhood for four or five days. There were two other little dogs nearby, and Corky likes to play with them.

In using the microcomputer to position the topic sentence in the three paragraphs given, students would perhaps go to another series similarly constructed. Three separate paragraphs might then be given, with different topic sentences. From these, students would choose where in the paragraphs on the *memory file* the topic sentences should be placed. Finally, students would practice constructing paragraphs with topic sentences shown in three different positions.

Sentence-combining activities also can be effectively done with a microcomputer, a point made by Fischer and Fischer.[66] Again, using the *memory-file* system of a word processor, frames can be developed in which students are asked to combine two, or in some cases, three short sentences. Some frames which call for different kinds of sentence combining follow:

Pattern 1

> I was sound asleep.
> The telephone rang.

I was sound asleep when the telephone rang.

Pattern 2

> It is a cold day.
> It is a rainy day

It is a cold, rainy day.

Sentence combining with the use of a microcomputer can be made more of an assessment-corrective activity when the teacher notes the types of short, choppy sentences that sometimes occur in students' writing. Specific patterns can then be developed to help students practice those patterns in which problems are occurring. For example, if it is noted that several students do not use double adjectives to describe nouns as is the case where a student writes, "It is a cold day. It is a rainy day." several examples of Pattern 2 can be developed on the *memory file* of the word processor. Students can then practice combining these sentences. In some cases, a worksheet can be developed in which the first combination is done for the student, and subsequent examples done on the microcomputer by the student needing help.

Another use of the microcomputer is the placing of different models of writing on the *memory file* and letting students try duplicating each model with a suggested topic or one that the student selects. Examples of a paragraph which combine narrative and descriptive writing follow.

Paragraph One

The young colt pranced around the barnyard. He could not be still. It was as if the bright, sunny day were made just for him to show how he could run, jump, and frolic.

Paragraph Two

Running! Jumping! Frolicking! The young colt could not be still. It was a bright, sunny day that seemed to be made just for him to show how he could prance around the barnyard.

Paragraph Three
Being still was out of the question for the young colt. He
pranced and frolicked around the barnyard. Jumping and
running, he showed off as if the bright, sunny day were made just
for him.[67]

Students are then given several topics such as "A Gathering Storm," "Entering a New School," or "Our Saturday Afternoon Game," to create paragraphs written in ways similar to the ones displayed on the microcomputer screen. Students may make up a topic. Students in groups may compare their paragraphs and revise them as necessary.

A number of innovative programs have been developed to utilize the microcomputer in language arts in general and writing in specific. Among these is a program called *The Bridge* which was developed to aid poor readers. The authors of the program identify the program as an "interactive learning environment designed to overcome the block caused by poor reading."[68] In this system, the student not only sees what text has been created but also hears the text read back to him/her. In addition, study materials which include a number of the reading skills and skills involved in writing, including punctuation and capitalization, are available for use.[69] Components of the system include a *Talking Text*, in which students read and hear text on a variety of topics found in reading programs; the *Talking Typewriter*, in which students use the microcomputer as a talking word processor; and the *Talking Tutor*, in which students are systematically taught vocabulary and concepts. Initial research has indicated the program to not only be more effective than traditional tutoring programs but also less expensive.[70] Stories written by a third grader and a fourth grader in an elementary school in Houston, Texas are shown in Figure 5–9. The handwritten stories and typed versions are shown together to indicate improvement made. While some spelling errors continue to occur in the first typed edition, further use of the *Talking Typewriter* will help in correction of these problems.

Activities/Strategies for Use in Correcting Problems in Writing

Many strategies suggested elsewhere in this book can be applied to corrective writing. Several are mentioned here specifically as they apply to writing. Included are modeling, cooperative learning, and special use of interests that students have demonstrated.

Modeling

While modeling, as presented by Graves, is given for a developmental program, the techniques suggested can be effective in a student-involved corrective writing program. Graves states that:

Third Grader

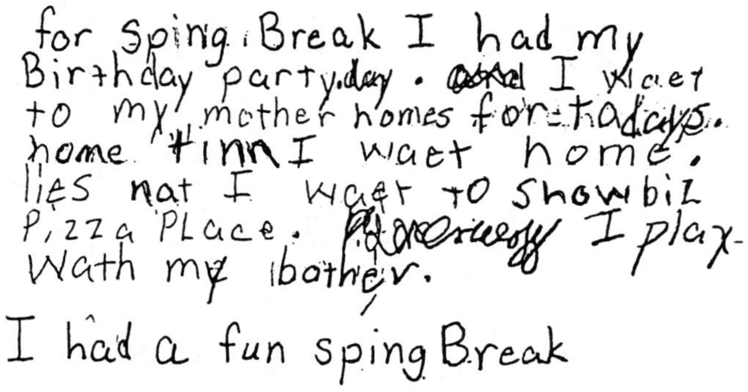

Fourth Grader

for Spring Break I had my
Birthday partyday. and I wcet
to my mother homes for todays.
home. #inn I waet home.
lles nat I woet to show biz
pizza place. Aoretuegy I plax-
wath my ibother.

I had a fun spring Break

One day I went
skiing first. I went to
my unkele in coliroto.
Then my cosent come
The next day I got
up and went to ski
i leend how to ski by
my self. Than the
next day I went to
Baver Crik. I got
on the lift aofd went
to the top. Than I
six down red buffulo.
Than we went to the
lift in the mjit I of
the montane off and brok
my sky. It was
a hordy Da and
I slep good.

For spring break, I had my birthday party. I went to my mother forto days. Thin I went home. Last nite I went home to shbizpizza place. I played weth my brother.

I had a fun spring break.

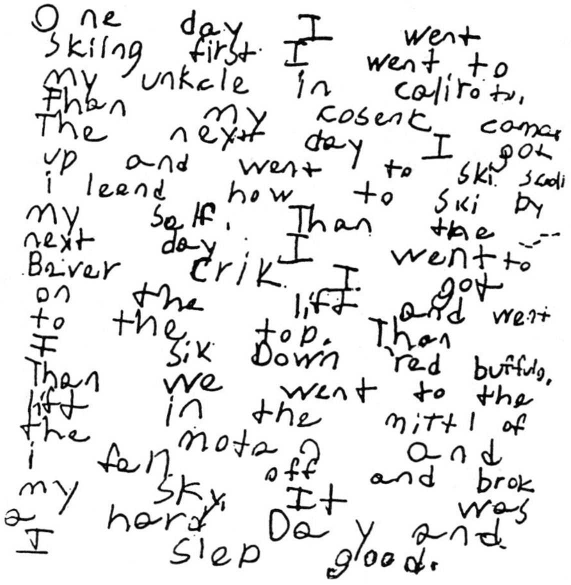

One day I went skiing. First I went to my unkcle in colorado. Than my cozents came. The next day I got up and went to ski scool. I lerned how mto ski by my self. Than the next day I went to Beaver creeck. I got on the left and went to the top. Than I ski down Red Buffulo. Than we went to the lift in the mitle of the mountane and I fel off and brook my ski. it was a hard day and I slep good

FIGURE 5–9 Written Compositions in Which the Microcomputer With Interactive Sound Was Used for Rewriting

173

> *... The tone for writing is set by what the teacher does, not by what the teacher says. In this instance, writing will be treated as a laboratory or studio subject. That is, instead of giving writing to children, you will share it with them. You will write with them.*[71]

Graves also points out rather explicit steps that involve the teacher as a lesson in writing is taught. These are summarized as follows:

1. *Give all in the room, including yourself (the teacher), a piece of lined and newsprint paper.*
2. *Tell the students that the newsprint is for writing down possible topics on which to write.*
3. *Number the newsprint from 1–4.*
4. *Tell the students that you are going to choose topics and then decide on which one you will write.*
5. *Have students write their four topics.*
6. *Choose a topic on which you, the teacher, will write.*
7. *Tell students why you chose the topic that you did.*
8. *Discuss with students what you hope to discover as you write about this topic.*
9. *Have students choose the topic on which they wish to write.*
10. *Let the students talk their topic over with a friend.*
11. *Have a brief (5 minutes) quiet period in which all in the room (including yourself) begin to write.*[72]

The teacher serves as a model in encouraging students to both read and write. With the connections clear between good reading habits and their effects on writing, the teacher takes every opportunity possible to demonstrate that he/she reads for pleasure and writes often.

Cooperative Learning Groups in Writing

In the *Cooperative Integrated Reading and Composition (CIRC)* model of a cooperative learning group, cited in Chapter 2, students work in pairs to improve the team's performance on a variety of language arts, including written compositions. One activity suggested was paraphrasing definitions of words in a dictionary. Yet another one specifically relating to written compositions was participation in writers' workshops where students brainstorm about a topic, learn form/technique in writing, write, and hold peer-review conferences.[73]

Writing Response Groups are discussed by Johnson, Johnson, and Holubec who suggest that students respond to each other's papers three times after reading a paper. Students use different codes (for example, a star by portions that they like; a question mark by a part not understood) for marking a paper before they discuss the entire paper with peer writers. Errors of mechanics and spelling are also marked, and the student who reads and marks the paper also proofreads final drafts.[74]

Group Reports is another writing activity recommended by Johnson, Johnson, and Holubec. Students jointly research a topic, with each team member responsible for one different source. At least three notecards of information are provided by each person. Students write and give oral reports together.[75]

Using Interests of Students in a Writing Program

Teachers can take advantage of students' interests in implementing cooperative learning groups for writing. One activity is developed around the most dominant interests that students in the same classroom have. For example, if the five most dominant interests in a fourth-grade classroom are horses, sports, travel, science fiction, and pen pals, students are placed in groups according to interest. For each group, a leader, a recorder, and a resource coordinator (or perhaps several coordinators) are assigned. Each role is clearly outlined by the teacher, but students are asked to redefine each role once they assemble in their respective group. For resource coordinators, some possible roles follow:

1. Check out as many library books on the group's topic as possible, using both the school's and the community's libraries.
2. Ask students in the class if they have magazines at home on their group's topic.
3. Continue to look for materials during the group's actual writing of the report.
4. Ask other teachers if they know of additional resource materials on the group's topic.

The students assemble in their group to begin their writing project. They must first decide the *focus* of the topic. Perhaps the group writing a report on horses might focus on the history of how the horse was domesticated, the many uses of horses in the world today, or the care and feeding of horses. An outline or plan for completing the report is formulated. A timeline may be formulated, indicating when the report and different phases of it is are due. The teacher serves as a consultant. Finally, the group divides up the various writing tasks, which may also include illustrations.

Summary

1. Writing programs should focus on both *functional* and *creative* aspects of writing. A point that should be remembered is that there are many factors common

to both, such as sentence building. A student-involved corrective program provides attention to problems common to both types of writing but also includes help in overcoming problems unique to functional and creative writing.

2. Nine areas of research on writing provide direction for a student-involved corrective writing program. These include the giving of attention to writing as a process, viewing writing as a recursive process, using sentence-combining techniques for writing growth, distinguishing between maturity and immaturity in writing, knowing the place of grammar instruction in writing programs, using models and modeling in writing, connecting reading and writing processes, giving appropriate feedback to writing, and establishing appropriate environmental conditions for writing.

3. Writing processes that appear to be important are pausing before writing various segments of a composition, planning, reviewing segments of writing, revising drafts, and discussing what one is writing.

4. Writing is a recursive, rather than a linear, process. This means that various processes such as revising are used over and over again throughout a composition—not at one point or one stage only.

5. Students should have opportunities to expand sentences in a variety of ways, using a number of transformations to do so. Among several kinds of transformations are deletions and rearrangements.

6. Research indicates that mature writers are more aware of and accommodate their audiences more than do immature writers. Mature writers care more about the results of their compositions and are more reflective than are immature writers.

7. Studies do not support grammar instruction as a way to improve writing, although students taught grammar may indeed know more grammar than those not taught grammar. Thus, students in a corrective writing program should have more instruction on fundamentals of writing than on grammar instruction *per se*. When grammar is taught, it should be taught inductively, taught in relation to reading/writing, and taught when students can do abstract reasoning.

8. Models for writing are useful and can be found in various forms, including discourse schema, story grammars, and framers. Such devices help the writer see the structure of a story or other form of writing.

9. Research indicates that a number of reading and writing processes are similar. A goal for effective reading and writing is to make students more active and less passive as they participate in these language arts. Effective writers and effective readers are more capable of using their background experiences than are their peers who are not as adept at writing and reading. Good writers read more than do poor writers. Teachers in a student-involved corrective writing program should pay attention to these relationships, such as attempting to increase the reading of students who are in need of improving their writing.

10. Feedback in writing should be given throughout writing, not just when a composition is completed. Conferencing is an effective way to provide feedback.

Comments on content and ideas are more helpful than comments on mechanics of writing.

11. The writing environment should include a positive attitude on the part of the teacher, an environment of support, an informal classroom, and much stimulation (as with pictures, books, and audio-visuals). A sense of community is also an important factor to consider in a writing program.

12. A writing curriculum can be developed around the broad-bands concept in which several skills/subskills are introduced as appropriate. The clusters of skills can be organized in four levels of increasing difficulty (background to formal writing, advanced).

13. Base groups can be formed through informal testing of skills and other content to be taught, through analysis of daily writing assignments, through observations of students as they write, and through a combination of writing sample analysis and observation.

14. Flex groups can be formed through analysis of syntactic maturity, through analysis of students' papers, through a codes-in-margin writing system, through a desirable-features-codes-in-margin system, and through a prerequisites-skills approach to analysis of content in writing.

15. A portfolio for assessing writing should be kept on each writer in a classroom. A portfolio should indicate overall growth as well as growth (or lack thereof) of specific kinds of writing (narrative, descriptive, expository, and argumentative).

16. The microcomputer is most useful to writing programs. A primary way that microcomputers are helpful is in the rewriting/editing stage of writing, although microcomputers can help in understanding plot, setting, and other characteristics of particular forms of writing.

17. Modeling by the teacher is an effective strategy for writing instruction. Cooperative learning strategies can also be effective in writing instruction. Also, knowing and using interests of students is important in a corrective writing program.

Reviewing, Connecting, and Expanding What You Have Learned

(Directions) The activities that follow should help you better understand writing in a student-involved corrective writing program. The paragraph number refers to the numbers in the summary section of this chapter.

1. (Paragraph 1) Make two columns on your paper. One should be labeled creative writing and the other functional writing. Under each, define the term, list its major characteristics, and give at least two examples. If you cannot do this, go back to the introductory section of Chapter 5 for help.

2. (Paragraph 2) Select any two research findings that have been presented in this chapter as basic research practices for writing. Write a brief essay on each practice, and have a partner critique what you have written. In turn, critique what your partner has written on his/her two research practices.

3. (Paragraphs 3 and 4) Develop a set of guidelines for a corrective program in writing in which attention has been paid to both the process and product of writing. Be sure to focus on themes that have been advocated for a corrective program in this book.

4. (Paragraph 5) In your small group or with a partner, select one of the following short sentences and develop a lesson to teach your peers how to expand the sentence. Develop your lesson around basic principles on "effective demonstrations" discussed in this book. The sentences are:

    a. John saw it.
    b. Susan is going.
    c. The horse ran.
    d. Cows "moo."
    e. Tony took it.

5. (Paragraph 6) In a corrective writing program, a goal should be to develop as many characteristics as possible of mature writers. First, name these characteristics. Second, analyze a sample of a student's writing (a story), and plan strategies for helping the writer of the paper become a more mature writer.

6. (Paragraph 7) List practices for teaching grammar that keep grammar instruction in proper perspective.

7. (Paragraphs 8 and 9) Using some suggested frameworks, such as story frames, presented in this chapter, explain how you would use these in teaching some of the relationships between reading and writing.

8. (Paragraphs 10 and 11) With a partner, develop a description of the ideal environment for providing feedback on writing instruction. Explain how the implementation of procedures for giving feedback may well be the first step toward the development of a sound corrective writing program.

9. (Paragraphs 12, 13, and 14) Curriculum and organization for instruction go hand-in-hand. Explain how a curriculum based on the broad-bands concept in which there is a gradual increase in difficulty level and base and flex grouping schemes go together.

10. (Paragraph 15) Select a student, examine his/her written compositions over a period of several weeks, and develop a writing portfolio for this student. If the situation allows, assign compositions to this student. Be sure to include in the portfolio any record forms or procedures for analyzing papers written by the student.

11. (Paragraph 16) Develop a set of guidelines for using the microcomputer in a writing program. Be sure to include in your guidelines all aspects of writing, including early work on a composition through the editing stage.

12. (Paragraph 17) Select *one* of the following strategies, and develop a lesson plan for writing in which the strategy is emphasized:

a. Using a paper that is a model of how to write
b. Modeling a form of writing as done by the teacher
c. Implementing a cooperative learning strategy
d. Using students' interests in writing

Endnotes

1. Walter T. Petty, "Writing of Young Children," In *Research on Composing*, Charles R. Cooper and Lee Odell (Urbana, Illinois: National Council of Teachers of English, 1978), p. 75.

2. Ann Humes, "Putting Writing Research Into Practice," *The Elementary School Journal* 84 (1983): 5–6.

3. Ibid.

4. Ibid., 6.

5. Ibid.

6. Ibid., 4.

7. Ibid.

8. George Hillocks, Jr., "Synthesis of Research on Teaching Writing," *Educational Leadership* 45 (1987): 71.

9. Ibid., 79.

10. Ibid.

11. Peter Mosenthal, "On Defining Writing and Classroom Writing Competence," in *Research on Writing—Principles and Methods*, eds. Peter Mosenthal, Lynne Tamor, and Sean A. Walmsley (New York: Longman, 1983), p. 26.

12. Stephen D. Krashen, *Writing—Research, Theory, and Applications* (Oxford, England: Pergamon Press, 1984), pp. 18–19.

13. Hillocks, "Synthesis of Research," 72–73.

14. Humes, "Putting Writing Research into Practice," 5–10.

15. Barbara Fassler Walvoord and Hoke L. Smith, "Coaching the Process of Writing," in *Teaching Writing in All Disciplines*, ed. C. Williams Griffin (San Francisco: Jossey-Bass, 1982), p. 6.

16. John H. Bushman, *The Teaching of Writing* (Springfield, Illinois: Charles C. Thomas, 1984), pp. 93–115.

17. Ibid., p. 102.

18. Ibid., pp. 102–104.

19. Hillocks, "Synthesis of Research," 75.

20. Bushman, *The Teaching of Writing*, pp. 104–105.

21. Ian S. Fraser and Lynda M. Hodson, "Twenty-one Kicks at the Grammar Horse," *English Journal* 67 (1978): 49–54.

22. Hillocks, "Synthesis of Research," 76.

23. Ibid.

24. Ibid.

25. Marlene Scardamalia and Carl Bereiter, "Research on Written Composition," in *Handbook of Research on Teaching*, 3rd ed., a project of the American Educational Research Association, ed. Merlin C. Wittrock, (New York: Macmillan, 1986), p. 778.

26. Robert J. Tierney, John E. Readence, and Ernest K. Dishner, *Reading Strategies and Practices—A Compendium*, 3rd ed. (Boston: Allyn and Bacon, 1990), p. 259.

27. Marilyn Smith and Thomas W. Bean, "Four Strategies That Develop Children's Story Comprehension and Writing," *The Reading Teacher* 37 (1983): 295.

28. June Cannell Birnbaum, "Reflective Thought: The Connection Between Reading and Writing," in *Convergences—Transactions in Reading and Writing*, ed. Bruce T. Petersen (Urbana, Illinois: National Council of Teachers of English, 1986), p. 30.

29. Ibid., p. 31.

30. Sandra Stotsky, "Research on Reading/Writing Relationships: A Synthesis and Suggested Directions," *Language Arts* 60 (1983): 628.

31. Ibid., 628–631

32. Ibid., 636.

33. Krashen, *Writing—Research, Theory, and Applications*, pp. 4–6, 8–12.

34. Barbara Eckhoff, "How Reading Affects Children's Writing," in *Composing and Comprehending*, ed. Julie M. Jensen (Urbana, Illinois: ERIC Clearinghouse on Reading and Communication Skills, 1984), pp. 105–109.

35. Krashen, *Writing—Research, Theory, and Applications*, p. 11.

36. Sister M. Joan Lickteig, "Research-Based Recommendations for Teachers of Writing," *Language Arts* 58 (1981): 45.

37. Ibid., 46.

38. Ibid., 48.

39. Charles R. Cooper, "Holistic Evaluation of Writing," in *Evaluating Writing: Describing, Measuring, Judging*, eds. Charles R. Cooper and Lee Odell (Urbana, Illinois: National Council of Teachers of English, 1977), p. 3.

40. Ibid., pp. 4–14.

41. Carol Greenhalgh and Donna Townsend, "Evaluating Students' Writing Holistically— An Alternative Approach," *Language Arts* 58 (1981): 811–814.

42. Ibid., 814–15.

43. Ibid., 816.

44. Ibid., 817.

45. Ibid., 818.

46. Ibid., 822.

47. Kellogg W. Hunt, "Recent Measures in Syntactic Development," *Elementary English* 43 (1966): 732–733.

48. Ibid.

49. Kellogg W. Hunt, "Early Blooming and Late Blooming Syntactic Structures," in *Evaluating Writing: Describing, Measuring, Judging* eds. Charles R. Cooper and Lee Odell (Urbana, Illinois: National Council of Teachers of English, 1977), pp. 95–96.

50. Paul C. Burns, *Assessment and Correction of Language Arts Difficulties* (Columbus, Ohio: Charles E. Merrill, 1980), p. 150.

51. Ibid., 154.

52. Shawn M. Glynn, "Computer Environments for Managing Writers," in *Computer Writing Environments—Theory, Research, & Design*, Bruce K. Britton and Shawn M. Glynn (Hillsdale, New Jersey: Lawrence Erlbaum Associates, 1989), p. 1.

53. Olga Howard Fischer and Chester A. Fischer, "Electrifying the Composing Process: Electronic Workplaces and the Teaching of Writing," *Journal of Teaching Writing* 4 (1985): 114.

54. Ibid., 115.

55. Ibid., 116.

56. Ibid., 117–118.

57. Ibid., 118.

58. Ibid., 119–120.

59. Ibid., 119.

60. Gerald L. Fowler, "Developing Comprehension Skills in Primary Students Through the Use of Story Frames," *The Reading Teacher*, 36 (1982): 177.

61. Ibid.

62. Ibid.

63. Joseph A. Alvarez, *Elements of Composition* (New York: Harcourt Brace Jovanovich, 1985), p. 238.

64. Ibid. pp. 243–244.

65. Dorothy Grant Hennings and Barbara Moll Grant, *Written Expression in the Language Arts, Ideas and Skills*, 2nd Ed. (New York: Teachers College Press, 1981), p. 158.

66. Fischer and Fischer, "Electrifying the Composing Process," p. 117.

67. Tennessee Department of Education, *Basic Skills First, Language Arts Curriculum Guide, Written Composition Skills*, (Nashville, Tennessee, 1984), Skill Number 63317, Grade Six.

68. Bergman, Eldo W. Jr., *The Bridge*, (Houston, Texas: Intelligent Learning Systems, 1990), p. 1.

69. Ibid.

70. Ibid., p. 2.

71. Donald H. Graves, *Writing: Teachers and Children at Work* (Portsmouth, New Hampshire: Heinemann Educational Books, 1983), p. 12.

72. Ibid., pp. 12–13.

73. Robert E. Slavin, Nancy A. Madden, and Robert J. Stevens, "Cooperative Learning Models for the 3 R's," *Educational Leadership* 47 (1990): 24–27.

74. David W. Johnson, Roger T. Johnson, and Edythe Johnson Holubec, *Cooperation in the Classroom* (Edina, Minnesota: Interaction Book Company,) 1990, p. 4:25.

75. Ibid.

Bibliography

(Technology)

Collins, James L. and Sommers, Elizabeth A. *Writing On-Line—Using Computers in the Teaching of Writing* (Upper Montclair, New Jersey: Boynton/Cook Publishers, 1985.)

Olson, Nancy S. "Using the New Technologies in Language Communication Education," In *Speaking and Writing, K–12, Classroom Strategies and the New Research*, edited by Christopher Thaiss and Charles Suhor (Urbana, Illinois: National Council of Teachers of English, 1984), pp. 188–207.

Solomon, Gwen. *Children, Writing, and Computers, An Activities Guide.* (Englewood Cliffs, New Jersey: Prentice-Hall, 1986).

(Evaluating/Revising Writing/Correcting Problems)

Brown, Jane Lightcap. "Helping Students Help Themselves: Peer Evaluation of Writing," *Curriculum Review* 23 (1984): 47.

Haley-James, Shirley M., "Revising Writing in the Upper Grades," *Language Arts* 58 (1981): 562.

Moffett, James and Wagner, Betty Jane. "Evaluating," Chapter 21 in *Student-Centered Language Arts and Reading, K–13—a Handbook for Teachers,* 2nd ed. by Moffett and Wagner (Boston: Houghton Mifflin, 1976) pp. 415–435.

Shaughnessy, Mina P., *Errors & Expectations—A Guide for the Teacher of Basic Writing* (New York: Oxford University Press, 1977).

Simmons, Jay, "Portfolios as Large-Scale Assessment," *Language Arts* 67 (1990): 262.

(Teaching Strategies/ Organization)

Hall, Nigel and Duffy, Rose. "Every Child Has a Story to Tell," *Language Arts* 64 (1987): 523.

Olson, Gary A. ed., *Writing Centers—Theory and Administration* (Urbana, Illinois: National Council of Teachers of English, 1984).

Suhor, Charles, "Thinking Visually about Writing: Three Models for Teaching Composition, K–12," In *Speaking and Writing, K–12, Classroom Strategies and the New Research,* edited by Christopher Thaiss and Charles Suhor (Urbana, Illinois: National Council of Teachers of English, 1984), pp. 74–103.

(Research/Writing Development in Children)

Farr, Marcia. "Writing Growth in Young Children: What We Are Learning from Research," In *Speaking and Writing, K–12, Classroom Strategies and the New Research,* edited by Christopher Thaiss and Charles Suhor (Urbana, Illinois: National Council of Teachers of English, 1984), pp. 126–143.

Harris, John and Wilkinson, John. *Reading Children's Writing—A Linguistic View* (London: Allen and Unwin, 1986).

Kamil, Michael L.; Langer, Judith A.; and Shanahan, Timothy. *Understanding Research in Reading and Writing* (Boston: Allyn and Bacon, 1985).

Temple, Charles; Ruth, Nathan; Burris, Nancy; and Temple, Frances. *The Beginnings of Writing* 2nd ed. (Boston: Allyn and Bacon, 1990).

(Miscellaneous Topics)

Duin, Ann Hill. "Implementing Cooperative Learning Groups in the Writing Curriculum," *Journal of Teaching Writing* 5 (1986): 315.

6

A Corrective Approach
to Handwriting Instruction

Focus

Handwriting serves somewhat the same purpose in written composition that spelling does. Both are taught because they help students communicate more efficiently through the medium of writing. At one time, handwriting was taught more as an art form than it is today. Beautiful penmanship was a desired attribute, and teachers devoted a considerable number of hours during the school week to handwriting. Today, the focus has shifted from beautiful penmanship to legibility. Thus, handwriting is seen as important, but attention given to it in the curriculum is more correctly focused on the proper role it serves in the total writing program.

In Chapter 6, attention will first be directed toward the handwriting curriculum and organization for handwriting as found in today's schools. Following this brief introduction, research of significance to a student-involved corrective approach to handwriting will be reviewed. Other major points to be covered in Chapter 6 include:

1. Analysis of handwriting errors made by students
2. How the handwriting curriculum can be organized to focus on a student-involved corrective program
3. How base and flex groups can be implemented in a handwriting program
4. How to modify evaluative techniques to make a handwriting program more corrective
5. The use of multidimensional materials and equipment for teaching handwriting in a corrective program

While reading Chapter 6, recall handwriting instruction that you had in grade school. Did you spend long hours practicing single letters? Did you have the same handwriting practice lesson as all other students in your class? Did you begin cursive (called *real* writing by children) at the same time that all others in your class started this form of writing, which is usually the second month of third grade? If you answer "yes" to these questions, you will find in this chapter that there are other ways of teaching handwriting which focus on more student-involvement and assessment/corrective strategies than did traditional strategies.

What is Taught in Handwriting Today?

The handwriting curriculum today is remarkably alike in schools throughout the United States. While some changes are beginning to take place as a result of some new forms of handwriting, the majority of schools still follow a curriculum that has six basic phases. These are:

1. Readiness for manuscript writing
2. Beginning of manuscript writing
3. Continuous development/maintenance of manuscript
4. Transition from manuscript to cursive writing
5. Beginning of cursive writing
6. Continuous development/maintenance of cursive form

Each broad phase of the handwriting curriculum is broken down into specific skills, concepts, and other components. Some school systems outline these thoroughly, while others depend primarily on the skill outlines of the commercial handwriting program that the school follows.

In Tables 6–1 and 6–2, three handwriting forms are shown. The first two forms are the well-known manuscript and cursive forms. In Table 6–2, a relatively new form, the D'Nealian Handwriting form, is shown. A number of school systems have moved from manuscript to D'Nealian handwriting in the primary grades because this form, made up of oval and slanted letters, is believed to be easier to transfer from than is the manuscript form.

While making the letters correctly in whatever form is being learned is a major legibility factor, there are several other factors that constitute legibility and will be used throughout this chapter. These are briefly defined:

1. *Spacing*—Spacing refers to spacing between words and spacing between letters. Both types of spacing are critical if handwriting is to be legible.

2. *Alignment*—Alignment is how letters are placed on the bottom guide or baseline and the appropriate height of the letters as they relate to the top guideline (headline), or the appropriate relationship of parts of the letters (such as, The horizontal stroke for some letters may be placed on the middle guideline.).

TABLE 6–1 Manuscript and Cursive Forms of Handwriting

(Manuscript)

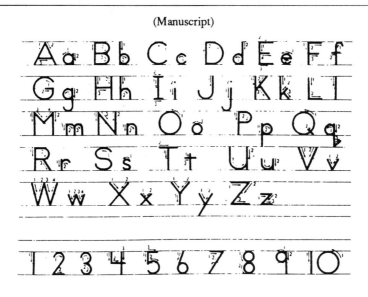

(Cursive)

Lower Case Cursive Alphabet

Upper Case Cursive Alphabet

Reprinted with permission of Macmillan/McGraw-Hill School Publishing Company from Palmer Method Handwriting, Grade 1 (Manuscript) and Grade 5 (Cursive), by Fred M. King. Copyright 1984.

TABLE 6–2   The D'Nealian ® Handwriting Alphabet

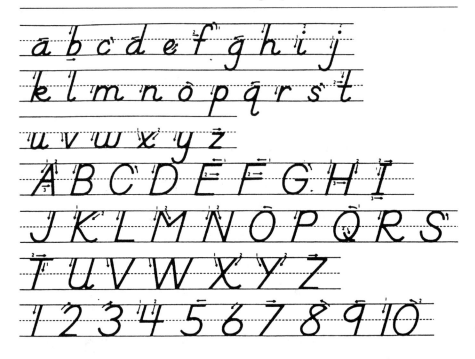

Donald Neal Thurber, "The D'Nealian® Handwriting Alphabet," *D'Nealian® Handwriting, Second Addition, K-Kindergarten* (Glenview, Illinois: Scott, Foresman and Company, 1987). Copyright (1987). Reprinted by permission of Scott, Foresman and Company.

3. *Slant*—Slant is the way in which a letter slopes to the right, away from the vertical or straight up-and-down position. Manuscript letters are designed to be completely vertical, while cursive and D'Nealian letters slant to the right.

4. *Uniformity*—Uniformity refers to the consistency of any of the legibility factors in handwriting. For example, consistency in pressure usually results in writing a letter which has uniform pencil or pen pressure as opposed to variations in pressure.

5. *Size*—Letter size refers to whether or not a letter is the size that it is intended to be. For example, "   " and "   " should both be the same size, coming to the middle guideline in manuscript writing.

In a later section of Chapter 6, each of these legibility factors will be explored. Focus will be on identifying the causes for problems with these factors and how to correct the problems.

Research of Significance to a Corrective Handwriting Program

Handwriting research is extensive and covers a broad spectrum of study. In particular, there are six areas which should be considered in building a student-involved corrective handwriting program. They are:

1. Copying letters from a model as an effective approach to initially learning how to make letters
2. Setting up individualized, corrective approaches for group instruction
3. Making evaluation of handwriting multidimensional
4. Using a variety of sensory modalities to provide instruction in handwriting
5. Identifying errors in both manuscript and cursive handwriting
6. Paying special attention to the problems of the left-handed writer

Research findings in these areas are presented as practices that should be followed in a corrective program. Where appropriate, some elaboration of the research is made to better understand the implications of the research.

Practice Number 1: Copying Letters From a Model to Initially Learn How to Make Letters

Askov and Peck state that the most common instructional technique for teaching new letter formation is copying of the letter by looking at a model, although such practice is more tradition oriented than research based. However, several studies have been done to compare copying with other techniques, such as tracing. In these studies, the superiority of copying was demonstrated. In one study (J. Williams, 1975), a need was demonstrated to have children learn copying of all letters rather than depending on transfer of what is learned from one letter to another.[1]

While copying of letters from a model should be the predominant way for children to initially learn to make letters, the question is still unanswered as to whether or not the model should be placed across the chalkboard or placed on a plane that is the same as the paper on which students write. For students having trouble following a model, a copy of the letter being learned might be taped to the desk. Not only can the student more readily see the strokes and the sequence in which they appear, the model is more personalized.

Another technique for initially learning how to make each letter is connecting dots. While this alternative procedure, like tracing, has not proven to be as effective as copying of letters from looking at a model, these procedures still may be of use when a student is having extreme difficulty in forming a troublesome letter by copying. Teachers should be willing to use these techniques, especially tracing, when copying appears to have failed.

Practice Number 2: Setting up Individualized, Corrective Approaches for Group Instruction

There has been some research to indicate that students should not be taught the same lesson at the same time. Yet, too often the whole class is provided instruction in just that way, even though teachers recognize that wide differences in ability to form letters exist among students.

Over the years, a number of studies suggest that there is an advantage in setting up and following an "individualized, diagnostic-prescriptive" procedure for teaching handwriting. The results of these studies suggest that there should be a limit placed on teaching the same handwriting lesson to all students at the same time.[2]

Practice Number 3: Making Evaluation of Handwriting Multidimensional

Froese states that 70 percent of schools depend on teacher observation as a way to evaluate handwriting.[3] While admitting that procedures for evaluating handwriting are "largely unresolved," Froese further states that some value can be derived from the use of scales if their current use is modified. The work of J. Noble (1965), L. Ayres (1957), F. Freeman (1959) and P. West (1957) has promoted the use of scales for handwriting assessment. When such scales are used, each student's writing samples are judged against or matched with the quality of the work in the scales.

To make scales more diagnostic in nature, Froese points out that:

> . . . *it is possible to adapt the scaling idea to more localized conditions and obtain diagnostic information as well. A teacher or group of teachers collect many samples of handwriting for each grade level and then sort them in to several categories of global legibility, i.e., excellent, very good, good, fair, poor). From each category, one or two representative samples are mounted as the models to be used for comparison. For each level, a range of attributes (uniformity of slant and size, letter formation, alignment, etc.) may be illustrated. The teacher then assigns a value of 5 to 1 for each attribute and compiles the total score for an overall rating.*[4]

Practice Number 4: Using a Variety of Sensory Modalities to Provide Instruction in Handwriting

Although several studies indicate the value of using various sensory modalities to provide handwriting instruction, B. Furner's work is perhaps best known. Her studies demonstrated that visual cues for forming letters are enhanced through verbalization, leading to the conclusion that handwriting is a perceptual, not just a motor, skill. In B. Furner's studies, students were taught to verbalize the starting points for each stroke in letters being formed, the direction of the strokes, the size of the letter being made, and the stopping point of each stroke.[5] N. Sovik's studies also demonstrated that, "verbal instruction combined with demonstration improves copying performance."[6]

When verbalization and visualization are combined in handwriting lessons, learning styles of students are being given more attention. Coupled with attention to hand movements required in handwriting instruction, the attention to learning styles increases considerably.

Practice Number 5: Identifying Errors in Both Manuscript and Cursive Handwriting

Several studies have led to documentation of the most common types of handwriting errors in manuscript and cursive writing. In an early study by T. Newland, it was found that only 14 forms of illegibility accounted for 50 percent of all elementary and high school illegibilities. The study revealed that four letters (*a, e, r,* and *t*) are among the most frequently-occurring letters and account for most of the illegibilities in cursive writing.[7] In L. Horton's study of sixth graders' handwriting, it was revealed that six letters (*h, i, k, p, z,* and *r*) accounted for nearly one-third (30 percent) of illegibilities in writing. In E. Lewis and H. Lewis' study of difficult manuscript letters for first graders, it was revealed that lowercase *q, g, p, y, j, m,* and *k* were the most difficult for students whose papers were examined. Of the uppercase letters, *U, G, R, Y, M,* and *S* were the most difficult.[8]

Teachers, armed with knowledge of the most prevalent handwriting errors, should be able to do some "preventive teaching." An example is the descending manuscript letters (*q, p, g, y,* and *j*) which, as cited, are among the most troublesome letters to make. Before these letters are introduced to students, special attention should be given to how strokes of each letter are made. Students might be asked to do more verbalization of each stroke, with the teacher highlighting how each stroke is made by using different colored marking pens on overhead transparencies or large charts (use of green for the first stroke to indicate "go" and red for the last stroke to indicate "stop"). More coaching and/or one-on-one instruction might be given than normally would be given. Students might do more checking of how they have formed these letters, using such devices as plastic overlays of the letters.

Practice Number 6: Paying Special Attention to the Problems of the Left-Handed Writer

In a well-known study of left-handed writers, the most effective hand-arm position was determined. Quality of the writing product, rate of writing, ability to produce neat, smear-free papers, and healthful body posture were considered. The most efficient left-handed position was number one shown in Figure 6–1, followed by position number two. The most troublesome position was the hook position, shown as position number three in Figure 6–1.

Alston and Taylor state that for left-handed writers:

1. *The paper is placed to the left of the body midline*
2. *The paper is tilted approximately 32 degrees to the right*
3. *The paper is supported by the right hand*
4. *The writing tool is held in a below-the-line position*
5. *The writing tool is held sufficiently far from the point to enable the writer to see what he is writing*
6. *The writing tool allows smooth movement across the paper.*[9]

Among several tips for left-handed writers, given by the Zaner-Bloser Company, is the advice of having students write at the chalkboard. Such practice

(Most Efficient Position..Number 1)

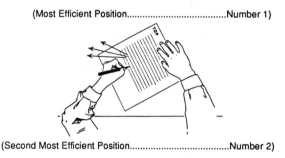

(Second Most Efficient Position.....................................Number 2)

(Least Efficient Position.....................................Number 3)

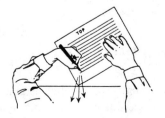

FIGURE 6–1 Most Efficient and Least Efficient Positions for Writing with the Left Hand

Jean Alston and Jane Taylor, *Handwriting-Theory, Research, and Practice* (London: Croom Helm, 1987) pp. 86–87. Reprinted by permission of Routledge Publishing Company.

". . . is important because it lends itself to full, free arm movement and allows both the student and the teacher to easily spot incorrect habits."[10] For the left-hander who has already established the hooked position for writing, an aid or frame has been developed by the Zaner-Bloser Company (Diagram 6–1).

The Handwriting Curriculum

In setting up a student-involved corrective handwriting program, one should begin with some of the myths or fallacies now existing in the elementary school. One, referred to earlier, is the myth that all children should have the same lesson at the same time each day of the year. It is not uncommon to find all students in a classroom at the same time copying the same sets of sentences from the chalkboard or a copybook. A second fallacy is that all students should change from manuscript to cursive at the same time, regardless of students' progress in manuscript.

The handwriting curriculum should be organized in such a way that students move through the curriculum at individual speeds, although small clusters of students should be grouped for instruction in common areas of the curriculum and/or on similar problems.

The same broad bands of the language arts curriculum earlier advocated for spelling and written composition should be observed for handwriting instruction. These are *Developing a Background for Formal Handwriting, Formal Handwriting: Introductory, Formal Handwriting: Intermediate,* and *Formal Handwriting: Advanced.* Some special emphases in each area are given as follows:

Stage 1, Developing Background: Attention is focused on readiness for manuscript which includes making various shapes that parallel the basic strokes of this form of writing. Attention is also given to scribbling, drawing, eye-hand coordination, learning alphabet letters, and concepts such as "touching the line" and left to right.

Stage 2, Formal Handwriting, Introductory: Students learn how to make letters in groups with similar strokes, such as straight-line or *i l t* letters. The functional aspect of handwriting is emphasized, with students moving as quickly as possible to

DIAGRAM 6–1 A Writing Frame for Helping Left-Handed Writers

Reprinted with permission from the publisher, Zaner-Bloser, Columbus, OH).

word and sentence writing. Various legibility factors (alignment, spacing, and so on) are introduced. Attention is given to proofreading letter forms made by students.

Stage 3, Formal Handwriting, Intermediate: Students begin to transition to cursive handwriting, moving through several readiness procedures for what students call "real writing." Students move through an orderly series of cursive letter clusters, and the focus is on using the letters, not just making them. Proofreading and checking of errors continue, with the students as key players.

Stage 4, Formal Handwriting, Advanced: Maintenance of cursive writing continues, but with some attention to maintaining manuscript forms (Please print activities). Students learn to show individuality in their handwriting, but continue to write legibly. Monitoring of all legibility factors continues.

Error Analysis in Handwriting

Factors other than letter formation leading to illegibility in handwriting include such errors as retracing, lack of alignment, and incorrect size of letters. One study which continues to be repeated in current literature, was conducted by Lewis and Lewis and dealt with first-graders' performance in manuscript.[11] In Table 6–3, each type of error, an example of the error, and a brief description of the error are shown. Specific errors found in the Lewis and Lewis study included:

1. *The letters* N, d, q, *and* y *were the most frequently* reversed *letters.*
2. *The letter* m *had the greatest number of* partial omissions, *followed by* U *and* I.
3. Incorrect size *was the most frequent type of error. Although more evenly distributed among the letters than any other type of error, it was more prevalent among the descending letters,* p, g, y, q, *and* j.
4. *Letters most frequently misshaped were* j, G, *and* J.
5. Incorrect relationship of parts of letters *was a common error and occurred most frequently in* k, R, a, M, *and* m *in decreasing order of frequency.*
6. Incorrect placement relative to line *was a common error in the descending letters but less frequent in other letters.*
7. Additions *were more frequent in letters* q, C, k, m, *and* Y.
8. *Errors were more common where curves and vertical lines merge* (J, U, f, h, j, m, n, r, *and* u).
9. *Boys were more prone to error than were girls.*[12]

TABLE 6–3   Errors Made in Manuscript by First Graders

Errors	Description	Example(s)
1. Reversal	the mirror image of a letter form	Ͷ for N
2. Partial omission	any part of a letter form missing	ı for i
3. Addition	inclusion of a part not shown on the model	ɤ for y
4. Incorrect relationship of parts	any letter in which a part is not correctly oriented	K, Δ, Є
5. Incorrect size of letter form or parts of it	a letter form (or part) that is too large or too small in relation to the guide lines	̄є̲F̲ı̲Ħ̲
6. Incorrect placement relative to line	incorrect orientation to the writing line	G̲c̲h̲
7. Misshapenness	distortion of all or part of a letter form	_є̱ for e
8. Rotation	a letter form rotated more than 15 degrees from an imaginary line drawn vertically through its axis	_ɤ
9. Retracing	any letter form (or part) that has been reconstructed after an initial effort	̱ẖ, O̱
10. Inversion	any letter form upside down	⊥ for F
11. Total omission	any letter form not attempted	

Edward R. Lewis and Hilda P. Lewis, "An Analysis of Errors in the Formation of Manuscript Letters by First-Grade Children," *American Educational Research Journal* 2 (1965), p. 27. Copyright (1965) by the American Educational Research Association. Adapted by permission of the publisher.

The easiest letters to make, as expected, had the fewest errors. These were *l, o, L, O,* and *H*.[13] These letters are easy to make because they are composed of the simplest strokes, (vertical and horizontal lines), and the "o" requires no merging of different kinds of strokes.

In a study that was more recent than the Lewis and Lewis study, R. Stennett, P. Smithe, and M. Hardy report that their K–3 subjects had more trouble copying lowercase manuscript letters than uppercase letters. The most difficult letters for the subjects in this study were *r, u, h,* and *t* which have been identified as letters requiring more visuomotor control. The easiest letters to make were *o, l, s,* and *c,* all letters made with a single stroke.[14]

The Horton study on illegibilities of sixth graders' writing is one of the most recent studies in which errors in cursive writing were identified. Over 1000 specimens of writing were collected. As reported earlier, *h, i, k, p, z,* and *r* accounted for 30 percent of all errors made.[15] While Horton primarily concentrated on error malformations (of lowercase letters only), some information was provided about left-handed versus right-handed boys and girls. This information, plus some additional information on errors made in general, follow:

1. *Errors on forming letters* a, b, c, i, l, m, n, u, v, *and* x *accounted for only 12 percent of the total errors made by the group studied (compared to* r *which alone accounted for 12 percent of the errors made).*

2. *Left-handed boys made a higher percentage of illegibilities than did any other group, with letters* d, e, h, z, g, n, q, *and* r *presenting the most trouble for these students.*

3. *Left-handed girls had more trouble with* r, o, h, *and* q *than with other letters.*

4. *Right-handed boys had the most difficulty with formation of letters* r *and* g, *with malformations of these two letters accounting for 25 percent of these pupils' problems.*

5. *Right-handed girls had more trouble with* r, h, *and* z *than with other letters. Problems with these three letters accounted for 37 percent of the problems of this group.*[16]

Case #1   Major Problems

Spacing between
  words (not enough)
Some misformed
  letters

Case #2

Spacing between
  words (too much
  space)

Case #3

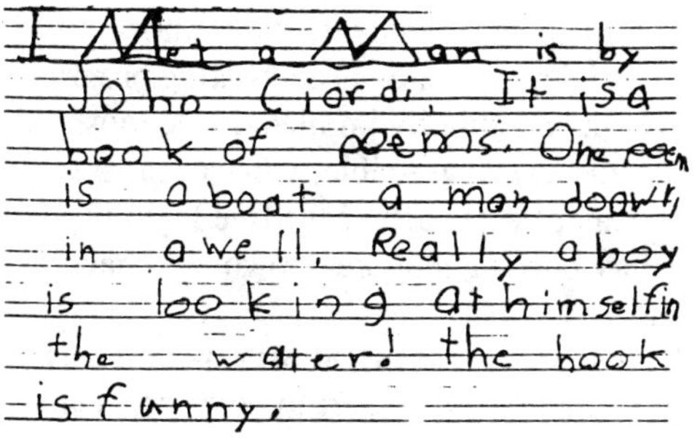

Alignment
Spacing between
letters

Case #4

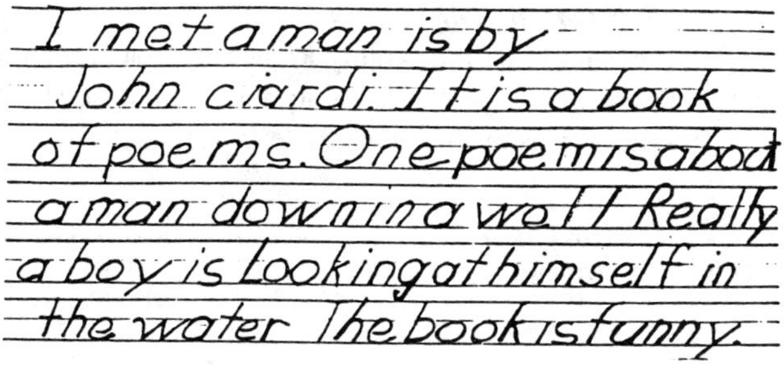

Slant (letters tend to
slant instead of
being straight)
Spacing between
words

Case #5

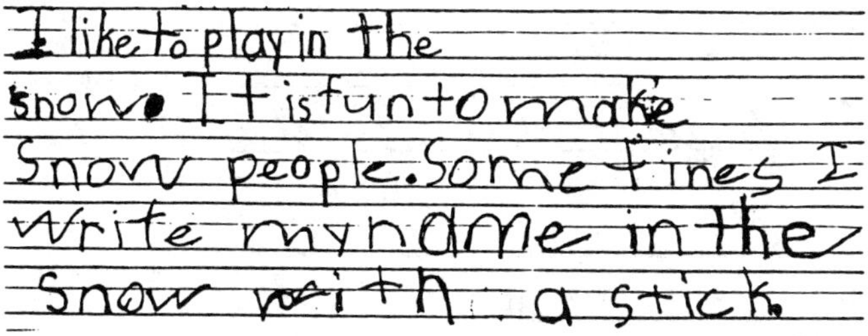

Inconsistent
arrangement on
line (words
bunched together
and then spread
out)
Some misformed
letters
Alignment

Case #6

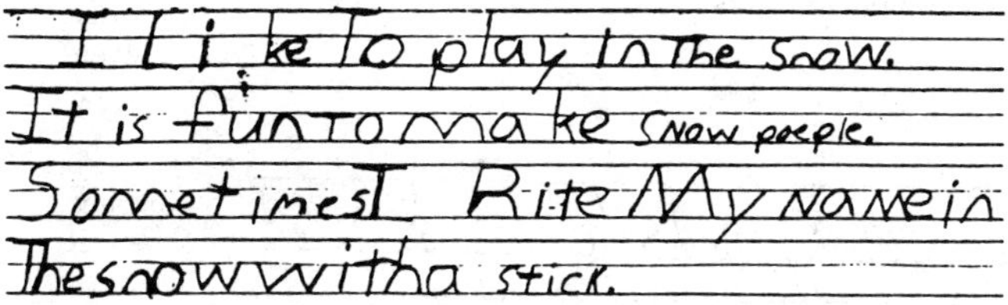

Spacing between
words
Spacing between
letters
Inconsistent letter
size

FIGURE 6–2   Problems with Legibility Factors in Manuscript Handwriting

Note: These examples of manuscript writing are from second grade students at the beginning of the
eighth month of the school year.

Assessment of Other Legibility Problems

The legibility factors identified earlier—spacing, alignment, slant, uniformity in writing, and letter size—must be given special attention in a handwriting program. The first step is to determine specifically which legibility problem is the most critical. The second step is to determine, to the extent possible, what is causing the problem. In Figures 6–2 to 6–4, several examples of each of the five legibility factors in manuscript, cursive, and D'Nealian handwriting are shown. For each legibility factor, several problems that occur are given.

These examples do not exhaust the variations that might exist within each of the problems depicted. Teachers should continuously be alert to other problems or variations of the five problems identified.

Identifying Probable Causes of Handwriting Difficulties

Causes of handwriting illegibilities should be thoroughly known by teachers in a student-involved corrective handwriting program. In Table 6–4, four illegibility factors/problems in manuscript writing, reasons for their existence, and activities to

D'Nealian Writing	Major Problems
Case #1 *She went home because she thought it was dinner time. Will Daddy be gone when I get up?*	Alignment (especially within middle guideline)
Case #2 *Did you take a boat ride in the fall? I made three cakes and five pies.*	Letter size (uneven) Spacing between words (uneven)
Case #3 *I think I saw his lost dog. She went home because she thought it was dinnertime.*	Spacing between words (Not enough space)

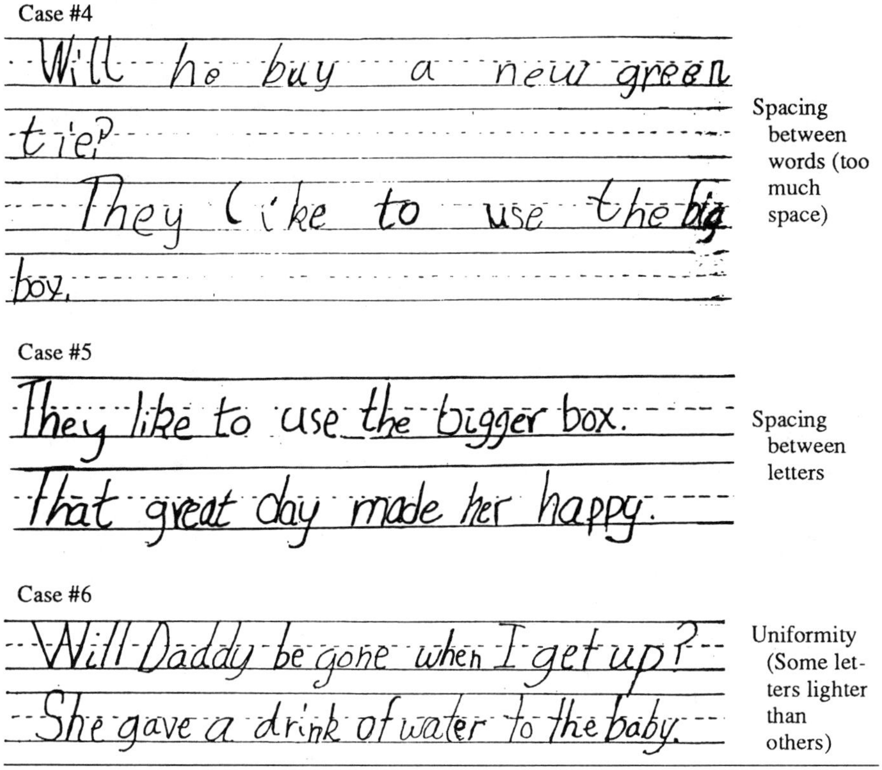

Case #4

Spacing between words (too much space)

Case #5

Spacing between letters

Case #6

Uniformity (Some letters lighter than others)

FIGURE 6–3 Problems with Legibility Factors of Students Using the D'Nealian® Form of Handwriting

Note: These examples of handwriting are from second-grade students at the end of the seventh month of the school year.

correct the problems, as defined by one company, are shown.[17] In Table 6–5, six illegibility factors/problems in cursive writing, probable causes, and activities to correct the problems, are shown.[18]

An example of yet another identified set of problems with cursive writing and solutions for correcting the problems is shown in Table 6–6. Hackney, the author of this chart, calls on teachers to know the eleven common problems and corrective strategies in working with students "in the later grades."[19] Hackney also calls for teachers to: (1) set a clear standard through modeling good handwriting themselves; (2) have desk strips that show correct letter formation; (3) have students rewrite assignments turned in if the writing is unacceptable; and (4) get students to evaluate their own handwriting, including each legibility factor such as size, shape, slant, spacing, and smoothness.[20]

Major Problems

Case #1

Snow

One day I was doing my work at school and I saw snow and I quit doing my work.

Inconsistency in
letter size
Mixed slant/no
slant

Case #2

Spring - Break

I bet everyone loves Spring. You get to sleep. You get to go places. You get to play in the leaves. What I like best is to go swimming. Now that is what I like abot Spring Break.

Mixed letter size
Incorrect size of
letters
(especially t's)

Case #3

Pledge to The Flag

"I pledge adgiance to the flag of the United States of america and to the republic for which it stands, one nation under God, indivisible with liberty for all".

Spacing between
words (uneven
spacing)
Spacing between
letters-messy
Mixed slant
(slight)

Case #4

Pledge to the Flag

I pledge allegiance to the flag of the United States of America and to the republic for which it stands one nation under God individual with liberty and justice for all

Alignment
Misformed letters

Case #5

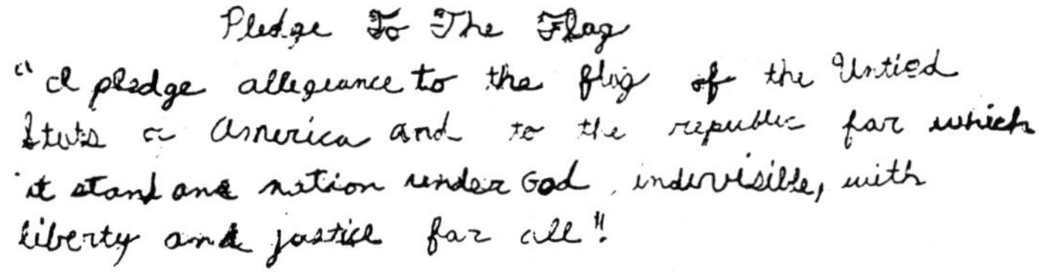

Line quality
Letter size (too
small)

Case #6

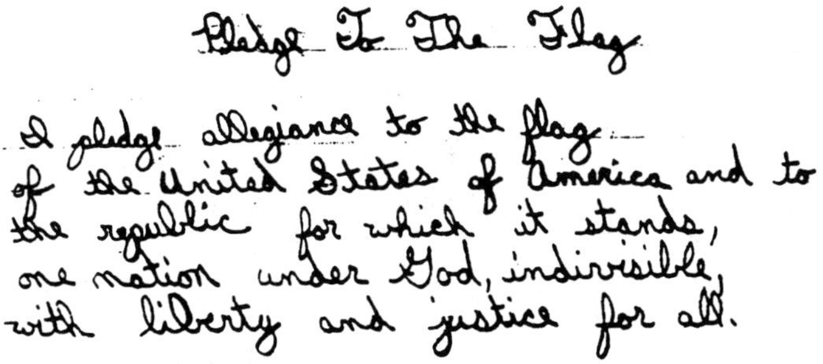

Incorrect slant
(tendency to
left)
Spacing between
words
(too much in
some cases)

Case #7

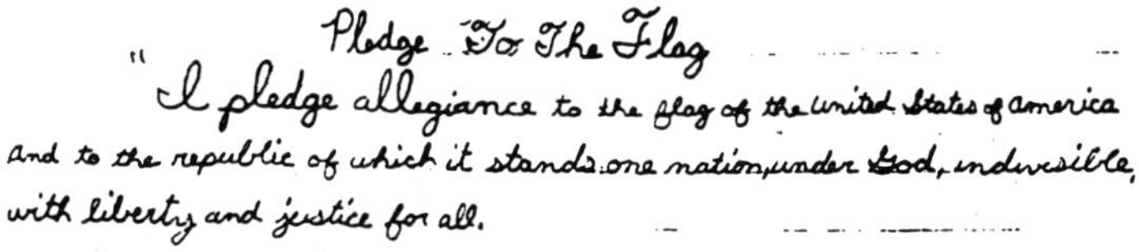

Letter size (too
small)

Case #8

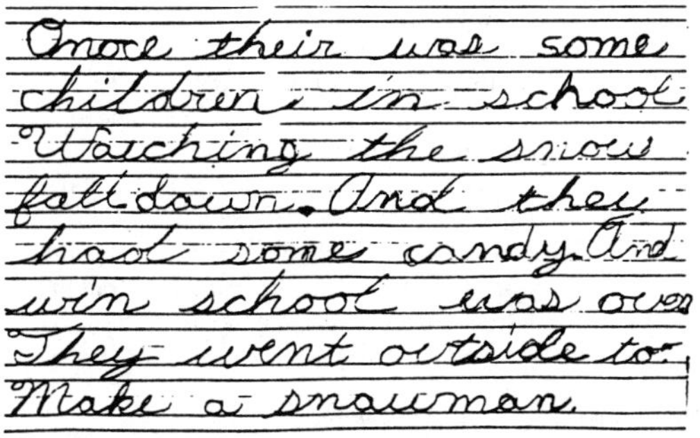

Letter size (too
large)

FIGURE 6–4   Problems with Legibility Factors in Cursive Handwriting

Note: These examples of cursive writing are from fourth-grade students at the beginning of the seventh
month of the school year.

TABLE 6–4   Handwriting Diagnostic and Prescriptive Chart (Manuscript)

Factor	Problem	Reason	Remediation
Size	Too small	Pencil held too close to the point	Have the pupils hold the writing instrument 3/4" to an inch from the point
		Over-emphasis of finger movement	Check hand-pencil and arm-desk positions; stress arm movement
		Improper concept of writing lines	Point out how the various letters fit between the designated lines
		Poor mental image of letter size	Revert to chalkboard activity, reteaching problem letters
	Too large	Exaggerated arm movement	Emphasize finger control, reduce arm movement
		Improper concept of writing lines	Point out how the various letters fit between the designated lines
		Poor mental image of letter size	Revert to chalkboard activity, reteaching problem letters
Shape	Too wide	Over-emphasis of arm movement	Stress finger movement; check arm-desk movement
	Too narrow	Finger-writing	Stress arm movement; check arm-desk position
Space	Crowded letters in words	Poor understanding of space concept	Reteach uniform spacing between letters in words and between words in a sentence (finger or pencil width)
	Too much space between letters	Improper letter size and shape	Review these concepts by having pupils closely follow given word models
	Erratic spacing between words	Poor understanding of space concept	Fold paper in quarters down the length of the paper. Have students then write the same word in each quarter of the page filling the space from fold to fold. (3 or 4 letter words are most appropriate for manuscript writers.)
Alignment	Letters not sitting on baseline	Poor understanding of baseline function	Demonstrate how various letters sit on the baseline, especially those with descending strokes. Also stress bringing the straight line strokes all the way down to the baseline.
	Inconsistent heights of relative letters	Poor understanding of size concept	Review groupings of letter sizes in relationship to the lines on writing paper

Bowmar/Noble Publishers, "Handwriting Diagnostic and Prescriptive Chart, Manuscript Writing," (Los Angeles: Bowmar/Noble Publishers) 1 (Reprinted with permission of the Macmillan Company).

TABLE 6–5   Handwriting Diagnostic and Prescriptive Chart (Cursive)

Factor	Problem	Reason	Remediation
Size	Too small	Pencil held too close to the point	Have the pupils hold the writing instrument 3/4" to an inch from the point
		Over-emphasis of finger movement	Check hand-pencil and arm-desk positions; stress arm movement
		Improper concept of writing lines	Point out how the various letters fit between the designated lines
		Poor mental image of letter size	Revert to chalkboard activity, reteaching problem letters
	Too large	Exaggerated arm movement	Emphasize finger control, reduce arm movement
		Improper concept of writing lines	Point out how the various letters fit between the designated lines
		Poor mental image of letter size	Revert to chalkboard activity, reteaching problem letters
Shape	Too wide	Over-emphasis of arm-movement	Stress finger movement; check arm-desk movement
	Too narrow	Finger-writing	Stress arm movement; check arm-desk position
Line Quality	Too light	Improper writing pressure	Demonstrate desired line quality; check hand-pencil position
	Too heavy	Excessive finger pressure on pencil	Place wadded paper in palm of writing hand to relax grip
	Shaky lines	Movement too slow	Increase speed; check hand-pencil position
Space	Crowded letters in words	Too much slant	Demonstrate letters that utilize a downstroke; emphasize parallel uniformity
		Finger movement	Check hand-pencil and arm-desk positions; stress arm movement
		Failure to move paper	Advise students to keep their writing within their line of vision
	Too much space between letters in words	Too little slant	Demonstrate letters that utilize a downstroke; emphasize parallel uniformity
		Exaggerated arm movement	Check arm-desk position for over-movement of forearm
	Irregular spacing between words	Long beginning and end strokes	Have the students curve beginning and ending strokes on a standard slant
		Poor understanding of between word spacing	Stress that spacing between words should be the width of a small "o"

TABLE 6–5 *Continued*

Alignment	Writing above the baseline	Paper too straight	Check all positions, stress good writing habits and point out that all letters must sit on the baseline
	Writing below the baseline	Paper too slanted	
	Irregular alignment	Not enough movement of paper	Move paper to enable student to keep the writing directly in the line of vision
	Uneven heights of relative letters	Poor understanding of size concept	Review how the various families of letters fit between the writing lines
Slant	Too little	Improper positioning of the paper	Check paper-desk position. If the writing runs uphill, you may not have the paper turned enough. If it goes downhill, the paper is too much on a slant to accommodate the natural sideward motion of the hand and arm*
	Too much		
	Lack of slant uniformity	No movement of the paper	Move paper often enough to keep the writing directly in the line of vision
	Back slant	Lefthandedness	Check paper-desk, hand-arm, and pencil-finger positions. Have the student hold the pencil an inch to an inch and one-half from the point, thus allowing him or her to see over his or her hand to observe what is being written.

Bowmar/Noble Publishers, "Handwriting Diagnostic and Prescriptive Chart, Cursive Writing," (Los Angeles: Bowmar/Noble Publishers) 2–3 (Reprinted with permission of the Macmillan Company).

*After proper angularity of the paper for both the right- and left-handed students has been accomplished, emphasize the following regarding downstrokes:
    1) For right-handed students, this stroke should be pulled toward the center of the body.
    2) In the case of left-handed students, it should be pulled to the left elbow.

TABLE 6–6 Corrective Strategies for Common Problems in Cursive Handwriting

Handwriting is so small that it cannot be read easily.	When two maximum undercurves are joined (**ll**, **fl**), letter formation suffers.
too small	*parallel*
• Use ruled paper with a midline, or rule a midline on standard writing paper. Explain that minimum letters touch the midline.	• Emphasize that the undercurve stroke must be made correctly.
• Practice large writing at the chalkboard or on the classified ads section of the newspaper.	• Make slant strokes parallel to each other.

The height of the lowercase letters is not consistent.

Write freely

- Use paper that has midline, or rule a midline on standard paper.
- Have the student identify maximum, intermediate, and minimum letters.
- Evaluate writing for size by drawing a horizontal line across the tops of the letters that are supposed to be of the same height.

The maximum letters (**b, f, h, k, l**) are made without loops.

little

- Demonstrate and explain proper formation of undercurve that begins loop of letter.
- Demonstrate and explain proper formation of the slant stroke.

The slant of the writing is irregular

flight

- Check for correct paper position.
- Pull strokes in the proper direction.
- Shift paper as writing progresses.
- Evaluate slant by drawing lines through letters to show the angle at which they are made.

When an undercurve joins an overcurve (**in, um**) the letters are poorly written.

instrument

- Show how the undercurve to overcurve is a smooth, flowing doublecurve
- Explain that the undercurve ending continues up and then quickly overcurves into the downward slant stroke.

The spacing of the writing changes within a single word.

laboratory

- Shift both the paper and the hand as the writing progresses. The paper moves toward the student, and the hand moves away.
- Improve the joinings and you automatically improve spacing.

The letters **a, d, g, o,** and **q** are not closed

bout amount

- Begin the downcurve stroke at the one o'clock position.
- Practice deep undercurve strokes to connect with the downcurve strokes.

Non-looped letters (e.g., **i, t, w, d**) are looped and become difficult to read.

little

- Emphasize the stop at the top of these letters before starting the retrace.
- Emphasize the retraces in these strokes.

Checkstroke joinings (e. g., **br, we**) are poorly made.

break weather

- Demonstrate the letters **b, v, o,** and **w** and explain the strokes as you form them.
- Demonstrate correct joinings in which the first letter has a checkstroke.
- Point out the letterforms that change when they are preceded by a checkstroke: **br, os.**

Joinings involving overcurves, such as **ga** and **jo,** are not well made.

baggage job

- Show how the overcurve connections cross at the baseline, not above or below it.
- Make the overcurve motion continuous. Do not change its direction in midstroke.

Clinton S. Hackney, "Corrective Strategies for Common Problems in Cursive Handwriting," Reprinted with permission from the publisher, Zaner-Bloser, Columbus, OH.

Tables such as 6–4, 6–5, and 6–6 can be used as sources for developing an easy-to-use card-file system on handwriting problems and what to do about them. A card file for mixed or irregular slant might contain the information cited in Diagram 6–2, which comes from Tables 6–4 to 6–6 (with some modifications/extensions). It should be noted that in some of these checkpoints (*1, 2, 3, 4, 5,* and *8*), the teacher is asked to observe student behaviors in handwriting. In two (*6* and *7*) students are asked to self-analyze their writing.

Organizing for Instruction

Handwriting is one of the easiest language arts to adapt to the kind of organizational structure advocated in this book. Students in any elementary school classroom, with their differences in handwriting abilities and achievements, can easily be divided into base groups. As individual problems are identified across base groups, it is easy to cluster the problems according to instructional needs and thus to form flex groups.

Forming Base Groups in Handwriting

Base groups permit clusters of students to be grouped for the same general instruction for much of a given week. The teacher in a corrective classroom should determine which students can be placed in the same group, ready to be taught at a similar level in the curriculum. Some ways that this can be done are:

1. Checklists that parallel a curriculum or portion of a curriculum can be kept in a portfolio to either determine how well a student is doing or if the student is ready to move to the next segment of the curriculum. For example, prerequisites for initial handwriting instruction can be broken down into subskills and be used to

DIAGRAM 6–2 Tips on How to Correct Slant (Cursive)

1. Check position of paper and desk.
2. Check to see if student's writing arm is too close to the body.
3. Check and correct posture if a problem exists.
4. Check to see if thumb is too stiff.
5. Check grip of instrument to determine if writing instrument is being held too tightly.
6. Have student draw lines through letters to help evaluate appropriateness of angle.
7. Have students use plastic overlays (templates) with appropriate slants to self-evaluate handwriting.
8. Check to see if strokes are being pulled in appropriate direction.

determine if a student is ready for handwriting to begin. Lamme has identified six prerequisites for beginning handwriting instruction as small muscle development, eye-hand coordination, holding of utensils or tools, basic strokes, letter perception, and orientation to printed language.[21] Using the various curricular activities for each of these prerequisites, a checklist can be used to help determine which students are making progress satisfactory enough to begin handwriting instruction. In Figure 6–5, such a checklist is shown. As can be seen, observation of students across these six basic areas is not limited to the handwriting program.

    2. Informal tests that follow the levels idea discussed earlier can be devised to incorporate any segment of the handwriting curriculum. If a school or school system is following a corrective approach to teaching, these tests can be developed by teachers as a group and kept on file for use at various times of the school year. Teachers may spend portions of the first month of the year determining handwriting levels. Teachers may spend one class period during each nine-week grading period reassessing levels. Students can be examined individually with the informal tests, or they can be examined in groups.

    3. Handwriting scales can be used to determine at what level students best perform in handwriting. Students are asked to write a selected passage several times. The samples then are grouped into categories, ranging from best to poorest in the class. The samples are further analyzed by comparing them to the scales being used. One company's scales are particularly helpful in that they include not only an easy-to-use checklist that includes the basic legibility factors, but examples of the five categories of handwriting achievement, ranging from poor to excellent for each grade level, 1 to 6. Scales for grade 2 (manuscript) and grade 4 (cursive) are shown in Figure 6–6.[22] Base groups would be formed after several sets of papers have been examined. Students whose papers rather consistently fall into the fair and poor categories for most of the legibility factors identified on the scales would form one base group. Those whose papers fall into another category would likewise form a base group.

    4. An analysis of students' papers over a period of several weeks can also be used to group students into base groups. Such a practice is facilitated if a portfolio is kept of students' writing samples. Where analysis of handwriting papers is to be done to set up base groups, the teacher might start with two groups (top and bottom half of students). Later, each group could then be divided into two groups, making a total of four groups which represent handwriting abilities ranging from the bottom to the top fourth of students in the class.

    Teacher analysis of handwriting levels via observation of papers, while not as precise as determining reading or spelling levels, can still result in fairly accurate placement of students in base groups. However, the teacher should remember that the focus of the handwriting program is on legibility, not beautiful penmanship. Thus, papers are grouped according to how readily they can be read.

(Directions: Answer *yes* or *no* for each student in class if the task called for can be performed with relative ease.)

Small Muscle Development   Can the child:

_____   perform manipulative tasks (put together jigsaw puzzles; play with Legos and/or Tinker Toys etc.)?

_____   handle common daily functions of buttoning, zipping, tying bows, screwing caps on jars, etc.?

_____   perform molding tasks of playing with clay, play dough, papier mache, etc.?

_____   cut paper with scissors?

Eye-Hand Coordination   Can the child:

_____   balance objects such as blocks?

_____   build houses, fences, and other structures with blocks, Legos, or similar toys?

_____   push buttons, work puzzles, string beads, and similar tasks?

_____   draw, color, paint, paste, finger paint?

_____   follow a series of dots, copy, trace?

_____   hammer a nail into wood?

Holding Utensils or Tool   Can the child:

_____   use shovels and pails?

_____   use garden tools such as rakes and hoes?

_____   use kitchen utensils such as beaters, spoons, spatulas, and pancake turners?

_____   use paint brushes and sponges to paint?

_____   hold and use a felt tip marker, chalk, crayon, and pencil (in that order)?

Basic Strokes   Can the child:

_____   draw objects (e. g., wagons, people, cars) in which circles are round and closed?

_____   draw straight lines that intersect properly (e. g., kites to their strings)?

_____   naturally use basic strokes of handwriting in drawing/painting, stirring, playing in sand/water, and finger painting?

_____   repeat patterns in letters and words over and over?

Letter Perception   Can the child:

_____   detect likenesses and differences in letters and words?

_____   detect likenesses and differences in the process of making letters and words?

_____   recognize alphabet letters, including both upper and lower case letters?

_____   follow the movement of the teacher as letter formations are modeled?

_____   detect directionality needed for letter formation (up, down, around, to the right, to the left)?

Orientation to Printed Language   Can the child:

_____   use writing (drawing) to make books, greeting cards, pictures with labels, signs, etc.?

_____   "read" favorite stories, rhymes, and class books (that were written in the child's presence)?

_____   tell left from right?

FIGURE 6–5   A Checklist of Prerequisites for Beginning Handwriting Instruction

Linda Leonard Lamme, "Handwriting in an Early Childhood Curriculum," *Young Children 35* (1979) pp. 20–27. Adapted from the article with permission of the Publisher, the National Association of Young Children, Washington, DC 20009.

Grade

2M

Evaluation Scale: Manuscript

How to evaluate handwriting with this scale:

1. The teacher writes the sentences from the Evaluation Scale on the chalkboard, or uses the transparency from the Teacher Resource Binder.
2. Students practice writing the sentences on paper ruled like that on the Evaluation Scale.
3. Students use their best handwriting to write the sentences again.
4. Compare the students' writing with the examples on the Evaluation Scale, using the keys to legibility. The evaluation should be done as follows:
   If all keys to legibility are correct, the writing is rated EXCELLENT, as in Example 1.
   If four keys are correct, the writing is rated GOOD.
   If three keys are correct, the writing is rated AVERAGE.
   If two keys are correct, the writing is rated FAIR.
   If only one key is correct, the writing is rated POOR.
5. Repeat the evaluation procedure at least once each grading period.

CHECKPOINT

	Satisfactory	Needs Improvement
Shape	✓	
Slant	✓	
Spacing	✓	
Size	✓	
Smoothness	✓	

Example 1—Excellent for Grade Two

This is my best manuscript writing. Can you read it easily?

CHECKPOINT

	Satisfactory	Needs Improvement
Shape	✓	
Slant	✓	
Spacing		✓
Size	✓	
Smoothness	✓	

Example 2—Good for Grade Two

This is my best manuscript writing. Can you read it easily?

CHECKPOINT

	Satisfactory	Needs Improvement
Shape	✓	
Slant	✓	
Spacing		✓
Size	✓	
Smoothness		✓

Example 3—Average for Grade Two

This is my best manuscript writing Can you read it easily?

CHECKPOINT

	Satisfactory	Needs Improvement
Shape	✓	
Slant		✓
Spacing		✓
Size		✓
Smoothness	✓	

Example 4—Fair for Grade Two

This is my best manuscript writing. Can you read it?

CHECKPOINT

	Satisfactory	Needs Improvement
Shape		✓
Slant	✓	
Spacing		✓
Size		✓
Smoothness		✓

Example 5—Poor for Grade Two

This is my BesT manuscripT wriTing. Can you read iT?

FIGURE 6–6 Scale for Evaluating Manuscript Handwriting at Grade 2 and Cursive Writing at Grade 4

Grade 4

Zaner-Bloser
Evaluation Scale: *Cursive*

How to evaluate handwriting with this scale:
1. The teacher writes the sentences from the Evaluation Scale on the chalkboard, or uses the transparency from the Teacher Resource Binder.
2. Students practice writing the sentences on paper ruled like that on the Evaluation Scale.
3. Students use their best handwriting to write the sentences again.
4. Compare the students' writing with the examples on the Evaluation Scale, using the keys to legibility. The evaluation should be done as follows:
   If all keys to legibility are correct, the writing is rated EXCELLENT, as in Example 1.
   If four keys are correct, the writing is rated GOOD.
   If three keys are correct, the writing is rated AVERAGE.
   If two keys are correct, the writing is rated FAIR.
   If only one key is correct, the writing is rated POOR.
5. Repeat the evaluation procedure at least once each grading period.

CHECKPOINT

	Satisfactory	Needs Improvement
Shape	✓	
Slant	✓	
Spacing	✓	
Size	✓	
Smoothness	✓	

Example 1—Excellent for Grade Four

Legible writing can be read with ease. I want to improve my handwriting

---

CHECKPOINT

	Satisfactory	Needs Improvement
Shape	✓	
Slant	✓	
Spacing		✓
Size	✓	
Smoothness	✓	

Example 2—Good for Grade Four

Legible writing can be read with ease. I want to improve my handwriting

---

CHECKPOINT

	Satisfactory	Needs Improvement
Shape	✓	
Slant		✓
Spacing		✓
Size	✓	
Smoothness	✓	

Example 3—Average for Grade Four

Legible writing can be read with ease. I want to improve my handwriting.

CHECKPOINT

	Satisfactory	Needs Improvement
Shape		✓
Slant	✓	
Spacing	✓	
Size		✓
Smoothness		✓

Example 4—Fair for Grade Four

Legible writing can be read with ease I want to improve my handwriting.

CHECKPOINT

	Satisfactory	Needs Improvement
Shape		✓
Slant		✓
Spacing		✓
Size		✓
Smoothness	✓	

Example 5—Poor for Grade Four

Legible writing can be read with ease. I want to improve my writing.

FIGURE 6–6 *Continued*

Used with permission from the publisher, Zaner-Bloser, Columbus, OH 43215

Forming Flex Groups For Handwriting Instruction

As base groups become operational, the teacher will note that there are some common problems requiring special-needs instruction. Regrouping into flex groups takes place for this instruction. These groups can be formed in several ways, as follows:

1. Keep the organizational structure flexible enough to regroup students as often as needed. Although individual folders or portfolios will help systematize the identification of problems that students have, it will be necessary for teachers to keep a running chart showing progress of the entire class. The charts can be arranged in a way similar to the charts suggested earlier for spelling and writing. For handwriting, the letters/legibility factors are placed on the left axis of the charts and the names of the students at the top. An example is shown in Figure 6–7.

2. Students can be asked to write several passages for the purpose of determining specific problems in handwriting. Some passages have been devised in which most, if not all the letters of the alphabet, are used when the passage is written. The most widely used passage is, "The quick brown fox jumps over the lazy dog." Every letter of the alphabet is contained in this one sentence, although all but one of the letters are in the lower-case form. Some handwriting copybooks also contain passages that, when written, zero in on a cluster of similar letters. These, too, can be used for testing purposes. Usually, when passages are used to determine how well students form letters or any of the legibility factors, the passage is written from two to four times in order to get enough tries of the same letter or letter group to make the correct decision about how well each student does.

Cooperative Learning in the Handwriting Program

Cooperative learning activities can effectively be implemented in a student-involved corrective handwriting program. Some activities follow:

1. *Jigsaw in Handwriting* Jigsaw, as stated in Chapter 2, is a system where students are assigned a segment of materials to teach other students. Students with the same materials to be learned are grouped to discuss the materials to be taught, with a focus on returning to their original team to teach what they have learned to their team.[23] In the case of handwriting, a new cluster of letters to be learned, spacing, or some other legibility factor would constitute the materials to be learned and then taught to other team members. Another modification of Jigsaw in handwriting is to let students who have already learned a letter sequence work as tutors with students in a group who are being introduced to the sequence. The teacher provides initial instruction to students learning the letter cluster, and then assigns each student a tutor who already knows how to make the letters being learned.

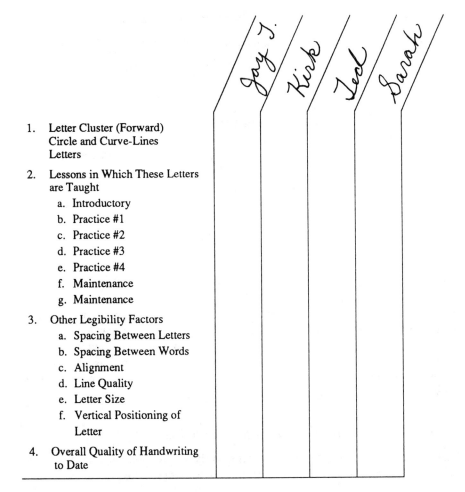

1. Letter Cluster (Forward)
   Circle and Curve-Lines
   Letters

2. Lessons in Which These Letters
   are Taught
   a. Introductory
   b. Practice #1
   c. Practice #2
   d. Practice #3
   e. Practice #4
   f. Maintenance
   g. Maintenance

3. Other Legibility Factors
   a. Spacing Between Letters
   b. Spacing Between Words
   c. Alignment
   d. Line Quality
   e. Letter Size
   f. Vertical Positioning of
      Letter

4. Overall Quality of Handwriting
   to Date

FIGURE 6–7   A Tracking System for Letter Formation and Other Legibility Factors (Manuscript)

2. *Small Group Teaching* (SGT)   As described in Chapter 2, this technique calls for students to be grouped heterogeneously into teams of 2 to 6 students per team and to work first on broader topics and, after regrouping, to work on individual tasks. Presentations are later made by each team with other students and the teacher evaluating each presentation.[24]

For review, students from various base groups are assigned selected legibility factors such as alignment, spacing between words, slant (if cursive), and spacing between letters. The teacher regroups the students according to the assigned legibility factor. Thus, all students who are to work on spacing between words are together, while others across base groups working on the same identified legibility factor are likewise regrouped. The teacher reviews elements of the assigned legibility factor. Students then concentrate on making a model paragraph along with a chart which illustrates the assigned legibility feature. Students then return to their team, and the team as a whole makes a "model" passage (perhaps longer than a paragraph) showing all legibility factors that various team members learned or reviewed in their new groups. Each team then presents its "model" to the class, demonstrating each legibility factor.

Reaching the Individual in the Handwriting Program

It is imperative that the focus of the handwriting program be that of reaching each individual student on his/her level of achievement and special needs. However, through base and flex groups, individuals can be reached.

Getting Students to Analyze Their Own Handwriting

A major theme that has been advocated in this book is the importance of self-analysis of all phases of the language arts. A major way to examine one's own work is through proofreading which must be systematically taught. In handwriting, special charts can be devised to help in self-analysis/proofreading. Burns has recommended that charts be available for both manuscript and cursive, complete with jingles or sentences that call for all letters of each form of handwriting to be used. In Figure 6–8, these charts are shown.

These charts, as designed, focus on student assessment and correction, in that they call for a handwriting sample to be written and self-analyzed prior to turning the sample in to the teacher.[25] Students are asked to check their papers and answer all questions on the chart "yes" or "no" before submitting the sample to be turned in for checking. Another procedure would be to have students check designated items on the chart and attach the form to the writing sample to be submitted to the teacher for review. Index cards with questions about the legibility factors, one question per card, can be used. An example follows: A student who is having trouble in spacing between words might concentrate on spacing between words for that day and use card #12 (Do you have room for the letter *o* between words?). This card would then be turned in with the student's handwriting sample, thus incorporating proofreading as a preventive aspect of assessment.

If the portfolio idea is used in handwriting, as advocated in written composition, students might be asked to complete charts such as the handwriting-analysis chart shown in Figure 3–6. In this chart, students were asked to compare earlier writing samples with later samples on factors such as the formation of *c's* and *e's*, alignment, margins, spacing, and so on.

Observing Students as They Write

What should a teacher look for as students are observed during handwriting class? Generally, how each student holds the writing instrument, posture, and arm position are the factors teachers look for when students complete a handwriting lesson. Stott, Moyes, and Henderson suggest additional physical factors, such as how close to the paper the head is held, pen grip, and how the paper is arranged.[26]

Such factors could be kept in a profile in each student's file and adjustments/corrections made and recorded as appropriate. The profile would follow the student to the next grade.

Students' Interests/Past Experiences in the Handwriting Program

Compared to other language arts, incorporating students' interests and past experiences into the handwriting program, is difficult. This is especially true in the initial stages of handwriting instruction when letter formation is being introduced. Later, when students can choose topics on which they might write for practice, the problem is easier to handle. Nevertheless, some strategies can be used to tap students' interests and experiences.

One way to appeal to students' interests and to tap experiences is to ask students to contribute some words that they know which contain the letter clusters being introduced or on which they are to practice. For example, in cursive writing,

---

(Manuscript)

Write the Sentence: The quick brown fox jumps over the lazy dog. Do not try to write more slowly than you do on your daily paper.

Then answer these questions with Yes or No.

1. Are *a*'s, *o*'s, *d*'s, and *g*'s, closed? _____
2. Do any *o*'s look like *a* or *u* ? _____
3. Does *k* look like *h* ? _____
4. Is each letter so plain that it doesn't look like any other letter? _____
5. Are letters the height of *b* all the same size? _____
6. Are letters the height of *a* all the same size? _____
7. Are *d* and *t* the same height? _____
8. Do *g, f, j, q, p, y,* and *z* come the distance below the baseline? _____
9. Do all letters sit on the baseline? _____
10. Do all letters have a uniform slant? _____
11. Are letters spaced evenly in words? _____
12. Do you have room for the letter *o* between words ? _____

(Cursive)

Write this jingle. Use the questions that follow to check your writing.
Thirty days hath September,
April, June, and November;
All the rest have thirty-one;
February twenty-eight alone,
Except in leap year, at which time
February's days are twenty-nine.

Check points:

1. Are all the letters made correctly? Are they easy to read? _____
    a. Are all your *a*'s, *o*'s, and *d*'s fully closed? _____
    b. Are the *i*'s dotted directly above the letters? _____
    c. Are your *a*'s written so they do not look like *o*'s or *u*'s? _____
    d. Is their an open loop in your *e*'s ? _____
    e. Are *b*'s and *l*'s the same height? _____
    f. Is your *n* written so it does not look like *u* ? _____
    g. Are the tips of *r*'s and *s*'s *a* little taller than letters such as *u* or *o* ? _____
    h. Are the *d*'s and *t*'s taller than *a* and shorter than *l* ? _____
    i. Are the *l*'s, *b*'s, *h*'s, *k*'s, and *f*'s about the same height as the capitals? _____
    j. Do *y* and *p* come the same distance below the baseline? _____
2. Are your letters the proper size? _____
3. Did you leave enough spaces between the letters so that your writing is not crowded? Are your words spaced correctly? _____
4. Do all letters sit on the baseline? _____
5. Do your letters have a uniform slant? _____

FIGURE 6–8 Self-Analysis of Handwriting (Manuscript and Cursive)

Paul C. Burns, *Assessment and Correction of Language Arts Difficulties* (Columbus, Ohio: Charles E. Merrill 1980) pp. 220, 222. Used with permission of Shirley A. Burns Baldridge.

if students are practicing how to connect downcurve, lowercase cursive letters such as , , and   in the word   , the students could be asked to think of words that they know which can be used for practice. It should be easy for most students at this stage of cursive writing to think of such words as *dad, do, odd, go,* and *add.* To practice making these downcurve-letter connectives, students might come up with a small sample of words and write each one, two, or three times for practice. As formations of more and more letters are learned by students, the range of options from which students can recall words expands.

Students who have used single words for practice are asked later to write sentences with the words, thus reinforcing some other letter clusters that they have learned. Eventually, students are asked to construct passages longer than single sentences to be used as a model. Students can also be asked to give sentences which contain as many targeted letters as possible. Where students are to practice the letter *l* in manuscript or cursive writing, such a sentence as "Sally is really ill." could be given as an example. When each student in a small group (flex or base) has made up a sentence, the sentence can be placed on the chalkboard, and sentences with the largest number of targeted letters can be the practice sentences. Each student in the group would write the sentences two or three times, thereby practicing the targeted letter a sufficient number of times. In some cases, targeted letters being learned can be omitted from the rest of a sentence, thus providing only instruction on the targeted letters. This is especially helpful where students have not learned most of the letters in a sentence.

It is very important that students not be taught in such a way that they forget why they are learning how to write letters of the alphabet. Practice in context of words and sentences that students come up with should move easily and as rapidly as possible into everyday writing—the reason for learning how to form the letters in the first place.

Whole Language and Handwriting

Since proponents of whole language incorporate all of the language arts (and sometimes other subjects as well), it is important to look at handwriting instruction in a student-involved corrective program and how it relates to whole language. The detailed procedures of learning letter formation and early writing are presented since they appear to be two areas in which potential conflict might emerge.

Handwriting: A Bottom-up Approach With Attention to Meaning

In some ways the highly detailed, lock-step, skill-oriented approach to handwriting instruction appears to be the opposite of what whole language teaching is all about. Often, the teaching of handwriting is a "bottom-up" approach to teaching, rather than a "top-down" approach. However, the initial formation of letters of the alphabet must have specific, direct instruction. This does not mean that attention to meaning is lacking in a handwriting program. In handwriting, the goal of learning to write to communicate with others should be a continuing focus. Handwriting should be presented as a functional subject. As children learn to form the letters of the alphabet in handwriting, what they are reading and writing about in the whole language classroom can be increasingly incorporated into handwriting lessons. Children can practice handwriting skills by describing a story read or by creating a story, using a setting of a story read to the class by the teacher. Passages worthy of writing such as a description of a character in a story read by the teacher can be used for students to practice their handwriting skills. At the same time, students are learning about describing characters in reading or writing materials.

Early Writing

Students should be encouraged to "write" or compose their thoughts on paper, even before they can technically write or spell. While the writing is little more than scribbling with invented spellings in some cases, to the child doing the "writing," it is much more than that. Thus, attention to meaning is indeed present and the whole language goal with emphasis on literature and natural language is not impaired by students' lack of writing skills.

Materials and Equipment for Corrective Teaching of Handwriting

Several of the leading handwriting companies have developed specialized materials for teaching handwriting. Included among these materials are "look-through" models for seeing/correcting problems with letter formation and other legibility factors, booklet-type materials for guiding letter formation, and desktop models of letters to follow.

Overlays

Shown in Diagram 6–3 are the impressions of the plastic overlays that the Zaner-Bloser Company recommends for students to check their letter formation when using a paper that is 3/8-inch in size and slant when writing cursive handwriting. Students place the overlay over their writing to compare the writing on the model with their own writing. If the writing is off more than it should be, the student tries again, paying special attention to problem areas.

Copybook Diagrams and Charts

Copybooks and/or workbooks often contain very detailed diagrams that help students form letter clusters. These diagrams not only show specific strokes of letters to be made but also include descriptive information on what to do. While the explicit directions and diagrams are usually well done and easy to follow, they usually contain only the visually- and kinesthetically-oriented activities. They too often leave out the audio component. B. Furner's work on verbalization can easily be adapted to copybook charts on letter formation. As stated earlier, in B. Furner's research it was demonstrated that students gained in skill development by

DIAGRAM 6–3 Diagnostic-Corrective Overlays

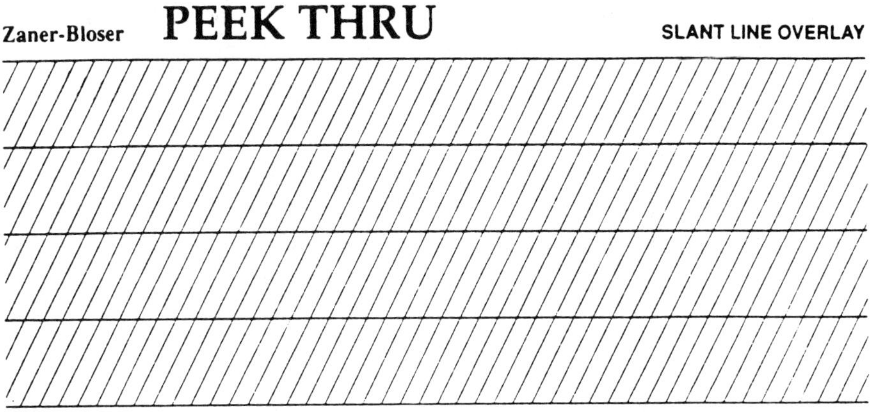
Zaner-Bloser
PEEK THRU
SLANT LINE OVERLAY

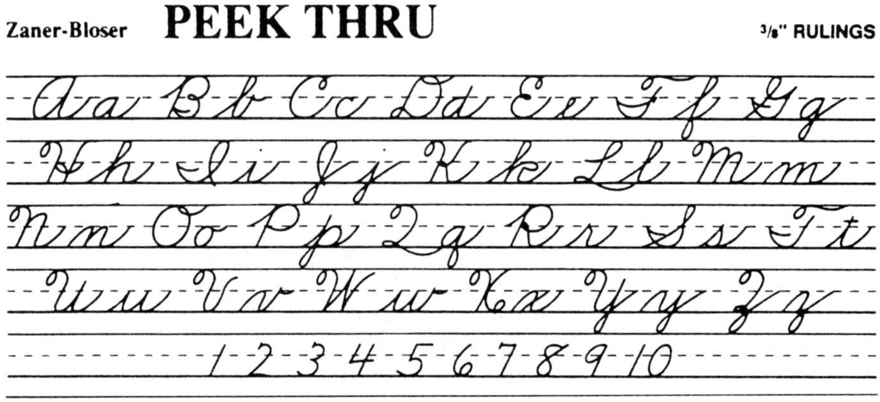
Zaner-Bloser
PEEK THRU
3/8" RULINGS
1 2 3 4 5 6 7 8 9 10

Used with permission of the Publisher, Zaner-Bloser, Columbus, OH.

verbalizing the starting points for each stroke being made, the direction of the stroke, and other points that are made in the formation of letters.[27]

In Diagram 6–4, instructions are provided on how to incorporate the audio modality of learning into the making of lower-case manuscript *a, c,* and *e*. Audio can be incorporated by having the first two columns placed on either electronic card reader sets of cards or on audio tape. The student looks at the letter to be made, runs the card reader materials through, repeats (with or without recording the verbalization, column 3), and then on paper, forms the letter as he/she verbalizes. For many letters, only one card would be necessary. However, where there are multiple

DIAGRAM 6–4   A Multisensory Approach to Initial Letter Formation

	Student hears: 1. I start just below the middle guideline. 2. I make a backward circle. 3. I stop when I come to where I started. 4. Then I start on the middle guideline and pull downward. 5. I stop on the bottom baseline.	Student repeats what is heard in forming ___ α ___ .	*a*
	Student hears: 1. I start just below the middle guideline. 2. I make a partial, backward circle. 3. I stop just above the bottom baseline.	Student repeats what is heard in forming ___ C ___ .	*c*
	Student hears: 1. I start just below the middle guideline. 2. I make a partial backward circle. 3. I stop just above the bottom-baseline. 4. Then I draw a straight line from left to right to connect the top part of my partial circle.	Student repeats what is heard in forming ___ e ___ .	*e*

strokes, more than one card would probably be needed. Card sizes vary for electronic card readers, and this factor would be considered in making audio instructions via these machines. As in any systematically-developed program, sets of materials must be well organized and packaged for use with groups of students who would be involved in using the materials independently.

Alphabet Desk Cards

A complete copy of the alphabet is provided for each individual in McDougal-Littell and Company's alphabet desk cards. The card recommended for use in Grades 1 and 2 is 4 1/2 by 11 inches and contains all upper- and lower-case letters and numbers 0 through 9. When a card is used, it is placed on the desk of each individual student for easy reference.[28] One advantage of having such a card, in addition to the easy reference it provides, is that the model of each letter is on the same level as the paper on which the student is to write. There has been criticism of having students (1) look at models of letters above the chalkboard or some other vertical plane in the room and (2) attempt to transfer the interpretation of how to make the letters to a flat surface on desktops.

The Microcomputer in the Handwriting Program

Although some uses of the computer have been made in analysis of handwriting movements,[29] there are few suggestions for how the microcomputer can be used in the teaching of handwriting. Those which follow are directed to some of the major themes in this book.

   1.   Use the microcomputer to provide yet another medium for students to see how a letter is formed. The following illustration of how to make the simple "straight-line" letters (*i*, *l*, *t*) of the manuscript form is just one example of what the teacher can put on a disk for individual or small groups to use. While the copy can be without voice, the use of digitized voice on interactive disk can provide yet another medium to provide students with directions on how to form letters. In some cases, directions using digitized voice may have to be shortened to parallel memory capacity, but such adjustment can be made without limiting the capacity to use voice with the microcomputer.

The *l* begins on this line.
Move down through this line.
The *l* ends here.

The *i* begins on this line.
The *i* ends on this line.

The *t* begins halfway between the top two lines. The *t* is crossed on the middle line and ends on the bottom line.

Students observe the straight-line letters and use paper at their desks to start and stop each stroke. While the making of other letters is not as easy to do on the microcomputer for purposes of showing where strokes start and stop, some new technology is emerging that should make all letters easier to illustrate on the microcomputer.

2. One problem that teachers have is the diversification of passages for students to emulate. If a classroom has a sufficient number of handwriting copybooks, different passages can be used for students to write. Teachers can put on microcomputer disks a string of passages that includes letter clusters on which a small group of students or an individual needs to practice. Two passages are shown below. Sample one is for practice on the letter *s*. Sample two is for practice on the letter *f*.

Sample One	*Sample Two*
Sally, my sassy cat, sleeps a lot. She sleeps six and seven hours a day. If you wake her up, she hisses at you.	Fred's dog, Fifi, is five years old. Fred says that Fifi is his best friend. Fifi is Fred's furry friend.

As students increase their uses of the microcomputer, it should be easy to use a disk for a series of handwriting lessons. Small groups of students, either in base or flex groups, can work together on a series of lessons, as long as there is one machine per small group and each student has his/her writing space.

3. Students can analyze handwriting passages for illegibility problems. A passage is printed on the monitor's screen with work space left on the right of the passage. Students place codes to show illegibility problems, line for line. In cases where there are two or more problems on the same line, the codes are typed on the line in sequence of their occurrence. The passage and directions are placed on the *memory file*. An example of one passage with illegibility problems is shown below, with directions.

Directions: Use the codes *SW* (spacing between words), *SL* (spacing between letters), and *ILF* (incorrect letter form) to tell what is wrong on each line of the passage "My Best Friend's Visit." Some lines may require more than one code.

(My Best Friend's Visit)
Herman, my   best   friend,   _____
is visiting me.   He i s fr om   _____
detroit, Michigan.   W e   have   _____
been friends many Years.   _____

If students are individually working on the analysis of this passage, they code their answers (*SW* for line 1; *SL* for line 2; *ILF, SL,* and *SW* for line 3; and *ILF* for line 4), in the passage. The passage, with codes, is saved for teacher review, unless the answers are checked immediately.

4. The microcomputer can be used to show students their progress in handwriting if they have been working on a problem since the beginning of the year. When students have shown improvement, the teacher and student examine the improved sample and the teacher, using digitized voice on interactive video, identifies in a very focused, succinct statement, progress noted. Combined with the portfolio idea of assessment and interactive video, the teacher can make brief statements about the positive features of the sample such as, "Your slanting is excellent here." or "This shows more consistent spacing between words." Throughout the year, verbal comments can be made about different samples each student places on a personal disk, resulting in a cumulative evaluation over some or all of the school year.

Assessment Activities for Handwriting Problems

Assessment activities in handwriting go beyond those already presented in this chapter. The following include several activities that call for student involvement:

Four-Square Review
In this activity, attention is focused on getting students to analyze their handwriting to see if specified legibility factors are presenting problems. A diagram such as the following four squares (two if the teacher wishes to reduce the specific factors being examined) is drawn and labeled.

Alignment	*Letter Spacing*
Slant	*Word Spacing*

Each student scans his/her paper, looking for problems in the four categories. The following directions are given for marking the paper and using the four-square design:

1. Draw a line under any letter which is not placed as it should be on the baseline. In the appropriate square, write the number of times that you found a letter not sitting on the base line.

2. Use the appropriate overlay and check your slant. In the *slant* square on the four-square diagram, place the number of times that a word does not have all letters in it slanted the right way.

3. Circle any letters that run together. Count the number of circles that you have drawn, and enter the number in the *letter-spacing* square.

4. Draw a set of vertical lines between words that are not spaced correctly. Place the number of these lines in the *word-spacing* square.

If students have no errors specified in one of the squares in the four-square diagram, they either write "no problems," or draw a smiling face. The next step is to have a designated partner for each student examine the paper and four-square diagram to see if the assessment is accurate. The four-square review might become part of a portfolio and serve as the basis for a conference with the teacher. Over a period of several weeks, this system can lead to a long-range evaluation of handwriting legibility progress.

Handwriting Bulletin Board

When students perform exceptionally well in any particular area of handwriting, their papers might become models for others to follow. A bulletin board can be divided into several sections. Each section has a heading according to the factor that has been emphasized in handwriting instruction. For example, if a lot of emphasis has been on alignment, a section of the board might be labeled *Proper Alignment* with papers that are particularly good in that area placed in that section. Another section of the bulletin board might be labeled *Good Formation of Letters i, l, t.* Students in their base groups might decide who in their group has a paper in one of the categories on the bulletin board that all others in the class should see. In some cases, each small group (base or flex) might have its own small bulletin board or chart for displaying work.

Overhead Projector Analysis

The overhead projector is an excellent machine for helping analyze a handwriting sample to either identify the kinds of problems that students should avoid or to teach students how to analyze their own papers. A transparency is made of a sample, and students examine the projected image with the teacher. Problems are identified in the sample, with students doing much of the analysis.

Codes-in-Margin

In Chapter 5, a "codes-in-margin" scheme was discussed for analyzing a student's written composition. The same type of system can be used in the handwriting program. The teacher introduces the codes to be used such as those shown in the chart that follows:

Legibility Factors	Codes
1. Alignment	*a*
2. Slant	*sl*
3. Letter spacing	*ls*
4. Word spacing	*ws*
5. Uniformity	*u*

As in the codes used in the writing activity, the teacher would place a code or series of codes on the line to the right where the error occurs. Students find the problem and correct it by writing the word or letter with the problem either on the back of the paper on which the lesson was written or on another sheet of paper.

Corrective Activities for Use in Handwriting Programs

While the following activities conceivably could be focused on assessment of problems, they are designed more to be used to correct problems in handwriting. They are but a few that can be developed and used in corrective teaching.

Color-coded Desk Models of Letters

When students are learning letter formations, a close-up model of the letters can be taped to the desk. Some additional help can be provided here if the strokes of a troublesome letter need special attention. Using magic markers, each stroke might be drawn with a different color. Thus, the first stroke might be green and an ending stroke might be red (traffic light signals). If there is a stroke in between the first and last strokes, this might be marked with a yellow marker. For easy filing and use of model letters, each letter in a cluster of similar letters to be introduced at the same time (such as cursive letters that begin with the same downcurve [*a d g q o c*] can be placed on small squares of tagboard, laminated, and placed in a small manila envelope. These are then easily used by either a small group of students or by an individual.

Chart Practice

Samples for practice, instead of being placed on the chalkboard for a class or small group to follow, can be placed in a large 3-foot x 4-foot chart tablet. Several pages in a tablet could contain selections dealing with a target letter or group of letters. Other pages would contain different target letters or letter groups. These pages would never be torn out and would be available for use throughout the year as well as the following years. Such charts make it possible for several students to work on a given lesson at the same time. When several tablets of charts have accumulated, it would be an easy matter for the teacher to have several small groups working simultaneously on different lessons.

Audio Instructions

Audio tapes can easily be developed to assist student with letter formation, spacing, alignment, and other legibility factors. While a single letter can be placed on a card for an electronic card reader, it might be more appropriate to have a cluster of letters to be introduced as a unit (for example, similar strokes as in i l +) placed on audio tape. On the audio tape, the teacher asks the students to first get a certain packet of letters and to get their paper and pencils ready to write. The first letter to be written is placed on the desk, and the instructions begin. For example, "We start on the middle guide line and pull down to the baseline. Then we make a dot over what we have written.") The teacher then gives the directions a second time, and asks the student listening to the audio (via earphones) to say the directions for making the letter with the teacher. Practice time is provided with students allowed to go back and listen to how the strokes are made.

Correction of Errors in Letter Shapes

The author of a handwriting resource book for the Province of British Columbia's schools suggest that for students who are having problems "in recognizing and producing simple letter shapes,"[30] a lesson such as that shown in Figure 6–9 be devised. It should be noted that the shapes suggested parallel the basic strokes for manuscript writing.

Letter Features Activities

For diagnostic and remedial instruction, Burns recommends that special attention be given to each letter, including analysis of strokes in the target letter, slant, and other features needed to form the letter as an individual letter and in context of writing. For example, to help with the formation and use of "cursive a," the activity in Figure 6–10 is recommended.[31]

Summary

1. Instructional programs in handwriting are remarkably alike in schools. Usually, they include six broad phases: readiness for manuscript writing, beginning of manuscript writing, continuous development and maintenance of manuscript form, transition from manuscript to cursive handwriting, beginning of cursive form, and continuous development and maintenance of cursive writing.

Stage One Lesson (Diagnostic/Remedial)

Objectives:
This diagnostic/remedial lesson can be used if you find that students have trouble recognizing and producing simple letter shapes. Specifically this lesson will teach them to
 • follow directions (both oral and visual);
 • reproduce simple shapes and forms with a variety of media.

Materials:
Have available unlined chalkboard space, larger unlined desk size paper, cleared sand box area, large paint brushes and easels, finger paint and paper, etc.
Prepare identical sets of (8 1/2" x 11") cards showing examples of simple shapes and forms in thick felt pen with directional arrows.

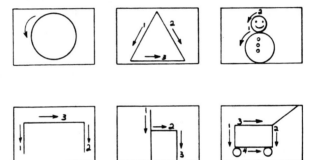

Motivation and Preparatory Activities:
Follow this procedure:
 • hold up cards and have students name the shapes (e. g, circle, line, triangle);
 • discuss reason for arrows (e. g., up, down, left, right);
 • as each card is shown, have the students draw shapes in the air following the arrows.

Instruction, Practice, Evaluation:
Set up a number of classroom centres and divide students into groups according to numbers of centres. Then give these directions to students:
 • choose a card;
 • take it to your centre;
 • put it to where you can see it easily;
 • copy it, remembering to follow the arrows;
 • have a friend watch you make a shape to see that you follow the arrows; then you watch your friend make a shape;
 • return the card and take another one.

Remediation:
Allow students who have difficulty to copy several different cards. Then repeat this activity on another day to allow students the use of different media. As students work, move around and observe that they are performing correctly.

FIGURE 6–9   Diagnostic Procedure for Correcting Letter Shapes

Reprinted with permission–Ministry of Education, Province of British Columbia (Victoria, British Columbia, Canada: Learning Resources Branch)–*Handwriting Resource Book* (1981) CG 0090.

CURSIVE "a"

1. Write this word and see how well you made the a.

road

a. Where does a begin?
b. Is "a" closed or open?
c. Is the up stroke retraced or looped?
d. Does the concluding stroke sit on the base line?

2. Make a row of a's. Make each one look like the one at the first of the row.

a

3. Look at the letters at the right.
   a. Are a and d the same width?
   b. What is the only difference between the a and d?
   c. Write a, d, and o in the space.

   a d o

4. Write these words. Make good a's.

gray draw gave

5. Write this sentence. Make your a's correctly.

I had to read it again.

6. Are you making better a's?
   a. Are you closing all your a's?
   b. Are you retracing, not looping, the upstroke?
   c. Does the connecting stroke sit on the base line?
   d. Do any of your a's look like o's, u's, or i's? They should not.

FIGURE 6–10   Examining Features of Individual Letters

Paul C. Burns *Improving Handwriting Instruction in Elementary Schools*, Second Edition (Minneapolis: Burgess Publishing Company, 1968), pp. 108–109 (Reprinted with permission).

2. A major focus of handwriting instruction is legibility. Legibility is measured in terms of correct letter formation, spacing between letters, spacing between words, alignment, uniformity in line quality, correct letter size, and appropriate slant in cursive and D'Nealian.

3. Copying of letters using a model or guide is considered the most effective way to learn how to make letters. Other techniques such as tracing letters and connecting dots, while not as effective as copying, might prove to be useful when copying is not working for an individual student.

4. Although total-class instruction prevails, there is some evidence to suggest that individualized-diagnostic teaching is a more effective way of teaching handwriting.

5. Teacher observation is the predominant approach to the evaluation of handwriting. The use of scales in which samples are used to judge against can be a part of observation for evaluative purposes. Scales, however, should be used more for assessment purposes than they now are used.

6. Handwriting instruction should not be considered a motor skill alone, since the act of handwriting requires the use of perceptual skills. Adding verbalization to visualization as another mode of learning enhances the teaching of letter formation.

7. The most-frequently misformed letters in handwriting have been identified for both manuscript and cursive forms. In some instances, errors occur in a limited number (four to six) of letters, accounting for up to a third or more of errors made by students. Teachers should know which letters cause the most problems and take special care to see that students are given extra help (more one-on-one instruction) when these letters are introduced.

8. Left-handed writers need special attention. Studies have led to the identification of a "non-hooking" position that results in more effective writing by left-handers. Several guidelines should be considered when working with the left-handed writer, including tilting the paper 32 degrees to the right and holding the writing tool in such a way that writing is seen as it is produced.

9. The handwriting curriculum should include skills that help in the development of a background for formal handwriting instruction and should advance through the stages of formal handwriting—introductory, intermediate, and advanced. Although skills and other curricular components are listed in broad bands, they should be clustered for teaching where possible. Handwriting should be functional, and the clustering of skills adds to this goal.

10. In addition to noting which letters are the most troublesome to make, other problems should be noted. These include omission of letter parts, incorrect relationship of parts of letters, and letter reversals. Handwriting samples should be carefully analyzed to note all kinds of handwriting problems as well as to determine probable cause of the problems.

11. Base groups can easily be formed for handwriting instruction. Teachers may use curricular checklists, informal tests made for a particular school or system, and handwriting scales for each grade level. In addition, teachers should analyze handwriting papers over several weeks, using the portfolio approach for assessment.

12. Flex groups can be formed through analysis of specific legibility factors over time or through analysis of selected passages that contain most or all letters of the alphabet.

13. Cooperative learning strategies can be implemented in the handwriting program. Two strategies in particular appear to be useful. One is Jigsaw in which students in a small group may each be assigned a letter in a cluster of letters having similar strokes. Each student learns the assigned letter and steps for making it and then instructs and helps monitor other students as they learn the letter. Small Group Teaching (*SGT*) can also be adapted to handwriting instruction. Students can be reassigned to a specialized group which focuses on a legibility factor. The regrouping leads to a model handwriting paragraph (or larger passage) in which the assigned legibility factor is prominently exhibited. Students then return to their original team for the purpose of writing a model passage in which all legibility factors are shown.

14. Self-analysis and proofreading of one's handwriting is important in a student-involved corrective program. Specially-designed charts can be developed to help students focus on self analysis of each handwriting paper. The charts, with all or selected items checked, are submitted with each sample students write. Some charts can become part of students' handwriting portfolios.

15. Observation of students as they write should include observation for physical factors that help in the handwriting process. These include correct body position, correct pen grip, appropriate arm movement, and position of paper.

16. Although not as easy to do as in the other language arts, students' interests, and past experiences can be incorporated into a handwriting program. Students can write a sentence in an area of their interests and one which has a large number of the letters being learned. Students can also provide single words which have target letters being learned such as *ill* when *l* is being learned. These become practice words.

17. Handwriting equipment and materials for use in a corrective program should include look-through overlays, diagrams showing specific sequence and direction of letter strokes, audio equipment for giving oral directions on how to form letters, and desk cards showing correct letter formation. The microcomputer can also be used in a corrective handwriting program. A primary use is the development of varied samples for students to write.

18. Bulletin boards can also be used for instructional purposes in handwriting. Selected, highly focused examples of ideal or model writing in which a particular legibility factor stands out, can be placed on the bulletin board and attention called to the particular feature in question.

Reviewing, Connecting, and Expanding What You Have Learned

(Directions) Read each numbered paragraph in the summary. Then do the activities that follow, either in small groups as assembled by your college professor/in-service education director or as an individual.

1. (Paragraph 1) Make six columns on your paper. For the headings of each, place one of the broad phases of handwriting programs identified as typical of programs across the country. Write a few key words that help identify what goes in each phase.

2. (Paragraph 2) If the situation permits, select one child's sample of manuscript writing (or D'Nealian) and one sample of cursive. Review each sample for legibility factors that you have learned. Focus on how well the papers rate on the major legibility factors.

3. (Paragraph 3) While most students learn to form letters initially through copying, there may be times when tracing and connecting dots could be helpful to a student. On what occasions might these other techniques be helpful?

4. (Paragraph 4) Speculate on why total-class instruction in handwriting continues to prevail. Write your ideas in notes to share with others in your class.

5. (Paragraph 5) Develop a set of guidelines for using handwriting scales in a student-involved corrective program. Make the guidelines as comprehensive as you can.

6. (Paragraphs 6, 7, 8) Select one of the following topics and prepare a lesson to teach other members of your group. Emphasize what is known from the research on your topic and how the content of your topic can be useful in a corrective handwriting program.
    a. Handwriting is a perceptual skill.
    b. Teachers should know which letters are the most difficult for students to form.
    c. Left-handed writers need special attention.

7. (Paragraph 9) Write a brief description of what kinds of handwriting skills one might find in each of the four broad bands of handwriting curricular design advocated in this chapter (development of a foundation for formal handwriting instruction, introduction to formal handwriting instruction, intermediate level of handwriting instruction, and advanced level of handwriting instruction).

8. (Paragraph 10) In your own words, tell what each of the following means:
    a. Omission of letter parts
    b. Incorrect relationship of parts of letters
    c. Letter reversals
    d. Inverted letters

9. (Paragraphs 11 and 12) Identify two ways to set up base groups in handwriting. Do the same for flex groups. Which kind of grouping do you feel would be the most difficult to establish and why? Which would be the most difficult to maintain all year?

10. (Paragraph 13) Develop a handwriting lesson using either Jigsaw or Small Group Teaching (cooperative learning strategies). Do not use the examples given in the summary.

11. (Paragraph 14) Develop a system for having students self-analyze their handwriting papers. Tell how you would implement the system.

12. (Paragraph 15) Select five students in a class whose handwriting abilities range from very poor to very good. Observe each child as he/she writes over several days. Write a brief description of the physical factors affecting handwriting that you noted about each child.

13. (Paragraph 16) In a 10–15 minute period, brainstorm with several of your peers on ideas for using children's interests in a handwriting program. Write your ideas on paper and then rank them from most to least effective (how your group ranks them).

14. (Paragraphs 17 and 18) Write one or two (no more) sentences on each specific kind of materials or piece of equipment that you recall discussed in this chapter. Share what you write with others. Discuss the merits of each kind of materials or piece of equipment.

Endnotes

1. Eunice N. Askov and Michaleen Peck, "Handwriting," in *Encyclopedia of Educational Research*, 5th ed., a project of the American Educational Research Association, ed. Harold E. Mitzel, (New York: Macmillan, 1982), p. 764.

2. Ibid., p. 765.

3. Victor Froese; "Handwriting; Practice, Pragmatism, and Progress," in *Research in the Language Arts—Language and Schooling*, eds. Victor Froese and Stanley B. Straw (Baltimore: University Park Press, 1981), p. 237.

4. Ibid.

5. Markhoff, Annabelle Most, *Teaching Low Achieving Children Reading, Spelling, and Handwriting* (Springfield, Illinois: Charles C. Thomas, 1976), p. 218.

6. Askov and Peck, "Handwriting," p. 764.

7. Froese, "Handwriting," p. 234.

8. Ibid., pp. 234–236.

9. Jean Alston and Jane Taylor, *Handwriting; Theory, Research and Practice* (London: Croom Helm, 1987), p 89.

10. Clinton S. Hackney, Ed.D. "The Left-Handed Child in a Right-Handed World," (Columbus, Ohio: The Zaner-Bloser Company, panel 6.

11. Edward R. Lewis and Hilda P. Lewis, "An Analysis of Errors in the Formation of Manuscript Letters by First-Grade Children," *American Educational Research Journal* 2 (1965): 27.

12. Ibid., 27-30, 34.

13. Ibid., 28, 30.

14. Michaleen Peck, Eunice N. Askov, and Steven H. Fairchild, "Another Decade of Research in Handwriting," *Journal of Educational Research*, 73 (1983): 284.

15. Froese, "Handwriting," p. 236.

16. Lowell W. Horton, "Illegibilities in the Cursive Handwriting of Sixth-Graders," *The Elementary School Journal*, 70 (1970): 446-50.

17. Bowmar/Noble Publishers, "Handwriting Diagnostic and Prescriptive Chart, Manuscript and Cursive Writing" (Los Angeles: Bowmar/Noble Publishers) p. 1.

18. Ibid., pp. 2-3.

19. Clinton S. Hackney, "Corrective Strategies for Common Problems in Cursive Handwriting," (Columbus, Ohio: Zaner-Bloser Handwriting Company), panel 2.

20. Ibid., panels 2-4.

21. Linda Leonard Lamme, "Handwriting in an Early Childhood Curriculum," *Young Children* 35 (1979): 20-27.

22. The Zaner-Bloser Handwriting Company, "Evaluative Scale for Grade 2 (Manuscript) and Grade 4 (Cursive), (Columbus, Ohio: The Zaner-Bloser Company).

23. Robert E. Slavin, "Cooperative Learning," *Review of Educational Research*, 50 (1980): 320-321.

24. Ibid., 321.

25. Paul C. Burns, *Assessment and Correction of Language Arts Difficulties* (Columbus, Ohio: Charles E. Merrill, 1980), 220, 222.

26. Denis H. Stott, Fred A. Moyes, and Sheila E. Henderson, *Diagnosis and Remediation of Handwriting Problems*, (Guelph, Ontario, Canada: Brook Educational Publishing, 1985), Part 3 of Diagnostic Record Form , p. 4.

27. Markhoff, "Teaching Low-Achieving Children."

28. McDougal, Littel and Company, "Alphabet Desk Cards," *Building Handwriting Skills*, Teacher's Edition (Evanston, Illinois, 1986), T1.

29. Hans-Leo H. M. Teulings and Arnold J. W. M. Thomassen, "Computer-Aided Analysis of Handwriting Movements," *Visible Language* 13 (1979): 218-231.

30. Ministry of Education, Province of British Columbia, *Handwriting Handbook* (Victoria, British Columbia, Curriculum Development Branch, Ministry of Education, 1981) p. 74.

31. Paul C. Burns, *Improving Handwriting Instruction in Elementary Schools*, 2nd ed. (Minneapolis: Burgess Publishing Company, 1968), pp. 108-109.

Bibliography

Strategies for Instruction

Hall, Janice K. "Improve Handwriting," Chapter 12 in *Evaluating and Improving Written Expression—A Practical Guide for Teachers*, 2nd ed., by Janice K. Hall, (Boston: Allyn and Bacon, 1988). pp. 199–207.

Wasylyk, Thomas M. and Milone, Michael N., Jr. "Corrective Techniques in Handwriting: Cursive," In *Handwriting: Basic Skills for Effective Communication*, edited by Walter Barbe, Virginia H. Lucas, and Thomas M. Wasylyk (Columbus, Ohio: Zaner-Bloser, 1984), pp. 334–38.

Issues/Research in Teaching Handwriting

Farris, Pamela J., "Views and Other Views: Handwriting Instruction Should Not Become Extinct," *Language Arts* 68 (1991): 312.

Graves, Donald H., "How to Keep Handwriting in Perspective," In *Handwriting: Basic Skills for Effective Communication*, edited by Walter Barbe, Virginia H. Lucas, and Thomas M. Wasylyk (Columbus, Ohio: Zaner-Bloser, 1984). pp. 70–77

Koenke, Karl. "Handwriting Instruction: What do we Know?" *The Reading Teacher* 40 (1986): 214.

Trap-Porter, Jennifer et. al., "D'Nealian and Zaner-Bloser Manuscript Alphabets and Initial Transition to Cursive Handwriting," *Journal of Educational Research* 77 (1984): 343.

Trap Porter, Jennifer et. al., "Space, Size, and Accuracy of Second and Third Grade Students' Cursive Handwriting," *Journal of Educational Research* 76 (1983): 231.

7

A Corrective Approach to
Listening Instruction

Focus

It is easy to get total agreement among a group of educators about the importance of listening. Yet, listening instruction in the schools is grossly neglected. In this chapter, you will look at the reasons for this neglect, definitions relating to listening and listening instruction, different kinds of and purposes for listening, major components of a listening curriculum, and how listening can best be taught in school. You will also look at how to determine listening skill-level development, corrective activities for listening instruction, and how basic principles of student-involved assessment and correction emphasized in this book can be applied to listening instruction.

A particular focus of Chapter 7 will be how listening instruction can be taught across the curriculum and integrated with other language arts. However, some attention will be given to separate lessons for listening *when such lessons are needed.* Other major points are:

1. Identifying research in listening that should be considered in a student-involved corrective program
2. Learning how base groups in listening instruction differ from base groups in spelling, writing, and handwriting
3. Determining when students should be placed in flex groups for special-needs instruction in listening
4. Learning about formal and informal tests that are available for determining listening-skill development

5. Setting up special activities for listening
6. Identifying problems that students have with listening
7. Identifying different approaches to instruction in listening

> As you read Chapter 7, recall any listening instruction that you might have had in elementary school. Most people, when they are asked to do this, recall a few incidents where teachers asked students to pay attention or to listen carefully, where "good listeners" received some type of special recognition, or where a few games were taught for the purpose of improving listening. But there is considerably more to listening instruction than this. Procedures for listening improvement, including assessment/corrective strategies, have been developed, and teachers should know about them.

What is The Status of Listening Instruction in Schools Today?

Listening is taught sporadically in schools today. It definitely does not have a systematic, identifiable place in the language arts curriculum as does spelling and handwriting. Nor is listening given the attention that writing is today being given. These conditions are interesting, given the fact that students (1) spend considerably more time listening in school than they do in reading, writing, and speaking, and (2) listening is a major way that students learn.

One reason for the neglect of listening instruction is the assumption that everyone knows how to listen, since it is a form of communication used early in life. From the very early months of a child's life, listening, unlike talking, reading, and writing, is in operation. Another reason for the neglect of listening instruction is the fact that listening has never been a part of *literacy*, a primary focus of schools. Historically, *literacy* has been defined, in part, as the ability to read and write. Had oracy (speaking and listening) been embraced in the same way that literacy has been attended to, it is possible that listening would be more established in the curriculum.

Although listening instruction has not been a major part of school curricula, some say that in today's schools, the importance of listening is increasing. Steil points out that three events in the late 1970s have enhanced listening education worldwide. These are the identification by law of listening as a basic competency through the passage of Public Law 95–561 as part of the Primary-Secondary Education Act, the Sperry Corporation's efforts to promote listening development as a business and managerial commitment, and the formation of the International Listening Association.[1] Steil also adds that state departments of education, specialists in listening, and teachers have contributed to the growth of listening effectiveness.[2]

Some Definitions of Importance in Listening

The lack of clear definitions of listening and related terms has long been one of the major problems in the provision of listening instruction in schools. Several terms such as listening and hearing are used interchangeably. The following terms should be understood:

1. *Hearing*—Hearing is the physiological act of receiving sounds. Thus, when one hears a booming sound, the mere act of sound waves reaching the ear which enables one to receive a message (not to understand what it is) results in hearing.

2. *Listening*—Listening refers to the act of zeroing in on, sorting out, focusing on, or paying special attention to an oral message or to a portion of it. Thus, listening goes further than hearing in that listening refers to an activity that goes beyond the physiological to the mental.

3. *Auding*—Auding, a term coined by Don Brown in 1954, refers to listening with comprehension or understanding.[3]

4. *Attending*—The process of paying attention to what is said or staying with a speaker as opposed to tuning out.

5. *Auditory discrimination*—The act of identifying whether or not sounds are alike or different.

6. *Auditory acuity*—The capacity to hear sounds or the degree to which sounds are received by one's hearing mechanism.

7. *Critical listening*—The act of evaluating what one listens to according to a standard or set of appropriate data.

8. *Auditory processing*—Auditory processing refers to the total act of hearing, listening, and auding. Froese uses this term in discussing several theoretical models for examining what happens during listening.[4]

In each of the basic processes involved in listening, there are critical factors and conditions to be considered if listening instruction is to be effective. A case in point is the area of hearing where teachers must be knowledgeable of those factors that impede the receiving of sound waves. Teachers must know how to cut down on distractions that keep students from hearing what is intended to be heard. Another case in point is in listening where teachers must know how to keep students' minds from wandering. Techniques developed for this include getting students to summarize a speaker's message at various intervals of a presentation and/or to project the speaker's next points.

Research of Importance to a Student-Involved Corrective Program for Listening Instruction

Research of significance to a student-involved corrective program for listening and listening instruction includes:

1. Students spend more time listening than they do in speaking, reading, or writing.

2. Listening is a complex rather than a unitary skill, dependent on and related to many factors.

3. Attending to or staying with a speaker is dependent on a number of factors, including those which pertain to the listener and factors related to the content/delivery of the message.

4. Auditory processing and visual processing, working in tandem, are dependent on some common factors at work to produce comprehension.

5. Non-linguistic factors such as a speaker's enthusiasm and gestures affect auditory processing.

6. Communication patterns for listening (as well as speaking) used in the classroom differ from those used by some children from different socioeconomic backgrounds.

7. There is a significant differential between speed of talk (speech speed) and speed of thought (thought speed), with the latter being considerably faster.

These findings along with practices evolving from them are summarized here.

Practice Number 1: Focusing on the Amount of Time Students Spend in Listening

In early studies by P. Rankin, and later, M. Wilt, it was found that people, including students in school, generally listen considerably more than they speak, read, and write. In school, the percentage of time spent in listening was found by M. Wilt to be almost 60 percent.[5] Devine states that more recent studies that extended to the use of radio and television indicated that "ours is a society of listeners."[6]

While it is true that in many instances listening is overused and students are being forced to be too passive, listening in school can be greatly sharpened and thus be used more effectively for learning. The conditions of listening, compared to reading, makes listening instruction even more critical. Listeners, unlike readers, have little time to criticize what they hear, making listeners highly vulnerable.[7]

Practice Number 2: Understanding the Complexity of Listening and How Interrelated it is with Other Factors

All factors influencing listening must be considered by teachers as they plan for effective instruction. Auditory processing has various functions working to produce comprehension, indicating that listening is a complex process, rather than a unitary skill. Kachur points to research indicating this complexity and states that listening should be better understood.[8] A number of factors are correlated with listening, including intelligence, thinking, and reading, although higher levels of reading and listening may have a common "thinking base."[9] According to S. Lundsteen, listening proficiency is dependent on several factors, including: (1) previous knowledge held by the individual; (2) the material to be listened to; (3) physiological factors such as hearing and sensation; (4) concentration; and (5) thinking that leads to integration of the message when it is heard and extension beyond the actual time that it is heard.[10]

Practice Number 3: Understanding How Listeners Attend to or Stay with a Speaker Helps in the Teaching of Listening

Attending to or "staying with the speaker" is dependent on the extent to which the message is effectively delivered and on the needs/values of the listener. According to Friedman, among the factors related to the message being presented are background or setting which can take away or add to the attention given to the message, the intensity of the stimulus in the message, and the concreteness (as opposed to the abstractness) of the stimulus. Friedman also adds another factor which he identifies as "extensity" or the size or amount of the stimulus.[11] Inner needs of the listener cited by Friedman are those that deal with physical needs, including hunger or fatigue as well as social needs such as the need for peer approval.[12]

The delivery of any oral message should begin with some type of analysis of who the listeners are and what, at the time the message is to be presented, might be more important to the listener than the content of the message. If an oral presentation is to be made during an early morning school hour (such as 8:30), it may indeed be wise to let students turn and buzz for five minutes about a big event that took place the night before or an upcoming event that most, if not all of the students, are to attend. Some presentations may well be more suited for afternoon as opposed to just before lunch time. Teachers must also be conscious of how they (or the students themselves) introduce an oral presentation, how variations in an oral presentation can be implemented, and how questions can be introduced in such a way that they involve the listeners as much as possible.

Practice Number 4: Knowing Common Factors That are at Work During Auditory and Visual Processing

Identifying common factors at work in both auditory and visual processing makes it easier to integrate certain aspects of teaching and reduce redundancy. Froese points to a number of studies that have been done which tend to suggest that:

> *Layering on of auding instruction is probably not necessary. Making inferences and making comparisons likely involve the same processes whether the input is visual or auditory; hence they need not be taught twice, once in "listening" instruction and once in "reading" instruction. This is a good reason for integrating the language arts.[13]*

As will be discussed later, listening instruction (here used in the same way as auding instruction is used in the preceding quote) should not be, for the most part, taught as a separate class. Knowing how to pay attention to listening in other subject areas and when, on occasion, to have separate listening lessons will add to the effectiveness of listening-skill development.

Practice Number 5: Identifying Non-linguistic Factors That Affect Auditory Processing

It is not uncommon to hear someone remark that while they liked what the speaker had to say, they did not like the way the speaker looked or acted. There is a need to recognize the importance of non-linguistic factors, since they obviously influence how one receives a spoken message.[14] Teachers should discuss such non-linguistic factors with students and plan strategies to help students avoid the pitfall of these factors.

As a class approaches a unit on oral-book reporting, students as a group might be asked to list nonverbal mannerisms that could interfere with what a speaker is trying to say. A class discussion follows, focusing on how some of the mannerisms can be ignored, such as listeners maintaining eye contact with the speaker at all times as opposed to letting their eyes wander around the room and back to the speaker. While the focus might be on tips for helping students stay tuned as listeners, there could be some spinoff effects for those students making oral presentations. Offensive mannerisms of speakers might be identified and avoided by the students when they make presentations.

Practice Number 6: Identifying Different Communication Patterns for Listening (and Speaking) Brought to the Classroom

Kean points to the work of anthropologists, linguists, psychologists, and sociologists who have studied language used in selected communities (American Indians, African-Americans, and Spanish-speaking communities) and concludes that differences in speaking and listening patterns may vary enough to interfere with classroom interaction.[15] This is a very sensitive area. Oral language is personal language, but with an understanding teacher who does not "put down" any child's language or in any other way suggest that the child's language is inferior, the difference between classroom language and other patterns of speech can be prevented from being a barrier.

Practice Number 7: Compensating for the Differential Between Speech Speed and Thought Speed

If a person's thinking could be translated into words, the speed of words per minute via thinking would be greater than how fast people actually speak. Friedman says that people talk at the rate of 120 words per minute, but that spoken materials can be comprehended up to 250 words per minute.[16] Wolff and others give a slightly different ratio, saying that the difference is 120–180 words per minute for speech speed with minds processing words at a rate of 400 to 800 or more words per minute.[17] The difference between thought speed and speech speed is called the speech-thought differential or *listening time.*[18]

What people do with the extra time between thinking and speaking is very significant. Friedman points out that, "Some students may be using that surplus time for deepening their comprehension of the message being received, while others are reflecting on unrelated past or future events that concern them."[19] Techniques developed for helping students cope with the differential between thought speed and speech speed should be included in a listening curriculum and will be presented later in this book.

A Curriculum for Listening Instruction

Listening skills often parallel reading skills. Thus, one skill might be to detect the main idea of a spoken passage which in concept is similar to detecting the main idea of a passage in reading. Sometimes listening is divided into purposes for listening and skills follow. The curricular framework in Table 7–1 follows this concept. The purposes for listening, some specific listening skills, and applications of the design of this framework are shown.

It should be pointed out that setting up skills in listening might again be attacked by those who believe in the "top-down" curricular design. Advocates of this system might indeed say that when listening instruction is based on extremely interesting topics, skill development is fostered as the listening activities are carried out.

Devine defends the establishment of specific skills by saying that . . . "teachers designing listening programs do need some master plan; otherwise instruction may become random and repetitive."[20] Devine lists a set of skills that teachers might use in designing a year-long program. These skills are shown in Table 7–2. Such a list could easily be woven into the objectives of what is being taught (units, stories, projects) in the language arts, whether the overall curricular design is "top-down" or "bottom-up."

Backlund states that the essential listening skills are those of the Educational Policies Board of the Speech Communication Association. These skills, according to Backlund, should be used as guidelines rather than competencies to be mastered for grade advancement.[21] While the speaking and listening skills are presented together, several of the essential skills focus primarily on listening and the receptive aspect of oral communication. These are: (1) listens effectively to spoken messages (hears the speaker, understands meaning, follows sequence of ideas and

TABLE 7–1 Listening Framework: Purposes/Kinds of Listening; Applications

Broad Purposes for Listening	Focused, Specific Listening	Applications of Listening
Appreciative Listening	to enjoy music to appreciate music to enjoy rhythm in poetry to appreciate imagery to appreciate story form	Listening to a waltz Listening to folk songs Listening to Wordsworth's "Daffodils" Listening to a couplet Listening for imagery in Haiku Listening to an Aesop's fable
Informative (Literal) Listening	to detect the main idea to detect details to follow sequence to follow directions	Listening to a paragraph on dragonflies Listening to a weather report on the radio Listening to "How to Make a Swing" Listening to directions on giving a book report
Informative (Analytical) Listening	to detect the unstated to relate the stated and the unstated to project the speaker's next point to separate fact from opinion to determine cause and effect to recognize points of support	Listening to a ghost tale Listening to a report on an "unusual river" Listening to how World War I began Listening to a radio report on how a fire started Listening to a report on how water freezes
Critical Listening	to detect bias to recognize "hard sale" tactics to recognize propaganda to recognize emotionally-laden words to recognize unfair statements	Listening to a speaker on the topic of deadly illnesses Listening to a radio talk show host downgrade a rival Listening to a salesman's speech about his/her product Listening to an enemy broadcast during the war Listening to a coach give a pep talk Listening to a television commercial about the best toothpaste

TABLE 7–2 Skills for a Year-long Listening Program

1. Determining one's own purpose for listening
2. Guessing the speaker's purpose for speaking
3. Following the sequence of ideas
4. Noting details accurately
5. Following spoken directions
6. Guessing the speaker's plan of organization
7. Noting transitional or signal words and phrases
8. Recognizing a speaker's main points or ideas
9. Noting the speaker's supporting details and examples
10. Using a study guide or outline when provided
11. Keeping track of main points by notetaking or mental recapitulation as the talk proceeds
12. Distinguishing between new and old material
13. Distinguishing between relevant and irrelevant material
14. Noting possible speaker bias
15. Noting emotional appeals
16. Distinguishing between fact and opinion
17. Predicting possible test questions in a lecture
18. Recognizing speaker inferences
19. Predicting outcomes of a talk
20. Drawing conclusions from the talk
21. Asking one's own personal questions (mentally or on paper) as the talk proceeds
22. Summarizing the speakers main points (mentally or on paper) after the talk
23. Relating the speaker's ideas and information to one's own life and interests

Thomas G. Devine, *Listening Skills, Schoolwide-Activities and Programs* (Urbana, Illinois: ERIC Clearinghouse on Reading and Communications Skills and the National Council of Teachers of English, 1982), p. 5. (Used with permission).

draws inferences); (2) recognizes and interprets non-verbal cues given by others; (3) describes others' points and recognizes how they differ; (4) distinguishes between different purposes in communication; (5) provides effective and appropriate feedback; and (6) critically evaluates spoken message.[22] The development of each skill is encouraged not only in the school setting, but also in the home and community.[23]

What then should be the listening curriculum in a corrective program? Can the design suggested for corrective teaching in earlier chapters of this book (*developing a background, formal instruction: introductory, formal instruction: intermediate,* and *formal instruction: advanced*) be adapted to listening instruction? The answer is "yes" provided that the skills, concepts, and other curricular components be, for the most part, embedded in the school curriculum at large. Thus, teaching the main idea and details as listening skills would indeed be done in the context of oral reporting in several subject areas such as social studies or science, with separate practice sessions and/or units focused on listening *per se* only when necessary. A curriculum that encompasses the four broad bands that have been identified might be built around the curriculum framework found in Table 7–1 and include the schoolwide listening skills in Table 7–2.

For younger students, skill development in stage one (*Developing a Background for Listening*) would focus on not only the importance of listening but foundations for focusing on attending to the spoken word as well as rudiments of comprehending through listening. Foundations for critical listening would be established in activities that get children to begin questioning what they hear. As students move through the elementary-school grades, formal lessons would begin in whatever subject area appears appropriate. Eventually, students would be at a more advanced level of listening to detect truth, propaganda, false advertising, and so on, in spoken messages.

Identifying and Correcting Problems in Listening

Listening instruction should include the identification of problems along the total spectrum of auditory processing. Determining only the problems associated with the part of the listening continuum that deals directly with comprehending what one hears would leave out a major segment of instruction. In listening, minds wander just as they do in reading. Thus, improving hearing, getting students to stay on track, and getting students to focus on what the speaker is saying, must all be given attention.

In Table 7–3, some of the major problems in listening are identified, followed by some possible causes, and corrective strategies. The problems identified include, among others, problems with inattention, overreacting to emotionally-laden words, and taking of notes from oral presentations. The list is not exhaustive, and the reader is encouraged to add additional problems that he/she might learn.

Inability to Follow a Speaker's Line of Thought
Although written for older students, *Perceptive Listening* by Wolff and others has some implications for student-involved corrective teaching of listening in the elementary school. The techniques of anticipating the speaker's next points, summarizing what the speaker has said, and evaluating the information—all focused on wise use of the differential between speech speed and thought speed—can be adapted to elementary-school students. The key objective in using these three techniques is to get students to keep up with the speaker by using the time available between speech speed and thought speed. For example, if students are right when they anticipate a speaker's next point, their anticipated idea is reinforced. If students are wrong, there is time to speculate on why they were wrong. In either case, students have remained on task in so far as paying attention to the speaker. These three techniques are briefly summarized, followed by instructions on how they can be adapted for use in the elementary school.

TABLE 7–3 Some Listening Problems, Possible Causes, and Suggested Corrective Strategies

Problems	Some Possible Causes	Corrective Strategies
1. Misinterpretation of oral symbols	Inadequate auditory acuity Problems with auditory discrimination	Have students give word that begins like the teacher's word. Gives students chances to mimic speaker's voice.
2. Misinterpretation of main idea and key concepts	Insufficient experience/background knowledge to comprehend key concepts/main ideas Inability to use context cues in oral setting	Develop/build necessary concepts/vocabulary. Identify beginning, middle, and ending phases of speech, using prearranged hand signals. Have students (a) make three sections on paper, labeled "Beginning," "Middle," and "Ending." (b) listen for and write key words in each section. (c) discuss the results.
3. Inattention	Short attention span Lack of interest in what is being said Home/interpersonal problems Lack of mental set	Build lesson to children's interests. Hold individual conferences to eliminate distractions. Employ good coaching strategies.
4. Inability to retain key concepts/ details in spoken context long enough to relate them to spoken information provided at a later time	Inability to focus and/or concentrate on points being made by speaker Tendency to daydream	Teach students how to periodically summarize (mentally) a speaker's key ideas/points. Teach students to ask mental questions about the speaker's point of view.
5. Lack of skill in taking notes during oral presentations	Tendency to write too much Poor or no training in how to summarize Little to no experience in "putting spoken messages into one's own words"	Teach schemes employed in oral presentations such as cause-effect, unfolding of an event, oral reporting, and compare/contrast. Teach how to detect key words/ideas in oral presentations. Teach telegraphic techniques for condensing speeches.

Continued

TABLE 7–3 *Continued*

Problems	Some Possible Causes	Corrective Strategies
6. Overreaction to emotionally-laden words	Bias/prejudice Lack of experience in listening to emotionally-laden oral reports or conversation	Identify with students a list of words that "make them cringe." (a) Use words identified in oral contexts that are different from the ones where students "cringe at certain words." (b) Gradually use the emotionally-laden words in oral activities for an extended period of time. Role play with students who have trouble with selected emotionally-laden words.
7. Inability to separate fact from opinion	Background experience unrelated to topic under discussion Inability to detect words/phrases that speakers use when giving fact and opinion	Identify signal words and phrases in speech used when someone gives opinions. Identify signal words and phrases in speech to state facts.

1. To anticipate the speaker's next points, have students:
   - Try to predict what directions the speaker's talk will take after listening to just a few sentences.
   - Listen for the central idea of the speech (also identified as the "thesis statement").
   - Predict the speaker's next point by listening for signals such as "I strongly believe," "Furthermore," "There are three steps in preparing for. ..."

2. To mentally summarize what the speaker has said, have students:
   - Identify key ideas and words, sometimes putting them in their own words.
   - Organize key ideas in their minds. Encourage students to tie early statements made with key words (such as central idea with key words now being stated).
   - Listen for pauses, changes in how a speaker is delivering a message (e.g., writing on chalkboard). Take time to add the speaker's ideas together.
   - Listen for clues that help summarize a presentation ("to sum up," "in conclusion," and so on).

3. To evaluate the information presented, have students:

- Mentally repeat what the speaker has said.
- Be as accurate as possible in asking questions of what the speaker has said (for instance, in speech on backpacking, did the speaker say "Backpacking is inexpensive" or "Backpacking isn't really too expensive"?)[24]
- Determine if the speaker is telling the truth. Relate message to own experience or what the listener knows.
- Determine if something has been left out and why it might have been left out.
- Ask if a conclusion other than the one made by the speaker might have been reached.[25]

To adapt these strategies to the elementary school, it is necessary initially to provide some structure and specificity in activities that focus on targeted listening skills. An example is given in a fourth-grade classroom in Case Study Number 1.

Another example illustrating specificity and structure is depicted in the passage on "Weeder Geese" on page 247. Read the passage, decide what you think the central idea (sometimes identified as the main idea) is, make notes on how you would present "Weeder Geese" to teach the central idea, and compare your notes with the suggestions that follow the passage.

Suggestions for teaching the central idea, using this passage follow:

1. Explain to students that often a sentence that gives the central idea is stated in an oral presentation.

Case Study Number 1

Miss Hill is teaching her students in third grade about animals and how they are protected in their natural habitat. Four groups are formed. Each group is assigned a different way that nature has provided for protection of animals. The four groups and their topics are:

Group I:	How Some Animals are Protected by Their Color
Group II:	How Some Animals are Protected by Their Ability to Flee From Their Enemies
Group III:	How Some Animals' Strength Protects Them
Group IV:	How Some Animals Inflict Pain on Their Enemies as a Way of Protection

The groups are instructed to use webbing, a system for guiding reading/exploring/researching a topic and its subtopics.

Continued

Case Study Number 1 *Continued*

Miss Hill shows all students in the class an incomplete diagram which has a central theme or focus in the center as shown below:

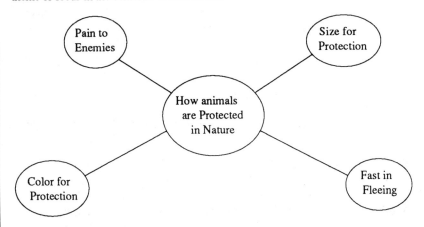

Students are told that in each group, the names of animals should be added, based on what students in the group find when they look in a collection of science books and reference books (e.g., The group working on color might have the lizard whose color changes to blend with different colors in the environment.). Students are to find, where possible, at least one animal per student in the group. On the diagram each animal is to be listed at the end of lines that radiate out from the appropriate category (e.g., lizard out from the "color category"). Brief mini-reports are to be made to the entire class. One group will report each day during science class. Students, when reporting on their animals, are to use pictures and diagrams.

Miss Hill feels that this would be a good opportunity to have students learn a technique for remembering details given in oral reports. Students are asked to listen carefully to each mini-report and quickly repeat to him/herself *key words* that will help them remember how each animal discussed is protected from its enemies. Miss Hill gives some examples such as "lizard: color changes-match-color surroundings." After a group finishes its report, Miss Hill asks each student listening to the report presented to jot down the name of each animal and a few words about how each animal is protected in its environment. Students put their names on their responses and turn them in for review.

Prior to the next group's report, Miss Hill asks students again to be sure to listen and repeat to themselves *key words* to help remember what each student giving a report has said. The same procedure is followed after this group finishes. The process continues the next day and the next day. By the end of the fourth group's report, Miss Hill has a good idea who is having trouble remembering details about animals' protective mechanisms. She plans a couple of lessons with about seven students (a *flex group*) who had trouble remembering details in the group reports. The focus for the lessons will be on identifying and silently repeating *key words* given in oral reports.

Weeder Geese

Farmers in some parts of the U.S.A. may have an alternative and cheaper way of keeping their crops free of weeds. The alternative is geese, developed in China some 2,000 years ago.

These wonderful birds, called weeder geese, are turned loose in a field. The geese eat weeds, but not the crop. They are prolific weed eaters. Weeder geese eat a lot and cost much less than other methods of weeding crops. In Idaho, it is estimated that to weed an acre, it cost $10 to $20 per acre, using weeder geese. Chemical herbicides would cost between $75 to $150 per acre.

---

2. Tell students to listen for the central idea in a speech on "weeder geese." Place the topic on the chalkboard to identify what the speech is about and to raise the curiosity level of students.

3. Ask several students to give their answers to what the central idea or point of the story is.

4. If the first and sixth sentences are given as answers, slowly repeat them, and let the students hear that the sixth one really gives a bit more detail than the first one. Avoid singling out any student's error, but discuss wrong answers in such a way that students learn how to detect the central idea. Approximated wording is accepted.

5. Discuss which sentences best support the central idea. Have students explain why they are the best.

To help students learn to detect central ideas and supporting ideas, Diagram 7–1 is suggested. Students are asked to place what they think the central idea and supporting ideas are in the appropriate columns. The form can be used in small groups or independently. In either case, discussion follows in which reasons are given why the central idea chosen is appropriate. The same discussions follow regarding supporting ideas. Using the Weeder Geese passage, it would be pointed out that a statement on how much it costs Idaho farmers to weed an acre with weeder geese as well as a statement on the cost involved to weed an acre with chemical herbicides would be supporting ideas (or supporting details).

If additional instruction is needed, have students listen for and combine specific details of *who, what, when, where,* and *how* in an attempt to get the central idea of the passage to which they are listening. This procedure is explained:

1. Ask students to make five columns on their paper.

2. Have students place one of the topics *who, what, when, where,* and *how* at the top of each column.

3. As the story of the "Weeder Geese" (as an example) is read to the students, ask them to jot down details under the appropriate column. Thus, under the "who" column, U.S. farmers, weeder geese, and Chinese would appropriately be placed.

(Name of Student)	(Name of Listening Passage)	(Date)

State the Central
Idea of This Passage

DIAGRAM 7–1   Noting the Central Idea and Supporting Details in Listening

Who	What	When	Where	How
Farmers	may have cheaper ways to weed crops	now, today, or the current time	some parts of the U.S.A.	through geese
Chinese	developed Weeder Geese	2,000 years ago		
Weeder Geese	eat weeds		in a field	

First Combination (18 words):   Farmers may have a cheaper way to weed crops in some parts of the U.S.A. through weeder geese.

Second Combination (15 words):   For farm crops, Chinese weeder geese may be cheaper way to get rid of weeds.

Third Combination (10 words):   For crops, geese from China may be cheaper weed eaters.

FIGURE 7–1   Combining Details in Listening to Derive the Central or Main Idea

4. After appropriate words have been placed in each column (and there may be one or two columns without any words), students begin combining the columns.

5. Words in each column are combined to form the central idea, but each combination is reduced as much as possible by the students as shown in Figure 7–1. The goal is to state the main idea in as few words as possible, without omitting any essential element.

As can be seen, the first attempt at combining what has been placed in the columns results in a rather long (18 words) main idea. On reducing some nonessential words (as some parts of the U.S.A.), the passage can be reduced to 15 words, and then to ten. This technique, developed and used successfully in listening and in reading, is easy for students to do. The initial introduction of the activity should be limited to paragraphs. Later, a longer passage should be used. The focus remains on relating the major details in the passage to determine its central idea.

Another passage, this also about geese, might be used to teach students to mentally summarize every few seconds what the speaker has said.

Goose Pimples

Geese played an important part in the life of medieval Britain, as well as other European countries. A prosperous farmer in some English counties—notably Norfolk and Lincoln—was likely to keep a thousand adult birds. Each produced on the average about seven goslings a year.

Flocks were regularly taken to pasture and water, much in the fashion of sheep. It was therefore logical that the man who tended them should be known as a "gooseherd." In autumn, birds were driven to market in London, waddling along at about one mile an hour.

Good strains of geese produced so many feathers that they were usually plucked five times a year. With its soft, downy covering removed a near-naked goose reacted quickly to any drop in temperature.

Like many other birds the goose is equipped with elaborate sets of muscles whose purpose is to pull feathers erect and form a "dead air" blanket. This natural insulation system is activated by thousands of tiny muscles, placed obliquely in the skin, that contract at the first breath of cold air.

Plucked geese react just like fully feathered ones—with the important difference that skin reactions of bare fowls are clearly visible. From gooseherd to housewife and from broker to farm boy, everyone was familiar with the queer, pimpled skin of a plucked goose exposed to cold. The bodily reactions by which humans respond to a draft by involuntary contraction of tiny muscles, despite the scanty hair on the human body, were long ago seen to be much like those of geese. That being the case it was natural that the minute bumps raised on the skin by a draft should be called *goose pimples.*[26]

Each student would be provided a chart like the one shown in Diagram 7–2. The chart is divided into three major parts, although it could have been divided into five parts to correspond to the five paragraphs in this passage.

The teacher, in reading (telling would be even better) this story would give a hand signal about one-third of the way through the passage, about two-thirds of the way through the passage, and at the end of the passage. Students would be asked to jot down some key words that would help them summarize what had just been said or read when the hand signal is given, although the teacher does not stop reading. Students are encouraged to write fast, and only to write key words/phrases to help in summarizing.

The teacher then reads (tells) the passage a second time and asks students to look at their key words and mentally summarize what has been said when the hand signal is given. This time, no writing is to be done. In a follow-up discussion students summarize segments of the story or the total story itself. The students might also be asked to jot down the central idea of the total story on the back of their chart and then to discuss their central idea with others in a small group, formed for the purpose of checking out what others came up with as their central idea. In addition, students could be asked to write down reasons why they chose their central idea, which is not stated in any one sentence as directly as the passage on weeder geese. In other words, students must defend their central idea.

Charts similar to Diagram 7–2 can be used in getting students to detect cause and effect, fact and opinion, sequence of events, and other specific listening skills. In selecting or constructing passages to be used, teachers should gradually move from easy to more complex passages and have students depend less and less on writing key words. The secret is to have students repeat key words to themselves as

DIAGRAM 7–2 Periodic Summarizing of What a Speaker Has Just Said

(Name of Student)	(Name of Listening Passage)	(Date)
Key Words and Phrases (1st Third)	Key Words and Phrases (2nd Third)	Key Words and Phrases (3rd Third)

the presentation is being made. Two brief examples are provided which can be used to provide instruction in listening for cause and effect. In the first one, "Fainting Goats," the causes and effects are more obvious than in the second one, "A Strange Little River."

In the first passage, students listen and identify several cause and effect segments, such as why the "fainting goats" are being eliminated. Both cause and effect statements are actually stated in the passage, but in the second passage, the reason why motorists cross Caney Fork River five times must be inferred.

Fainting Goats

Although rare, there is a breed of goats that, when suddenly frightened or surprised, appears to faint. Their hind legs become immobilized. The goats simply cannot move for a few seconds. Although temporary, such disability has led to the elimination of a number of herds of "fainting" goats. Even a few seconds of being unable to move allows a predator to catch and devour helpless goats.

A Strange Little River

About twenty-five miles east of Nashville, Tennessee, on Interstate 40, motorists cross a very short bridge that is marked "Caney Fork River." In about a minute a second bridge is crossed. Again, the sign on the bridge reads "Caney Fork River." This happens a third time. It happens a fourth time, and it happens a fifth time. Within less than five miles of interstate a small bridge is crossed five times, each with a sign stating "Caney Fork River." Motorists who do not know the area must indeed be puzzled about crossing Caney Fork River five times.

Overreaction to Emotionally-Laden Words

Wolff and others, in writing on being objective when listening to someone speak, give a French proverb that identifies the source of much of the problem of objective listening: "The spoken word belongs half to him who speaks and half to him who hears."[27] Thus, the speaker by his/her way of speaking, mannerisms, or dress, can influence what the listener hears. On the other hand, what the listener hears is influenced by past experiences with the content of the message, the listener's mindset, and how objective the listener has learned to be during a conversation or oral presentation.

Several suggestions that should help students remain objective when they are listening to someone speak are identification of selected words/emotions, reasons why one reacts to these words and emotions, the importance of the identified words and emotions to one's life, and whether or not the listener is reacting to the tone of voice, rather than the message (which could keep someone from being an objective listener).[28]

In the classroom, a teacher might read a story which tells about the school bully who is named Butch. Butch is repeatedly in trouble with the principal because he picks on the smaller children. In the story, one small boy named Carl is Butch's favorite target. Prior to reading the story, students could be asked questions in general about bullies, thus drawing on students' experiences as well as establishing mindset for the story to be read. The students could be asked to identify words/emotions/actions associated with bullies they have known (such as "threat" words used by bullies). A good question to stimulate thinking is one which deals with some of the "threat words" used by people they like. What if your friend said the same threatening words to you that the bullies you have known said to you or others? Following this discussion, the story is read, followed by students filling out individual response cards such as the one shown in Diagram 7–3. Then students might be grouped for discussion, on which a chart would be prepared in each group. Students may again listen to the story, read this time by one of the students in each group. Each chart is shared with the total class.

Students can also be involved in structured role-playing activities in which one student in a small group reads the description on one side of a card of how the person delivering the message is dressed (for instance, Mr. Smith's clothes are too big on him. His shoes are not polished. His hair is greasy and needs combing.) A picture of Mr. Smith might even be shown. The student describing the messenger and reading the message then turns the card over and reads Mr. Smith's message which gives students some figures about the dangers of drugs. The message contains some statistics about the number of elementary-school students who use drugs, and even some grim figures on those who are arrested for selling drugs. Students in the group

DIAGRAM 7–3 Reacting to Emotionally-Laden Words

1. How did you feel when Butch the Bully called Carl a runt?	2. How did you feel when someone like Butch calls you names?	3. What are other words in this story that *really* turned you off? Who said them? Rank the characters who said them from "least liked by you" to "best liked by you."

then discuss the message and the speaker. Basically, the students are focusing on what they think of Mr. Smith's message. Is it creditable? Can they believe him? Why or why not?

Without knowing it, students in another group are going through the same procedure, except the Mr. Smith they hear about is well-groomed, wears a suit that appears to have been made just for him, has on an expensive-looking tie, and wears shoes that appear to be freshly polished. After the group discussions, students then compare their feelings/ discussions about the messages read to them.

Students in each group respond to the questions in Figure 7–2 for activity one. In all probability, it is likely that there would be more positive responses to the Mr. Smith who is a picture of good grooming. The variations in responses should lead to meaningful discussions about the importance of separating the message from the messenger. Variables could also be thrown into each situation. The unkempt Mr. Smith hypothetically, could have lost a child to drug overdose, a situation which led to his appearance and mannerisms. If this is the case, discuss with students if Mr. Smith's message would have been received differently? Why?

A student-involved corrective listening program will take advantage of such techniques as those just described. When a technique is introduced, a series of lessons should follow on a given skill. A listening folder for each student with responses such as those on the chart in Figure 7–2 can give a good picture of listening and reacting to emotionally-laden words. Situations in social studies, science, literature, and other subject areas can easily be developed, using the same procedures outlined.

Activity 1

(Directions) After you have participated in Activity 1 on "Mr. Smith's Fight Against Drugs," answer the following questions "yes" or "no." If you wish to do so, write how you feel about this activity in the "comments" section.

_____ 1.   I listened to Mr. Smith's message about the dangers of drugs.

_____ 2.   My impressions of Mr. Smith were negative.

_____ 3.   My impressions of Mr. Smith were positive.

Comments

FIGURE 7–2 Progress Report for My Listening Portfolio

Organizing for Listening Instruction

There are a number of questions to be answered about grouping patterns for teaching listening. Should there be base and flex groups? How should listening groups be started?

Base and Flex Groups in Listening

Should base and flex groups be implemented in a corrective listening program in the same way advocated for spelling, written composition, and handwriting? This question has been partially answered in Chapter 2 in reference to Table 2–2. First, it was advocated that listening be primarily taught in context of other subjects. Second, it was advocated that base and flex groups in listening would be organized less frequently than in some of the other language arts. There comes a point in the curriculum where separating the different language arts segments the curriculum more than it should. While separate spelling, writing, and handwriting curricula are well-established and will probably continue to be so, listening has not reached this status. With relationships among the language arts more clearly recognized than ever before, now is the time to integrate listening and other curricular areas. As indicated earlier, Froese says that the overlap of processes between language arts areas should lead to integration of listening instruction with other subject areas.[29]

Backlund states that given an already-busy curriculum, teachers have expressed concern about beginning new programs that would encompass listening (and speaking). Backlund, too, says that skill development in listening (and speaking) can be achieved in other content programs and cites an example of a social studies unit where a student is giving an oral report that, for other students in the classroom, turns into a listening exercise. A reading lesson in which one student reads a passage orally followed by other students paraphrasing the passage is given as another example.[30] While Backlund states that imagination and creativity applied to the rest of the curriculum leads to a number of opportunities for teaching listening, "students should see speaking and listening as a content area by itself."[31]

Being Specific About What is Taught in Listening

Lundsteen, who has done pioneering work in both listening taxonomies and critical listening, provides some insight into the need to be specific in planning for listening instruction and avoiding the teaching of listening in isolation. She states that skill in listening is achieved more rapidly when the teacher plans specific activities with consideration to what skill is to be taught as well as a method for observing responses to questions asked.[32]

Devine calls for listening instruction to be integrated, but points out that some separate listening lessons are necessary ". . . in short units and extended daily practice sessions. . . . "[33] In calling for listening instruction to "permeate all studies," Devine gives specific ways of doing so, stating that students should practice notetaking skills in their history and science classes, discuss problems that they encounter when listening to televised newscasts and other out-of-school listening situations, and carry into content-area classes the listening guides developed in their listening lessons. Devine also states that students should report back their observations and examples from other classes and from home and practice their listening skills on school announcements, radio news and weather forecasts, proclamations, and messages from the principal's office.[34]

Understanding Where Listening Can be Taught in the Total Curriculum

To facilitate the teaching of listening as an integral part of the total curriculum, it is necessary to have a good understanding of a listening curriculum. It is also necessary to have a solid understanding of relationships that exist across skills. Thus, knowing that some of the subskills for following sequence in listening are also found in reading helps in teaching sequencing in both language arts. Knowing that there are relationships between main idea and details in listening and reading facilitates integration of listening with reading.

In a self-contained classroom where one teacher is responsible for teaching most if not all subjects to be taught, the integration of listening instruction with other subject areas is relatively easy. However, a conscientious effort must be made in planning where best to integrate listening with other subjects taught.

If teachers note that a number of students in the class are having trouble with particular listening skills, students (1) may be taken from their base groups if this is where the skills have been noted as deficient, and (2) may work together for several days in flex groups on a listening lesson or short series of lessons. An example is in order. If it has been noted that a number of students across several base groups in reading have trouble following the flow of the story when other students retell the story that has been read from the basal or from a trade book, the students having trouble are placed in a flex group and taught special lessons for following an oral sequence of events. They may be taught signal words/phrases such as "at first," "finally," "at last," "in the beginning," and "next." They may use specially-prepared charts that help them listen for and jot down key words and phrases in different parts of a story, or they may listen to commercial lessons on audio tape that provide appropriate instruction.

In social studies, if students appear to have problems keeping on track when special reports are being made by other members of the class, some of the techniques previously discussed for making wise use of the differential between thought speed and speech speed can be taught. If the number of students appear to be most of the class, a listening lesson might indeed be substituted for the next social studies class. If the number is small, a flex group can be formed for the teacher to provide instruction (including reteaching where necessary) some of the skills described, such as anticipating the speaker's next points, mental summarizing, or evaluating information.

Assessment and Corrective Activities for Teaching Listening

While most of the activities available for teaching listening are for developmental programs, some activities are helpful for teaching listening in a corrective program. Such activities as having students attend to or keep focused on what the speaker is saying; listen for sequence of sounds, words, ideas; combine listening and visual images; listen for multiple meanings of words; and make listening a homework assignment should be in a corrective program. While the activities are skill-focused, they are performance-based and call for the teacher to observe behaviors of students. To make the activities more assessment/corrective oriented, progress charts on each student should be kept and where necessary, students should be regrouped and taught appropriate skills. In addition, specific activities in appropriate content fields should be developed and taught, specific/separate listening lessons should be devised if necessary, and students should help in self-evaluating their own progress.

Testing Students on Listening Skills can be both informal and formal. Many of the activities already presented in this chapter deal with teacher observation, a primary way of determining how students are doing in listening. Keeping checklists or having students keep checklists are informal ways of recording progress being made in listening. Formal tests can, however, be useful if the teacher has some flexibility in administering the test. One listening test available on the market is the *CTB/McGraw-Hill Listening Test*. This test, according to its developers, " . . . is a norm-referenced test for Grades 3 through 12, designed to measure the ability to follow directions and interpret connected discourse."[35] Students have an answer sheet and listen to the examiner read passages. Students mark their answers based on the passages that are read. Levels 1 through 4 of this test are designed to measure following directions and interpreting oral passages.[36] In Figure 7–3, a section of a work sheet, response form, and oral directions read by the examiner are given for selected items on levels 2 and 4.

Getting students to attend to oral language being used is often a first step in improving listening. Otto, McMenemy, and Smith offer several suggestions:

1. *While engaged in individual social conversation or instruction, ask a student to repeat your last sentence in his own words.*
2. *Say something absurd in the course of talking to a class, small group, or individual and note who does not react to the absurdity.*

3. Use a nonsense word while giving directions to an individual and note the reaction. For example, "Put the book on the framler when you finish."

4. Play a short, tape recorded story and ask students to summarize the story in their own words when it is finished. Do not tell the students beforehand that they will be asked to do this.

5. After a short speech, ask students to (1) describe the speaker's appearance and mannerisms, and (2) tell the major ideas presented. Note which students attended to the speech more carefully.[37]

Level 2

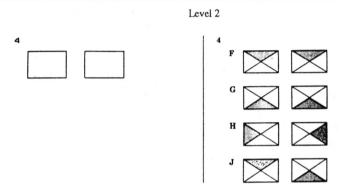

Item 4
SAY   Look at number 4 on the work sheet. Draw an X from the corners of each box. Fill in the top triangle of the first box and the bottom triangle of the second box. What do the boxes look like when you finish? Mark your answer.

SAY   Numbers 14 through 16 are based on the following passage:

One day a little grasshopper told his father about the fantastic creature he had seen. "It is long and narrow and can slide on the ground and wrap itself around trees."

The father grasshopper said he, too, could become long and narrow and wrap himself around trees. He stretched and stretched himself, and very soon he became so thin that . . .

Item 14
SAY   Number 14. What animal was the father grasshopper trying to copy?

          F   a frog   H   a lizard
          G   a fly   J   a snake

Mark your answer.

FIGURE 7–3 Sample Questions and Student Response Forms on a Standardized Test of Listening

Listening Test by CTB Macmillan/McGraw-Hill, 2500 Garden Road, Monterey, California 93940–5380. Copyright © 1985 by McGraw-Hill, Inc. Used with permission.

Level 4

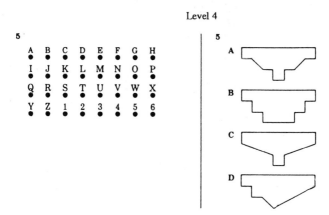

Item 5

SAY   Look at Number 5 on the works heet. Put your pencil on A, draw a line to I, and then go to J. From J, go to S, and from S to T. Then from T, go to number 2, and over to number 3. Go up to U, over to V, and then up to O. From O, go to P and to H. From H, go to A. What does the completed drawing look like? Mark your answer.

SAY   Numbers 11 through 13 are based on the following passage:

Have you ever given any thought to what life would be like without some of the machines and inventions we use every day? How would you like to have to walk to get every place you go? Maybe if you were rich enough, you could be carried around on a chair attached to a platform. If you could handle them, you could ride horses or mules or camels.

To get from one place or another these days, we still often depend on our feet, but now we have bicycles, airplanes, automobiles, and ships to help. Several of these methods of transportation made possible the discoveries that explorers made while traveling on land, on the sea, and in the air.

Item 11

SAY   Number 11. What is the main purpose of the passage?

A   to show that life is made easier by some inventions

B   to show that people are spoiled by new inventions

C   to show that life was much more fun before machines were invented

D   to show that people do not like anything that seems like work

Mark your answer.

FIGURE 7–3   Sample Questions and Student Response Forms on a Standardized Test of Listening *Continued*

Listening for Sequence of sounds, words, ideas, and phrases can be taught with any number of activities. In most of the ones that follow, students are placed in small groups of 3 to 5 students each.

Listening for sequence in sentences   Tell each small group that turns will be taken in which a student is to make up a sentence that has sequence in it, similar to the ones that follow:

1. I went to town, and then I rode the bus home.
2. I played ball, and then I went swimming.
3. I washed my car, and then I went to the movie.
4. I baked a cake, and then I made some coffee.

Make sure that the students in each group understand the sentence pattern which, in this case, is simply an activity performed by an individual followed by a second activity in sequence. Also, stress that sentences to be made up should not be written and shown to others. Only when a student is asked to give his/her sentence should others in the group know what it is. Now play a game by designating any student in a group to begin by giving his/her sentence. The first student repeats his/her sentence (for instance, I watched television and then I went to bed.).

The second student says: "Roy (or whoever said the first sentence) watched television and then went to bed. I ate some soup and then I listened to some records."

The third student repeats what the first two students did and then gives his/her own sentence. Points can be scored if the activity is turned into a game with each correctly-sequenced sentence earning one point.

This activity continues into a more complex type of sentence such as, "I dug a hole in the ground, I put a flower seed into the hole, and then I covered the hole with dirt." Yet an even more complex sentence might be "We raked the leaves, put them into a sack, hauled them to the city dump, and then returned home."

While this activity may appear to be a rather repetitive task that calls for sheer memory, much teaching can be done. In each group, students can be trained to immediately repeat what the students preceding them have done *and in sequence.* Students can also be trained to associate names of their peers and the food they ate, activities they performed, and so on. In addition, students can be trained to remember only the key words such as dug hole, seed in, covered hole for the last sentence. The more students are trained to listen for key words, the more efficient they can become in remembering each activity and the sequence of occurrence. An example can be given to show how students can be taught to associate activities with individuals, thus taking advantage of the differential between thought speed and speech speed. Imagine that the four sentences in the first activity were those made up by students named Douglas, Sally, Sheila, and Kevin who gave their sentences in the order their names are listed. While each of the first three students were giving their sentences, Kevin would be repeating to himself the names of each student and only the key words that indicated the activities in sequence for that person (Douglas—went town, rode bus home; Sally—played ball, went swimming; Sheila—washed car, went to a movie; Kevin—baked cake, made coffee). By the time Kevin gave his sentence, he would have repeated activities for Douglas three times, those for Sally twice, and those for Sheila, once.

Prepare a 5" X 7" index card with one side containing the name of the specific listening skill to be learned (as listening for sequence of ideas). On the reverse side of the card, list the specific points that one should remember to learn the skill in question. Specific points for listening for sequence might be:

1. While listening to an oral presentation, try to detect when the speaker has reached the first third of his/her speech, the second third of the speech, and when the speech is about to end.

2. When the speaker gets to the first third of the speech, quickly summarize (in your mind) what has been said.

3. When the speaker gets to the end of the second third of his/her speech, quickly summarize (again, in your mind) what has been said thus far (including first third also).

4. At the end of the presentation, quickly summarize the speech, making sure to identify events in each third of the presentation. Another listening for sequence 5" X 7" card might have on the back of it such points as:

   a. Listen for specific signal words/phrases such as, "Once upon a time. . . ," "Let me begin by. . . ," "At last. . . ," "Finally." Jot these down on a piece of paper that is divided into three sections labeled "First third," "Second third. . . " and "Last third."

   b. Now summarize the total presentation, using the signal words that you jotted down. Use the signal words in each section of your paper (first, second, third sections) to help you remember the events in each part of the story.

Combining listening and visual images helps students remember what has been or is being said. Armstrong outlines one unique way of doing this. Students do contour drawings by closing their eyes while holding a pencil on a large sheet of newspaper. Each step is given by the teacher which results in describing a figure the students are to draw. Students do not let their pencils leave the paper and do not open their eyes until the figure is drawn. Example: Have students start at the top of their paper and draw a round hat "with a huge curving feather." Then let the students place the hat on a "tall, skinny clown who is riding on a fat camel which is hobbling along a tightrope—on crutches." Outlandish drawings result and are fun, but at the same time, students are concentrating on listening.[38]

Newspaper interviews, according to Armstrong, are helpful ways to get students to listen carefully. Let students conduct interviews for the school or classroom newspaper. Questions are written beforehand and replies are written afterward. Interviews have to be oral, thus putting students in the position of careful listening. Armstrong goes on to say that students first interview each other within the same classroom, then they interview students in other classes, and then staff members. The focus is to sharpen prowess in listening to others.[39]

Listening and filmstrip viewing help develop and/or determine problems in listening. A filmstrip is shown twice. The second time that it is shown, it is shown without sound. Then questions are asked about the most important parts.[40]

Making listening a homework assignment can be helpful. Students are asked to name and list the sounds that they hear from the end of the school day until dinner. The next day activities can be developed using the sounds that the students listed. Included among these are poetry writing in which the sounds are used.[41]

Multiple meanings of words can be used to sharpen students' listening prowess. Lundsteen suggests the use of sentence pairs in which students must orally insert the target word in the second sentence. Examples:

1. *If you **lean** against that glass, it might break.*
   I want a piece of _____ steak.
2. *He used a **switch** to make the mule go.*
   Why don't you _____ to another TV station.[42]

Storytelling can be used to develop imagining, according to the authors of *Basic Listening Skills.*[43] Procedures for using storytelling to develop imagining, adapted from the full description are:

1. Select a brief story that has a dominant mood such as one that is scary or funny.
2. Arrange lighting and play music to help create the appropriate mood.
3. Tell the story, using much expression to create strong visual images.
4. Follow up the story with any of several appropriate activities by having students:

   a. Draw pictures of characters in the story
   b. Discuss the theme of the story and its mood
   c. Discuss details of the story that helped students get the "picture"
   d. Act out the story
   e. Create a story, using the same mood as the story read[44]

Reading to students can be effectively used to develop the skill of inferring. Alvermann advocates the use of a listening guide.[45] She gives as an example the reading of Ezra Jack Keats' *The Snowy Day* for teaching inference. The procedures follow:

1. Tell the students that the story to be read is *The Snowy Day* by a famous author, Ezra Jack Keats.
2. Read aloud to students three literal-level statements, one which is a distractor. Tell the students that "Here are some things he (the author) *might* tell you about Peter, the boy in this book."[46]

   a. Peter took his dog for a walk in the snow (the distractor sentence).
   b. Peter made a snowball and put it in his pocket.
   c. Peter went inside his warm house.[47]

3. Tell the students to listen as the story is read and raise their hands when they hear a part that says "Peter took his dog for a walk in the snow." or "Peter made a snowball and put it in his pocket." or "Peter went inside his warm house."[48]

4. Stop reading when it appears a mistake has been made such as children raising their hands when the part is read about Peter going for a walk in the snow (but by himself—not with his dog). Guide students to see that there was no reference to a dog.

5. Let students pretend to be detectives. The part where students infer that the snowball in Peter's pocket melted is one where they can figure out what happened to the snowball since some clues (but no direct answer) are given.

6. Let students discuss their experiences which may help them understand the disappearance of Peter's snowball. For example, students who have seen the warm sun melt snow or have noticed how fast a snowcone melts on a warm summer day can lend their experiences to help solve the mystery of Peter's disappearing snowball.[49]

The case was made earlier that much of listening instruction should be taught in various subjects as opposed to being a separate content field. Using Alvermann's listening guide, inferences can be taught in any subject. Science is an example. The following passage on termites, intended for students who are older than those *The Snowy Day* is for, can be given as an example.

Termites are often called white ants, but they are not really ants at all. They belong to a different group of insects. However, termites are social animals. Some of the workers are much larger than the others. They act as soldiers and protect the colony.

In many parts of the country, termites are pests. They get into buildings and eat away the wood. Sometimes buildings fall in after termites have weakened them in this way. Termites cannot digest the wood that they eat. They depend on other animals to do it for them. Inside their abdomens are many protozoans. These tiny one-celled animals change the wood into materials that the termites can use for food.

In the warmer parts of the earth, termites build huge mounds of soil for their nests. Some of these nests are so strongly built that only explosives will break them apart.[50]

Reprinted by permission of Scott, Foresman and Company.

The teaching strategy for using this passage and Alvermann's listening guide would be to:

1. Ask the students if they know what termites are. Other questions might be asked that relate to what termites do that homeowners fear or if termites are ants.

2. Have students listen carefully to the three literal-level statements that follow:

a. Termites are insects.
b. Termites and ants live together. (the distractor sentence)
c. Termites build strong nests.

3. Ask the students to raise their hands when they hear a part of the passage read which tells that termites are insects, that termites and ants live together, or that termites build strong nests.
4. If some of the students have trouble with the distractor sentence (Termites and ants live together.), reread paragraph one. Ask students to listen carefully for the *exact* place where it says that termites and ants live together. Since it does not say this, try to determine the source of the confusion by asking probing questions.
5. Use Alvermann's detective scheme to have students listen for clues in paragraph one that tell the listener why ants are insects. If students have trouble, ask them to listen very, very carefully to sentence two (They [termites] belong to a different group of insects.). The detective scheme and students' background experiences can be used in this same paragraph to tell what is meant by *social animals* which is not directly defined.

Identification of common sounds can make the listener more alert to just how many sounds the ear is bombarded with and can lead to identification of sounds in the environment not noted before. Wolvin and Coakley suggest the following in *Listening Instruction* which is designed for older students but contains some activities for younger students:

A Fog Horn?*

Objective. *To provide students with practice in auditory discrimination of everyday sounds.*

Exercise. *Put together a listening tape of everyday sounds that would be familiar to virtually all students from either personal experience or from some medium such as TV. The tape should include sounds such as the following: telephone busy signal, door buzzer, Ping-Pong game, lawnmower, zipper, vacuum cleaner, turkey, car skidding, baby crying, bottle opening, ballpoint pen clicking, bowling, knocking on a door, writing on chalkboard, finger snapping, car door closing, bacon frying, Venetian blinds closing, etc. These sounds can be taken from records of*

*By Andrew D. Wolvin and Carolyn G. Coakley in *Listening Instruction* (Urbana, Illinois: ERIC Clearinghouse/Reading-Communication Skills and the National Council of Teachers of English). (Used with permission).

sound effects and or can be "homemade." Play the tape, and have students identify the sounds by listing them on paper.

Discussion. *How many sounds were identified? Were common sounds recognized more frequently than the less common sounds?*[51]

Diagrams to aid listening comprehension are encouraged by Ur. Among the diagrams advocated are maps and grids.[52] One map activity is called Ground-plans, which Ur stresses is a "very easy exercise for younger learners."[53] The directions and diagrams follow for this activity:

. . . The students are given copies of the plan (with the pools marked as in [Diagram 7–4] and told it is a zoo. They are also given a written list of the animals in the zoo—the teacher should of course make sure they know

DIAGRAM 7–4   A Map for Ground-Plans (an Activity for Teaching Various Listening Skills)

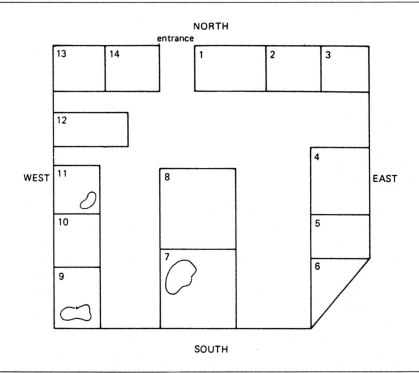

Penny Ur, *Teaching Listening Comprehension* (Cambridge, England: Cambridge University Press, 1984), p. 109. (Used with permission.)

what they all are, and what a "cage" is—and told to write them in the appropriate spaces according to information given in the dialogue that follows the list of animals given to the students.

(List of animals given to students): zebras, pelicans, dolphins, hippos, lions, tiger, camels, pandas, giraffes, monkeys, fox, llamas)

(Dialogue):
A: *Please tell me where the animals are in your zoo.*
B: *Well, tell me what animals you want to see.*
A: *I love lions.*
B: *That's easy. The lions are in the biggest cage, the first one you see in front of you as you come in. Behind it is another big cage, the hippos are in that—they have a pool to swim in.*
A: *What animals are in the smaller cages?*
B: *Well, near the hippos in the corner is a small cage with a pool in—can you see it?*
A: *Yes.*
B: *The dolphins live in that. And next to them is the fox.*
A: *Only one fox?*
B: *Yes. Then there are the pelicans; they live between the monkeys and the fox. The monkeys have a bigger cage, they need room to climb.*
A: *I see. The pelicans have the fox on one side and the monkeys on the other. What about the cages near the entrance?*
B: *Well, on one side of the entrance are three cages and on the other side—two. Right?*
A: *Right.*
B: *Well, in the two cages are giraffes and zebras.*
A: *Which is which?*
B: *The giraffes are nearer to the entrance. On the other side of the entrance are the pandas. Then there's an empty cage, then the camels.*
A: *The empty cage is between the pandas and the camels.*
B: *That's right.*
A: *There are three more cages you haven't told me about.*
B: *Oh yes, well, the big cage near the camels has llamas in it. And behind them is a smaller cage with a tiger. The very smallest cage in the corner is empty at the moment.*[54]

The correct answers are shown in Diagram 7–5. Although not suggested by Ur, an option for this activity would be to develop a series of playing boards that correspond to Diagram 7–4. Names of the animals would be placed on small strips

DIAGRAM 7–5   A Completed Map for Ground-Plans (an Activity for Teaching Various Listening Skills)

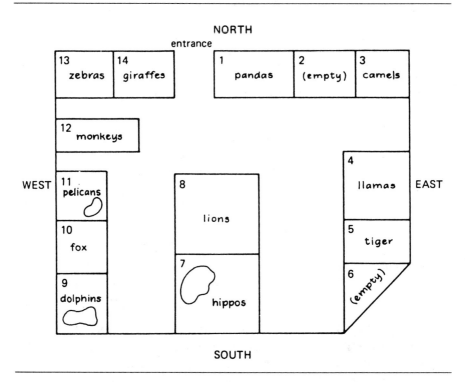

Penny Ur, *Teaching Listening Comprehension* (Cambridge, England: Cambridge University Press, 1984), p. 110. (Used with permission.)

of tagboard, one set per board. As the dialogue is given, students who are participating would have to listen carefully in order to place the names of the animals in the right cell (cage) on the board. The use of a game board and small tagboard markers could help provide manipulative experiences, thus being appropriate for learners who need this type of activity.

Either observing students during this activity or examining the results that students come up with would reveal whether or not students have listened carefully to note details, whether they can locate parts of a diagram (map) when they are dependent on conversation, and the completion of a diagram where they must depend on both listening and seeing. With some changes in the directions, concepts of north, south, east, and west can be added, thus assessing/developing the concept of directionality.

Through teacher observations when students work with grids and maps, records can be kept to help identify students who do not respond appropriately when listening. Students can be placed in flex groups as the need arises. Parent volunteers can be trained to help teachers note how well students respond when working with grids and maps and to help record problems that students have in listening.

Summary

1. Among the important terms in listening are hearing (the physiological act of taking in sounds), listening (focusing on what one hears), auding (listening with understanding), and critical listening (evaluating what one listens to according to standards or data known by the listener). If corrective teaching is to be successful, there must be attention to all aspects of the listening process.

2. Listening is sporadically taught in most schools today, despite the fact that listening is the most used of the language arts. Reasons for this neglect are the assumption that everyone knows how to listen and listening is not a part of literacy, the primary focus of schools. However, in recent years, some additional attention has been given to the teaching of listening in schools.

3. Studies have shown that nearly 60 percent of a person's waking hours are spent listening. Therefore, it is imperative that listening be given more attention than it now is in schools. Listening itself is a complex area. Proficiency in listening is dependent on a number of factors, including background experience of the listener and listening materials used. Teachers must consider the many factors that influence listening if there is to be improvement in the language arts in which so much time is spent.

4. Two basic factors influencing how one attends to what someone is saying are how effective the message is delivered and needs of the listener. Teachers must present their oral messages in a well-organized way. Teachers must also know students and what needs they have that may prevent listening for understanding.

5. Non-linguistic factors also influence listening. These include a speaker's mannerisms or how the speaker looked. Students must be taught how to deal with such factors, focusing on listening to the message more than on the speaker. Teachers must also know how listening (and speaking) patterns differ in selected communities, such as Spanish-speaking communities or neighborhoods. Efforts must be made to keep differences from interfering with how these students interact in the classroom.

6. The differential between how fast a person thinks and how fast a person speaks allows a listener to let his/her mind wander. In a student-involved corrective language arts program, it is important to pay attention to this difference and work to help offset any negative consequences that are the result of the difference. The problems caused by the differential can be lessened if students are taught to anticipate what the speaker will say next, summarize what has been said, and evaluate what has been said.

7. Designing a listening curriculum for a student-involved corrective program is influenced by how one believes language arts should be taught (top-down vs. bottom-up approaches). Positions taken in this book include the identification of specific skills and other components of the listening curriculum; the teaching of curricular components in listening, for the most part, in tandem with content of other subjects (including the language arts); the organization of skills/other components in broad bands, beginning with foundations for formal instruction in listening and moving through listening instruction to the introductory, intermediate, and advanced levels; and grouping of curricular components in listening for instruction. Separate skills are taught when there is a need for emphasis and better understanding of a particular skill.

8. There are similar processes at work in listening and other language arts such as reading. This suggests that listening lessons may be integrated with reading and other subjects.

9. There are specific problems in listening that must be dealt with, beginning at the causal level. Among these are inattention, overreacting to emotionally-laden words, inability to take notes during oral presentations, inability to separate fact from opinion, misinterpretation of oral symbols, misinterpretation of key concepts/central or main ideas, and inability to retain key concepts heard in oral context long enough to relate them to information given earlier or that will be given later.

10. Students should be provided with a number of listening passages which provide practice in listening for the central or main idea, which relate the main idea to details in the passage, and which are to be mentally summarized throughout the passage. Noting key words and using them in summarizing helps with these skills. Students can also hear messages given by quite different characters and learn to focus more on the message than the messenger.

11. There are several ways that listening instruction can be carried out within the total curriculum, including notetaking in various subjects, the stressing of listening standards or guidelines across the total curriculum, and taking advantage of everyday opportunities to teach listening. While base and flex groups should probably not be organized for week-after-week instruction, there will be opportunities, on occasion, to group students in flex groups for listening instruction as the need arises in other areas of the curriculum.

12. Keeping up with progress students make in listening, letting students help evaluate how well they "attend" in situations where listening is called for, and building files that contain creative, focused strategies to help improve listening effectiveness should be focal to student-involved corrective teaching. Diagrams, maps, games and small-group activities should be utilized to teach listening.

Reviewing, Connecting, and Expanding What You Have Learned

(Directions) Read the numbered paragraphs in the summary section of this chapter. Do the corresponding activities that follow, either in a group that your college professor or in-service director assigns you to or do them independently.

1. (Paragraph 1) On the continuum that follows, place where you think the terms *auding, attending, hearing, listening, auditory processing,* and *critical listening* should be:

    Cognitive Processes ◄──────────► Physiological Processes

    In your own words, define each term on the continuum.

2. (Paragraphs 2 and 3) Build a convincing argument that you could use to persuade your employer (your principal perhaps) of the need to teach listening at the grade level you hope to teach or are already teaching.

3. (Paragraphs 4, 5, 6) Make three columns on your paper. Label one "The Message," a second one "The Messenger," and the third column "The Environment." Under each column, list as many factors as you can that relate to the topic and how it influences listening.

4. (Paragraph 7) List what you consider to be the basic guidelines for developing a listening curriculum specifically designed for a student-involved corrective program.

5. (Paragraph 8) Write two brief case studies of a classroom (The grade level is your choice.) in which you identify (a) a situation where listening-skill development should be integrated with another subject and (b) a situation in which a listening lesson might be a separate lesson. Be specific.

6. (Paragraph 9) Identify two specific listening problems presented in this chapter and explain what might cause them. Go further. Find appropriate resources and write a brief essay on each problem, identifying the problem, probable cause for the problem, and some corrective strategies.

7. (Paragraph 10) Make four columns on your paper and label them as follows:
    a. Periodically summarize a speaker's points.
    b. Periodically anticipate a speaker's next point.
    c. Mentally verify what a speaker has said.
    d. Relate details and main or central idea.
    Under each column, list as many ideas as you can think of for carrying out each skill. Then share ideas with your group members or partner. A list of six to eight ideas under each topic would be helpful for classroom teaching.

8. (Paragraph 11) As a group or with a single partner, divide a typical elementary-school student's day into 30–minute intervals. Show what might be taught during each interval and in some instances, across intervals. Divide the intervals up equitably and let each

person in your group develop a hypothetical situation where listening may be taught as part of the lesson designated for the interval.

9. (Paragraph 12) Select one diagram, chart, or grid presented in this chapter, and develop a lesson with its use. *Do not duplicate the activities presented.*

Endnotes

1. Lyman K. Steil, "Listen and Learn: Improving Listening Across the Curriculum," *Curriculum Review*, 23 (1984): 15.

2. Ibid.

3. Sara W. Lundsteen, *Listening—Its Impact on Reading and the Other Language Arts* (Urbana, Illinois: ERIC Clearinghouse on Reading and Communication Skills and the National Council of Teachers of English, 1979), pp. 63, 151.

4. Victor Froese, "Hearing/Listening/Auding: Auditory Processing," in *Research in the Language Arts—Language and Schooling*, eds. Victor Froese and Stanley B. Straw (Baltimore: University Park Press, 1981), p. 123.

5. Thomas G. Devine, *Listening Skills Schoolwide—Activities and Programs* (Urbana, Illinois: ERIC Clearinghouse on Reading and Communication Skills and the National Council of Teachers of English, 1982), p. 1.

6. Ibid.

7. Ibid., pp. 1–2.

8. Donald S. Kachur, "Having Ears They Hear Not," in *Interpreting Language Arts Research For the Teacher*, ed. Harold G. Shane, James Walden, and Ronald Green (Washington, D. C.: Association for Supervision and Curriculum Development, NEA, 1971), pp. 28–29.

9. Thomas G. Devine, "Listening: What Do We Know After Fifty Years of Research and Theorizing?" *Journal of Reading*, 21 (1978): 299-302.

10. John M. Kean, "Listening," in *Encyclopedia of Educational Research*, 5th ed., ed Harold E. Mitzel (New York: American Educational Research Association, The Free Press, a Division of Macmillan, 1982), p. 1102.

11. Paul G. Friedman, *What Research Says to the Teacher—Listening Processes: Attention, Understanding, Evaluation*, 2nd ed. (Washington, D.C.: NEA Professional Library—National Education Association, 1986), pp. 10–11.

12. Ibid.

13. Froese, "Hearing, Listening, Auding," p. 138.

14. Ibid.

15. Kean, "Listening," p. 1103.

16. Friedman, *What Research Says*, p. 6.

17. Florence I. Wolff et al, *Perceptive Listening* (New York: Holt, Rinehart and Winston, 1983), p. 154.

18. Ibid., p. 159.

19. Friedman, *What Research Says*, p. 6.

20. Devine, *Listening Skills Schoolwide*, Ibid., p.5.

21. Philip Backlund, "Essential Speaking and Listening Skills for Elementary School Students," *Communication Education*, 34 (1985): 187.

22. Ibid., 190–192.

23. Ibid.

24. Wolff, et al, *Perceptive Listening*, pp. 162–163.

25. Ibid.

26. Webb B. Garrison, *What's in a Word?* (Nashville, Tennessee: Abingdon Press, 1965), p. 258.

27. Wolff, et al, *Perceptive Listening*,.p. 130.

28. Ibid, pp. 143–144

29. Froese, "Hearing, Listening, Auding," p. 138.

30. Backlund, "Essential Speaking and Listening," p. 192.

31. Ibid.

32. Lundsteen, *Listening*, pp. 53–54.

33. Devine, *Listening Skills Schoolwide*, p. 8.

34. Ibid.

35. CTB/McGraw-Hill, *Listening Test*, Examiner's Manual, Levels 1 Through 6, (Monterey, California: CTB/McGraw-Hill, 1985), p.1.

36. Ibid.

37. Wayne Otto, Richard A. McMenemy, and Richard J. Smith, *Corrective and Remedial Teaching*, 2nd ed., (Boston: Houghton Mifflin, 1973), p. 316.

38. Linda Armstrong, "Is Anybody Listening?" *Learning*, 13 (1985): 33.

39. Ibid.

40. Ibid.

41. Ibid.

42. Sara W. Lundsteen, *Listening—Its Impact on Reading and the Other Language Arts*. Revised Edition (Urbana, Illinois: National Council of Teachers of English and ERIC Clearinghouse on Reading and Communication Skills, 1979), p. 43.

43. Illinois State Board of Education, Curriculum Improvement Section, *Basic Listening Skills*, (Springfield, Illinois: Illinois State Board of Education, 1987), p. 13.

44. Ibid.

45. Donna E. Alvermann, "Teaching the Process of Inferring Through a Listening Guide," *Reading Horizon*, 24: (1984) 243.

46. Ibid., 245.

47. Ibid.

48. Ibid.

49. Ibid., 245–246.

50. Scott, Foresman, *Science Problems 1*, (New York: Scott, Foresman, 1957), p. 356.

51. Andrew D. Wolvin and Carolyn Gwynn Coakley, *Listening Instruction*, (Urbana, Illinois: ERIC Clearinghouse on Reading and Communication Skills, 1979), p. 23.

52. Penny Ur, *Teaching Listening Comprehension*, (Cambridge, London: Cambridge University Press, 1984), pp. 103–121.

53. Ibid., p. 108.

54. Ibid., pp. 108–110.

Bibliography

Strategies/Materials

Delaware State Department of Public Instruction. *State Content Standards for English Language Arts, Volume I: Instructional Activities for Effective Teaching, Grades 1–3* (Dover, Delaware: State Department of Public Instruction, 1989).

Shoop, Mary. "Inquest: A Listening and Reading Comprehension Strategy," *The Reading Teacher*. 39 (1986): 670.

Spiegel, Dixie Lee. "Materials for Developing Listening Skills: A Review of Five Criteria," *The Reading Teacher*, 43 (1990): 674.

Issues

Michaels, Sarah. "Listening and Responding: Hearing the Logic in Children's Classroom Narratives," *Theory Into Practice* 23 (1984): 218.

Watson, Kittie W. "Listening: Who's Testing What?" *Curriculum Review* 23 (1984): 20.

Research

McMahon, Margaret L., "Development of Reading-While-Listening Skills in the Primary Grades," *Reading Research Quarterly* 19 (1983): 38.

Marten, Milton. "Listening in Review," In *Classroom-Relevant Research in the Language Arts*, coordinated by Harold Shane and James Walden (Washington, D.C.: Association for Supervision and Curriculum Development, 1978), pp. 48–60.

8

A Corrective Program for Instruction in Oral Communication (Speaking)

Focus

Speaking, like listening, is neglected in most schools. The reasons are perhaps the same as stated for listening: Children learn to speak before coming to school and speaking is not an integral part of literacy. At one time, however, some systematic and focused attention was given to speaking as a part of the school curriculum. Attention was given to speaking before the public and lessons in "oratory" were given with that aim.

Chapter 8 begins with a discussion of the status of oral communication in the elementary school today. The focus then shifts to four research conclusions and practical implications that they have for the curriculum. In this chapter, the promotion of various kinds of verbal communication in the classroom will be addressed, as well as grouping patterns which facilitate such communication. Corrective activities that focus on a number of themes presented in this book (student involvement, multi-modal teaching strategies, and using students' interests) will be given.

Oral Communication in Today's Classroom

While there has been a neglect in oral communication or speaking as an integral part of the school curriculum, there are some activities involving this language arts found in most schools. However, all too often, these activities are taught sporadically.

> As you read Chapter 8, contrast what you are reading with what you know about oral communication taught in today's elementary school. Pay special attention to what objectives are to be taught in such a program, for all too often the objectives are not clear. A special effort should be made, as you read, to understand the value of teaching oral communication in the elementary school. Also, you should focus on how the various themes of this book apply to an oral-communication program.

The oral-communication activities typically found in the primary grades include sharing, creative dramatics, some small-group work where students plan and talk together on projects to be carried out, and conversations among students. In the upper-elementary-school grades, oral communication often is more structured than in the primary grades and has more complicated rules. In the upper grades, one might find panel discussions, formal book reporting, debate, more structured small-group discussions, and reporting before the total class.

Research of Importance to a Student-Involved Corrective Program for Oral Communication (Speaking)

Research in oral communication lags behind research in most of the other language arts. However, this status may be changing. The 1986 *Handbook of Research on Teaching* contains a chapter by Cazden on "Classroom Discourse," with attention given to such topics as classroom discourse and student learning, cultural differences and oral language in the classroom, and interactions among peers.[1] While the topics are not focused on the teaching of oral communication in the classroom, the existence of a chapter on classroom discourse could signal a shift in the importance being given to oral communication in the elementary school.

There are four basic research practices in oral communication that should have implications for a student-involved corrective program in oral communication. Two of them are the influence of social conditions in the classroom and their effects on verbal interaction of cultural groups often considered "different" and how a teacher can better facilitate small- and large-group discussions where the focus is on children's use of hypothetical language, prior knowledge, and questioning. Two other research practices include how verbalization and drama affect the learning of various language arts.

Practice Number 1: Understanding that the Classroom Environment May Have Negative Effects on Verbal Interaction of Children from Some Cultural Groups

This is the same as a research area identified in Chapter 7 (Listening) in which it was stated that some children's speaking and listening patterns are so different from those found in the school that verbal interaction is inhibited. Through ethnographic and linguistic research studies, it has been found that children from some cultures choose not to talk in classrooms as a result of differences between social conditions in the classroom and those in the children's communities. African-Americans, Spanish-speaking children, and American Indians are among the groups that have been cited.[2] Cazden cites the need for teachers to not only be aware of language and other cultural differences in their classrooms, but to work toward eliminating problems that are often created in the schools. S. Heath, an ethnographer, working in rural communities (including rural African-American communities and communities made up primarily of rural white children), used the forms and functions of questions asked by children in their home settings and encouraged teachers to try out new patterns of classroom discourse.[3]

Cazden further points out that providing differential treatment for groups whose language is different from that found in schools can have negative effects. She says that "The most important question is whether differential treatment is helpful individualization or detrimental bias."[4] This can be asked about reading groups where a question can be raised: Do children in low reading groups (which of course have participants from all cultural groups) receive the kind of help that children in high reading groups receive?[5]

Practice Number 2: Facilitating Small-Group and Total-Class Discussions

Research shows that the usual classroom pattern of verbal interaction is a triad of teacher question/student response/teacher judgment.[6] The prevailing model of teaching has been found to be a transmission-of-knowledge model which greatly limits the quantity and purpose of children's language use.[7] What is called for is a teacher who is or can be a true facilitator of classroom discussion. Such a teacher gets students to

> . . . *test their understanding against other sources and their own knowledge for consistency and truth. During this type of discussion, risk-taking and error-making, both integral parts of learning, occur with feedback in an atmosphere of trust. By focusing attention, posing questions, pointing out problems, suggesting alternatives or providing information at the teachable moment, a teacher can heighten awareness and facilitate learning.*[8]

In student-involved corrective classrooms, teachers pay much attention to total-class and small-group discussions. Working to move away from the model previously cited where the teacher questions, students respond, and teacher judges or evaluates, teachers strive to involve students by getting them to interact with one another, rather than with just the teacher.

The teacher, as a facilitator of group discussions, serves as a model for asking questions, continuously asking probing questions such as "Why?", "How-do-you-know-that?", and "But-don't-you-think-that?" The questions are inquiry-type, upper-level kinds of questions.

The teacher also pays close attention to children's interests. Such interests are systematically used in all kinds of discussions. In addition, the teacher provides many resources on topics for discussion, including resources for pre- and post-discussions on a topic.

Models of good discussion should be provided, with students having opportunities to develop their own skills of oral communication before, during, and after the model is observed. Students may observe a videotape of one group's discussion that has been judged to be a model discussion. During the observation, students who are watching are instructed to write *why* and *how* questions that they would ask if they were participants in the group. These questions could then be the center of a lesson on good questions during discussions.

Practice Number 3: Letting Children Verbalize During the Learning Process

In Chapter 6, it was pointed out that verbalization of letters of the alphabet, as they are made, aids in the formation of the letters. Research by B. Furner demonstrated that when students verbalize starting and stopping points of each stroke as well as the direction of each stroke in handwriting, initial letter formation is helped.[9] In addition, N. Sovik's research demonstrated that copying of letters was improved when verbal instruction was combined with demonstration.[10]

Research by R. Gagné and E. Smith demonstrated that verbalization by children as they performed problem-solving tasks produced superior results.[11] Johnson and Johnson cite numerous studies, dating back to 1971, which reveal the value of what they call "oral rehearsal." They state that:

> *Explaining what one knows and is thinking has important cognitive benefits for the explainer. In one of the earlier studies on this issue, Johnson (1971c) found that one's understanding of an issue and level of reasoning were enhanced by the combination of explaining one's knowledge and summarizing and paraphrasing the other person's knowledge and perspective. More recently, a number of studies have found that orally summarizing, explaining, and elaborating one's information, ideas, and conclusions provides a review that seems (through further encoding and networking) to consolidate and strengthen what is known and to provide relevant feedback about the degree to which mastery and understanding have been achieved.*[12]

The extent to which the teacher in a student-involved corrective language arts program uses verbalization is dependent on a number of factors. In initial skill development, students should be encouraged to "say and listen to yourself" as the task at hand is being undertaken. In small groups or in pairs, one student might verbalize steps to be taken in learning a skill while other students in the group listen and give comments about the task. An example is changing the form of a verb such as *sing* to *singing*. A student can be asked to use the words *sing* and *singing* in an oral sentence (or sentences) composed on the spot ("Gene will *sing* tomorrow.", "He is *singing* in the glee club in his school.") and then verbalize how the word *sing* was changed. Other students would take their turns. Later, the more difficult changes (*make* to *making*; *sun* to *sunning*) are made, following the same procedure.

In some cases, students may verbalize a skill being learned initially and place the results on audio tape for the teacher to hear. In such cases, however, the taping session would probably be more than a single skill such as changing *sing* to *singing*. It might be a sequence or procedure that has been taught, such as study steps to accomplish a task. For example, it might be spelling where students take a group of new words to be learned and explain on tape how they used the study steps to learn how to spell the new words.

There are numerous ways that verbalization can be used in teaching. The use of this modality, however, should not become so routine that students tire of doing it. Neither should verbalization be substituted for the use of experiences calling for imagery, acting out or doing to learn, nor other constructive ways of learning.

Practice Number 4: Using Drama, which Includes Talk, Gesturing, and Acting Out, is a Productive Way to Learn the Language Arts

Drama, according to Wagner, is highly productive in the learning of language arts. A meta-analysis* study by C. Kardash and L. Wright revealed that drama has a positive effect on reading, communication, and a person's perception of self.[13] Other studies revealed positive effects on personal attitudes often associated with language growth, self-confidence, self concept, self-actualization, empathy, helping behavior, and cooperation.[14] The work of Jean Piaget on how children move from egocentric symbolic play to social symbolic play has been cited by Wagner to underscore the importance of drama elements in learning:

> . . . *The child symbolizes experiences from the real world by engaging in object substitutions (as substituting a box for a house) and "decontextualized behavior" (i.e., behavior, including talk, that occurs*

---

*Meta-analysis refers to a statistical procedure for analyzing a group of research studies in the same area of study. Central to such analysis is the effect size.

outside its real world context). Since the acquisition of literacy is dependent on the manipulation of symbols and increasing decontextualizing of language, social symbolic play provides a useful bridge to literacy.[15]

L. Vygotsky states that drama helps children separate the signifier from the signified and attach meaning to symbols, while A. Pelligrini and C. Wolfgang, in separate studies, found that drama correlates with literacy skills (especially in kindergarten and first grade).[16]

Drama also has an effect on writing. C. Bereiter and M. Scardamalia concluded that the main problem with writing is ". . . assessing and giving order to what they (children) know and . . . drama should help them discover and shape their ideas."[17] One specific way in which drama helps in writing is in the use of gestures to help in persuasive writing.[18]

While drama can be used in assessing problems in oral communication, it would appear that the real value of drama to a student-involved corrective program is in the development of corrective activities that push children to be more emphatic, precise, descriptive, and imaginative. An example in writing can be given. Two students are told how to walk across the front of the room, one at a time. However, the rest of the class does not hear the instructions. The first student is told to walk very slowly as if lost. The second student is told to walk very briskly as if he/she "knows exactly where to go and why." The teacher asks other students to write sentences which describe how each of the two students walked across the room. The focus is to get students in the class to say more than "Jill walked slowly across the room." and "Beth walked rapidly across the room." Students can be coached to not only write sentences that follow, but see how they are far more descriptive than those given:

1. Jill walked slowly and aimlessly across the room as if she had lost her way.
2. Jill, looking as if she were in a fog, walked ever-so-slowly across the room.
3. Beth walked briskly across the room to meet her dearest friend.
4. Beth, looking as if she had won a million dollars, walked across the room at a clip.

Identifying Skills and Other Components of the Oral-Communication Curriculum

The oral-language curriculum in the corrective classroom can follow the same model as the curricula for other language arts, with emphasis on first the development of a background for teaching/using oral communication, formal introductory teaching of oral communication, formal intermediate teaching of oral communication, and formal advanced teaching of oral communication. In each case, students are asked to proceed through four levels of content, although the curriculum is not totally linear. Students may be taught several skills in a level at the same time or in the same lesson. Also, flex groups may be organized.

As in listening, oral-communication skills can and should very frequently be taught in the context of content fields such as social studies, literature, and science. Where needed, separate lessons are taught to strengthen oral-communication and listening skills, but such lessons do not constitute the heart of instruction in these two language arts.

Not every oral-communication activity has to be focused on a specific skill to be learned. Indeed, there are any number of oral-language activities that children should participate in throughout the school year for the purpose of enjoying the activities. Children enjoy activities such as choral speaking, reciting poetry, and reading to others, and these activities should be a part of the curriculum.

The Promotion of Effective Talk/Discussion in the Elementary School Classroom

Much of the attention to oral communication in the elementary school classroom should center on the promotion of effective talk and good discussions. This is particularly true of a corrective classroom in which problems cited are to be dealt with in the regular classroom as opposed to a clinic-type class taught by a specialist. The first step toward the promotion of effective talk and good classroom discussions is the adoption of a philosophy that embraces talk as a pivotal point in learning. Such a philosophy has been embraced by educators in British schools. Green explains the practices in British schools emanating from the acceptance of a philosophy which places talk as central to learning:

> *As with writing, talking exists in abundance in the British Schools—all kinds of talking. Children seem to be tacitly encouraged to share ideas and problems with each other as they work because they do so openly and in a noncompetitive and helpful way. Talking is not considered an illegal enterprise and consequently, the frequent murmurings of the classroom seem facilitative rather than disruptive. The informal talk is not the total substance of it, however, because from the earliest age there seems to be significant time given each day to class discussions. Teachers frequently encourage children to exchange, examine, and develop ideas in more than just a random fashion. . . . [19]*

Several kinds of oral-communication practices are presented in this section of Chapter 8. These include collaborative talk, small-group discussions, oral language in cooperative learning settings, and the more formal types of oral communication which include oral reports, panels, and debates. These practices are given attention because the author feels that they have the most promise for making talk a more viable tool for learning than it now is and because they are diverse enough to be used as examples. For each practice cited/discussed, some attention will be given to assessing-correcting problems that students might have in the area.

Collaborative Talk

Collaborative talk is defined as "... talk that *enables* one or more of the participants to achieve a goal as effectively as possible."[20] Characteristics of and roles taken by students and teacher as well as an example of the dialogue between two elementary-school students engaged in collaborative talk are given in Table 8–1. This dialogue took place in a third- and fourth-grade combination classroom in an inner-city school in Toronto. The students, *Joao* and *Eric* are engaged in building a model of Dawson City, a project that grew out of the reading of "The Cremation of Sam McGee," a poem by Robert Service.[21]

In reviewing the initial dialogue in Table 8–1 (1–23 in the Student-Student Talk section of column 1 between the two participants in collaborative talk), it can be seen that the goal of building a model is given in explicit terms. Also, it can be seen that both students have an understanding of what each is thinking, a point that is important in collaborative talk.[22] While the goal set for this activity is action oriented, Chang and Wells state that the goals in collaborative talk can be more abstract such as talking to understand a principle learned in science.[23]

In Table 8–1, the role of the teacher can be further explained by examining selected points of dialogue (1–23 in Student-Teacher Talk in the first column). The teacher's comments such as "uh-huh" are intended not to evaluate what the students are saying/doing but to get them to amplify what they have said. Questions asked by the teacher are also intended to clarify/amplify the dialogue, not to add new information or to in any way interfere with the students' collaborative talk. Such types of comments and questions help carry out the teacher's role which Chang and Wells identify as one to "lead from behind."[24]

In promoting collaborative talk, there are five areas in which the teacher can unobtrusively carry out some of the corrective strategies central to the themes in this book. The first has to do with grouping students for getting maximum effectiveness out of collaborative talk. The second is knowing/using students' interests in promoting collaborative talk. The third area is helping students self-evaluate their participation in situations where collaborative talk has been implemented. The fourth area is establishing a relationship of helpfulness so that students can feel free to seek advice on ways to improve their reactions/responses in collaborative talk. The fifth area in which the teacher can carry out a student-involved corrective approach to collaborative talk is in the evaluation of needs of students either from observation or reading narratives on self-evaluation or from both and following up with activities that correct problems.

Grouping students for collaborative talk is an important first step for the teacher to take. Following the reading of a selection that might serve as the vehicle for collaborative talk, students are placed in pairs and/or small groups, ready to define their goals and strategies for carrying them out. Students should be grouped in such a way that one student does not dominate the discussion, thus putting his/her partner/group members in the role of merely carrying out the dominant member's decisions. While one person may take a leadership role, such a role must not be dictatorial.

TABLE 8–1 Collaborative Talk in Elementary School Classrooms

Student-Student Talk	Characteristics of/Roles Taken in Collaborative Talk (Students)
1 *Joao:* Eric, look! See, here is going to be the small mountain.	1. Specify goal (problem) in explicit/precise terms.
2 We're going to build it up how it is in the book.	2. Plan means for achieving goal.
3 Where's the book? (*He picks it up to show to Eric*).	3. Generate/choose between alternatives.
4 You know, building it up and everything.	4. Review achievement to date (periodically).
5 *Eric:* Yes.	
6 *Joao:* Here it is, see. It says 'Building it up'.	5. Modify what has been done as necessary.
7 *Eric:* No, it doesn't mean—	
8 *Joao:* So the small one then the big one (*referring to the already cut	
9 pieces of cardboard*).	
10 We can make a little river and the town on the edge too.	
11 *Eric:* Yes, that's what I mean.	
12 *Joao:* Yeh, OK.	
13 *Eric:* That's what we were talking about.	
14 *Joao:* Yes, we're starting.	
15 *Eric:* And we can do little boats because of the little trees.	
16 *Joao:* Yes. OK. So we have to glue this (*the cardboard*)	
17 *Eric:* And these are the <*****>	
18 *Joao:* Yes. No, we're not going to put a church.	
19 *Eric:* I know I know.	
20 *Joao:* No, we're not going to do any of that, OK?	
21 We are going to plan it how we planned it in the paper.	
22 *Eric:* Yes.	
23 *Joao:* OK, let's go.	

Continued

TABLE 8–1 *Continued*

Student-Teacher Talk	(Teacher)
1 *Joao:* We're going to—we're going to cover it with white tissue paper, Eric.	1. Takes participants seriously as each works through problem that has been chosen.
2 *Eric:* <That's what we've got to do>	
3 That's for when they have snow. and after. by mistake it	2. Listens carefully to participants.
4 could avalanche on here (*pointing to the base of the mountain*	3. Requests amplification/clarification of ongoing talk as necessary *to understand.*
5 *on the model*) and some houses will be crushed	
6 *T:* I wonder if that's a danger here (*pointing to the equivalent place on the photograph*)	4. Makes contributions aimed at getting participants to talk through and come up with their own solutions (as opposed to teacher-imposed solutions and/or new information).
7 I think you're quite right about some <u>mountains</u>	
8 *Joao:* <u>I thought</u> it was summer (*meaning in the photograph*)	
9 *Eric:* Yeh but in winter—but if it's in winter	
10 *Joao:* Yeh. yeh the seasons could change.	
11 *T:* That's true	
12 And they don't move their houses here .. do they?	
13 *Eric:* <u><**></u> Yeh they can't like lift it and go 'ow ow' (*miming*	
14 *lifting a very heavy weight*) unless they just go 'da da da	
15 da' (*said in a sing song voice, which seems to represent the use of magic*) (*all laugh*)	
16 T: I don't think they're going to do that..	
17 Well if you have a look here (*pointing to photo in book*)..	
18 See where the houses are. along the river. and then.	
19 What does this look like?	
20 *Joao:* That's a mountain	
21 *T:* Part of the mountain	
22 *Eric:* (*pointing to model*) These are one of these mountains	
23 *T:* Uh-huh uh-huh	

Gen Lang Chang and Gorden Wells, "The Literate Potential of Collaborative Talk," in *Oracy Matters: The Development of Talking and Listening in Education,* eds. Margaret McLure, Terry Phillips, and Andrew Wilkinson (Milton Keynes, England: Open University Press, 1988), pp. 96–105 (Adapted from and used with permission).

In collaborative talk, when it is noted that one student dominates others, the problem should not be compounded by putting these students together in activities calling for collaborative talk. The teacher might group two students together who tend to be overly assertive in order that there is some balance between giver-receiver language-sharing roles. While such grouping can backfire and result in more argument than collaborative talk, the risk of having this occur can be better controlled by the teacher than the situation where one student totally dominates others in his/her group.

Knowing and using interests of students can facilitate effective collaborative talk. As stated in Practice Number 2, such interests should be systematically used in classroom discussions. If several students in the classroom are interested in race cars, meaningful collaborative talk may evolve from these common interests. Students may work together on building a model racetrack. They may work together on planning a hypothetical race. Students may work together on writing a description of, "The Most Exciting Finish in the History of Racing" or on developing/carrying out a radio broadcast in which the race is described. Other students in the classroom will have different interests such as making plans for remodeling an old house, traveling to a distant land, making plans for a gourmet dinner, and learning about the domestication of animals.

Self-evaluation of participation in collaborative talk activities can be handled in such a way that what the students say not only gives them an insight to areas that they might work on, but also helps the teacher in plans for future collaborative talk. Such self-evaluation should be more open-ended than has been advocated for some of the other language arts (handwriting, spelling). While some checklists might, on occasion, be used, the author of this book is of the opinion that narrative statements would in most situations be more helpful for self-evaluation of collaborative talk. An example of a form that might be used is presented in Figure 8–1. On this form, students may examine their own participation. On other occasions, students who were together in collaborative-talk activities might assess joint efforts. Forms can also be developed and used by the teacher. These forms help make teacher observation more systematic than it otherwise might be.

Establishing an appropriate relationship of helpfulness where students feel comfortable seeking help from the teacher is important. While the teacher is not to interfere during ongoing talk, it is important for students to feel that they can come to the teacher for information that might be helpful in preparation for their talk with a partner. Thus, in the situation where race-car enthusiasm among several students is to be utilized as a base for collaborative talk, the teacher should serve as a resource person prior to the beginning of projects on which students will be involved. The teacher explains to students that there are several books and sports magazines about race cars in the school's media center. The teacher might also suggest sources for getting photographs of race-car tracks. The teacher does not necessarily provide the information, but he/she does help with pointing out possible sources of information.

_____

_____

(Names of the Participants in your Group)

_____

(Name of your Project)   (Project Dates)

Activity 1   In the space below, explain how you feel about how your project
              developed?

Activity 2   When you do another project in which you talk through and carry out
              activities similar to those you have just completed, what are some things
              that you want to do differently?

_____

FIGURE 8–1   Self-Evaluation of Collaborative Talk

Following up on problems noted can be handled without creating problems
when students are again engaged in collaborative talk. Teachers should record specific problems observed when students are engaged in collaborative talk. One
example is where students are not explicit enough in defining goals that they hope
to accomplish. Prior to the next time that collaborative talk is to take place, the
teacher could use a prepared overhead transparency which shows some contrasts of
"fuzzy" and "very explicit" goals, as shown in Figure 8–2. These examples should
be given in such a way that they do not embarrass the students who were not
explicit enough in stating goals. In some cases, examples from classes previously
taught might be given.

Small-Group Discussion

Small-group discussion refers to groups of usually three to five students together
exploring a topic. There are several types of small-group discussions such as buzz
groups and brainstorming groups. Each type will be explored in this section of
Chapter 8 with special attention to how each group can be organized for maximum

Fuzzy Goals	Very Clear (Explicit) Goals
1. We are going to study about evaporation.	1. We will make a table display that explains the process of evaporation.
2. The model frontier village that we will build will be the best in the class.	2. We will build a model of a frontier village found in the late 1700s.
3. We are going to make a scrapbook on horses.	3. We are going to make a scrapbook of magazine pictures on race horses.
4. Our topic to explore is how air expands when heated and contacts when cooled.	4. We will demonstrate how air expands when heated and contracts when cooled.
5. The speech that we are preparing is on women and their right to vote.	5. We will outline and then write a speech on how women have received the right to vote in the United States.
6. We will explain how an airplane stays up in the air.	6. We will make a diagram to show the scientific reason why an airplane can stay up in the air.
7. We will bake a cake that everyone will surely like.	7. We will bake a cake that has been judged to be the favorite in the United States.

FIGURE 8–2   Fuzzy and Very Clear (Explicit) Goals in Collaborative-Talk Situations

student-involvement in the corrective classroom. While there are differences in purposes, organizational structures, and procedures for implementing small-group discussions, there are some common tips that cut across the various kinds of small groups. Klein has identified thirteen such tips:

 1. Keep groups small, ideally three to five members. With practice, size can be increased somewhat, but generally it should not exceed seven members.
 2. Be certain group member roles are clear, and the assignment is understood by all. In nearly every type of small group activity, there should be a chairperson assigned the responsibility of facilitating smooth operation of the group, and a secretary to record the group efforts and conclusions. These roles, of course, should be moved around among the students.
 3. Consider the size of your room, number and arrangement of chairs, and location of physical obstacles, etc., then design an orderly system for moving the class into and out of small group settings. Each child should know the specific job and route to follow. Remember that one of the more troublesome matters to

overcome in small group operations is the physical rearrangement procedures. If they are clean and orderly, it helps set a tone for the rest of the operation.

4. *Begin with task-oriented, problem-solving types of small group activity with a very specific charge. Exploring groups should come only after experience in other formats.*

5. *Keep the first small group activities short, 15–20 minutes, perhaps less in the primary grades. Lengthen time gradually. Eventually, some small group activities can be extended through several weeks, with groups researching particular issues or problems.*

6. *Assign groups and leadership roles within groups in the beginning stages. Strive for group balance, so that there will be less likelihood of frustration for individuals who happen to get in with ill-matched membership. Be aware of personality differences, and try to keep these from frustrating the entire group.*

7. *In later stages, consider interest groups where youngsters interested in a similar theme or issue can work together. Be very careful, however, not to allow the groups to become a matter of friends vs. enemies.*

8. *Although the teacher role is essentially one of learning instigator and group operations facilitator, once internal group rapport is developed, move into and out of groups as a member on occasion. Be careful not to allow your presence to intimidate group operations, however.*

9. *Remember that two-person argumentation within a group is often the source of frustration and can cause the collapse of group processes. Work toward developing smooth techniques for cutting off such debate, e.g., draw in other group members so that consensus can conclude one way or the other. Move digressors back to the issue at hand when group process appears to be breaking down.*

10. *Be sure necessary resources and materials are available when groups need them. Try to anticipate needs as much as possible.*

11. *Do not make quick and total changes in group memberships. Interaction patterns and internal group rapport can break down completely. Make changes gradually and few at a time.*

12. *Remember that small groups represent an activity where some sense of closure is desirable. Structure situations to assure maximum likelihood of such closure.*

13. *Remember, when designing small group activities, the factors of talk models and the abilities of the talkers. Try to coordinate the two.[25]*

Knowing the basic kinds of groups and the purpose for using each is necessary if the discussion in each group is to have meaning for the students involved. Lundsteen has identified three basic kinds of groups. These include *bull* or *buzz* groups, *brainstorming* groups, and *task-group* discussion groups.[26]

A *bull* or *buzz* group is ". . . a casual, free and uninhibited rap session on any topic of great interest to the group."[27] There is little teacher involvement. The focus is on providing students an opportunity to interact, express themselves, and share ideas. Lundsteen points out that teachers can learn much about children through such a group (participants' needs such as a need for more background in an area, language processes, interests, trouble with listening skills, and ability to synthesize ideas).[28] Thus, observing participants in *buzz* sessions would have two basic, inter-related purposes. One would be to help students advance their knowledge in an area under discussion such as in science where students get together to discuss topics such as the most beneficial scientific discovery since 1900 and why. The other purpose would be to determine and help correct problems that students have in organizing and implementing strategies for advancing discussion skills.

An example of how the two purposes for *buzz* sessions identified can be carried out is given in Case Study Number 1, where a *buzz* session is going on in a fifth-grade classroom about a topic of concern to many, the War in the Persian Gulf.

As noted in Case Study Number 1, the purpose established for breaking the class up into *buzz* groups was, through discussion, to learn more about the objective of the Allied Forces in the War in the Persian Gulf. However, the teacher, Mr. Hammonds, took advantage of this opportunity to observe and note several important skills teachers should look for when students work in discussion groups.

Case Study Number 1

Mr. Hammonds' fifth-grade class held discussions daily during the War in the Persian Gulf. Since some students appeared to be confused about the real objective of the Allied Forces fighting Iraq, Mr. Hammonds broke the class into five groups of six students each to discuss the question of "What is the real objective that the Allied Forces are fighting for in the Persian Gulf?"

Students in each group were furnished a map of the Middle East. The students discussed the August 1990 invasion of Kuwait by Iraq, the United Nations' denouncement of the invasion, the massing of troops in Saudi Arabia and other Persian Gulf regions, the ultimatum/deadline given Iraq to evacuate troops from Kuwait, and the conditions that the Allied Forces imposed on Iraq.

Each group in Mr. Hammonds' class was asked to place the Allied Forces' objective on a chart and to be able to tell *why* this objective was chosen as the *real* objective. A total-class discussion followed in which the class came to an agreement that the *real* objective of the Persian Gulf War was to have Iraqi troops leave Kuwait. One group, however, did argue that the *real* objective was to keep the flow of oil from Kuwait open to countries needing this oil to run industries.

A skills checklist such as the one in Figure 8–3, used by Mr. Hammonds, helps keep up with both strengths and weaknesses which are needed in teaching oral-communication skills. However, in order to avoid inhibiting students from freely participating in group discussions, the skills checklist should be used in a subtle way, with students rarely seeing the teacher write on it.

Brainstorming is identified as a free, uninhibited, but organized group discussion whose purpose or use is to get students to verbalize hypotheses around a problem that has been identified. Lundsteen says that there are certain rules for using *brainstorming*. These are:

1. *The group needs to be made up of enough people in order to get a group of heterogeneous skills. The range of skills needs to be relevant to the problem area. Some arbitrarily set the number of participants in the group at around 12 (thus departing from the usual three to five members in small-group discussion groups). In other words, the groups need to be just large enough in order to contain people with the kinds of competencies needed.*

Content Skills	Jack	Ann	Bob	Juan	Jim B.	Ellie	Carlos	Sara
1. Identifies on map where the following are located:								
a. Persian Gulf								
b. Saudi Arabia								
c. Kuwait								
d. Iraq								
e. Baghdad								
f. Basra								
2. Knows the following:								
a. Who invaded Kuwait								
b. The Allied Forces' objective in the Persian Gulf War								
c. Terms laid down by the Allied Forces when the war ended.								
d. The role of the United Nations in the War								

Participants in Group

Discussion Skills	*Participants in Group*							
	Jack	Ann	Bob	Juan	Jim B.	Ellie	Carlos	Sue
Performs the following:								
1. a. Listens to others								
b. Takes orderly turns without disrupting discussion								
c. Utilizes resources in making discussion more effective								
d. Stays on task (the topic at hand)								
2. a. Asks relevant questions								
b. Asks appropriate "why" and "how" questions								
c. Relates ideas in logical way								
d. Reaches generalizations needed on data presented in discussion								
e. Uses prior knowledge of topic to elaborate on points made in discussion								

FIGURE 8–3   A Checklist of Skills for Observing Students in Buzz Group Sessions

2. *Wild ideas are welcomed; none are excluded.*
3. *Quantity is sought, stressed, and desired. The group works quickly.*
4. *Group members seek to combine ideas, to hitchhike on others' ideas, and to improve them.*
5. *Adverse judgment of ideas is held off until later, until all ideas have been entered and reviewed. There is no attempt during the process to sort out the good solutions from the bad ones.*[29]

While an observation form like the one proposed in Figure 8–3 for *buzz* groups can be developed, it probably is best to use a shorter form and one that calls for the student to self-assess him/herself. The focus might be more on the questions like those in Figure 8–4 on *brainstorming*. Each student in the group would make an assessment whether or not he/she offered solutions to the problem raised, asked questions of others for clarification or expansion of ideas that they presented, and offered ideas to expand someone else's suggestion. In addition, each student assesses his/her designated role and whether problems, if identified, need further attention.

_____	_____
(Your Name)	(Topic Discussed)
_____	_____
(Date of Discussion)	(Your Designated Role)

_____
(Other Members in Your Group)

In my group today, I did the following that are checked and did each to the degree circled in parentheses in each sentence.

_____ I listened (all, most) of the time to what was said.

_____ I looked at others (all, most) of the time when I listened and spoke to others in my group.

_____ I contributed to the discussion by giving (one, a couple, several) new idea(s) to the problem that we discussed.

_____ I contributed to the discussion by expanding (one, a couple, several) idea(s) given by others in my group.

_____ I contributed to the discussion by asking (one, a couple, several) question(s) during our discussion.

_____ If you had a role such as discussion leader, recorder, or summarizer, tell how well you think that you carried out your role.

How well I did my role _____

_____

_____

Problems I need help on with this role _____

_____

_____

FIGURE 8–4   Assessment of How I Participated in a "Brainstorming" Session

In *brainstorming*, students hypothesize about a number of problems in any subject area. Students might discuss ways that an unusually large number of mosquitoes can be eradicated in a marshy area of the community, what the government can do about the problem of acid rain, how best to build a doghouse with a limited (but specified) number of square feet of lumber, or how to go about preparing a meal for 100 guests. Lundsteen points out that students need to see each other when they are in *brainstorming* groups, that a chalkboard should be available for recording ideas, and that the teacher does not necessarily have to be in the group (but might be to serve as a recorder).[30]

A *Task-Group Discussion* is one in which students, through focused discussion and shared responsibilities, carry out a task set up by the students themselves or by the teacher. As identified by Lundsteen, *task-group discussions* have several components, including: (1) a clearly defined and understood task; (2) clearly defined individual assignments; (3) necessary resources or books, known about and available; (4) a schedule and a close supervision of progress within a limited amount of time; and (5) a final reporting to a larger group on the product.[31] Two settings for *task-group discussions* have been mentioned earlier. One is project teaching as found in many British schools (Chapter 2); another is cooperative learning (also Chapter 2).

In project teaching, one or more themes are selected for the class to pursue (Example given earlier: "Words and Expressions that We Have Borrowed From Many Lands"). Students plan not only how they go about searching for "borrowed words" but how they are going to present these to others in the class. In cooperative learning, students work together in small groups to reach team goals. Of the several cooperative learning strategies identified, all involve small, heterogeneous groups involved in discussion and have well-defined tasks.[32]

Like Klein, Lundsteen asserts that specific roles are important components of discussion groups. A number of roles are identified, including some of the more important roles of group facilitator, clarifier, evaluator, summarizer, and recorder.[33]

In some situations, discussion can best be carried out through the use of structured discussion forms. Especially is this true when students are just learning small-group discussion skills. Later, the forms can be less structured. The intent of these forms is to keep students on task and moving through a series of questions that help reach the objective established for the type of discussion in question. In Figure 8–5, a discussion form on the topic of weeder geese, introduced in Chapter 7, is shown. This topic, which has much appeal to elementary-school children, is one developed from a ready source of good small-group discussion topics, a newspaper story.

Sometimes the newspaper story itself can be used. Each participant in a small group is given a copy to silently read along as a designated group member reads the story orally. Students become quite interested in stories such as the newspaper story on weeder geese shown in Figure 8–6.

Passages in textbooks can often be better understood when small-group discussions take place. The passages are read together in a small group, one student

Directions: In your small group, discuss the questions below and in the order (1–6) that they are given. The group should try to reach consensus on what goes in each cell on this form. This consensus statement(s) is to be written in the appropriate cell by the recorder.

1. In 1980, Chinese weeder geese were introduced to parts of the state of Idaho to help farmers with their crops. How do you think these geese were supposed to help Idaho farmers?	2. If your group decided that weeder geese help the farmer by eating weeds around crops, discuss why such a way of weeding crops might be better than spraying the crops with chemicals or having humans use hoes to weed the crops.	3. Why do weeder geese not eat the young plants that the farmer is growing? Do you think the young plants might look the same way as weeds look?
4. In what other ways do geese help man? In what ways do you think weeder geese differ from other geese?	5. What all would you need if you were going into the business of raising weeder geese?	6. What else would your group like to know about weeder geese? Discuss some ways of finding additional information.

FIGURE 8–5   A Discussion Form on Chinese Weeder Geese

reading orally while others follow. Students then work through a discussion form. The earlier passage on termites in Chapter 7 is an example. Students could easily be grouped to read this passage and use an appropriate discussion form to begin a unit on insect pests. Not only would the discussion help motivate students, but a number of facts would be learned in a good discussion. Students could also follow up with meaningful research on termites or other insect groups.

In using discussion forms, it is important that students discuss the questions and arrive at some consensus on what should be written in each cell of the form rather than see the activity as one of merely answering questions on the form. A student whose role has been designated as a questioner could keep this focus in proper perspective. If several groups within a classroom are working on the same topic, a discussion with the total class should follow. This should lead to further discussion when it is seen that there are different conclusions reached.

When students use discussion forms, specific objectives can be established by the teacher. These objectives then become the basis for assessing whether or not students in a small group are learning what is intended for them to learn. As with *buzz* sessions, some type of evaluative form can be used to determine which students are learning the objectives. An example of objectives established for a

Honk and peck: taking a gander at weed eaters

BURLEY, Idaho (AP) — They waddle down rows of crops gobbling up everything green but the plants they are hired to protect.

"They are eating machines. They live to eat," says Dennis Sewald of the Chinese weeder geese he introduced to Idaho this year as an alternative to chemical herbicides. "They are like a sheep dog that's bred to herd sheep."

The birds were developed 2,000 years ago in China to combat the bane of a farmer's life — the common weed. Recently they have been used by organic farmers in the Pacific Northwest and California, where Sewald, principal owner of Idaho Organic Farms, first saw them.

Weeder geese will eat their own weight or more in greenery every day, and Sewald says 1,500 of the birds will weed 500 acres of crops within a week. They are most effective in the spring "when the weed is a mouthful rather than a meal."

Some of those familiar with weeder geese insist the birds sense that they aren't supposed to eat anything planted in rows, but Sewald says that's ridiculous — they just prefer weeds to crops.

"There's a point at where

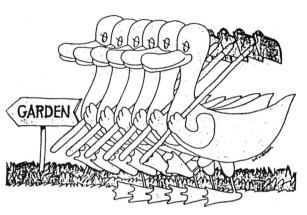

they're hungry but they want something else to eat, and then you have to pick them up. If you leave them out there, they'll eat your crop," he said.

That point comes when between 75 percent and 90 percent of the weeds have been devoured, he says.

One of the advantages to using weeder geese, Sewald said, is that "they turn all the green into instant fertilizer."

Since Jan. 1, when Idaho Organic Farms received 8,000 day-old

geese from California, Sewald has leased the birds to two dozen farmers. He charges $10 to $20 an acre if the farmer has learned to handle the geese, but more if Sewald must use his own handlers.

He said chemicals would cost between $75 and $150 per acre.

Sewald said response to the birds has been enthusiastic. He plans to have two 5,000-egg incubators at the company's Goose Creek Ranch and 125,000 birds by next spring.

FIGURE 8–6   A Newspaper Story that Forms the Basis for a Small-Group Discussion

From *The Tallahassee Democrat*, Tallahassee, Florida. Reprinted with permission of the Associated Press.

small-group discussion in which a discussion form has been developed appears in Case Study Number 2. The case study is broken down into three parts which include the teacher's objectives for developing oral-communication skills, the discussion activity/form used, and analysis of how the teacher decided that some students had reached the objectives while others had not. Some suggested follow-up also appears.

It is necessary that students learn how to move through discussion groups independently. This can be done when roles to be taken in small groups are taught to students and when rules for each type of discussion group are well known. Initially, the teacher is involved in teaching roles and rules. However, as students become accustomed to knowing what to do and how to do it, the assignment of participating in small-group discussions becomes streamlined by using cards that

Case Study Number 2

Mrs. Sydney teaches fourth grade and wants all of her students to get involved in small-group discussions whenever this mode of teaching is utilized. Mrs. Sydney breaks the class into five small groups and appoints a *leader* and *recorder* for each group. On a chart, Mrs. Sydney places three main objectives that she hopes each group will carry out during its discussion. However, Mrs. Sydney says that she will give out individual objectives to some students. The individual objectives are those Mrs. Sydney thinks these students ought to work on, based on analysis of small-group discussions previously held. The group or overall objectives are:

1. To increase the number of why and how questions in small-group discussions,
2. To practice giving all members in the group ample opportunity to participate in the discussion taking place,
3. To establish a strong oral defense for the position the group takes in its discussion.

Mrs. Sydney then distributes the discussion form marked "Form Number 1" and shown below:

Form Number 1

1. Sometimes the herring gull digs in the sands of the beach and finds clams. HOW DO YOU THINK THE GULL GETS THE MEAT FROM THE SHELL?	2. What do you think the gull will do if it cannot get the clam meat out of the shell after trying to do so for a long time?
3. How will you defend your position to the rest of the class?	

When the groups are in place, Mrs. Sydney quietly hands a few students a small piece of paper with tasks these individuals are to do (in addition to participating in the group's objectives). Some examples are:

(1) For Johnny, a shy boy, the instructions are to "Johnny, speak a bit louder in your group so that all can hear you."
(2) For Susie, a very talkative ten-year-old, "Susie, slow down when you talk."
(3) For Betsy, a girl who constantly daydreams, "Betsy, listen carefully to what is said because I am going to call on you to defend your group's decision. You will have to know why your group reached the decision that it did."

The groups talk for about twenty minutes. They reconvene and argue their reasons for deciding "how the herring gull gets meat out of the shell of the clam." Then Mrs. Sydney asks each student to evaluate the group's work as well as how he/she contributed to the objectives. The form used for this is shown as Form #2.

Form Number 2

1. In the space below, write how well your group did on this topic.	2. Write your answers in the space below each item. How did you help your group: a. ask more *why* and *how* questions? b. give everyone a chance to participate? c. build a good defense for the position taken?

give (1) the task to be accomplished, (2) the roles to be assumed (one card per role), (3) the rules to be followed for the particular type of discussion that is to take place (for example, *task-group discussion*), and (4) the procedure to use for evaluating the discussion.

Each card is laminated so that it can be used again. A set of cards for a discussion is placed in a manila envelope (7 ^{1}/$_2$ inches by 10 ^{1}/$_2$ inches suggested earlier as an ideal size). When a group has been identified, the appropriate envelope is procured and the group leader reads the task card to his/her group members, distributes the role cards to the appropriate person, and begins with the group to discuss the task to be accomplished and how it is to be done. The group leader may coordinate all the proceedings, calling on each student to perform his/her role when it is appropriate to do so.

Oral Reporting (Talks)

The objectives for teaching oral reporting, or talks as identified by some writers, are twofold. First, oral reporting follows the same objectives as written discourse but via oral communication. Oral reporting is for informing others, for persuading others, and/or for presenting (telling) a story or an event. But oral reporting has another valuable objective, the attainment of a sense of comfort in speaking before an audience, including first individuals known by the speaker, and then an audience not known by the speaker.

When oral reporting is taking place, there are specific skills the speaker should be developing. These include such physical features as poise, good posture, a pleasing voice, appropriate enunciation and pronunciation, and effective or well-chosen vocabulary. There are also organizational skills to be developed, such as good sequencing of ideas presented, effective relationships between parts of the oral presentation, a strong or inviting beginning, and an effective summary.

In the elementary-school classroom, oral reporting begins with sharing during the earliest years. An example is "show-and-tell" where students have the opportunity to bring an object from home and tell peers about it, tell about a project completed at school, and/or tell about a trip taken. Unfortunately, "show-and-tell" has become overly routinized, and sometimes calls for too much of the same from students. "Show-and-tell" should be a time when students are not put into a situation of having to listen to everyone share in the same day. It should be a time when students are instructed to think through what they are going to share ahead of the time that they are to share. It should be a time when students see/hear different ways to share, thus avoiding the *sing-song* type of round robin sharing that causes conflicts with listening objectives. And last, it should be a time when the teacher serves as a model, listening to each child (four or five a day) rather than grading papers or other types of teacher work.

As students move through the grades, attention should be given to various forms of oral reporting, including talks in the content areas of the curriculum, talks on books read, oral reporting on school events, and numerous other kinds of activities. The reports given should be rather brief (five to seven minutes) for younger students, but by the time they reach fifth and sixth grade, students should plan for and feel comfortable in giving oral reports that are as long as fifteen or more minutes.

Self-analysis and evaluation of oral reporting is an important part of the oral-communication program. How is such analysis and evaluation started? To begin with, objectives for each activity must be carefully thought out by the teacher and communicated to the students. Much emphasis should then focus on these objectives, with students determining how well they have reached them.

One way of initiating self-evaluation is to let students keep diaries or journals and write how they feel about oral reports that they make. Each student self reports on how he/she feels about oral reports given, what he/she thinks needs improvement, how the current oral report given compares to the last report that was similar in structure, and/or what might be done differently on the next report. Gradually, the giving of oral reports can be critiqued by peers in small groups, or for some students, by partners. The teacher and then in some cases, other adults in the school and/or community, can be asked to critique oral reports that students give (but only when each student feels comfortable in having this done).

When oral reporting becomes more formalized and evaluation more sophisticated, students should still be involved in assessing their own reports. One way of doing this is similar to what teachers have long been told they should do in grading a short answer or essay-type test question. Teachers should write out what is desirable for short answer and/or essay-type questions ahead of the grading of answers to such questions. Thus, if students are writing on a question about the reasons why the United States was drawn into World War II, the teacher should write the major points he/she expects for an answer (for example, the bombing of Pearl Harbor). In giving oral reports, a similar approach can be adopted, with students guided by the teacher to the criteria for making effective reports.

Diagram 8–1 contains an example of a card that students could use (back and front) prior to making an oral book report. On side one, students list the major points (or in some cases, a few of the major points to consider) of good oral book reporting covered in class. Five major points shown in Diagram 8–1 include creative opening, appropriate voice, eye contact with the audience, clear descriptions, and a good summary for the closing. On the back of the card, students list specific

DIAGRAM 8–1 Major Points in a Good Book Report and My Personal Goals on this Report

Front of Card

Back of Card

points on which improvement will be sought. In other words, the student lists from previous oral book reports the points on which there should be improvement. The card is handed to the teacher (or group leader if in a small group) just prior to the talk to be given. These cards and notes made on them become a part of each child's portfolio and a focal point for student-teacher conferences on oral communication.

Using Students' Interests is critical in oral reports. To begin with, the teacher must know interests that students in the class have. If, for example, an interest inventory such as the Alexander Interest Inventory in Figure 1–2 has been used and seven or eight dominant interests (for instance, horses, trains, basketball, football, gardening, dogs, and flowers) emerge, students can be organized to give mini-talks as follows:

1. Students in a group whose dominant interest is horses prepare to give separate (or in some cases group) mini-talks on horses. They might first give their reports to others with the same interests (horses) and then to a group where the dominant interest is another animal group, such as dogs.

2. Criteria for giving a mini-talk are set and known by all members of the class who, at a given time, are giving or listening to mini-talks.

Using Students' Interest Leads to the Development of Effective Listening and Speaking Skills (*Photograph by Robert Heller*)

3. The groups reporting to each other get together for two talks per day (in some cases three), but never are all talks given in the same period.

4. Later in the week, the process is repeated until all students in the group liking horses have given a mini-talk to the group that likes dogs. As soon as each member of the group has given his/her mini-talk, the roles are reversed with the dog group giving mini-talks to the group liking horses.

5. If the students have had enough experiences and feel comfortable in making an assessment of talks by their peers, students can be asked to do a critique at the end of each talk. In some cases, however, it might be more appropriate for students to write two-to-four global statements on each talk and discuss some of these statements when all mini-talks given by one group have been completed. Such statements as, "What I liked best about Amos' talk on poodles as pets was

_____

_____ ;

One suggestion that I have for Betty's talk on the great race horse, Citation, is to

_____

_____ ."

Cooperative Learning

The cooperative learning strategies described in Chapter 2 all involved small-group discussion. Cooperative learning groups are excellent not only for helping promote specific content to be learned, but because they help develop oral-communication skills. Oral summarizing, elaborating, giving feedback, and evaluating verbal interchange are but a few oral-communication skills identified as basic elements of cooperative learning.[34]

Oral language is seen as a vital component in even the introductory cooperative learning strategies. Johnson, Johnson, and Holubec suggest a number of what they call "Quick Cooperative Starters," several which appear to be particularly useful for getting students to immediately use oral language in small-group work. These include:

1. Reading Buddies: *In lower grades, have students read their stories to each other, getting help with words and discussing content with their partners. In upper grades, have students tell about their books and read their favorite parts to each other.*

2. Composition Pairs: *Student A explains what s/he plans to write to Student B, while Student B takes notes or makes an outline. Together they plan the opening or thesis statement. Then Student B explains while Student A writes. They exchange outlines and use them in writing their papers.*

3. Book Report Pairs: *Students interview each other on the books they read, then they report on their partner's book.*
4. Skill Teachers/Concept Clarifiers: *Students work with each other on skills (like identifying adjectives in sentences or showing proof in algebra) and/or concepts (like "ecology" or "economics") until both can do or explain it easily.*
5. Summary Pairs: *Have students alternate reading and orally summarizing paragraphs. One reads and summarizes while the other checks the paragraph for accuracy and adds anything left out. They alternate roles with each paragraph.*
6. Elaborating and Relating Pairs: *Have students elaborate on what they are reading and learning by relating it to what they already know about the subject. This can be done before and after reading a selection, listening to a lecture, or seeing a film.*[35]

Since some students will have problems with skills and roles to be learned in cooperative learning, it is appropriate to regroup students on occasion for special-needs instruction. Such regrouping constitutes flex groups that would stay together for appropriate lessons. Students would not necessarily be taken away from activities in their cooperative learning group, since flex groups can be organized during activities other than what cooperative teams do together. An example is given in Case Study Number 3. The specific skill being taught is oral summarizing, and an increasingly popular teaching medium, videotapes, is utilized by the teacher in this case study.

Panel Discussions

Panel discussions are natural for social studies and science, where the purpose of such discussions is to expand and/or enrich what is being learned. Textbooks often provide only a skeletal framework for topics covered. Supplementary materials can be used to prepare for panel discussions, thus building depth and interest in the topic covered.

In a corrective language arts program in which panel discussions are used, teachers should start with points covered in a unit or chapter that students really want to know more about. Questions such as "What topic in our study of England have you liked best?" or "What topic on England would you have liked to know more about?" should be asked for the purpose of getting students interested in searching the literature for additional information on a targeted topic and planning a panel discussion with peers. Students who learned just a sentence or two from their textbooks about Stonehenge, about the Queen of England's role in governing her subjects, about the famous English "Bobby" or policeman, or about England's legendary castles, should find it intriguing to explore these topics more in depth and share their findings via panel discussions.

Case Study Number 3

Miss Barton's sixth-grade class has been working in cooperative learning groups several times during the past three weeks. One goal that Miss Barton has had is to teach several roles, including *group leader, recorder,* and *summarizer.* Although Miss Barton gave some instruction on each role, she has noted that three students in the six cooperative learning groups set up are having trouble with the role of *summarizer.*

Miss Barton calls the three students having trouble carrying out the role of *summarizer* together and lets them view a videotape of a good discussion group in which an excellent summary is made by a student appointed to this role. After viewing the complete video, Miss Barton plays the brief summary two times. However, before doing so, she asks the students to write down separate strategies that the *summarizer* uses in making a good summary. The students write down several statements and Miss Barton puts them on a chart. Here is what is placed on the chart:

The Summarizer:
1. Briefly tells the problem the group is faced with solving, "How the City Council Must Find More Resources for Street Repairs."
2. Identifies three possible solutions to the problem given by the group participants.
3. Tells which solution the group decides is the best and the reason why the students chose this solution.

The next time that the three students meet for help on summarizing, they first review what the *summarizer* did that made the summary effective. Then the students see a videotape of another cooperative learning group in which a small group is trying to tackle another problem similar to the one on the first video. However, this time, the part of the *summarizer* is not seen. Students in the small group discuss and practice making a summary of the group's discussion.

In preparation for panel discussions, many skills that students have learned in working together in such activities as webbing, cooperative learning, and joint oral book reporting can be used as a base. However, the format for conducting panel discussions should be taught. As students plan in groups for their panel presentations, the teacher visits each group and talks briefly about panel discussions. Or, if it appears to be more expedient, a formal, more direct approach can be taken with a large-group discussion.

Students should look at their audience when presenting each part of the panel and when interacting with each other on a panel. Panel members should speak clearly, with words distinctly enunciated. Students should refrain from reading to their audience, but outlines and/or notes may be used. Finally, panel members should tie in what they present with preceding remarks of panel members. An example: "John told you how Stonehenge was started. I am going to tell you of some interesting events that have taken place at Stonehenge."

Points to remember in making panel presentations should be placed on small index cards and taped on the table in front of each panel member. Students should read these silently just before they begin the panel discussion and glance at them whenever it is appropriate. Later, these same points can become a checklist for each student assessing either how the group did in making its presentation or how each individual did. A group conference with the teacher following the presentation should focus on the major points one should remember in panel discussions.

Demonstrations

In Chapter 3, demonstrations were mentioned as an effective approach for the teacher to use in working with students. However, it was also indicated that demonstrations can be made by students. Demonstrations are particularly useful in the content fields and can be carried out before small groups as well as the total class. Demonstrations are more effective for older elementary-school students, but some foundation work can be laid for primary students who demonstrate to others how a newly-acquired toy works, how one should clean the classroom gerbil's home, how to write a paragraph, and similar topics.

Of special significance in making demonstrations are the ten research findings on effective demonstrations as outlined by Rosenshine.[36] While these ten findings as listed pertained more to the teacher's role in using demonstrations, some of them can be used as a basis for teaching students to give effective demonstrations. They should be included in the oral-communication curriculum. For students, the most important points to remember (in the writer's opinion) are: the sequential organization of materials; varied and specific examples of what is being demonstrated; presentation of basic points in small steps; focusing on one thought at a time; avoiding digressions; modeling skills that are a part of demonstrations; and fielding questions to help monitor others' understanding of the materials being presented.[37] These criteria can be used as a checklist for students to self-assess their effectiveness in making demonstrations. The criteria can also be used for assessment of demonstrations by peers as long as the teacher is skillful in letting students focus on the positive points, as well as points that need improvement. Students who are having trouble on the same criteria for effective demonstrations should receive special help as members of a flex group.

Debates

According to Petty, Petty, and Salzer, debating is usually considered for secondary school and college, but also has appeal as "formalized argument" for some students in the upper elementary grades.[38] Fisher and Terry also indicate that debate is an appropriate activity for some elementary-school children. They suggest that debates first be informal and then later, formal; that experiences be provided in making decisions about which side to take, and that children have experiences in getting/organizing information.[39]

If debate as an oral-communication activity is to be successful in the elementary school, it should be built on experiences in the lower grades in which students had opportunities to give oral arguments in other contexts. Students who have had experiences defending their opinions in informal and formal speaking roles and who have been taught to use "appropriate voice" to do so as well as how to be objective should have little trouble in debate. These activities/skills are prerequisite to debating skills.

Preceding the introduction of debate to any group of students, the skills to be taught should be clearly identified. To formerly introduce debate, viewing a video of an effective debate, perhaps from a previous class, should help students see the overall organization of how a debate operates as well as specific techniques that both the proponent and opponent use. While small groups can operate simultaneously in a debate, it might be more appropriate for one group, and then another, to have a debate before the entire class. Not only will this give more students an opportunity to see how a formal debate is conducted, but will also help students in making oral presentations before a large group. Inviting another class in to witness a debate should also be helpful.

Noting/Dealing With Errors Made in Speech

This is one of the most sensitive areas the teacher faces in working with children. Oral language is personal and the possibility of hurting children's feelings is so great that many teachers ignore problems that occur when children speak. It is probably best to ignore problems if the teacher does not know how to tactfully help children with oral-language problems. It is far better to have children feeling free to talk and talking plentifully than to have them clamming up for fear of being criticized.

Several practices should help the teacher as he/she notices oral-language problems and attempts to help children with them. First, the teacher should recognize that children have learned their speech in their home community and the speech used is quite functional in that setting. Second, the teacher should approach any speech pattern not typically considered "standard" as different, not inferior and in need of correction. Third, the teacher should provide ample models for students to hear "another way" of saying words and phrases. Fourth, the teacher should provide group instruction in helping students with speech problems, thus lessening the probability that students will feel singled out. Such group work should not include only those students who have oral-language problems, since students need to hear peers talk "that different way." Fifth, the teacher should work with students to help them self-analyze and self-correct their speech patterns where problems exist. This should be very much in line with self-analysis/self-correction in which students are involved in all school work.

Three major areas of concern are *enunciation*, *articulation*, and *pronunciation*. Problems in these areas are sometimes treated as if they are the same. While there are some overlaps, there are differences among them. Teachers should know these differences, spot which ones are problems for students, and set up corrective activities to help with the problems.

Articulation refers to correctly using, in speech, the vowel and consonant sounds. When sounds are correctly made with no substituting or omitting, articulation is said to be effective. Pronunciation refers to the choice one makes or learns in the environment for pronouncing a word. A person who pronounces "either" as "ither" is choosing to pronounce the word that way or has learned to pronounce it that way in his/her community.*

Some examples of poor articulation are *pedging* for *pledging, wabbit* for *rabbit*, and *wot* for *what*. Petty and Jensen (citing L. Scott and J. Thompson) indicate that examples of articulation difficulties young children have are:

1. w *for* r—*wabbit for rabbit*
2. y *or* w *for* l—*yamp or wamp for lamp*
3. th *(voiceless) for* s—*Tham for Sam*
4. th *(voiced) for* z—*thoo for zoo*
5. d *for* g—*doat for goat; dough for go*
6. t *for* k—*tum for come; tea for key*
7. f *for* th *(voiceless)*—*fank for thank*
8. b *for* v—*balentine for valentine*
9. t *or* ch *for* sh—*too or chew for shoe*
10. sh *for* ch—*shoe for chew*
11. w *for* wh—*watt for what*
12. l *or* w *for* y—*less or wess for yes*
13. *omission of initial sounds*—*es for yes*[40]

Sometimes poor articulation is a developmental problem, as when very young children do not yet have facility to produce certain sounds but know and use the word having the sound in it. Age of the child is a critical factor to consider and some children need more time than others for the appropriate speech facility to develop. If, however, the problem needs attention, the teacher can work in class to handle mild problems. For severe problems, however, services of a speech therapist should be sought.

Enunciation refers to slurring and/or omitting syllables when speaking. When "What are you up to?" becomes "Wot cha up ta?" poor enunciation is being practiced.

*The author recommends Chapter V of *The Teaching of Speaking and Listening* by Wilbert Pronovost and Louise Kingman (Longmans, Green, and Co.) as an excellent source for distinguishing among the three areas of articulation, enunciation, and pronunciation.

Some examples of enunciation problems include the following:

1. *gonna* for *going to*
2. *doncha* for *don't you*
3. *wot cha* or *what cha* for *what you*
4. *kinda* for *kind of*
5. *gotcha* for *got you*

Pronunciation problems reflect another way to pronounce a word. In the case previously given, saying "ither" for either is one way of saying this word. It can also be pronounced with the first vowel sound being the *long e* sound. Such flexibility does not always exist since some words are just simply mispronounced. An example is *jist* for *just*. Some pronunciation problems one might hear are *own* for *on*, *cain't* for *can't*, *thang* for *thing*, *ainswer* for *answer*, *git* for *get*, and *gittin* for *getting*.

In some situations, work with speech problems can be informal. Jingles and poems can be listened to by students who need help in hearing sounds/syllables/words. Opportunities to hear how others say certain sounds/syllables/words and to practice them in an incidental way should help correct problems that are in need of help. More formal lessons might be organized in groups, but without putting all children with a particular problem together. For example, suppose that six students are having problems with the enunciation problem of "Wot cha doin?" These students might be divided and placed in two groups. In addition to the three in each group who have this problem, two others who have no problem with saying "What are you doing?" are placed in each group. *There is no indication of why the group members are together.* The students are told that they are to create new endings to oral sentences. There is some attention to saying each word clearly, but the teacher does not specify the objective of the activity in such a way that it is obvious which students are having problems. All students are equally encouraged to clearly enunciate the words in the sentences they make. The beginning part of the sentence is "What are you doing?" which students are to expand with a phrase different from any given in the group. One student might say, "What are you doing after we eat dinner?" This might be followed by "What are you doing tomorrow at eight?"; "What are you doing after graduation?"; "What are you doing to help raise money?" and so on. Since these are repetitious and students may soon tire of them, the activity can be relatively short, competition can be introduced between the two groups, the mode of sentence making can be made funny (for example, "What are you doing about exercise now that you are the largest person in the county at 1300 pounds?")

To hear model sentences in which "What are you doing?" is enunciated correctly, an electronic card reader set can be organized, with students listening to perhaps seven or eight "What are you doing _____ ?" sentences prepared by the teacher. Students are asked to record the sentences on the student-track side of each card and turn them into the teacher.

Assessment/Evaluation in Oral Communication

Self-assessment and evaluation have been cited as meaningful in a student-involved corrective language arts program. These procedures can be carried out in small groups. In addition to these procedures, other activities for determining oral-communication problems can include analysis of children's oral-language production, use of scales for recording different oral-language factors, use of comprehensive checklists, the recording of anecdotes, and use of standardized tests. These are presented in the text that follows.

Analysis of Children's Oral-Language Production

During the past thirty years, a number of procedures have been developed for eliciting and recording oral-language production. Among these are Loban's "communication unit" defined by Hopkins as "the grammatical independent clause with any of its modifiers."[41] Hopkins chronicles a number of such techniques used to measure children's oral language, including several measures for determining oral syntactic development (e.g., Hunt's T-unit [previously discussed in Chapter 5], adapted to oral language) and vocabulary diversity (Carroll's type/token ratio—the number of different words [types] divided by the total number of words).[42] Hopkins discusses the implications of these procedures:

> *In view of the fact that it is so time consuming to elicit and evaluate language samples using existing measures and procedures, it is the opinion of this writer that it is probably not worth the classroom teacher's time to undertake such analyses. Moreover, there is no support for using these language complexity measures for diagnostic purposes or for curriculum evaluation....*[43]

This does not mean, however, that some of these techniques advocated for measuring oral-language production are void of value in other settings. They are valuable as a research tool for determining more about oral-language development. Furthermore, they have some value in clinical settings. Glazer and Searfoss, for example, point to the value of using the T-unit measure in a clinical setting and provide a rather extensive analysis with examples of its use.[44]

While formal analysis of language production measured by these techniques may indeed be unwise, some informal analyses may prove valuable. An informal, diagnostic approach based primarily on observation of children as they verbally interact in a variety of settings can lead to a better understanding of how well oral-language production is progressing. Teachers can note the following in students' speech:

1. Do students tend to give mostly elementary or basic sentences when they speak? Example: "My dog is sick." rather than "My dog is sick, and she is going to the vet today."

2. How well do students combine short sentences in their speech, using conjunctions to do so? "Betty is my sister, and she is older than I am."

3. Can students embed grammatical elements in their speech? Example: "My brother, who is a policeman, is on duty tonight."

4. Can students use different ways to orally express the same thought? Example: "We ate lunch after we played basketball. We played basketball and then ate lunch."

Rating Scales

Rating scales in which some degree of how well students perform in selected areas can be used with oral language. Kubiszyn and Borich recommend that scales be used to rate oral performance in the oral-language areas of enunciation, pronunciation, loudness, word usage, pitch, rate, and gestures. They suggest separate scales for these factors, and provide a five-point, three descriptors per item, format. The "Word Usage" scale appears in Diagram 8–2.

Scales for all elements identified appear as Appendix 8–1. It should be noted that for each scale, Kubiszyn and Borich recommend that plenty of space be left for recording comments.[45]

Comprehensive Checklists

Keeping a comprehensive checklist of the development of major oral-language factors can be an excellent way for teachers to get an overall picture of how students in a classroom are progressing in this language arts area. Such a list can be developed by the teacher, although several are available. One presented by Phelps-

DIAGRAM 8–2 Rating Scale for Word Usage

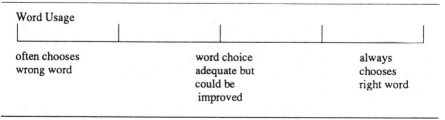

Word Usage		
often chooses wrong word	word choice adequate but could be improved	always chooses right word

From *Educational Testing and Measurement: Classroom Application and Practice,* 2/e by Tom Kubiszyn and Gary Borich. Copyright © 1987 by Scott, Foresman and Company. Reprinted by permission of HarperCollins Publishers.

Terasaki, Phelps-Gunn, and Stetson is called the "Language Screening Checklist." It has three major sections: *semantic content, grammatic form,* and *use in content.* An example of semantic content is "has difficulty formulating sentences to express self."[46] Teachers are encouraged to use the checklist by observing a child for several days "within the context of everyday classroom activities."[47] The entire checklist appears in Appendix 8–2.

Another checklist that classroom teachers might find useful in a corrective program is "Assessing Oral Controls" by Glazer and Searfoss. This checklist includes several interesting sections such as "interdependent/interactive language" on which teachers are asked to observe students to determine if they encourage conversation by saying: "You tell me." and "What do you think?"[48] The checklist appears as Appendix 8–3.

Anecdotal Records

Anecdotal records have long been advocated for use in classrooms. They are easy to keep and, over time, present very interesting information. Kubiszyn and Borich advocate the use of anecdotal records in the evaluative process of oral performance through the recording of "critical incidents" in which students' strengths and weaknesses evolve.[49]

Anecdotal records are kept over a period of time on one or more students. On some occasions, teachers should focus on specific objectives such as observing how relaxed a student is (1) when speaking as a member of a small group, (2) when giving a book report, and (3) when speaking before the total class. On other occasions, there may be impromptu situations in which the student being observed displays certain oral-language behaviors. Over a period of four or five weeks, a picture of strengths and weaknesses in oral language should emerge.

Summary

1. Oral communication (speaking) in the elementary school is not a systematically-taught part of the curriculum. Yet, there are some valuable oral-communication activities at both the primary- and upper-grade levels. At the lower-grade levels, oral-communication activities tend to focus on sharing and creative role playing. At the upper-grade levels, oral communication becomes more structured and roles tend to become more specific, as in roles for students participating on panel discussions or debates.

2. Teachers must understand and accept the oral language of all students. Students' oral language should not be criticized. It has been learned as naturally as anyone's oral language has been learned, and, within the cultural group where it is spoken, is effective.

3. Teachers must move away from a model of classroom discussion in which the teacher asks a question and only a few students respond. Such a model lacks real thinking and spontaneous discussion. Teachers must work to be facilitators of dynamic discussion.

4. Verbalization is an important dimension to learning. Tasks such as learning to make letters of the alphabet and problem solving are aided when students verbalize as they learn the tasks.

5. Drama, as part of the language arts curriculum, leads to such positive effects as improved cooperation among students and self-confidence. Drama can also be effectively used in teaching the other language arts, such as writing.

6. As in listening, oral communication should most often be taught in context of other subjects. However, some separate lessons may be necessary. Oral-communication skills should be presented in a curriculum that encompasses four broad bands: *foundational, formal introductory, formal intermediate*, and *formal advanced*. Skills can be taught together.

7. Talk should be a primary focus of an oral-language curriculum. Such talk takes a number of forms, including collaborative talk, small-group discussions, oral communication in cooperative learning, the more formal oral reports, panels, and debates.

8. Small-group discussions, to be effective, should have structure and role responsibilities well defined. Often, it is helpful to have forms to guide the discussions, but as students become more adept at interacting in small-group settings, the forms or discussion sheets can become less structured.

9. Oral reporting should have specific objectives that are clearly communicated to students who should be involved in assessing their own oral reports. Tasks, defined on cards, help students focus on the goals of a particular kind of oral report, as well as help students determine how well the goals have been met. Using students' interests also helps make oral reporting more effective.

10. Cooperative learning strategies are ideal for use in an oral-communication curriculum. Such group work may start out with very informal "starter tasks" and progress to the more focused and structured cooperative learning strategies.

11. Foundations for panel discussions, demonstrations, and debates are started long before students learn these forms of oral communication. Learning to state one's point of view, sharing, and using factual information to back up points made in oral reports are but a few of the prerequisite skills important to panel discussions and debates.

12. Errors that children make in oral communication should be noted by the teacher, but without any hint of criticism. Students who make errors should have an ample number of models to follow to help correct the errors. Students can be taught to self-correct their own errors in oral communication. Problems with articulation, enunciation, and pronunciation are different kinds of problems and may require different kinds of help.

13. Much of the assessment of oral-communication problems can take place in the regular classroom on an informal level. Teacher observation is a prime way to identify problems. Oral-language scales, checklists, and anecdotal records are three ways to record existing problems.

Reviewing, Connecting, and Expanding What You Have Learned

(Directions) The numbered paragraphs in the summary section of this chapter should help stimulate class discussion on the activities that follow. Do these activities either as a part of a group designated by your college professor or in-service education director or independently.

1. (Paragraph 1) Explain to a peer or to all members of your group what the major difference is between the oral-communication curriculum found in most primary grades and that of upper-elementary grades. As a group, identify several effective activities for use at each level of an elementary school.

2. (Paragraphs 2, 3, 4, 5) Four basic practices for a student-involved corrective program in oral communication were identified, based on research in the area. Write a two-page summary of the most significant findings and their impact on the oral-communication curriculum.

3. (Paragraph 6) Develop two hypothetical situations in a school of your choice in which oral communication is taught as an integral part of some other aspect of the school curriculum (science, mathematics, social studies, and so on) and as separate lessons. Describe each situation in terms of grade level, rationale for your description, and the design of the lessons that you propose.

4. (Paragraphs 7, 8, 9, 10, 11) Select from the oral-communication activities that follow, the two activities that you feel are the most diverse. Describe each activity, tell how you would implement each in a corrective classroom, and explain the value of each: (a) collaborative talk, (b) small-group discussions, (c) cooperative learning, (d) oral reporting, (e) panel discussions, and (f) debates.

5. (Paragraph 12) Error analysis has been discussed in each chapter of this book. Explain how errors in oral language differ from other errors, how the teacher must treat oral-language errors differently, and the major types of errors that students make in oral language.

6. (Paragraph 13) Discuss the use of scales and checklists for use in oral communication.

Endnotes

1. Courtney B. Cazden, "Classroom Discourse," in *Handbook of Research on Teaching*, 3rd ed.; ed. Merlin C. Wittrock, American Educational Research Association Project (New York: Macmillan Publishing Co., 1986), pp. 432–463.

2. John M. Kean, "Listening," *Encyclopedia of Educational Research*, 5th ed.; A project of the American Educational Research Association, ed. Harold E. Mitzel (New York: The Free Press, a Division of Macmillan, 1982), p. 1103.

3. Cazden, "Classroom Discourse," p. 445.

4. Ibid, p. 447.

5. Ibid, p. 448.

6. M. Trika Smith-Burke, "Reading and Talking: Learning Through Interaction," in *Observing the Language Learner*, Angela Jaggar and M. Trika Smith-Burke, eds. (Newark, Delaware: International Reading Association; Urbana, Illinois: National Council of Teachers of English, 1985), p. 202.

7. Kathleen S. Berry, "Talking to Learn Subject Matter/Learning Subject Matter Talk," *Language Arts* 62 (1985): 34.

8. M. Trika Smith-Burke, "Reading and Talking," p. 202.

9. Markhoff, Annabelle Most, *Teaching Low Achieving Children Reading, Spelling, and Handwriting* (Springfield, Illinois: Charles C. Thomas, 1976), p. 218.

10. Eunice N. Askov and Michaleen Peck, "Handwriting," in *Encyclopedia of Educational Research*, 5th ed., a project of the American Educational Research Association, ed. Harold E. Mitzel, (New York: The Free Press, a division of Macmillan, 1982), p. 764.

11. Bette L. Cook, "The Spoken Word," in *Interpreting Language Arts Research for the Teacher*, eds. Harold Shane, James Walden, and Ronald Green (Washington, D.C.: Association for Supervision and Curriculum Development, 1971), p. 14.

12. David W. Johnson and Roger T. Johnson, *Cooperation and Competition —Theory and Research* (Edina, Minnesota, Interaction Book Co., 1989), pp. 65–66.

13. Betty Jane Wagner, "Research Currents: Does Classroom Drama Affect the Arts of Language?" *Language Arts* 65 (1988): 46–55.

14. Ibid, p. 48.

15. Ibid, p. 49.

16. Ibid, pp. 49–50.

17. Ibid, p. 50.

18. Ibid.

19. Frank Green, "Language Arts Instruction: Lessons from the British," *Language Arts* 63 (1986): 381.

20. Gen Ling Chang and Gordon Wells, "The Literate Potential of Collaborative Talk," in *Oracy Matters: the Development of Talking and Listening in Education*, Margaret MacLure, Terry Phillips, and Andrew Wilkinson, eds. (Milton Keynes, England: Open University Press, 1988), p. 96.

21. Ibid, p. 95.

22. Ibid, p. 98.

23. Ibid, p. 96.

24. Ibid, p. 98.

25. Marvin L. Klein, *TALK in the Language Arts Classroom* (Urbana, Illinois: ERIC Clearinghouse on Reading and Communication Skills and the National Council of Teachers of English, 1977), pp. 44–46.

26. Sara W. Lundsteen, *Children Learn to Communicate—Language Arts through Creative Problem-Solving* (Englewood Cliffs, New Jersey: Prentice Hall, 1976), pp. 175–177.

27. Ibid, p. 175.

28. Ibid, pp. 175–176.

29. Ibid, p. 176.

30. Ibid, p. 177.

31. Ibid.

32. Robert E. Slavin, "Cooperative Learning," *Review of Educational Research*, 50 (1980): 315–42.

33. Lundsteen, "Children Learn to Communicate," p. 148.

34. David W. Johnson, Roger T. Johnson, and Edythe Johnson Holubec, *Cooperation in the Classroom*, (Edina, Minnesota: Interaction Book Company, 1990), p. 1:25.

35. Ibid, pp. 4:24–4:25.

36. Barak Rosenshine, "Teaching Functions in Instructional Programs," *The Elementary School Journal* 83 (1983): 339.

37. Ibid.

38. Walter T. Petty, Dorothy C. Petty, and Richard T. Salzer, *Experiences in Language—Tools and Techniques for Language Arts Methods*, 5th ed. (Boston: Allyn and Bacon, 1989), p. 128.

39. Carol J. Fisher and C. Ann Terry, *Children's Language and the Language Arts—A Literature-Based Approach* (Boston: Allyn and Bacon, 1990), pp. 485–486.

40. Walter T. Petty and Julie M. Jensen, *Developing Children's Language*, (Boston: Allyn and Bacon, 1980), p. 333.

41. Carol J. Hopkins, "Evaluating Children's Oral Language," in *Research in the Language Arts—Language and Schooling*, Victor Froese and Stanley B. Straw, eds. (Baltimore: University Park Press, 1981), p. 43

42. Ibid, pp. 49–52.

43. Ibid, p. 53.

44. Susan Mandel Glazer and Lyndon W. Searfoss, *Reading Diagnosis and Instruction: A C-A-L-M Approach* (Englewood Cliffs, New Jersey: Prentice Hall, 1988), pp. 56–71.

45. Tom Kubiszyn and Gary Borich, *Educational Testing and Measurement: Classroom Application and Practice,* 2nd. ed. (Glenview, Illinois: Scott, Foresman and Company, 1987), p. 199.

46. Diana Phelps-Terasaki, Trisha Phelps-Gunn, and Elton G. Stetson, *Remediation and Instruction in Language—Oral Language, Reading, and Writing* (Austin, Texas: Pro Ed, 1983), pp. 83–84.

47. Ibid, p. 82.

48. Glazer and Searfoss, *Reading Diagnosis and Instruction*, p. 57.

49. Kubiszyn and Borich, *Educational Testing*, p. 199.

Bibliography

Strategies/Materials

Littlefield, Robert S. and Littlefield, Kathy M., "Debate Instruction at the Elementary School Level: An Opportunity to Build Legitimacy," Paper presented at the 75th Annual Meeting of the Speech Communication Association, November 18–21, 1989, San Francisco.

Illinois State Board of Education, Curriculum Improvement Section. *Speaking and Listening Activities in Illinois Schools: Sample Instructional and Assessment Materials.* (Springfield, Illinois: Illinois State Board of Education, 1989).

Morgan, Norah and Saxton, Juliana. "Enriching Language Through Drama," *Language Arts* 65 (1988): 34.

Wood, Barbara S. *Oral Communication in the Elementary Classroom—The Talking and Writing Series, K–12: Successful Classroom Practices* (Washington, D.C.: Dingle Associates, 1983).

Issues

Brossell, Gordon C., "Developing Power and Expressiveness in the Language Learning Process," In *The Teaching of English: The Seventy-Sixth Yearbook of the National Society for the Study of Education, Part I*, edited by James R. Squire (Chicago: The University of Chicago Press, 1977), pp. 39–65.

McCaleb, Joseph L., "Measuring Oral Communication," *English Education* 11 (1979): 41.

APPENDIX 8–1   Rating Scale for Speaking

1. Enunciation

most words inarticulate	some words inarticulate	all words clearly articulated

2. Pronunciation

few words pronounced accurately	some words pronounced incorrectly	all words pronounced accurately

3. Loudness

too soft, difficult to hear	appropriate level of volume	too loud, distracting

4. Word Usage

often chooses wrong word	word choice adequate but could be improved	always chooses right word

5. Pitch

too low	just right	too high

Continued

APPENDIX 8–1 *Continued*

6. Rate

|_____|_____|_____|_____|

too slow   just right   too fast

7. Gestures

|_____|_____|_____|_____|

distracting or   sometimes   natural and
monotonous   effective but   expressive
                   with some
                   distracting
                   mannerisms

Note: Where the central point on the five-point scale is the most acceptable behavior, the authors of these scales recommend that a 5 be given this rating and two 3s be given to the left and right of center. Two 1s are recommend for the extreme positions, No 4s or 2s would appear on scales where the center rating is 5.

Tom Kubiszyn and Gary Borich, *Educational Testing and Measurement: Classroom Application and Practice*, 2nd. ed. (Glenview, Illinois: Scott, Foresman and Company, 1987), pp. 198–99. Reprinted by permission of HarperCollins Publishers.

APPENDIX 8–2 Language Screening Checklist

Child _____ Date _____

Teacher _____ Grade _____

The following checklist contains many of the observable signs and symptoms that are often associated with a learning problem. Please read through this list and those items you have observed in this particular child.

SEMANTIC CONTENT

Observe if the child shows the following behaviors:
( ) 1. Does not know the meaning of spoken words on grade level or at age level
( ) 2. Has a spoken vocabulary that is inadequate for age or grade level
( ) 3. Has difficulty learning abstract words that are on grade level
( ) 4. Has difficulty thinking of a particular word needed for expression (word finding problems)
( ) 5. Does not always understand spoken messages (e.g., misunderstands or confuses directions or stories)
( ) 6. Has difficulty in listening comprehension tasks, for example, remembering a story, answering questions about a story, or relating story events in sequence
( ) 7. Cannot correctly remember or follow directions given orally
( ) 8. Has difficulty formulating sentences to express self
( ) 9. Tells stories that do not make sense, ramble, or are incomplete
( ) 10. Cannot always repeat or rephrase a spoken message

( ) 11. Confuses numbers, colors, quantity words, and quality words, for example, the words *same/different, equal, or empty*
( ) 12. Cannot categorize, relate, compare, or contrast ideas, events, and objects
( ) 13. Has difficulty with the manipulation of time, space, and number concepts, for example, telling time, understanding the *yesterday/today/tomorrow* differentiation, and sequencing events, as in *first/middle* or *next/last*
( ) 14. Has difficulty understanding cause and effect or mood words
( ) 15. Cannot make judgments or inferences about new information
( ) 16. Does not actively seek the meaning of what is heard or read (i.e., the author's or speaker's intent)
( ) 17. Inappropriately substitutes words when reading (e.g., The boy rode a *house.*)
( ) 18. May read orally but does not always comprehend the meaning of written grade-level words (word-caller), sentences, or stories

GRAMMATIC FORM

Phonology
Observe if the child shows the following behavior:
( ) 19. Cannot blend sounds together into syllables or words
( ) 20. Cannot break a word into its component sounds or syllables
( ) 21. Confuses words or letters that sound similar, for example, short *i* and short *e*, *th* and *f*
( ) 22. Cannot recognize rhyming words
( ) 23. Uses inappropriate rhythm, stress, pitch, tone, or intonation
( ) 24. Has difficulty producing some phonemes (misarticulates some sounds)

Morphology and Syntax
Observe if the child shows the following behavior:
( ) 25. Consistently makes grammatical errors when speaking
( ) 26. Has trouble using pronouns, plurals, descriptive noun phrases, possessives, prepositions, verb tenses, or other grammatical elements
( ) 27. Confuses prepositions, verb tenses, pronouns, and other grammatical structures
( ) 28. Uses sentences that have poor length, complexity, or structure

USE IN CONTEXT

Observe if the child shows the following behavior:
( ) 29. Does not differentiate egocentric and social speech
( ) 30. Does not understand verbal turn taking and how to initiate and close conversations
( ) 31. Does not comment on new ideas or information
( ) 32. Does not understand how to take a hint, relate to indirect requests or questions, or understand cynicism
( ) 33. Does not understand or use humor well
( ) 34. Does not understand or appropriately use gestures and facial expressions
( ) 35. Does not use a wide range of speech acts: giving or requesting information, answering or asking questions, making statements of factual information, recognizing or expressing feelings, exchanging greetings and other social comments

Diana Phelps-Terasaki, Trisha Phelps-Gunn, and Elton G. Stetson, *Remediation and Instruction in Language-Oral Language, Reading, and Writing.* Austin, Texas: Pro-Ed, Inc., 1983, pp. 83–84 (Used with permission).

APPENDIX 8–3   Assessing Oral Controls

Question	Yes	No	Need More Data
Fun Language Does the student mimic and play with oral language creating stories, poems, and nonsense words?			

Investigative Language
Does the student ask why?
Does the student notice specifics and ask, "What's that?"
Does the student demonstrate curiosity for learning by asking,
    "How do you do that?"
    "Show Me!"			

Language to Control
Command for Control
Does the student command or direct this demonstration with phrases including:
    "Give me that _____"
    "Come here _____"
    "You do it now."			

Concrete Phenomena Does the student describe things using objectives and comparisons?			

Emotional Descriptions
Does the student say, for example,
    "I hurt."
    "That feels sad."
    "I feel lonely."			

Interdependent/Interactive Language
Does the student encourage conversation by saying:
    "You tell me."
    "What do you think?"			

Susan Mandel Glazer and Lyndon W. Searfoss, *Reading Diagnosis and Instruction: A C-A-L-M Approach* (Englewood Cliffs, New Jersey: Prentice Hall, 1988), p. 57 (Used with permission).

9

A Corrective Reading Program

Focus

Reading is the most researched and written about of all the language arts. With so much written about reading, one might wonder why a book on corrective teaching of the language arts would have a chapter on this topic. There are two reasons for this. One is that the themes presented in this book have not been advanced as a unified approach to teaching reading. A second reason is that some teachers are integrating reading and other language arts (especially with writing), and including a chapter on reading in this book should provide some help in this effort.

Corrective Teaching: A Review

As stated earlier, a corrective language arts program takes place within the regular classroom as opposed to a separate, specialized room that is set up more as a clinic than a classroom. There is no specialized or remedial teacher in a corrective classroom, as there is in a remedial program. Furthermore, in a corrective program one deals with less severe cases of language arts problems than is the case in a remedial program.[1]

The contrast between remedial and corrective programs can be made more clearly in reading than in the other language arts. Many schools have remedial reading programs where the more critical problem readers leave the regular classroom for twenty-five or more minutes at a time for the purpose of working with someone specially trained in coping with severe reading problems. But what about those students whose problems are not severe enough to warrant special clinical help? What help will be provided within the regular classroom? While the regular classroom teacher does provide some extra help for these students, too frequently instruction within the regular classroom for these students is the same provided to all students. Thus, a refocusing of instruction is necessary to help these students.

To help you better understand the focus of this chapter, examine Table 9-1. Nine themes of this book are listed, along with eight knowledge components (such as, concepts, vocabulary, and so on). How to interrelate these components with each theme is a question that you should concentrate on as you read Chapter 9. For example, theme one is "Use of interests of students extensively/systematically." The teaching of concepts and vocabulary in reading is listed first on the horizontal axis of Table 9-1. As you read the section on these two components (presented together), you will learn how to include them in a student-involved corrective program. Other components and themes will similarly be covered. Focus on them.

Research of Importance to a Student-involved Corrective Reading Program

Research on reading instruction spans a continuum from physiological features such as eye movement in reading to reading attitude. Volumes, including entire issues of some journals, contain large amounts of research on reading, making it difficult to select a limited number of research findings and say that they are the ones of most importance to corrective teaching of reading. Nevertheless, six "findings" that appear to be appropriate to a corrective reading program have been selected from reviews of research. They include:

1. The *Informal Reading Inventory (IRI)* remains among the best approaches for finding reading levels.

2. Vocabulary can be taught both directly and from context of the printed page.

3. Reading comprehension is a process in which the reader, drawing on his/her experiences, interacts actively (rather than passively) with text.

4. Students better understand what they read when they perceive the structure of the materials, which can be developed through graphic frameworks.

5. Decoding (breaking the printed code) should be taught in such a way that meaning is not impaired.

6. Reading and writing appear to be related in a number of ways, including the possession of similar processes and subprocesses.

TABLE 9–1 Basic Themes in this Book and Content of the Reading Curriculum

Themes	concepts	vocabulary	decoding skills	generalizations	comprehension skills	critical reading skills	attitude toward and interest in reading	study skills
1. Use interests of students extensively/systematically.								
2. Set up *base groups* to meet developmental needs of students.								
3. Set up *flex groups* to meet special needs of students.								
4. Involve students in collaborative/cooperative learning.								
5. Involve students in activities calling for analysis of their progress/problems over a long period of time.								
6. Be aware of and accommodate different learning styles.								
7. Use many types of materials, including manipulatives.								
8. Use a variety of assessment techniques (observations, conferences, and informal testing.								
9. Use a variety of teaching strategies (coaching, modeling, demonstrating, small-group instruction, etc.).								

Practice Number 1: The Informal Reading Inventory (IRI) *Remains among the Best Instruments for Finding Reading Levels*

In any given classroom, there are several reading levels, and dealing with them is a challenge for teachers. The *Informal Reading Inventory*, to be discussed later in more detail, helps in the identification of reading levels.

Alexander and Heathington define the *IRI* as follows:

> *An informal reading inventory consists of sets of graded passages of text and sight word recognition lists. The text passages usually parallel book levels in a basal reading series. At each IRI level there is generally a list of twenty words to be recognized at sight, along with at least one passage of text to be read orally and one to be read silently* . . . [2]

Numerous research studies have been done on the *IRI*, including research on passages selected for students to read and comparisons of the *IRI* with other techniques for finding reading levels (for instance, norm-referenced approaches to finding reading levels). Farr and Carey, surveying the research on informal assessment in general and informal reading inventories specifically, point to the value of IRI's as part of informal tests when they state that:

> *Because informal tests use a wide variety of procedures to assess reading performance over a number of different occasions, it is not surprising that they can be more reliable and valid measures than criterion or norm referenced tests which cannot be used as often and are more divorced from daily classroom instruction.*[3]

Practice Number 2: Vocabulary Should Be Taught Both Directly and from the Context of the Printed Page

Several positive strategies for teaching vocabulary have been identified. It is probably true today, as Weintraub stated a number of years ago that, "Research evidence does not point to a single best approach to teaching vocabulary but rather indicates a variety of techniques are useful."[4]

Even where various techniques have been identified for teaching vocabulary, there tends to be a proclivity toward dependency on memorizing definitions. Pressley, Levin, and McDaniel, in giving examples of how vocabulary is taught, point out that from preschoolers (where pictures are to be labeled) to high school English and college-preparation classes, learning vocabulary terms and their definitions is a basic way to learn vocabulary and that such " . . . examples fly in the face of the claim that real world vocabulary acquisition follows principally from people inferring meanings from context. . . . "[5]

Chall points out that recent research indicates that meaning vocabularies can be taught directly, with special benefits to students of lower ability, but that word meanings are also learned when one reads or is read to.[6] Chall and Stahl state that evidence supports the claim that both definitional information, such as synonym study, and contextual information (use of words in sentences) are preferred to methods in which only one approach is used.[7] Calfee and Drum point out that

> ... *The nature of the passage, the relation between the words and the text, the type of assessment (and implicitly, the level of understanding of the word) are all candidates in determining the effectiveness of contextually based learning.*[8]

As reported in Chapter 1, it has been shown that the least effective strategies for learning vocabulary are those calling for few encounters with words and strategies in which stress is placed on word definitions.[9] Also, as pointed out in Chapter 1, students relating new words to known words and using experiential backgrounds to learn new vocabulary help in the learning of vocabulary.[10]

Practice Number 3: Comprehension Instruction Should Reflect Concept of Reading as an Active Process Where Students Interact with Text

Reading instruction in the past was focused more on students interpreting messages that the author of the materials intended, rather than in getting students to apply their background of experiences to text. Such a model was based on the mistaken idea that reading, like listening, was a receptive language arts in which the primary process was one of receiving messages. In more recent years, reading has been viewed as a process where the reader's ideas and thoughts interact with text. As Smith-Burke and Ringler have stated, "Research has shown that prior knowledge significantly influences how readers comprehend text. . . . "[11]

Pearson states that the reader is of equal importance to the text, and possibly more so.[12] Beck and McKeown, in describing reading as an interactive process, cite the work of several scholars and state that ". . . information from print and the reader's knowledge act simultaneously and influence each other."[13]

Research indicates that unlike poor readers who are passive, good and average readers are active in the reading process. Good readers more frequently: (1) monitor their comprehension behaviors; (2) apply "fix-up" strategies when comprehension is blocked; (3) use context cues for understanding; (4) reread materials in an effort to comprehend what is being read; (5) question the author of materials being read, and (6) correct miscues in reading.[14] Good and poor readers are different in that good readers see "meaning" as the objective for reading, whereas poor readers see decoding as the purpose for reading. Bristow points out that teachers respond to students differently, with poor readers getting more attention on word pronunciation and less attention to meaning than do good readers.[15]

Practice Number 4: Graphic Frameworks or Organizers Should be Used to Help Students Better Understand What They Read

A number of studies have demonstrated the importance of story structure in helping students retain information. Reutzel cites the work of J. Mandler and N. Johnson, L. McGee, and B. Taylor and R. Beach, among others, who demonstrated that perceiving the structure of reading materials aids children's capacities to restore and retrieve information.[16]

McGee and Richgels cite recent research based on schema theory to recognize characteristics of expository text. Accordingly, there is evidence that a clear organizational structure in which there is a hierarchy of related components aids in reading comprehension.[17] Citing the work of cognitive psychologists of the 1970s, Smith and Bean explain that story grammars can be effective in helping children comprehend stories. The interplay of reading, writing, speaking, and listening, all combined with visual diagramming (for which techniques will be presented later), are at work to help develop comprehension.[18]

Chall and Stahl cite a number of studies/theories dealing with the effect of schemata on recall of text read. They cite R. Anderson and others in stating that schemata have slots to be filled with textual information.[19] According to D. Rumelhart and other schema theorists, schemata relating to specific topics being read, are called into play during reading or during recall.[20] Chall and Stahl explain that the effect of D. Ausabel's advance organizers (information given to readers in advance of the reading itself) might be explained by schemata.[21]

In a corrective reading program, students should be taught in ways that help remove the abstractness of what is being taught. They should be led to see relationships among different parts of the text. Graphic structures serve to remove abstractness of text and help to relate different parts of text.

Practice Number 5: Decoding Should be Taught in Such a Way that Meaning is Not Impaired

Much has been written on the controversy between the teaching of decoding or breaking the printed code and teaching reading for meaning. The primary focus of the controversy is on the early teaching of reading. Should children start out learning about letter-sound relationships, or should they start out with early emphasis on deriving meaning from print? Some empirical studies indicate that it is advantageous for children to have direct and early instruction in decoding, that students not acquiring decoding skills by the mid-elementary school grades have trouble in reading, and that teachers support the teaching of decoding skills.[22] Chall and Stahl cite reviews of studies covering nearly a half century of beginning reading instruction and conclude that a "code emphasis" approach where relationships between sounds and letters are taught leads to increased achievement in word recognition and comprehension, compared to a "meaning emphasis" approach in which meaning was stressed from the beginning of initial instruction. More positive influences of "code emphasis" were prevalent for children through third grade, but there was no research evidence for differences beyond third grade.[23]

The "meaning emphasis" advocates stress the need to start students in the initial instructional phase of learning to read with meaning as a primary focus. Strong arguments have been advocated for teaching decoding and comprehension simultaneously.[24] In both a corrective and a developmental reading program, it would appear unwise to take an "either-or" position. Both the breaking of codes and the messages to be derived from the codes are important. Of great significance also is how reading, using both approaches, is taught. Calfee and Drum, reviewing studies that indicate the importance of early phonics, address this concern in stating that rote drill and practice should not be the primary vehicle for decoding instruction, and fluency and understanding should be part of decoding instruction.[25]

Practice Number 6: Relationships between Reading and Writing Should be Used in Teaching

This essentially is practice number 7 in Chapter 5 on writing. Better readers tend to be better writers and vice versa. The more proficient readers, like the more proficient writers, are more reflective, take better control of written language, formulate better questions/solutions about text being read, continually monitor how successful they are in obtaining meaning from print, use background experiences more efficiently, and use schemata more effectively for working with both form and content of discourse.[26]

In the upper-elementary school grades, W. Laban found that a high correlation existed between reading scores and indices of writing quality, and these relationships become more pronounced as students move toward secondary school. Good writers tend to do more leisure-time reading than do poor writers. Also, more complex sentence patterns appear in writing as reading comprehension increases.[27]

Finally, research indicates that increased reading in general is more important to the improvement of writing than is frequency of writing. In addition, reading/study of literature is more effective on writing improvement than is the study of grammar.[28]

Since there is a close relationship between reading and writing, it might be assumed that these two language arts should be taught together. In part, there should be integrated teaching. Shanahan identifies seven principles of reading-writing relationships which are based on research and have implications for instruction. These are:

1. *Reading and writing both need to be taught.*
2. *Reading and writing should be taught from the earliest grade levels.*
3. *The reading-writing relationship should be emphasized in different ways at different developmental levels.*
4. *Knowledge and process relations need to be emphasized.*
5. *The connections between reading and writing should be made explicit to children.*
6. *The communications aspects of reading and writing should be emphasized.*
7. *Reading and writing should be taught in meaningful contexts.*[29]

Shanahan points out that reading and writing, while related, are not so identical as to suggest total integration. He also points out that there is not automatic transfer between reading and writing, but that examination of relationships across the two areas might be useful.[30]

Corrective Teaching of Concepts and Vocabulary in Reading

Introduction

Although many lessons should be organized to teach vocabulary through associations with known words, direct teaching, and context of the printed page, much effort should be given to getting students to learn on their own. Strategies for life-long learning of vocabulary are critical. As Sternberg emphasizes:

> *. . . No matter how many words we teach them directly, those words will constitute only a small fraction of the words they will need to know, or that they eventually will require. They truly constitute a drop in the vocabulary bucket. It doesn't really matter a whole lot how many of those few words students learn or how well they learn them. What matters is how well they go on learning long after they have exited from our lives, as we have exited from theirs. . . .* [31]

Concepts, too, should be taught in such a way that students develop skills for learning new concepts. Direct instruction should include much attention to using the context of a sentence or larger passage to determine what a word not encountered and learned before means. In Figure 9–1, some of the major techniques are shown for direct teaching of meaning through the use of context. Passages are shown on the left with the unknown word in each in italics. On the right, the focus of questions that should be asked to help develop each strategy is shown.

Strategies	Focus of Questions for Teaching Use of Context
Strategy 1 (Contrast/Compare)	
The big cloud has a *tinge* of pink in it. It looked like a thin pink ribbon on a giant blue cotton ball.	Questions are asked to get students to find in the second sentence words that tell what *tinge* means. In this case, questions lead students to compare "thin pink ribbon" with "giant blue cotton ball."
Strategy 2 (Definition)	
The *crater* on top of the volcano is not solid like the top of a hill. It is a hole from which lava and hot steam might one day come spurting out.	Questions are asked to get students to put together key words in the second sentence with those in the first to define *crater*. In this case, the words are "hole" in sentence two and "top of the volcano" in sentence one.
Strategy 3 (Synonym)	
Estimate, or guess, what the answer will be before you work the problem.	This is simple and direct teaching where it is pointed out that in instances like this, the meaning of the unknown word is set off with commas following the word.
Strategy 4 (Antonym)	
She was far from the sweet person we thought she was. Instead of kind, she was *cruel*.	As stated here, the questions should lead to an examination of sentence two and the word "instead" which helps signal that the unknown word following can be contrasted with the description (the opposite of the unknown word) in the preceding sentence.
Strategy 5 (Rewording, Restating, Elaboration)	
Zeke could not find his *Frisbee™*. He looked everywhere for what he called his flying saucer. But the toy that looked like a plastic plate could not be found.	Although similar to the synonym strategy above, this is a bit different in that questions must lead students to examine the sentences that follow.

FIGURE 9–1 Strategies for Learning Concepts and Vocabulary From Context

Using Context for Teaching Vocabulary

Direct teaching of concepts/vocabulary through the use of context should include oral-reading sessions where the teacher asks students to explain an unknown word by (1) reading the sentence that contains the word, (2) going back to a preceding sentence, and/or (3) reading a sentence that follows the one in which the unknown word is located. Since some one-on-one instruction will be necessary, volunteers should be brought into the classroom to hear students read, although volunteers should be trained in how to help students use context to unlock word meaning.

Where students are grouped for learning vocabulary through context, everyone in the group should have opportunities to interact to probes aimed at getting meaning from context. While on occasion one student can be called on to give an answer to a question, in general, all students should be responding through such procedures as whispering an answer to another student in the group, jotting down key words called for, or holding a response card up when the signal is given to do so.

Word association activities are helpful in learning and expanding new concepts/vocabulary. Some examples of word association strategies follow.

Ongoing word association charts can be effective in getting students ready for vocabulary to be encountered in assigned reading and using current and/or past experiences to help students understand vocabulary. Such charts can be especially effective where several stories in either a basal or literature-based reading program are linked together by a common theme. For example, preceding a series of mystery stories, the teacher can develop a bulletin board or chart which contains a category on "mystery words," to which students supply words. These are periodically placed on the bulletin board and discussed, written about, and eventually read about. The teacher, too, may add words, and especially if some of the words to be read are not given by students. An association chart is shown in Figure 9–2, including a column for mystery words. The column contains two divisions. One is for words that are "known" while the other is for words that are "unknown." In writing and discussing words, more attention would be given to the unknown words (or words to be learned). Two other columns are shown in Figure 9–2, including one that could be developed when students listen to weather reports to learn new words and one about the environment.

Other ongoing word association activities are shown in Figure 9–3. These include collecting words in designated categories and matching words with pictures which depict concepts to be learned. These activities call for students to be actively involved collecting and discussing words, rather than passively participating in a paper and pencil task.

Word Association Charts/Diagrams (Direct Teaching)

Durkin stresses the importance of using known words and a category under which these words and the unknown words (words to be introduced) can be classified. Thus, unknown words *stalk* and *swagger* would be associated (on a chart) with known words such as *walk, dash, scamper, stroll,* and others.[32] Another technique that Durkin identifies is called *scaling*. An example of scaling is given for the word *gaunt*, which is not as commonly used as some of the words that help identify the meaning of *gaunt*. An example of *scaling* would be the use of a simple diagram that relates *thin   skinny   bony   gaunt*. Durkin states that *scaling* is appropriate when

Directions: In each column, list known words that students give when solicited. List as many words as the group can give in a specified timespan. Then add new words that the students will encounter in the story to be read. Take a few minutes to talk to the students about these words. Where possible, draw relationships with the words known by the students. Then have students read the story. Ask them to try to figure out what the words mean, make notes of what they think they mean, and later discuss the words.

Weather Words	Mystery Words	Environmental Words
(Known)	*(Known)*	*(Known)*
fog	ghost	garbage
dry	haunted	poisoning
hot	goblins	pollute
rain	creaking	
cloudy		
sunny		
snow flurries		
(Unknown)	*(Unknown)*	*(Unknown)*
humid	ghoul	ozone layer
barometric	intrigue	pollutant
overcast		

FIGURE 9-2 Association Chart: Known with Unknown Words

the meanings of words are different by degree. She also points out that if prefixes like *mal* have been introduced or are known, students can associate a word like *malnourished* with the new word (in this case, *gaunt*) being introduced.[33]

Manipulatives for Learning Concepts/Vocabulary

Manipulatives can be devised to help students who learn best through haptics or hand learning. One activity involves envelope definitions. Inside a small manila envelope, definitions (but not necessarily dictionary definitions) of selected words and phrases are placed on tagboard of different colors. Each word to be defined is written on the outside of the envelope and shaded with the color that corresponds to the color of tagboard used inside for defining a word. Thus, five words such as *island, peninsula, isthmus, inlet,* and *strait* might be written on the outside of one envelope, and shaded with a different color. The concept for each word can be learned by placing like colors together and arranging the cards to define each term to be learned. Thus, on yellow tagboard, cards that would go together might be

Body of land	surrounded	on three sides	by water	is a peninsula	.

(Word Collector)

Directions to Students: In each category below, find words that can be used as specified:

Words That Describe How one Athletic Team Defeated Another Team	Words That Explain How Meat Has Been Cut	Words That Tell How a Horse Might Move
routs	diced	trots
humbles	sliced	gallops
edges	ground	ambles
crushes	shaved	walks
annihilates		

(Matching Words and Meanings)

Directions to Students: Place the words on the right with the picture on the left that best explains what the word means.

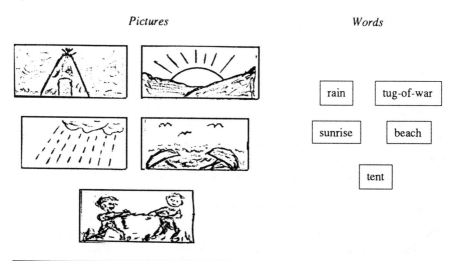

Pictures   *Words*

rain   tug-of-war

sunrise   beach

tent

FIGURE 9–3 Interacting With Words

Note: Cards with words can easily be placed on masking tape that has been folded under, thus exposing only the adhesive side.

Assessment Strategies for Concept/ Vocabulary Development

Among the identified strategies for assessing vocabulary are unaided recall where students check words for familiarity, use of words in a sentence, explanation of the meaning of words, giving of a synonym, and giving of an antonym. Aided recall of tests can be devised including matching, multiple choice, use-in-sentence tests, same-opposite, recall, and analogy tests.[34]

Use of the Cloze Test for Vocabulary Programs

Farr and Carey point out that the cloze* test can be used to measure vocabulary.[35] This test can be developed by the classroom teacher, can be revised, and is flexible. The cloze test forces students to use context of a sentence or larger passages. For corrective programs, a pool of cloze passages should be placed on index cards, one passage per card, and laminated. Passages selected can come from the text in use in the reading program, from supplementary programs, and from texts in various content areas.

The answers for the words omitted from a passage can be placed on the back of the index card which has the cloze passage on one side. Answers can be given either in numbers that parallel those placed in blanks on the side of the card with the passage or in a completed passage. To better understand what is meant by cloze, two sides of a card with words deleted on one side and not deleted on the other are shown in Figure 9–4. In this sample, every fifth word has been deleted, although some argue for other frequencies, such as every eighth word.

Front of Card	Back of Card
Some of the Maya _____ much time learning. They _____ down what they knew. _____ studied the stars and _____ planets. From their studies, _____ calculated that a year _____ equal to a little more _____ 365 days.	Some of the Maya <u>spent</u> much time learning. They <u>wrote</u> down what they knew. <u>They</u> studied the stars and <u>the</u> planets. From their studies, <u>they</u> calculated that a year <u>was</u> equal to a little more <u>than</u> 365 days.

FIGURE 9–4 Cloze Test for Assessing Vocabulary

David Reed, "Mexico's Mysterious Lost City," in *Reader's Digest Reading Skill Builder*, Part 1, Silver Edition, eds. Miriam Weiss Meyer and Peter Travers (Project Editors); Barbara Antonopulos and Jacqueline Kinghorn (Editors) (Pleasantville, New York: Reader's Digest Services, 1977), p. 32 (Used with permission).

*Cloze refers to the deletion of one word every few words, thus forcing the reader to insert a word that can be used in context of the passage. It is a technique that has been recommended for a number of uses in reading, including the finding of reading levels.

In testing for vocabulary using the cloze shown in Figure 9–4, students can independently test themselves and check their answers or students can test and check each other. The cloze test is used for different purposes, and each use calls for different procedures for developing materials for it. For using the cloze test to find reading levels, much larger passages would be selected than the passage found in Figure 9–4.

Use of Standardized Diagnostic Tests of Vocabulary

A number of standardized tests are available for assessing vocabulary. The *Iowa Tests of Basic Skills* for which a skills chart was presented in Figure 3–4 contains several tests on vocabulary. The *Stanford Reading Diagnostic Test*, discussed in Chapter 3 with samples given in Figure 3–5, has a test identified as an Auditory Vocabulary Test. As in standardized tests in general, tests for assessment of vocabulary should (1) have maximum flexibility as to when they are given, (2) be only one of several ways to assess vocabulary, and (3) have meaningful follow up.

Student Interaction With Concepts and Vocabulary

Eliminating tedious and boring drill and practice is the first step toward getting students in a corrective reading program to meaningfully interact with words. As stated earlier, isolated practice where students do not see the reason for or the value of drill and practice should be avoided. Also, as stated, the research on seatwork in which drill and practice most often take place, should be followed. This includes the giving of clear instructions, providing sufficient practice before seatwork begins, and the teacher circulating among students (actively explaining, observing, asking questions, giving feedback), and making short contacts with students.[36] Other suggestions for making concept-vocabulary drill and practice more meaningful include:

1. Have students keep a journal of new words that they have learned during a specified time (such as first six weeks, first semester, and so on). Have student partners discuss and use their "words."

2. Have students keep vocabulary that they have learned in a designated time period on small pieces of tagboard (one word per card), using either a manila envelope, box, or folder to deposit each new word learned. The words are used to learn new skills, such as lining the cards up on desk tops to make a "new kind of sentence being learned," reinforcing alphabetizing skills and so on.

3. Permit students to periodically take their word cards and/or words in a journal home to show their parents the words that they have mastered.

4. Let students use "their words" to make new class games to be played during free time. Have word lists changed periodically, thus adding new sets of words from time to time.

5. Have students use pictures frequently to learn new concepts/vocabulary. Pictures may be collected individually or by small groups of students.

The use of single concept cards has been identified by Culyer and Culyer as an effective technique for teaching concepts and vocabulary. For younger children's oral vocabulary and concept development, it is recommended that pictures which clearly represent concepts (picture of a banana) to be taught be placed on one side of a card (3 x 5, 4 x 6, or 5 x 8 inches). For more advanced pupils, words are printed on both sides of the card, including a word below the picture on one side of the card and the word by itself on the opposite side. Sets of cards are developed by categories such as food, clothing, and animals. Students are placed in groups of three, with one student being more proficient in exercises to follow than the other two students. Activities consist of discussions of the pictures in a set. Included could be students describing the pictures, telling as much as they know about a picture, or relating one picture to another. Students are encouraged to find new pictures to add to each set in use. Questions are raised such as: (1) What shape is a _____ ?; (2) How does it grow (vine, tree, bush, underground plant)?; (3) What do we call the outside (peel, husk, rind, crust)?[37]

In using single concept cards or other techniques in which a list of concepts/vocabulary is to be learned, a grid suggested earlier can be used. Such a grid is shown in Figure 9–5. Students can be encouraged to keep a personal grid in a journal or portfolio, students in cooperative learning groups can keep up with the group's progress on learning concepts/vocabulary, or the teacher can keep a running account of the progress of various students in the class by marking/writing in cells on the grid.

Corrective Teaching of Comprehension and Critical Reading Skills

Solving the Issues

Like the teaching of concepts and vocabulary, a number of approaches should be taken to teach comprehension and critical reading skills. As in vocabulary development, whole volumes have been devoted to these areas and the key to effective teaching of them is finding the most appropriate activities.

Making Poor Readers More Active and Involved in Reading

A major challenge in a student-involved corrective reading program is that of making poor readers more active, thus stimulating them to develop and/or change behaviors to be more like those of good readers. How can this be done? What can the teacher do to get students who are too passive more involved in the reading process? Bristow identifies five "potential solutions" for answering this question. These include: (1) placing students in materials at the correct instructional level; (2) focusing students on "sense-making" by continuously asking questions like, "Does that make sense?"; (3) developing children's background of experiences through additional pre- and post-reading discussions, use of conceptual frameworks (schemata), and teacher verbalization to demonstrate modeling, comprehension-

Concepts/Vocabulary to be learned	pronounce name of each picture?	match picture with right word?	use word in oral sentence?	use word in writing?
1. banana				
2. orange				
3. peach				
4. apple				
5. grapefruit				
6. tangerine				
7. pear				
8. pineapple				
9. nectarine				
10. plum				

(Packet 12)

What to Know About and do With Concepts/Vocabulary (Answer yes or no) Can you . . .

Some Questions:
1. How many fruits above did you answer "yes" to for all four questions? _____
2. Can you describe each fruit? _____

FIGURE 9–5 Charting Concept/Vocabulary Development

monitoring behaviors; (4) giving explicit directions during direct teaching of comprehension; and (5) helping students overcome "learned helplessness" through raising expectations for improving and building confidence.[38]

Strategies previously identified such as coaching, setting up meaningful goals for each student, and charting of progress all should be helpful in making poor readers more active in reading. In addition, eliminating problems that block success should help poor readers become more active readers.

Schema for Developing Reading Comprehension
As stated in research practice 4, graphic frameworks or organizers help promote understanding of what is read. Such frameworks help students see the myriad

relationships among different parts of a story, such as the plot and significant events in the story. In Figure 9–6, two similar, but different techniques are shown, along with a brief summary of the characteristics of each. These have been recommended by Smith and Bean. Both techniques call for more language arts than just reading. In Story Patterns, reading, writing, speaking, and listening are combined with visual diagramming. In Circle Stories, children comprehend, discuss, and write their own stories.[39]

In Figure 9–7, a story map is shown as presented by Reutzel. This is a main-idea, sequential detail map in which the main idea of a story in history is written in the center of the map, with major events and major characters sequentially placed around the main idea.[40] Maps can also be constructed to illustrate cause-effect, fact-opinion, or other relationships within a story as well as relationships between two stories.

(Story Patterns)	(Instructions)
Story pattern of "The Wonderful Feast" and a classroom story	The teacher:

The teacher:

1. reads story to children one or more times.

2. draws sketches in vertical sequence, one column at a time.

3. asks students to discover story pattern.

4. discusses pattern in story.

5. discusses idea of pattern to make sure children know what is meant by patterns.

6. lets students read and make their own story patterns.

Continued

FIGURE 9–6 Graphic Frameworks for Developing Reading Comprehension

Marilyn Smith and Thomas W. Bean. "Four Strategies that Develop Children's Story Comprehension and Writing," *The Reading Teacher 37* (1983): 296–97. Reprinted with permission of the International Reading Association.

(Circle Stories)

Circle story diagram of "The Runaway Bunny"   The teacher:

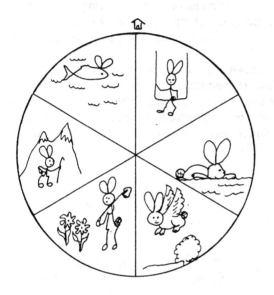

1. draws large circle on chalkboard or butcher paper.

2. divides circles into sections.

3. marks beginning place with small house ( )

4. reads story to class.

5. lets children decide which event goes in each section or "pie slice."

6. places students in small groups to illustrate a story in similar way.

FIGURE 9–6 *Continued*

In Chapter 5 on writing, it was pointed out that story sense could be learned by using different kinds of story frames. These were identified as "setting," "important idea or plot," "story summary with one character included," "character analysis," and "character comparison,"[41] Story frames can be used to develop comprehension in grades as low as first grade as reported by Cudd and Roberts. They indicate that story frames can be used in stories where there is no sequence as well as in stories where the sequence is rather specific. Frames can be used to help develop comprehension of a story where signal words are given to note sequence of events, such as first, then, and finally. Story frames can also be used to teach what is identified as the main episode of a story.[42]

Gemake reports that having students interact with stories stimulates interest and creativity for both able and disabled readers."[43] The teacher demonstrates how one interacts with characters in a story, asks questions about selected actions or events in the story, and relates to emotions developed. Students follow the teacher's lead (an example of teacher modeling) of interacting with materials in a story, create booklets as they interact, eventually design covers for their stories, and share them with peers.[44] An example of how students might interact with "Jack and the Beanstalk" is shown in Figure 9–8.

(Main Idea-Sequential Detail Map)

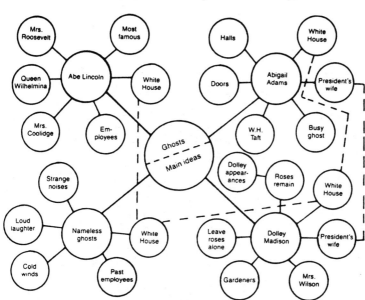

For Selected Story:

1. Construct in sequence a summary list of main idea, major events, and major characters.

2. Place main idea in center of map.

3. Use diagonal lines to make ties between main idea in center to all major events/characters on summary list.

4. Enter major concepts/events in circles attached to ties above. Do in sequence, clockwise.

5. Enter subevents/subconcepts around circles with major events/concepts in story map.

FIGURE 9–7   Story Maps to Improve Comprehension

D. Ray Reutzel, "Story Maps Improve Comprehension," *The Reading Teacher 38* (1985): 400–401. Reprinted with permission of D. Ray Reutzel and the International Reading Association.

In reading, students can be taught to use details of a story to learn the main idea, using the technique identified in Chapter 7 on listening. Students make columns for each of the details of *who, what, when, where, how,* and *why.* As students read, they write brief details under each category and then combine and reduce what has been written. Only the barest elements in each category should remain, resulting in the central or main idea. In this activity, short reading passages

Sample summary page from an interactive reading activity

Draw a picture of Jack, his mother and a huge beanstalk. Where do you think the beanstalk goes? What will Jack do next? Write some sentences that tell what Jack will do in the next part of the story.

Jack will go up there to see what he can find for his mother and him

Jack decided to climb the beanstalk. His mother told him to be very careful.

If you were Jack, how would you feel climbing the beanstalk? Write 5 words that tell how you would feel about this climb.

scared daring frightened afraid upset

Soon Jack saw another land and a large castle. There was a lady sweeping the stone steps in front of the castle. Jack asked the woman who lived in the castle. She said that a giant lived there. Jack was tired and thirsty, so the woman invited him into the castle for something to eat.

Answer these questions.

Who was your favorite character and why? *The wife giant because she was very patient and kind and gave food to Jack.*

Would you like Jack to be your friend? Why? *No because he only wanted more and more and that's bad.*

How do you feel about what Jack did? Should he have taken the money? *Maybe he could use the money for food.*

Should he have taken the chicken that laid the golden eggs? *He should have used the money smarter.*

Should he have taken the singing harp? *No that's not fair taking things he didn't make the harp just food.*

How do you feel about the giant? *Sorry because he want his Jack come and take all his things and he is waving and he didn't treat us anymore.*

Jack had other adventures. Take some paper and write another story for Jack. Draw pictures about your story too. Then, put your story on my desk.

Make a cover for this book. Place your book on the library shelf. Look at the other books. How are your classmates' ideas like yours? Find some books with ideas that are different from yours.

FIGURE 9–8 Story Booklets for Promoting Interaction in Reading

Josephine Gemake, "Interactive Reading: How to Make Children Active Readers," *The Reading Teacher* 37 (1984): 463, 465. Reprinted with permission of Josephine Gemake and the International Reading Association.

should be used first, followed by longer passages as students become more adept at noting and combining details.

Observing and writing about demonstrations can lead into reading passages to develop skills that parallel those found in listening/speaking. One example, identified earlier, involved fitting a balloon over the top of an empty bottle that is then placed in a pan of water and gradually heated. As the air in the bottle expands and the balloon slowly inflates, students write cause and effect statements in the appropriate columns. Students are then led to analyze these statements which are placed on a chart or overhead transparency. Some examples of what might be written follow:

Cause	*Effect*
1. It happened because . . .	1. Air molecules in the bottle expanded . . .
2. As a result of . . .	
3. The reason why . . .	2. . . . air in the bottle contracted.
4. When the air trapped in the bottle heated . . .	3. Air molecules bounced out of the bottle into the balloon.
5. When the air in the bottle and balloon cooled . . .	4. The balloon blew up . . .
	5. . . . the balloon began to shrink.

Students then move to a passage in a book in which cause-effect is presented. Students examine the passage to determine cause-effect language similar to what had been written during the balloon and bottle demonstration. A running chart of cause-effect language patterns should be kept over a period of a few weeks or longer, with explanations continuing as students write/read cause-effect passages.

Students who continue to have problems with cause-effect relationships can be taught as a flex group. Activities might include additional demonstrations and transitions to reading cause-effect passages, listening to cause-effect passages on audio tape, peer tutoring in cooperative learning groups, and/or collection of magazine pictures which clearly show cause and effect relationships.

Identifying Critical Reading Skills

Critical reading extends reading for understanding or comprehension. In one sense, reading comprehension skills are prerequisites for critical reading, although in some instances the skills in the two areas may develop concurrently. Critical reading moves the student into a deeper involvement with the text in that the student is to make a critical judgment about what has been read, focusing on validating the accuracy of the passage.

As in critical listening, the reader must use his/her background experiences to recall or formulate standards against which reading materials are evaluated. If, for example, a student is reading about a television set where the "picture is absolutely the sharpest yet developed," background experiences must be activated to help the student formulate a standard by which to judge the passage.

Among the most frequently-mentioned critical reading skills are those which can be classified as propaganda techniques. Cheek and Cheek cite the *Institute of Propaganda Analysis* in identifying seven basic critical reading skills that fall into this category. These include name calling, glittering generalities, transfer, plain folks, testimonials, bandwagon, and card stacking.[45]

Name Calling
This critical reading skill refers to the use of either negative or positive names to get one's point of view across. When a political candidate is referred to as a congenial family man, the candidate is being projected in a positive way. On the other hand, a candidate in a political race might be referred to as a conservative in such a way that he/she will be seen as one who is against changes that are needed.

Glittering Generalities
Glittering generalities are those broad-sweeping statements aimed at appealing to the reader's sense of wanting the very best. When a passage reads, "the sweetest ice cream ever made," the message is that ice cream should be very sweet and that buying the ice cream in question helps the buyer obtain this desired quality.

Transfer
When a technique is used to get the reader to apply a message being read to another situation, *transfer* is being used. An ad which stipulates that an *Algebra Made Easy* book will help develop study skills useful for other college subjects is an example of this strategy. While there may be some truth to what is advertised, there may also be much that is not true. The book may not be useful at all in helping students understand chemistry.

Plain Folks
When this technique is used in critical reading, it is an attempt to make readers think that being a "common man" is quite important. A statement such as, "They are ordinary folks," is an example of this skill in use. A restaurant that advertises "country cooking" is appealing to a return to simplicity that many people do indeed seek. It is a *plain folks* appeal.

Testimonials
This critical reading strategy is used to identify the very best about a person or product. When someone writes that, "She is like a mother to us all," a *testimonial* strategy is being used. When a company advertises that its product is good enough for a "king's feast" or is "the preferred dish of the White House chef," a form of testimonial is being used. Often, celebrities are used in advertisements to carry out this strategy.

Bandwagon
One of the most common propaganda techniques is *bandwagon*. In simplest terms, this refers to an appeal being made to get the reader to do what everyone else is doing, to not be the only one left out, to be like everyone else and buy "this automobile, this beauty aid, or this air conditioner."

Card Stacking
In this propaganda device, the writer has "stacked the cards" in that only the very positive features of a product are given focus. Some glaring deficiencies may exist in the product, but without reference to them. A toothpaste might really have an unpleasant taste when used, but the ad focuses on how white the toothpaste makes the teeth look.

Strategies for Teaching Critical Reading Skills

There are a number of strategies for teaching critical reading skills, but six are perhaps the most important in a student-involved corrective reading program. These are:

1. Intensify the use of students' background experiences for teaching critical reading.

2. Compare passages about the same topic in which a critical reading skill (such as *bandwagon*) is used in one passage but not the other, thus making the use of the skill more explicit.

3. Model a skill, demonstrating how one questions the validity or truth of what someone has written.

4. Teach students how to develop standards or "judgmental" statements that can be used in evaluating a written passage.

5. Teach signal or clue words to look for in making a judgment about a reading passage.

Intensifying Students' Background Experiences
In preparation for teaching critical reading skills, the teacher should start with experiences that are almost certain to have happened to most of the students being taught. For example, if *bandwagon* is the strategy being taught, a beginning point could be to have students react to a statement placed on the chalkboard such as, "Janie told her parents that she would be the only girl in her class without a bicycle if they did not buy one for her." Similar statements that other students have made to their parents are elicited and written on the chalkboard. The list of statements serve as a lead-in to reading passages where *bandwagon* has been used. The strategy is then defined and explained as the *bandwagon* strategy, followed by small-group work where students find other examples of the strategy in use in magazines or newspapers, and/or write other examples of this strategy. Other propaganda

strategies can be taught through a similar cycle of using students' experiences to develop an understanding of each strategy, defining the strategy, examining language used in each strategy, and finding/writing examples of each strategy.

Contrasting Passages

Contrasting reading passages written two different ways can lead to significant development of critical reading skills. Students are given background information which puts the analysis of the passages in proper perspective, such as determining which of two passages is best for a consumers' guide on buying wisely at a supermarket.

An example of a passage written two different ways in which the *bandwagon* technique is used is shown in Figure 9–9. For use in a corrective reading program, several passages should be available, both on overhead transparencies and laminated cards. In addition, students can be asked to write paragraphs on the same topic with a propaganda strategy in one but not the other paragraph. This can be done in small groups, in pairs, or individually.

Modeling Critical Reading Skills in a Corrective Reading Program

Using an overhead projection of a passage, the teacher can demonstrate how she/he begins to doubt the validity of a passage in a story, what kinds of statements trigger questions that lead to more critical reading of the passage, and how, in some instances, questions and doubts are confirmed in the passage through further

> John heard his classmates talking about getting microcomputers for their homes. He told his parents that night how much he really wanted a microcomputer, because he could do better homework if he had a microcomputer. "They are so neat for doing fancy homework," John told his parents.

> John heard his classmates talking about getting microcomputers for their homes. He told his parents that night how much he really wanted a microcomputer, because all of his friends at school will have their own microcomputer. "I will be the only one without one," John said. "And my homework won't be neat like their homework is," he said.

FIGURE 9–9 Contrasting Reading Passages with and without Bandwagon Strategy

reading. An example that might be used follows. The students are reading a story about "Medicine Men of the Old West." The following passage with sentences numbered for easy reference is placed on an overhead transparency:

> (1) The old man stood on the corner of a downtown street in Dodgewood, barking out the glories of his "Magic Medicine." (2) He said that his "miracle medicine" was made from a stream of water in the mountains, and is water that has "special powers." (3) The water had been mixed with desert sand "from a secret place nearby," and that the sand could cure any ailment. (4) "Everybody from miles around says that my 'Magic Medicine' has cured their rheumatism and arthritis," the old peddler cried out. (5) "Everyone is buying my 'Magic Medicine,' so don't you be left out!"

Sentences are read in order, with the teacher raising questions about sentences two and three in which it is stated that water from a stream in the mountains and desert sand are mixed together. The teacher reads sentence four and says to her class, "Now I know that this is a hoax. Not everyone from miles around (anywhere) would have arthritis or rheumatism. The old man should have worded his sales pitch differently." Then the teacher reads sentence five and says that this sentence just confirms what she had already discovered. "The old man is a phony. Not everyone (anywhere) would buy the same product, even where the product has been proven to be totally good for people." Students discuss the technique, identifying it as the *bandwagon* strategy and read ads where the strategy has been used. In much the same way that the teacher walked through the reading of the "Magic Medicine" passage, students in small groups, take turns walking through passages showing how they detected fallacies in the materials read.

Developing Standards/Making Judgmental Statements to Use Prior to Reading

Although a goal in critical reading is to get students to automatically draw on their experiences to formulate standards/criteria for evaluating what they read, an intermediate step can be the writing of projected standards *prior to* reading a passage. This would be followed with a critique of what is read and how the statements written prior to reading could be used to discount the passage. An example might be the reading of a story about a race horse that was mistreated by its trainer, in an attempt to make the horse run faster on race day.

After discussing what a trainer of a race horse does, students are asked to write the kind of behaviors a good trainer should display in working with a horse. Each student writes on a small card or piece of paper four or five ways that good trainers take care of their horses during training. Then the story is read, with students evaluating the behavior of the cruel trainer in respect to what they have identified as good standards of behavior for trainers of horses. After the discussion, more passages are read in the next few days, each preceded by students writing standards to judge each episode.

Teaching Signal Words and Phrases to Aid Critical Reading

As in listening, signal words in critical reading are important. Signal words and phrases that are most often used to distinguish opinion as opposed to fact include such words/statements as: (1) I believe; (2) In my opinion; (3) It could be this way; (4) It might have happened like this; (5) My guess is; (6) James said that he thought; (7) We think it important; (8) It could be one of several; (9) For a long time, the Earth was believed to be . . . ; and (10) One theory is that . . .

Words and phrases that signify fact as opposed to opinion usually include reference to: (1) an authoritative source; (2) believable statistics or other data for support; and (3) an appeal to reason or logic. In the first category, authoritative source, one might find such statements as: (1) The Surgeon General has determined . . . ; (2) A group of scientists at the Oak Ridge National Laboratory has found that . . . ; (3) It was reported in the *New England Journal of Medicine* that . . . In the second category, believable statistics, such words/phrases/statements as; (1) Four out of every five . . . ; (2) There are 249,000,000 people living in . . . ; and (3) Water freezes at 32 degrees Fahrenheit. In the third category, appeal to reason or logic, words and phrases that help distinguish fact from opinion might include: (1) A reasonable explanation was . . . ; (2) This is the way a witness saw it . . . ; (3) It is logical to . . . .

One way to involve students in learning signal words is to identify a few such words in categories being taught (*card stacking, glittering generalities, fact-opinion*) and have students continue to add words in the appropriate categories over the next several weeks. As each list grows, students discuss the words, write passages using some of the words, and read what each other has written. The objective is to learn the signal words and how they are used in each skill.

Corrective Teaching of Study Skills

Study skills are those skills that provide structures and/or processes for focusing and/or streamlining the reader's efforts in reading. An example of a study skill in which the reader both focuses and streamlines his/her efforts is *skimming*. A student who *skims* a passage focuses on key points under divisions of the content to be read (if divisions are given), rather than on all of the details in the body of the passage. Reading the legend of a map or graph is an example of a study skill which utilizes a structure to help focus on what is read.

Identifying the Study Skills

Cheek and Cheek state that there are three categories of study skills. These include reference skills, organizational skills, and specialized skills.[46] Reference skills are those skills which relate to finding information in designated source books/

materials, including the dictionary, the encyclopedia, specialized reference materials, the library card catalog, and selected software packages for the micro-computer. Organizational skills refer to those skills which help students understand and make meaningful relationships among the various facts/figures that they read. Included among these skills are the development of outlines, underlining key points/ideas, and the taking of notes. Specialized study skills are those skills within text that help the reader locate specific materials and/or better understand materials. These skills include using title pages, tables of content/lists of charts; locating the introduction, preface and foreword of a book; using the appendix; identifying bibliography/lists of suggested readings; using the glossary and index; using study questions; reading maps, tables, graphs, and diagrams; using footnotes, typographical aids, and marginal notes; previewing, skimming, and scanning materials; adjusting rate according to materials and purpose; understanding general and specialized vocabulary; and using appropriate study techniques, such as SQ3R.[47] It is important for all teachers to know the study skills, but especially is it important for teachers in a student-involved corrective program to know these skills.

Techniques for Teaching the Study Skills

How are the study skills taught in a corrective reading program? Some of the basic themes of this book help answer this question and are reviewed as they relate to instruction on study skills.

1. Where possible, teach each study skill in context of use. An example is showing a small group how to use a table of contents or an index as the group searches for information on a project that is being done.

2. Model the skill when introducing it, walking through each step for all students to see what is to be done. Let students walk through the steps.

3. Place the basic techniques for using a study skill on an index card for easy reference. For example, when students are learning to use the dictionary for pronouncing words, place the basic substeps of this process on an index card. Then when students want to use the skill, reference is made to the appropriate card. Multiple copies of the card permit group use of this technique. Also, laminating the cards will help preserve them.

4. Use a variety of techniques for assessing students' abilities in using study skills. A paper and pencil test is fine to measure outcomes or results of using a study skill, but observation of a student as he/she performs a study skill (demonstrates how to look up a word in the dictionary) helps assess processes involved.

5. Determine and assess prerequisites for learning a study skill. For example, prerequisites for outlining call for students to know coding systems (Roman numerals, upper-case letters, lower-case letters, and so on), and main topic/subtopic designations. A major prerequisite for finding words in a dictionary is alphabetizing.

6. When students are doing seatwork or small-group activities in which study skills are to be used, remind students of the study skills needed, and briefly discuss how they are performed. Also, remind students of the card file with steps for each skill, and allow students to use the skill cards at their desks.

7. Have materials available for students to practice study skills, independently or in small groups. Each activity should be specific and easy to read.

8. Reinforce the use of study skills by discussing with the class or a small group how a student used a particular reference book, and, with the help of one or more study skills, located information that would not have been found otherwise.

9. Use flex groups for special-needs instruction as often as is needed to teach or reteach specific study skills.

Paying attention to headings and subheadings often help students better comprehend what they are reading. As part of the way text is organized, headings and subheadings help break down content into smaller units that have a unique relationship. Therefore, it is important to provide direct instruction on how to use headings/subheadings.

Among the most frequently-identified techniques for teaching study skills is the *SQ3R Technique*. The formula, *SQ3R*, refers to surveying, questioning, reading, reciting, and reviewing. F. Robinson is credited for developing this formula which follows:

S = Survey   Read the title of the chapter, the introductory statement, and the main headings. Survey illustrations and read the summary at the end of the chapter. Try to construct a chapter outline in your mind.

Q = Question   Look at the main headings. Ask yourself what they mean. Formulate questions from your survey.

R_1 = Read   Read to find answers to your questions.

R_2 = Recite   Recite answers to your questions. Do the author's answers satisfy you? Do you have new ideas that could help answer the questions?

R_3 = Review   Review the entire chapter or selection in a survey fashion. Reconstruct your outline in your mind. Recall the author's important ideas. Think of ways to use the new ideas you learned.[48]

The Decoding Debate

Teaching young children to unlock words as part of the reading process is the most controversial area in reading instruction. There are basically two schools of thought on which is the best way of attacking words. On the one hand is the whole-word approach in which children learn to decode the word through repetition and memory, somewhat in the same way that sight words are learned. The application of knowledge about the sound system of the English language to teach reading (defined as phonics) is not a primary focus for beginning reading in this approach.

The other camp, the phonics group, has promoted the position that symbols and the sounds they represent should be learned initially. Thus, youngsters learning to read would begin to transfer to other words what they have learned. For example, knowledge that the symbol <b>* representing the beginning sound in *bat* and *boy*, would be transferred to *band* and *bus* when these words are encountered. In this approach, students are not taught to memorize whole words, but instead to concentrate on the sounds made when letters are used to represent words. Even here, there is some divisiveness with one camp wanting to start with letters and their sounds (as putting sounds together to form words) while others argue for starting out with words and breaking them down into their symbol-sound elements. Attacks made on the phonics group's position center on the criticism that more than one symbol is used to represent a number of sounds and that some symbols, especially those representing consonants, are distorted when one tries to teach the sounds these symbols represent. A case in point is the /b/† sound to which some phonics programs have given the "buh" sound which, of course, is distorted.

While critics of phonics approaches have attacked what is identified as the irregularity of English, a counter argument has been that English is more regular than previously believed. When students see the <gh> combination of letters, the sound of /f/ is indeed a predictable sound. Likewise, when students come across <ph>, there is a high predictability factor built into the pronunciation of the sound associated with this grapheme. Letters that typically represent consonant sounds have the highest level of predictability.

Predictability of not only symbol-sound relationships, but other systems in the language can be seen by looking at the nonsense story on p. 346. In this nonsense story, most English-speaking people who can read have no problem pronouncing *lell* or any words derived from it, such as *lelling* or *lelled*. Rules of the sound system of English as well as the morphological or word-building system are in operation. Those who read this story almost always pronounce other nonsense words used, including *brimpy*, *yob*, *zooky*, and *hiler*. They pronounce *lapes*, *loit*, *vindy*, and *ganny* with little or no difficulty because these words pattern

---

*In Chapter 4 (Spelling), the term grapheme was introduced to indicate a symbol that stood for a phoneme. As indicated, when enclosed with < >, reference is to the graphic symbol or grapheme, not the sound.

†The reader will remember that / / on either side of a letter or combination of letters refers to a sound or phoneme, not a symbol.

Going Lelling

The brimpy yob went lelling. It lelled by the ganny. It lelled by the vindy. It lelled and lelled.

One day while lelling, the brimpy yob met a zooky hiler. The brimpy yob and the zooky hiler became lapes. Wherever the brimpy yob went, you saw the zooky hiler.

Today, you can see the good lapes lelling zad of the loit. They lell by the ganny. They lell by the vindy. They lell and lell.

Would you like to go lelling with them?

---

in a way that letters used in real words pattern in the English language. Their pronunciation is predictable.

Questions can be answered about this nonsense story, although with no concepts attached to the nonsense words, the story is void of full meaning. In the first question, while we do not know what the *brimpy yob* did exactly, we can say that it went *lelling*. We know also where it went *lelling*. In fact, we can respond to the question of, "In what two places did the *brimpy yob lell*?" By looking in paragraph two, we can also respond to the question of, "Who did the *brimpy yob* meet?" And on it goes. Even though we do not know enough vocabulary to really comprehend this nonsense story, the syntactical pattern (stringing of words together) lets us answer questions about it.

An excellent activity in a student-involved corrective program is to let students take a few minutes to see how many nonsense words that pattern certain ways can be generated. Individually or in small groups, students generate words that most students in the class would pronounce only one way because of the letter patterns. The longest lists are written on the chalkboard. A similar activity can be done with a nonsense story. Students are asked to create a story using nonsense words as in "Going Lelling." Questions in the story are to be answered from the context, even though the nonsense words themselves are not known.

In decoding, some students will pick up symbol-sound relationships on their own, but there is a need for systematic instruction. Especially is this the case in a corrective program. How should symbol-sound relationships be systematically taught? Which relationships are of most value? Johnson and Pearson recommend that the letter-sound relationships shown in Table 9–2 are the most worthy of teaching. It should be noted that Johnson and Pearson point out that when patterns are taught, sample words are used.[49] Students use these words to recall how a target sound is pronounced.

Steps in Decoding

Decoding should be taught in such a way that students learn systematic and automatic steps for breaking words down. Where students have not learned to do this,

TABLE 9–2 A Recommended Symbol-Sound Curriculum

For each pattern sample words are used to illustrate the letter-sound relationships that need to be learned. Occasionally a rule is given.

Consonants

b—book	k—king	qu—queen	w—water
d—dance	l—lemon	r—roll	x—xylophone,
f—funny	m—money	s—sit or was	exam, tax
h—heart	n—new	t—top or nation	y—yes
j—job	p—party	v—violin	z—zebra

Other Consonants
Rule: *C* sounds like *s* before *e, i, y,*
and sounds like *k* elsewhere.

c— cent	c— cat
city	cot
cycle	cup

Rule: *G* sounds like *j* before *e, i, y,*
and sounds like *g* elsewhere.

g—gem	g—game
agile	gone
gym	guild

Double Consonants
Rule: Except for *cc* and *qq,* two
identical consonants have one sound.

digraphs	sh—shoe	th—thin	ch—chew
	ph—photo	this	choir
	ng—song	wh—while	chef

doubles	bb—rabble	ll—belly	nn—funny	rr—narrow	zz—dizzy
	dd—ladder	mm—dimmer	pp—happen	vv—savvy	gg—egg
	ff—jiffy	cc—buccaneer			suggest
		accept			

blends	bl—black	sl—slow	gr—ground	scr—screen	squ—squeak
	cl—clue	br—brown	pr—proud	sm—small	st—stump
	fl—flap	cr—cry	tr—trap	sn—snow	sw—swing
	gl—glass	dr—draw	sc—scat	sp—spot	
	pl—play	fr—friend			

Vowels
Rules: 1. "A vowel between two consonants is usually 'short'": pin, cap, hot, bug, bed.
2. "A vowel before two or more consonants is usually 'short'": wish, graph, much, blotter, lettuce, happen, itch, hospital, cinder, bumper.

Continued

TABLE 9–2 *Continued*

3. "A vowel followed by a consonant plus *e* is usually 'long'": pine, date, dope, cute, mute.
4. "The letter *y* sometimes is a vowel and it has two sounds": y—my; baby.

i— if	a— act	o—hot	u—much	e— bed
mild	about	of	cute	jacket
bird	ape	note	tube	blaze
	want	off	bull	often
	call	for	fur	she
	star			her

Double Vowels

io—nation	ai—pain	ou—ounce	au—because	ow—own
lion	said	though	laugh	cow
ea—each	ay—play	soup	oo—moon	oi —coin
bread		would	book	
great		ee—see		
		been		

(Adapted from Smith and Johnson, Teaching Children to Read, 1976) Dale D. Johnson and P. David Pearson, *Teaching Reading Vocabulary,* (New York: Holt, Rinehart and Winston, 1978), p. 61. (Used with permission).

corrective teaching is necessary. There are several basic decoding strategies, one of which is found in Table 9–3. In this strategy, students look for morphemes or meaning-bearing units* in words. In this decoding strategy, knowing syllables and some rules governing pronunciation of them is important. In addition, symbol-sound association is also important as found in Step 3. In using these steps together, context of a sentence is important. Reading is about getting meaning, and students should often ask themselves, "Does this word (as I am trying to say it) make sense?"

Another decoding strategy, identified as graphophonics with context, calls for more emphasis on Step 3 in the approach in Table 9–3. In this approach, fully described by Durkin, students try to sound out letters in words by using what they already know about symbol-sound relationships. Context of the sentence is used to determine whether or not the reader is successful.[50] In yet another decoding strategy, sound substitution, there is an emphasis on recalling patterns of words (*make, cake*) and substituting different sounds in various positions of the unknown word (for example, if *rake* is the unknown word).[51]

---

*There are two kinds of morphemes that students learn in school. In the word *singer,* the two kinds exist. The word *sing* is a free morpheme since it has meaning by itself. The *er* in *singer* is bound in that it must be attached to a free morpheme to have meaning.

TABLE 9–3 Steps in Decoding Unknown Words

Method 1–Morphemic Elements in Words

Step 1

Break the word down into meaning-bearing units (morphemes), unless the word is quite short (e.g., *Singer* has two morphemes—*sing* and *er*).

Step 2

Look for the number of syllables in a word. Vowels in a morpheme often determine how many syllables a word has. Vowels between consonants usually indicate a syllable as in *taken* (two syllables); *sunning* (two syllables). There are exceptions, but these should not be confusing.

Step 3

Sort out or think through sounds associated with letters <f> or letter combinations <ea> in each morpheme in a word. Try pronouncing the sounds that *you think* are associated with the letters in a word you are trying to say. Some words are easy as in *bat*; others are more difficult as in *teacher*. Test what you think the word is by using the rest of the sentence to see if it makes sense.

Robert Calfee and Priscilla Drum, "Research on Teaching Reading," in *Handbook of Research on Teaching*, 3rd ed. ed. by Merlin C. Wittrock (New York: Macmillan Publishing Company, 1986), pp. 813–814 (adapted with permission).

    The teacher in a corrective program should know a variety of such strategies and employ them as needed. The first step in reteaching decoding strategies is to help students learn symbol-sound relationships that they do not know. Intensive work may be necessary and should be done in flex groups. Some decoding strategies recommended for corrective reading programs are:

    1. Use pictures to help students learn words with the basic sounds (as a picture of a kite to learn the initial /k/). Make sure that pictures selected fit the age group, for older students resent pictures considered "babyish."

    2. Extend students hearing of a sound by having them collect and place appropriate pictures in a journal or other type of log.

    3. Have students recall words that they know and then write them (if they can write the word), and underline the symbol that represents the target sound. Write the word for them if they do not yet know how to write.

    4. Have students consistently use context of sentences to learn how to identify a word, including its meaning.

    5. Keep on file appropriate sets of pictures that help students identify target sounds. These should be on file in appropriate packets for individual or small-group use (in manila envelopes). Once students have learned or relearned the basic symbol-sound combinations, various techniques can be utilized to teach decoding strategies. Sets of words can be placed on audio tape and appropriate word lists provided for students to use in learning and/or practicing the strategies.* One-on-one teaching in which students have opportunities to demonstrate the decoding strategies is critical, although some small groups of students might be taught the strategies together. Again, trained volunteers can be an asset to a corrective reading program to provide individualized help.

The Teaching Of Generalizations

While there is controversy about the validity of some traditional generalizations taught in reading (as "When two vowels go walking, the first one does the talking."), there is some merit in teaching a limited number of the more productive generalizations. Position of letters in words, relationship of letters to other letters in words, and how words can be generated from other words are among several factors that are important in determining which generalizations are the most productive and should be taught. In Table 9–2, four productive generalizations are presented. These generalizations depend on two of the factors identified, position of letters and relationship of letters to other letters.

Like spelling generalizations, reading generalizations can be learned inductively in varied ways. However, in teaching reading generalizations, the focus is on identifying and pronouncing words, not in spelling them.

Teaching to Improve Attitude Toward and Interest in Reading

A number of strategies covered in this book can be applied to the improvement of attitude toward reading. The major one is assessing and using students' interests. Another theme is making drill and practice meaningful. Yet another important strategy is using children's experiences to teach or reteach various components of the language arts.

Measuring Attitude Toward Reading

A systematic plan should be devised for determining how children feel about reading. Such a plan should include the use of an established instrument for determining how students feel about reading, daily observations of how children react to both reading and activities for teaching reading, and conferences with students about what they like and dislike about reading.

*A colleague of the writer at the University of Tennessee, Dr. Donald Dickinson, and two of his graduate students (Pam Gross and Francine L. Reynolds), have had success with an audio component for Method 1 in Table 9–3. Taped directions with practice words in sentences are given via earphones. Students apply each step until they have learned to use the step to decode unknown words.

Several reading attitude scales have been developed. Some have appeared in a number of books on reading instruction. One is *A Scale of Reading Attitude Based on Behavior*, which first appeared in print in 1972. This scale (a Likert design with five response items, always occurs to never occurs) is used to record observed reactions of students to reading situations. There are sixteen items which can be divided into three broad categories: reading instruction (items 1–6), reading for pleasure (items 7–13), and reading in the content areas (items 14–16). For each item, the teacher or another rater observes a student (or two to three students at once, where possible), but over a period of time.[52] The reliability of the scale and its easy use within a "normal classroom setting" have been reported a number of years after its development.[53] The scale in its entirety is shown in Table 9–4. The scale can be used as a diagnostic instrument by assigning points to each item (5 for always occurs, 4 for often occurs, and so on) and by totaling scores in each of the three major categories (reading instruction, reading for pleasure, and reading in the content areas).

TABLE 9–4   A Scale of Reading Attitude Based on Behavior

Name of Student _____   Grade _____   Date _____

School _____   Observer _____

Directions: Check the most appropriate of the five blanks by each item below. Only one blank by each item should be checked.

	Always Occurs	Often occurs	Occa-sionally occurs	Seldom occurs	Never Occurs
1. The student exhibits a strong desire to come to the reading circle or to have reading instruction take place.	____	____	____	____	____
2. The student is enthusiastic and interested in participating once he comes to the reading circle or the reading class begins.	____	____	____	____	____
3. The student asks permission or raises his hand to read orally.	____	____	____	____	____
4. When called upon to read orally the student eagerly does so.	____	____	____	____	____
5. The student very willingly answers a question asked him in the reading class.	____	____	____	____	____

Continued

TABLE 9–4 *Continued*

6. Contributions in the way of voluntary discussions are made by the student in the reading class. ____ ____ ____ ____ ____

7. The student expresses a desire to be read to by you or someone else, and he attentively listens while this is taking place. ____ ____ ____ ____ ____

8. The student makes an effort to read printed materials on bulletin boards, charts, or other displays having writing on them. ____ ____ ____ ____ ____

9. The student elects to read a book when the class has permission to choose a "free-time" activity. ____ ____ ____ ____ ____

10. The student expresses genuine interest in going to the school's library. ____ ____ ____ ____ ____

11. The student discusses with you (the teacher) or members of the class those items he has read from the newspaper, magazines, or similar materials. ____ ____ ____ ____ ____

12. The student voluntarily and enthusiastically discusses with others the book he has read or is reading. ____ ____ ____ ____ ____

13. The student listens attentively while other students share their reading experiences with the group. ____ ____ ____ ____ ____

14. The student expresses eagerness to read printed materials in the content areas. ____ ____ ____ ____ ____

15. The student goes beyond the textbook or usual reading assignment in searching for other materials to read. ____ ____ ____ ____ ____

16. The student contributes to group discussions that are based on reading assignments made in the content areas. ____ ____ ____ ____ ____

C. Glennon Rowell, "An Attitude Scale for Reading," *The Reading Teacher*, 25 (1972), p. 444. Reprinted with permission of C. Glennon Rowell and the International Reading Association.

Two other scales that can be used to measure attitude toward reading are the *Heathington Primary Scale* and the *Heathington Intermediate Scale.* These scales call for students to respond to a series of questions about the way they feel toward reading, about their behavior toward library books, about their frequency of reading, and a number of other items which can be used to assess reading attitude. The *Primary Scale* calls for students to respond by marking a series of five faces (very happy to very unhappy) by each item. An example is shown in Diagram 9–1, along with an item on the twenty-item scale.

The *Intermediate Scale,* which appears in Table 9–5, contains twenty-four items which are read to students who respond by marking an answer sheet that is coded for five responses from "SD" for "Strongly Disagree" to "SA" for "Strongly Agree."[54] The scale can be used for diagnostic purposes by grouping items in specific areas.

For example, attitude toward free reading in the classroom can be determined by grouping responses to items 5, 6, and 15. Attitude toward general reading can be determined by examining responses to items 2, 8, 14, 16, 18, 19, and 22.[55]

Finding Reading Levels and Grouping Students for Daily Instruction

As previously described, the *Informal Reading Inventory* or *IRI* is one of the most efficient instruments for finding reading levels. The inventory, is useful for finding three basic levels of reading. These widespread levels are identified by McKenna:

- *The* instructional level *is the level at which students comprehend from 75–89 percent of what they read and have a 95 to 99 percent accuracy rate in oral reading.*

DIAGRAM 9–1   Sample Item on Heathington Primary Scale (Reading Attitude)

Sample Response Spaces   **Primary Scale**
                                              How do you feel...

6.

6. when you read to someone at home.

J. Estill Alexander and Ronald C. Filler, *Attitudes and Reading,* (Newark, Delaware: The International Reading Association, 1976) pp. 2–3. Reprinted with permission of J. Estill Alexander and the International Reading Association.

TABLE 9–5   Heathington Intermediate Scale (Reading Attitude)

	Items	Sample Response Form

1. You feel uncomfortable when you're asked to read in class.

SD   D   U   A   SA

2. You feel happy when you're reading.
3. Sometimes you forget about library books that you have in your desk.
4. You don't check out many library books.
5. You don't read much in the classroom.
6. When you have free time at school, you usually read a book.
7. You seldom have a book in your room at home.
8. You would rather look at the pictures in a book than read the book.
9. You check out books at the library but never have time to read them.
10. You wish you had a library full of books at home.
11. You seldom read in your room at home.
12. You would rather watch TV than read.
13. You would rather play after school than read.
14. You talk to friends about books that you have read.
15. You like for the room to be quiet so you can read in your free time.
16. You read several books each week.
17. Most of the books you choose are not interesting.
18. You don't read very often.
19. You think reading is work.
20. You enjoy reading at home.
21. You enjoy going to the library.
22. Often you start a book, but never finish it.
23. You think that adventures in a book are more exciting than TV.
24. You wish you could answer the questions at the end of the chapter without reading it.

J. Estill Alexander and Ronald C. Filler, *Attitudes and Reading*, (Newark, Delaware: The International Reading Association, 1976), pp. 31–32. Reprinted with permission of J. Estill Alexander and the International Reading Association.

- *The* independent level *is the level at which students comprehend from 90–100 percent of what they read and have a 99 percent accuracy rate in reading orally.*
- *The* frustration level *is the level in which students comprehend less than 50 percent of what they read and have an oral-reading accuracy rate of 90 percent or less.*[56]

The instructional level is the level on which materials are used to teach reading to students. At this level, students can read with relative ease. They have trouble pronouncing few words (less than 5 percent) and can answer correctly at least three out of every four questions asked of them. With guidance from the teacher, students can benefit from instruction at the instructional level.

The independent level, sometimes called the recreational level, is the level on which students can read books (such as trade books) for pleasure. Students on this level can read books quite well on their own, with relatively few errors in word pronunciation. Students reading at this level have a high degree of fluency and comprehension.

When students are reading at the frustration level, they are having severe difficulties calling words (decoding) and understanding what they are "reading." This level is characterized by stumbling over words unnecessarily. When students are at the frustration level, they should be provided with easier reading materials.

Another level is sometimes identified as the *listening comprehension* or *capacity* level. This is the level at which children comprehend through listening 70 percent or more of what is read to them by the teacher.

According to Cheek and Cheek, there is general agreement on steps to take in administering the *IRI*.[57] In abbreviated form, the steps suggested are:

1.   Use a graded word list such as the *Dolch Basic Sight Word List* to determine a student's word recognition level.

2.   Choose a reading passage approximately two grade levels below the estimated instructional level of the student being tested.

3.   Have the student read a selection orally. Mark errors, using codes (as *p* where the teacher must pronounce a word; *mp* over mispronounced words).

4.   Ask comprehension questions when the student has completed oral reading.

5.   Count errors (words teacher had to pronounce, mispronunciations, substitutions, omissions, and so on), and record on a summary response form.

6.   Use criteria for finding reading levels and determining instructional, independent, and frustration levels. (Note: All three levels may not be found with first passage used, as explained in step 11.)

7.   Use a second passage for silent reading. Make sure that the student understands the purpose for reading it.

8.   Record words that the student asks while reading.

9.   Ask comprehension questions (following silent reading).

10. Use criteria for finding different kinds of reading levels (as in step 6).

11. Continue testing in both oral and silent reading until appropriate levels are found. If materials first selected are at the frustration level, easier materials should be used to determine instructional level. If materials are extremely easy, higher materials should be used.[58]

The *Dolch Basic Sight Word List*, the graded word list identified in number 1 in the preceding list, has been used over fifty years to determine word recognition levels of students. There are 220 words on the *Dolch List*. These words are broken down by grade levels into shorter lists.

Burns and Roe have developed an *Informal Reading Assessment (IRA)*, a set of graded materials for determining reading levels from preprimer to grade twelve. Two kinds of materials from the *Informal Reading Assessment* are reprinted in Figures 9–10 and 9–11. These are shown to illustrate the kinds of recordkeeping systems needed not only for use with the *IRA*, but for use with any type of informal reading inventory. Such forms help teachers streamline recordkeeping, which is a "must" for busy teachers. In Figure 9–10, diagnostic information can be shown, along with comprehension skill analysis information. In Figure 9–11, a summary of a student's test results is shown. In using the *IRA*, not only are independent, instructional, and capacity (listening) levels given, but specific miscues or errors in reading are shown. These provide valuable diagnostic information about a student's oral-reading problems.

Another reading inventory available is the *Basic Reading Inventory, Pre-Primer–Grade Eight* developed by Johns. This inventory contains both graded passages and word lists for determining the student's independent reading level, instructional reading level, frustration level, strengths and weaknesses in word attack, strengths and weaknesses in comprehension, and listening level.[59]

Cloze Reading Inventory

As mentioned earlier, the cloze technique can be used to determine reading levels. One inventory available is *The DeSanti Cloze Reading Inventory*, for which the stated purposes are to: (1) measure reading achievement; (2) determine the independent, instructional, and frustration reading levels; and (3) diagnose an individual's reading strengths and weaknesses.[60]

Recognizing Oral Reading Errors

Different kinds of oral-reading errors or miscues that students make should be determined. The basic ones usually identified in the literature are given in Table 9–6. Usually, the system of noting errors is one of writing in codes or words above the place in a passage where the student made an error. The student reads from a copy of the passage that the teacher also has for marking errors. Specific patterns of errors are noted. A marked passage is shown in Figure 9–12. A coding

Word-Recognition Miscue-Analysis Chart

Miscue	PP	P	1	2	3	4	5	6	7	8	9	10	11	12	Total
Mispronunciation															
Substitution															
Refusal to pronounce															
Insertion															
Omission															
Repetition															
Reversal															
Total															

Comprehension Skill Analysis Chart

Skill	Number of Questions	Number of Errors	Percent of Errors
Main idea			
Detail			
Sequence			
Cause and effect			
Inference			
Vocabulary			

FIGURE 9–10   Examples of Word-Recognition Miscue-Analysis and Comprehension Skill Analysis Charts

Paul C. Burns and Betty D. Roe, *Informal Reading Assessment-Preprimer to Twelfth Grade*. (Boston, Massachusetts: Houghton Mifflin, 1980), p. 4. Copyright© 1980 by Houghton Mifflin Company. Used with permission.

system is given for marking answers to questions asked to check comprehension and for recording various kinds of reading levels.

Charts should be developed for keeping a running count of oral-reading errors. The nine errors identified in Table 9–6 can be placed on a vertical axis of a chart or grid, with names of students from each base group written on the horizontal axis. During oral reading, types of errors noted by the teacher would be marked appropriately.

SUMMARY ━━━━━━━━━━━━━━━━━━━━━ TEACHER

NAME _Melissa Harden_   GRADE _2_ ORAL _✓_ SILENT _✓_ FORM _X_

ADMINISTRATOR _Ms. Wilson_   DATE _9/4/79_   RATE _86_ HIGH _____ AVERAGE _✓_ LOW _____

INDEPENDENT LEVEL _1st grade_   INSTRUCTIONAL LEVEL _2nd grade_ FRUSTRATION LEVEL _3rd grade_ CAPACITY LEVEL _5th grade_

Strengths and weaknesses in word recognition: include information about use of or failure to use syntactic and graphic clues and about dialect-related miscues, which should not be considered serious recognition problems. Check items on chart.			
Single consonants	—	Word middles	—
Consonant blends	✓	Word endings	✓
Single vowels	—	Prefixes	—
Vowel digraphs	—	Suffixes	—
Consonant digraphs	—	Inflectional endings	—
Diphthongs	—	Compound words	—
Word beginnings	—	Syllabication	—
		Accent	—

In passage reading, most frequent miscues involved refusal to pronounce, substitutions, and omissions. On isolated word lists, a pattern of difficulty with medial vowels and word middles/endings was noted. There was no evidence of reversal difficulty or dialect-related miscues.

Strengths and weaknesses in comprehension: include information about use of or failure to use semantic clues.

Most frequently-missed questions were related to inference and cause and effect. All main idea and sequence questions were answered correctly, and few errors were made on detail and vocabulary questions.

FIGURE 9–11 Summary of Student's Test Results from an Informal Assessment

Paul C. Burns and Betty D. Roe, *Informal Reading Assessment—Preprimer to Twelfth Grade.* (Boston, Massachusetts: Houghton Mifflin, 1980), p. 21. Copyright© 1980 by Houghton Mifflin Company. Used with permission.

TABLE 9–6 Nine Types of Oral Reading Errors

Type of Error	Example
1. *Words told*: A word pronounced orally by the examiner when the student hesitates more than 5 seconds. Draw a line through the word told.	Everyone was ~~excited~~.
2. *Substitution*: a real word is substituted for another real word in the script. Write the substituted word over the word in script.	Dad was *away* always wanting to buy junk. *boy*
3. *Mispronunciation*: a word whose pronunciation is distorted to make it nonsensical. Write the mispronounced word phonically over the word in the script.	Mother enjoyed the old lamps and clocks.
4. *Omissions*: a letter, word part, word, group of words, or line omitted. Draw a circle around omitted parts.	The four ⟨of us⟩ head⟨ed⟩ for the flea market.
5. *Hesitations*: a word that stops the natural flow but is still pronounced within five seconds. Place an *h* above the word.	We went to the flea market.
6. *Insertion*: a word or word part added to or between a word. Write in addition and mark with a caret.	Mother *did* ^liked the lamps and one old clock. *s*
7. *Repetitions*: any word part, word, or phrase that is repeated. Draw a wavy line under repeated portion.	Jane enjoyed looking at old dolls.
8. *Disregarding Punctuation*: ignoring punctuation or inserting punctuation where it does not belong. Mark ignoring of or insertion of punctuation with X.	We were heading for the flea market/It was exciting.
9. *Reversals*: changing word order, or changing letter order. Draw curved line to show the reversal.	Did you like that?

Diana Phelps-Terasaki, Trisha Phelps-Gunn, and Elton G. Stetson, *Remediation and Instruction in Language-Oral Language*, Reading and Writing. Austin, Texas: Pro-Ed, Inc., 1983, p. 168 (reprinted with permission).

Passage A-3 (110 Words)

THE FLEA MARKET TRIP

The four of us headed for the flea
market. Everyone was excited. We went
to the flea market every other week
to look at the things that people
brought to sell. Some people sold
old junk items from their garages.

Others sold new things such as
jewelry, rugs, and other crafts.
Mother liked the old lamps and clocks
but never bought any. Dad was always
wanting to buy junk that wasn't good
for anything. We would laugh and he
would put them back. Jane enjoyed
looking at old dolls. I would always
try to find toy guns and old tools.
Although we seldom bought anything,
we had a great time.

ANALYSIS OF READING ACCURACY	
Type of Error	Number
Significant Errors	
1. Words Told	*1*
2. Substitutions	*II*
3. Mispronunciations	*I*
4. Omissions	*II*
TOTAL SIGNIFICANT ERRORS	*6*
Nonsignificant Errors	
5. Hesitations	*III*
6. Insertions	*I*
7. Repetitions	*III*
8. Disreg. of Punct.	*II*
9. Reversals	*I*
TOTAL NONSIGNIF. ERRORS	*10*
a. TOTAL WORDS	*110*
b. SIGNIFICANT ERRORS	*6*
c. RAW SCORE (a-b)	*104*
d. READING ACCURACY PERCENTAGE SCORE [C ÷ A]	*94.5%*

Questions:

F _T_ 1. Where was the family heading? (Flea Market)

F _+_ 2. What did Jane enjoy looking at? (old dolls)

I _+_ 3. Who is the writer of this story? (son, child, boy, etc.)

I _+_ 4. How many family members are there in this story? (4)

V _—_ 5. What is a flea market? (accept reasonable answer)

V _+_ 6. What does the word seldom mean? (not often)

M _+_ 7. What is this story mainly about? (trip to flea market)

READING ACCURACY SCORE = _95_ % [see d above]

COMPREHENSION SCORE = _86_ % [14 pts. off for each error]

RATING CHART	Frustration	Instructional	Independent
Reading Accuracy Percentage	0 - 93	94 - 98	99 - 100
Comprehension Percentage	0 - 69	70 - 89	90 - 100

FIGURE 9–12 Reading Passage: Analysis of Oral Errors and Reading Level

Diana Phelps-Terasaki, Trisha Phelps-Gunn, and Elton G. Stetson, *Remediation and Instruction in Language-Oral Language, Reading, and Writing.* Austin, Texas: Pro-Ed, Inc., 1983, p. 170 (reprinted with permission).

Computers for Reading Instruction

The microcomputer should increasingly be used in all reading programs, but especially in corrective programs. Since the microcomputer itself is becoming more available and software programs are increasing, well-thought-out guidelines are critical.

The International Reading Association (IRA) has established guidelines for the use of microcomputers in reading. Among the several guidelines for software are: (1) the design must be consistent with what research and practice have shown to be important in the process of learning to read or of reading to learn; (2) there should be clearly stated instructional objectives; (3) the activities should be ones that the computer can do better than traditional procedures/materials can do; (4) prompts used should be simple and direct; (5) screen instructions must be on appropriate readability level, be clear and unambiguous, with print, margin, spacing on the screen being quite legible; and (6) activities should call for effective involvement/participation by the learner. The IRA also says that hardware should: (1) be durable; (2) be capable of producing high quality text displays; (3) be compatible with the range of software available; (4) have sufficient memory capability; (5) have a functional keyboard; (6) have reasonable technical support from the manufacturers or distributors.[61]

In three major areas, drill and reinforcement, simulation of reading situations, and integration of writing and reading, the microcomputer is considered to be important in reading programs, and especially for student-involved corrective programs. Each is briefly discussed.

In the area of drill and reinforcement, Balajthy quotes D. LaBerge and S. Samuels in pointing out that some of the reading processes are more difficult for slower learners than they are for brighter students who readily synthesize the processes. Consequently, some subskill teaching is necessary for the slower learners, and the microcomputer is excellent for such teaching. Balajthy says that computers have advantages in drillwork in that they are very patient, and there is very little ego involved when a student is corrected by the computer (for instance, no teacher's frowns or giggles from classmates).[62]

In the area of simulated reading situations, Balajthy provides guidelines for choosing simulated activities for the microcomputer. He gives as examples of simulated activities the reader as "a pioneer on the Oregon Trail" and "the life of a fish in the ecological cycle of a lake." Teachers can maximize use of microcomputers in simulated activities when they have students work in small groups where a recorder has been appointed and where students think through and discuss the simulated event.[63]

In integrating writing and reading, the microcomputer should be used in a corrective program to have students create stories, read their created stories, and share the stories for others to read. Not only are students motivated to read and reread when they know the authors of the stories, but they are motivated to change their

The Microcomputer is an Excellent Tool for Teaching Reading and Writing in a Corrective Language Arts Program. *(Photograph by Robert Heller)*

own stories, thus rereading their own stories for a purpose often lacking when students are asked to reread stories in their books.

Special Microcomputer Materials/Programs

Casteel calls for the establishment of "computer banks" to use in reading. She says that there should be many different kinds of items such as skill banks (as for use in reinforcement of perceptual skills), assessment banks, materials banks, and diskettes with suggestions for teaching specific reading skills. Such materials on the computer saves time and leads to immediate use. Teachers can set up files for these four different kinds of reading items as they wish to do so for their school.[64]

There are numerous microcomputer software programs available for classroom use. One is *Toward Better Reading Skills, A-F.* This is a program in which the focus is on a variety of reading comprehension skills at grade levels 4–8. In addition, the program places emphasis on dictionary, vocabulary, and word-usage skills. In the program there are six disks, each containing a story divided into eight lesson modules. Each module has four reading passages and appropriate questions per module. Students are asked to complete an entire module and then to either proceed to the next module or stop at that point. Individual pacing is done via a "textscroll" system in which a student can scroll the text of a reading passage up and down on the screen. The program runs on Apple II, IIe, and IIc computers.[65]

IBM's *Writing to Read* program begins with a readiness program in which students use a number of approaches to learning the alphabet such as alphabet boards and "The Alphabet Song." The program also contains a "Writing to Read Center" in which students work on journals, make words, and learn about typing on the computer. Also incorporated in the center is a listening library. Using the *Writing to Read* program, students are involved in using their background knowledge and speaking vocabulary into stories that are written (and read) on the microcomputer screen. According to the author of the program, students learn best when they are in a responsive environment, feel in control of their own learning activities, and have no fear of failure.[66]

IBM's *Private Tutor Series* contains a wide variety of language arts skills, including capitalization, punctuation, spelling, grammar, reading comprehension, vocabulary, and word knowledge. This program is designed for middle and high school students.

Developing Fluency In Reading

Students, too frequently, do not read in phrases. Thus, "the little girl" becomes "the . . . lit-tle . . . girl." One way to tackle this problem is to give attention to phrase reading. Practice in phrase reading can begin with labeling of pictures when some words are being learned early in a reading readiness program. For example, instead of learning "desk" from a card attached to the teacher's desk, the card might read "the teacher's desk." "Our green chalkboard" might replace the single word "chalkboard," to identify the chalkboard.

A second way to deal with the slow, monotonous word calling problem is to have students practice recording their reading with a focus on reading smoothly and fluently. One activity seen years ago by the writer in a primary classroom, calls for students to periodically record a story on his/her own personal audio tape. Students had access to the recorder throughout the day, and when appropriate, took their book to the corner of the room to read their story. Students recorded their passage and listened to how smoothly they read. If they stumbled on a word, they got help from the teacher or a designated student helper.

Students, in recording themselves read each week, should have specific goals, such as reading words together, rather than slow, word-for-word reading. Conferences with the teacher before reading, where possible, should be held with each student being encouraged to read and concentrate on the goal set for that student. Follow-up work in flex groups might include practice on phrase reading, improvement of expression in voice, or other problems the teacher notes in listening to taped readings.

Videotaping of students reading can also be helpful in getting students to read fluently and with expression. Students who read fluently can be taped as models.

Summary

1. Six basic research practices on which to build a student-involved corrective reading program are using the *Informal Reading Inventory (IRI)* for: determining reading levels; the teaching of reading vocabulary both directly and from context of print; reading comprehension as an active (as opposed to passive) process; using graphic frameworks to help students understand the structure of what they read; teaching of letter-sound relationships in such a way that meaning of what is read is not impaired; and relating reading and writing.

2. The *IRI* remains the best-supported instrument for finding reading levels. *IRI's* are easy to administer and fare well compared to norm-referenced tests for finding what level is best suited for students for both instruction and leisure reading.

3. Reading vocabulary or knowing what words mean, is learned by direct teaching as well as through context of passages. Although frequency of exposure to words is critical to learning word meanings, there is a tendency to have students memorize definitions of words.

4. While the author's intent is important to the reading process, research has shown that the reader's reaction to what the author is saying is equally, if not more important, to comprehension. The reader's background of experiences interacts with what is on the printed page, helping make reading an active process.

5. Story structure is important in reading comprehension. Such structure can be attained through a variety of graphic frameworks such as story patterns and story maps. Graphic displays of how a story is constructed help develop schemata needed for understanding what is read.

6. Two schools of thought about beginning reading are the "codes emphasis" and the "meaning emphasis" approaches. Research indicates that decoding is important in learning to read. However, an emphasis on learning codes that are used to represent sounds should not be so all-encompassing that fluency and understanding in the reading process are lost.

7. There are a number of relationships between reading and writing that should influence reading instruction. As with good writing, good readers tend to be more reflective about what they have read. Good readers interact with the text in ways that poor readers do not. And in both reading and writing, students use their background experiences to construct meaning.

8. Reading vocabulary and concepts can be taught through word association charts where known words are called into play to learn unknown words. Classification schemes in which word relationships can be developed actively involve students in learning new vocabulary.

9. There are various strategies for assessing and evaluating concepts-vocabulary. Included are both aided and unaided recall, use of words in sentences, and giving synonyms/antonyms for words. Assessment/evaluative strategies for determining concept-vocabulary development also include the use of formal, standardized tests.

10. Concepts and vocabulary in reading can effectively be taught with the use of (a) journals where students keep words that they have learned; (b) a collection of words learned kept in file folders or envelopes; and (c) pictures to represent concepts for words.

11. Comprehension and critical reading skills are best taught when students are exposed to strategies in which they are asked to be active in the reading process. Important also is the careful placement of students in reading materials which closely match their reading levels. In some instances, background experiences must be expanded to aid comprehension. Graphic frameworks should be used to help students better comprehend materials being read. Modeling and effective demonstrations of comprehension and critical reading skills also help develop understanding. Specific critical reading skills must be known by teachers and taught in such a way that students see their application in everyday life. Such teaching includes the development of standards by which to judge reading materials and learning signal words/phrases which help identify critical reading skills.

12. Study skills in reading are those skills which focus on wiser, more effective use of reading. Included among these skills are reference skills, how to use headings/subheadings, use of table of contents, and other organizational skills. Study skills can be assessed/evaluated with paper/pencil activities, but also via teacher observation. Students should have ready access to how to use a study skill, once the skill is initially introduced. Placing separate skills on cards and having them nearby for use when needed is effective. Study skills should be modeled by the teacher, should be taught in context of use, and should be used often. Students should be taught how to use headings and subheadings effectively, and the *SQ3R* technique should be taught.

13. Decoding should focus on patterns used in the English language. There are several steps that should be systematically followed in learning decoding. Symbol-sound relationships should be learned by students. Pictures, audio input, use of context to recognize words, and examples of patterns of words being taught are all important in learning how to decode. Reading generalizations, like spelling generalizations, should be taught inductively, utilizing varied approaches.

14. Making drill and practice meaningful, knowing and utilizing students' interests, and using background experiences of students all contribute toward improved reading attitude. Reading attitude scales should be used as part of a systematic attack on developing more positive attitude toward reading.

15. Whether informal or commercially-prepared inventories are used to find reading levels, teachers must stress the placement of students on appropriate reading levels. Inventories usually require administration of graded word lists and graded passages. Questions are asked about materials read to determine comprehension levels. The cloze reading inventory may also be used to determine students' reading levels. Systematic noting of oral reading miscues or errors is important.

16. Microcomputers can be effective in a corrective reading program. Drill and practice and simulation activities can effectively be taught with microcomputers. Computer banks can be developed for ready access to materials for teaching reading. Commercial programs available should be wisely chosen, utilizing guidelines for selecting software packages as well as hardware itself.

17. Fluency in reading can be developed when attention is given to reading by phrases as opposed to word-by-word reading. Having students record their reading is also effective for developing fluency in reading.

Reviewing, Connecting, and Expanding What You Have Learned

(Directions) In the summary section of this chapter, each paragraph is numbered for easy reference. As you do the following activities, you may want to go back to the paragraph indicated in the activities and review what you have read. Or, in some instances, you may want to go back to the body of the chapter. These activities may be done in small groups or independently.

1. (Paragraphs 1–7) Write a one- or two-page summary of the six basic research practices on which one could build an effective student-involved corrective reading program. Then divide the six practices into segments, with each person in a small group asked to orally elaborate on the research in that area.

2. (Paragraphs 8–10) Make a chart that has three columns. Label one column, "Concepts-Vocabulary Defined," a second column, "Assessment/Evaluation of Concepts-Vocabulary," and the third column, "Teaching Concepts-Vocabulary." Under the appropriate heading, write what you remember about the topic.

3. (Paragraph 11) Write a defense for each of the following practices:
   a. Comprehension and critical reading skills are best learned when students are active in the reading process.
   b. Finding appropriate reading levels for each student is the first step toward effective teaching of comprehension and critical reading skills.
   c. Building backgrounds of students is sometimes needed for effective teaching of reading comprehension and critical reading skills.
   d. Graphic frameworks promote effective reading comprehension.

4. (Paragraph 12) Write a definition for study skills, list as many study skills as you can, and outline the steps in the SQ3R strategy.

5. (Paragraph 13) Explain how you would go about teaching students to decode three words of your choice.

6. (Paragraph 14) Explain why reading attitude is an important factor in teaching reading. List several ways that teachers might go about improving reading attitude.

7. (Paragraph 15) Identify the various steps one should follow in using the *Informal Reading Inventory*. Prepare a report to give to the class on a commercial *IRI* in use.

8. (Paragraph 16) Develop a "Do and Don't List" of how microcomputers can be used in a corrective reading program. Be prepared to add to your list when you hear other lists presented.

9. (Paragraph 17) Using the activity of having students keep an audio tape of their reading as part of a reading portfolio, set up several hypothetical objectives for a small group of students who are having trouble reading fluently.

Endnotes

1. Wayne Otto and Richard J. Smith, *Corrective and Remedial Teaching*, 3rd ed. (Boston: Houghton Mifflin Co., 1980), pp. 25–27.

2. J. Estill Alexander and Betty S. Heathington, *Assessing and Correcting Classroom Reading Problems*, (Glenview, Illinois: Scott, Foresman/Little Brown Co., 1988), p. 89.

3. Roger Farr and Robert F. Carey, *Reading—What Can be Measured?* 2nd ed. (Newark, Delaware: International Reading Association, 1986), p. 167.

4. Samuel Weintraub, "Research: The Development of Meaning Vocabulary in Reading," *The Reading Teacher* 22 (1968): 175.

5. Michael Pressley, Joel R. Levin, and Mark A. McDaniel, "Remembering Versus Inferring What a Word Means: Mnemonic and Contextual Approaches," in *The Nature of Vocabulary Acquisition*, eds. Margaret G. McKeown and Mary E. Curtis (Hillsdale, New Jersey: Lawrence Erlbaum Associates, 1987), p. 108.

6. Jeanne S. Chall, "Two Vocabularies for Reading: Recognition and Meaning," *The Nature of Vocabulary Acquisition*, eds. Margaret G. McKeown and Mary E. Curtis (Hillsdale, New Jersey: Lawrence Erlbaum Associates, 1987), p. 12.

7. Jeanne S. Chall and Steven A. Stahl, "Reading," in *Encyclopedia of Educational Research*, 5th ed., Edited by Harold E. Mitzel, Sponsored by the American Educational Research Association, (New York: The Free Press, a division of the Macmillan Co., 1982), pp. 1544–1546.

8. Robert Calfee and Priscilla Drum, "Research on Teaching Reading," in *Handbook of Research on Teaching*, 3rd ed., Merlin C. Wittrock, American Educational Research Project, (New York: Macmillan Publishing Co., 1986), p. 833.

9. Margaret G. McKeown et al., "Some Effects of the Nature and Frequency of Vocabulary Instruction on the Knowledge and Use of Words," *Reading Research Quarterly* 20 (1985): 522–535.

10. Dolores Durkin, *Teaching Them to Read*, 5th ed. (Boston: Allyn and Bacon, 1989), pp. 334–35.

11. M. Trika Smith-Burke and Lenore H. Ringler, "STAR: Teaching Reading and Writing," in *Reading Comprehension: From Research to Practice*, ed. Judith Orasanu (Hillsdale, New Jersey: Lawrence Erlbaum Associates, 1986), p. 220.

12. F. David Pearson, "A Decade of Research in Reading Comprehension," in *Research in the Language Arts—Language and Schooling*, eds. Victor Froese and Stanley B. Straw (Baltimore: University Park Press, 1981), p. 259.

13. Isabel L. Beck and Margaret G. McKeown, "Instructional Research in Reading: A Retrospective," in *Reading Comprehension: From Research to Practice*, Judith Orasanu, ed. (Hillsdale, New Jersey: Lawrence Erlbaum Associates, 1986), p. 115.

14. Page Simpson Bristow, "Are Poor Readers Passive Readers? Some Evidence, Possible Explanations, and Potential Solutions," *The Reading Teacher* 39 (1985): 318–20.

15. Ibid, 319–21.

16. D. Ray Reutzel, "Story Maps Improve Comprehension," *The Reading Teacher* 38 (1985), 400–404.

17. Lea M. McGee and Donald J. Richgels, "Teaching Expository Text Structure to Elementary Students, *The Reading Teacher* 38 (1985), 739–749.

18. Marilyn Smith and Thomas W. Bean, "Four Strategies that Develop Children's Story Comprehension and Writing," *The Reading Teacher* 37 (1983), pp. 295–301.

19. Chall and Stahl, "Reading," p. 1542.

20. Ibid.

21. Ibid.

22. Calfee and Drum, "Research on Teaching Reading," p. 812.

23. Chall and Stahl, "Reading," p. 1539.

24. Ibid.

25. Calfee and Drum, "Research on Teaching Reading," p. 813.

26. June Cannell Birnbaum, "Reflective Thought: The Connection Between Reading and Writing," *Convergences—Transactions in Reading and Writing*, Bruce T. Petersen, ed. (Urbana, Illinois: National Council of Teachers of English, 1986), pp. 30–31.

27. Sandra Stotsky, "Research on Reading/Writing Relationships: A Synthesis and Suggested Directions," *Language Arts* 60 (1983): 628, 631, 636.

28. Stephen D. Krashen, *Writing—Research, Theory, and Applications* (Oxford, England: Pergamon Press, 1984), pp. 4, 5, 8, 12.

29. Timothy Shanahan, "The Reading-Writing Relationships: Seven Instructional Principles," *The Reading Teacher* 41 (1988): 636.

30. Ibid, 637–641.

31. Robert J. Sternberg, "Most Vocabulary is Learned From Context," *The Nature of Vocabulary Acquisition*," Eds. Margaret G. McKeown and Mary E. Curtis (Hillsdale, New Jersey: Lawrence Erlbaum Associates, 1987), p. 97.

32. Durkin, *Teaching Them to Read*, p. 336.

33. Ibid.

34. Farr and Carey, *Reading—What Can Be Measured?*, pp. 96–97.

35. Ibid, p. 99.

36. Barak Rosenshine, "Teaching Functions in Instructional Programs," *The Elementary School Journal* 83 (1983): 348.

37. Richard C. Culyer, III and Gail B. Culyer, *Preventing Reading Failure—A Practical Approach* (Lanham, Maryland: University Press of America, 1987), pp. 133–135.

38. Bristow, "Are Poor Readers Passive Readers?", 321–24.

39. Smith and Bean, *"Four Strategies,"* pp. 295–298.

40. Reutzel, "Story Maps," pp. 400–404.

41. Gerald L. Fowler, "Developing Comprehension Skills in Primary Students Through the Use of Story Frames," *The Reading Teacher*, 36 (1982): 177.

42. Evelyn T. Cudd and Leslie L. Roberts, "Using Story Frames to Develop Reading Comprehension in a 1st Grade Classroom," *The Reading Teacher* 41 (1987): 74–79.

43. Josephine Gemake, "Interactive Reading: How to Make Children Active Readers," *The Reading Teacher* 37 (1984): 462.

44. Ibid, 463–65.

45. Martha Collins Cheek and Earl H. Cheek, Jr., *Diagnostic-Prescriptive Reading Instruction* (Dubuque, Iowa: Wm. C. Brown Company Publishers, 1980), p. 297.

46. Ibid, p. 310–311.

47. Ibid, pp. 311–320.

48. Arnold R. Davis, "Study Skills," in *Teaching Reading*, 3rd ed. ed. J. Estill Alexander (Glenview, Illinois: Scott, Foresman and Company, 1988), p. 261.

49. Dale D. Johnson and P. David Pearson, *Teaching Reading Vocabulary*, (New York: Holt, Rinehart and Winston, 1978), p. 61.

50. Durkin, *Teaching Them to Read*, pp. 199–205.

51. Ibid, pp. 280–282.

52. C. Glennon Rowell, "An Attitude Scale for Reading," *The Reading Teacher* 25 (1972): 442–447.

53. Christine A. McKeon and John W. McKeon, "Automated vs. Teacher Instruction: Applying Rowell's Attitude Scale for Reading," *The Reading Teacher* 32 (1978): 302–306.

54. J. Estill Alexander and Ronald Claude Filler, *Attitudes and Reading*, (Newark, Delaware: The International Reading Association, 1976), pp. 28–32.

55. J. Estill Alexander and Betty S. Heathington, *Assessing and Correcting Classroom Reading Problems*, (Glenview, Illinois: Scott, Foresman/Little Brown Co., 1988), p. 175.

56. Michael C. McKenna, "Informal Reading Inventories: A Review of the Issues," *The Reading Teacher* 36 (1983): 670–74.

57. Cheek and Cheek, *Diagnostic-Prescriptive Reading,* p. 65.

58. Ibid., pp. 65–67.

59. Jerry L. Johns, *Basic Reading Inventory—Pre-Primer-Grade Eight*, 3rd ed. (Dubuque, Iowa: Kendall/Hunt Publishing Company, 1985), p. 3.

60. Roger J. DeSanti with Renee Michelet Casbergue, and Vicki Gallo Sullivan, *The DeSanti Cloze Reading Inventory* (Boston: Allyn and Bacon, 1986), p. vii.

61. International Reading Association, "Guidelines for Educators on Using Computers in the School," *The Reading Teacher* 38 (1984): 80–81.

62. Ernest Balajthy, "Reinforcement and Drill by Microcomputers," *The Reading Teacher* 37 (1984): 490

63. Ernest Balajthy, "Computer Simulations and Reading," *The Reading Teacher* 37 (1984): 590–92.

64. Carolyn P. Casteel, "Computer Skill Banks for Classroom and Clinic," *The Reading Teacher* 38 (1984): 294–298.

65. Queue, *Toward Better Reading Skills, Teacher's Manual*, (Fairfield, Connecticut: Queue, 1985), pp. 1–2.

66. International Business Machines Corporation, *Writing to Read* (White Plains, New York: International Business Machines Corporation, 1990), p. 4.

Bibliography

Comprehension/Critical Reading

Carr, Eileen; Dewitz, Peter; and Patberg, Judythe. "Using Cloze for Inference Training With Expository Text," *The Reading Teacher* 42 (1989): 380.

Durkin, Dolores. "What is the Value of the New Interest in Reading Comprehension?" *Language Arts* 58 (1981): 23.

Fitzgerald, Jill. "Helping Readers Gain Self-Control Over Reading Comprehension," *The Reading Teacher* 37 (1983): 249.

Pearson, P. David and Johnson, Dale D. *Teaching Reading Comprehension* (New York: Holt, Rinehart, and Winston, 1978).

Rakes, Thomas A. and Choate, Joyce S., "Reading Comprehension," In *Language Arts— Detecting and Correcting Special Needs* by Rakes and Choate (Boston: Allyn and Bacon, 1989) pp. 100–113.

Schell, Leo M., "Dilemmas in Assessing Reading Comprehension," *The Reading Teacher* 42 (1988): 12.

Wagoner, Shirley A. "Comprehension Monitoring: What it is and What We Know About It," *Reading Research Quarterly*, 18 (1983): 328.

Teaching/Grouping Procedures

Gambrell, Linda B., Wilson, Robert M., and Gantt, Walter N., "Classroom Observation of Task-Attending Behaviors of Good and Poor Readers," *Journal of Educational Research* 74 (1981): 400.

Decoding

Adams, Marilyn Jager. "Issues in the Teaching of Phonics," In *Beginning to Read—Thinking and Learning About Print*, by Adams (Urbana, Illinois: Center for the Study of Reading, The Reading Research and Education Center, The University of Illinois, Urbana-Champaign, 1990), pp. 73–87.

_____. "Decoding, Context, and Fluency," In *Beginning to Read—Thinking and Learning About Print*, by Adams (Urbana, Illinois: Center for the Study of Reading, The Reading Research and Education Center, The University of Illinois, 1990), pp. 88–94.

Gaskins, Robert W., Gaskins, Jennifer, and Gaskins, Irene W., "A Decoding Program for Poor Readers—And the Rest of the Class, Too!" *Language Arts* 68 (1991): 213.

Freppon, Penny A. and Dahl, Karin. "Learning About Phonics in a Whole Language Classroom," *Language Arts* 68 (1991): 190.

Reading Attitude/Cooperative Reading Teams

Madden, Lowell. "Improving Reading Attitudes of Poor Readers Through Cooperative Reading Teams," *The Reading Teacher* 42 (1988): 194.

Miscellaneous

Armbruster, Bonnie B., Anderson, Thomas H., and Ostertag, Joyce. "Teaching Text Structure to Improve Reading and Writing," *The Reading Teacher* 43 (1989): 130.

Reutzel, D. Ray and Fawson, Parker C., "Using a Literature Webbing Strategy Lesson With Predictable Books," *The Reading Teacher* 43 (1989): 208.

10

*Implementing and Evaluating
a Corrective Language
Arts Program*

In implementing a new program in schools, the first step should be the establishment of specific, reachable goals. In a student-involved corrective language arts program, themes that have been consistently identified in this book can be developed into goals for a school or school system to strive for in the implementation of the type of program that has been outlined in the preceding chapters. The themes that have appeared throughout this book are:

1. Use students' interests in a systematic way and as extensively as possible
2. Establish *base groups* to meet developmental needs of students
3. Establish *flex groups* to meet special-instructional needs of students
4. Involve students in collaborative/cooperative learning
5. Involve students in activities in which they analyze their progress, identify their problems (where possible), and evaluate progress made in the language arts
6. Accommodate different learning styles of students
7. Use many types of materials, including manipulatives
8. Use a variety of assessment techniques, including observations, conferences, and informal testing
9. Use a variety of teaching strategies, including coaching, modeling, demonstrating, and small-group instruction

Upon accepting these themes as goals, the next step is to establish strategies for reaching the goals. Following this step, a school or school system should develop a procedure for evaluating progress being made. The evaluation procedure should not only be devised to focus on determining how well the strategies are implemented and functioning when the program begins, but continuously throughout the process and life of the new program. Evaluation of school programs is a never-ending process.

Strategies for Setting up Goals

The first phase of planning, after having studied a program such as the one advocated in this book, is to examine the accepted goals to see how they can best be developed and tried out in a school or school system. There are numerous ways. Teachers on one grade level may take one or two of the goals and develop systems for implementing the goals. For example, teachers in second-grade might volunteer or be encouraged to work on a system for implementing goals two and three (setting up base and flex groups). In consultation with other teachers in the school, these teachers would decide in which areas of the language arts both types of groups would be established. If they decided base and flex groups would be established in reading, spelling, and writing for the total year, and listening and speaking for selected units, a plan should be established by the second-grade teachers not only to set up systems to work in the second grade, but also systems that could be shared with other teachers. Where teachers in a school are working to implement a schoolwide system, everyone assigned to a task must consider how to carry out that task in all grade levels where the language arts are taught.

Some teachers in the school would select other goals that they would implement in their classrooms and share with other teachers as the school moves toward a corrective language arts program. Again, the focus of implementing and sharing strategies for reaching a designated or selected goal would not be on single activities or ideas but a system or procedure that ultimately the whole school might adopt. For example, if the fourth-grade teachers selected as one of their goals the using of students' interests in a systematic way, these teachers would either develop or find appropriate interest inventories; develop guidelines for using the inventories; provide examples of ways to use interests in: (1) separate lessons; (2) clusters of lessons; (3) units of study; (4) content fields; (5) lessons where the emphasis is on skill development; (6) vocabulary lessons; and/or combinations of these various responsibilities. They would find or develop strategies that could apply to children in the lower grades as well as those in the upper grades. The task of the fourth-grade teachers, as well as for other teachers, would be comprehensive.

Another approach to implementing goals would be to have teams of teachers across several grade levels working on the same goals, but again, with the focus that what they are doing is not only for their grade level, but for the total school. For example, a team made up of a first-grade teacher, a third-grade teacher, and a fifth-grade teacher might work on goals two and three which deal with establishing the two types of grouping systems aimed at meeting developmental and special needs of students.

If a total school system chose to move to the student-involved corrective language arts model outlined in this book, individual schools might select a small number of goals and work extensively to provide systems that other schools could adopt (perhaps with some modifications to meet localized needs).

An individual teacher in a school could likewise choose to implement a student-involved corrective language arts program as outlined in this book. While a teacher working alone might be forced to move more slowly than a group of teachers working together could move, a system still could be made operational within a relatively short period of time. One way that a teacher who is working solo on a corrective program could implement such a program is to select a language arts area per semester to begin setting up base and flex groups, developing appropriate materials, finding students' interests, and working on other goals outlined at the beginning of this chapter.

Whether a grade-level group, a combination grade-level group, a system, or an individual teacher plans to implement a corrective language arts program, a system should be established that incorporates the various language arts curricula in place. The system should indicate the model proposed as well as the language arts to operate within this model. For purposes of review, Figure 2–1 is reproduced as Figure 10–1. As can be seen, Model 1 calls for the total class of 25–35 students to be subdivided into smaller groups for special-needs instruction. In Model 2, developmental groups are already formed and smaller breakout groups are formed for special-needs instruction.

Initially, it might be more feasible for Model 1 to be made operable in one or two of the language arts, with a goal in mind of gradually moving these language arts subjects toward Model 2. For teachers who have spent a long time teaching to the whole class, rather than individuals in the class, transition may be difficult. Implementing Model 1 and gradually moving toward Model 2 might make these teachers feel more comfortable as they move away from whole-class teaching. In addition, the efficiency with which a student-involved corrective program is implemented would probably be higher.

The following schedule, based on how language arts are now organized and taught, is a suggested pattern:

1. Semester 1, *Reading*—selected because most schools now have developmental groups in reading. Model 2 in Figure 10–1 would probably be more appropriate for adoption of the student-involved corrective approach to instruction presented in this book. More focus in reading would be on developing and implementing flex groups, which for some teachers might be increasing the number and systematizing the operation of special-skills groups already in place.

2. Semester 2, *Spelling*—Continue what has been started with the reading program, but add spelling as a subject to be taught, using flexible grouping plans. Set up base and flex groups in spelling. Start out with a manageable number of base groups (perhaps just two to begin with) but then gradually increase the number of

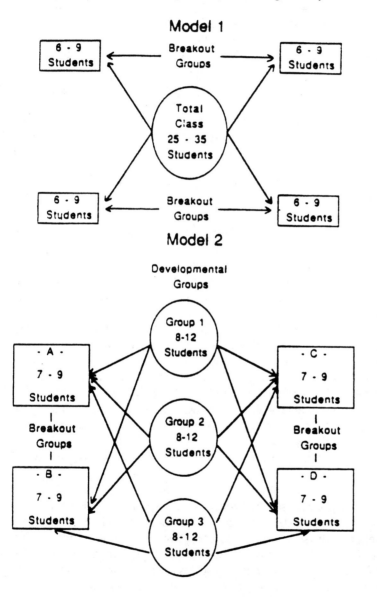

FIGURE 10–1   Two Models for Flexible Grouping

groups in order to have students operating on the most appropriate level. Thus, for spelling, Model 1 in Figure 10–1 may be followed initially but with a gradual movement toward Model 2.

3. Semester 2 (next to last six weeks in the semester)—Set up base and flex groups in yet a third area, perhaps handwriting for primary-grade teachers and written composition for upper-grade teachers. The purpose of adding this third area at this particular time is for teachers to get a feel for how one orchestrates these groups across three language arts areas. Having three base-flex group combinations going for a relatively short period of time (six weeks) will help teachers gradually learn management skills that they can sharpen and use later on when corrective teaching becomes standard in the school. Also, at this point, there may be some opportunities to see how some cross-subject areas can be taught, on occasion, together. Integration of the language arts is made easier when students in base and flex groups are moving into a wider variety of subject matter than when all students in a class are presented the same topic and move together (at least in motion, but not in learning) through the language arts.

During the following year, the same teachers should feel comfortable in the implementation of a student-involved corrective program in reading and spelling and ready to sharpen their skills in providing corrective instruction in a third area. Later in the second year, a decision can be made to begin reviewing the listening-speaking curriculum to see where there might be units or mini-units that would be better taught following a corrective approach. It might be appropriate at this point to combine listening-speaking with other language arts, thus teaching several subjects as a broad unit, but doing so while incorporating all or part of the nine themes advocated in this book as goals to be implemented.

How the second year of a student-involved corrective program might look is presented again in Table 10–1, adapted from Table 2–2, Chapter 2. Committees of teachers, armed with their assignments of developing strategies for carrying out specific goals, might set up a timetable that parallels this yearly plan for implementing base and flex groups.

Developing Procedures for Evaluating Goals Established For a Corrective Language Arts Program

Once goals have been identified, timelines developed for reaching the goals, and an equitable and logical division of responsibilities relating to the goals established, the next step is to work out a procedure for reaching the goals. Such a procedure should involve evaluation during the process of setting up and implementing strategies for carrying out the goals as well as evaluation when the goals have been fully implemented. An evaluation during the formative stages of development of a

TABLE 10–1   Yearly Plan for Implementing Base and Flex Groups

Language Arts Area	September	October-November	December-January	February-March	April-May
Reading	Three *Base Groups* Formed	⟶	⟶	*Base Groups* Reevaluated	Three *Base Groups* in Operation
	Several *Flex Groups* in Operation	- - ⟶	- - ⟶	- - ⟶	- - ⟶
Writing	Writing Needs of Students Studied		*Base Groups* Formed Linked to Base *Groups* in Reading	⟶	⟶
		Flex Groups in Writing in Operation	- - ⟶	- - ⟶	- - ⟶
Spelling	Four *Base Groups* Formed	⟶	*Base Groups* Evaluated	Three *Base Groups* in Operation	⟶
	Several *Flex Groups* in Operation	- - ⟶	- - ⟶	- - ⟶	- - ⟶
Handwriting	Three *Base Groups* Formed	⟶	⟶	*Base Groups* Reevaluated	Three *Base Groups* in Operation
	Several *Flex Groups* in Operation	- - ⟶	- - ⟶	- - ⟶	- - ⟶
Speaking*	Speaking Skills Assessed	Cooperative Learning Teams in Operation	⇒	⇒	
			Some Large Class Instruction	*Flex Groups* in Operation	- - ⟶
Listening*	Listening Skills Assessed	Listening Center Activities	⇒	Two *Base Groups* Formed	⟶
		Some Large Group Instruction	⇒	*Flex Groups* in Operation	- - ⟶

Key: ⟶ Base Groups Continue   - - ⟶ Flex Groups Continue

⇒ Other Instructional Groups in Operation

*May be primarily taught in context of other subjects as discussed in the chapters on these language arts areas

flex group system can be given as an example. Teachers who are working on a systematic procedure of setting up and using flex groups that the entire school will eventually adopt in reading and spelling, should establish plans for trying out the system. In some cases, these teachers might be trying out two slightly different systems. After a relatively brief period of operation in which they have observed each other as the system is implemented, the teachers come together and decide which approach is more effective and what adjustments are needed. They discuss with other teachers what they are doing in planning a flex group system for the school. They discuss what they are doing with their supervisors. Always, during the early stages of development and implementation of a defined goal, teachers should be open to change, remembering that their focus is on the development of a system that works in the teacher's busy work day. Streamlining of a system is necessary, and teachers on the committee setting up a flex group system should seek advice specifically on this topic from all teachers and administrators in a school. During the same time, teachers on a committee will have to be convincing, for there are always skeptics. Committee members might share with others how *students are involved in assessing/evaluating their problems/progress.* When teachers not on the committee see that this can be done, fears, doubts, and other factors that could interfere with the setting up of a flexible grouping plan should be lessened.

A hypothetical workplan is shown in Table 10–2 that might well be one that a team of teachers at an elementary school uses for the purpose of developing and implementing a flex grouping system at a large elementary school. The team consists of five teachers who have been assigned the goal of setting up a system of flex groups for the entire school. Three teachers come from the primary grades and two teachers come from the upper-elementary grades.

Teachers on the committee should also seek advice from teachers on the faculty who believe in and have implemented different kinds of language arts programs, not that these teachers would be excluded from various committees. For example, if teachers at a particular grade level have been studying and implementing a *whole language program,* these teachers should give input concerning how their "new" program would (and in some ways, would not) mesh with the student-involved corrective goals outlined for the school.

As can be seen in Table 10–2, the workplan is subdivided into specific tasks in spelling. For example, setting up a streamlined, systematic way to study students' weekly spelling errors is shown as a task that Mr. Carlson, sixth-grade teacher, is to do. Mr. Carlson, in carrying out this task, would be expected to read as much as possible on weekly spelling tests and how they are administered, graded, and used in schools. Mr. Carlson should do more than "think" about his task. He would actually be involved in finding out what other schools or school systems have done. Some procedures that he might learn in his efforts to find different ways for analyzing students' weekly spelling papers, and that, in part, have been discussed in this book follow:

1. Students use a form for recording their spelling errors, exactly as they are made. The form is kept in each student's folder and is periodically analyzed by the teacher.

2. Students write spelling tests on paper with six columns to the right of the space where the words are written. Each column has a title as shown: Column 1, *Letter(s) omitted*; Column 2, *Letter(s) added*; Column 3, *Wrong letter(s) used*; Column 4, *Wrong word spelled*; Column 5, *Other error.* Students analyze their papers and place a check mark in the appropriate column when a word is missed. Records of which problems are the most troublesome are kept and corrective strategies are planned by the teacher.

3. Students pair up and help analyze samples of each other's papers, including both written work in various subjects and the weekly spelling test papers. Each student writes what he/she thinks is a major problem the other student is having such as "errors with endings of words," or "doesn't appear to be able to spell words with *long a* sounds." This is done each week for several weeks and the notes made on each other's papers are placed in a spelling folder for the teacher to see.

4. The teacher keeps a card file of major kinds of spelling errors made. He/she selects five to seven students for individual, brief (five-minute) conferences for the purpose of looking at the last three or four spelling papers to determine what problems are most critical for each student. The teacher enters errors identified on the appropriate cards, along with which student appears to be having the problems.

TABLE 10–2   Setting Up Flex Groups in Spelling

Teacher	Tasks to do	Date to be Accomplished
Mr. Carlson 6th Grade	Task 1—Determine most efficient ways to analyze students' written work to determine types of spelling errors made	September 30
Miss Jennings 2nd Grade	Task 2—Develop a system for keeping up with progress students make in several *base groups* and errors made in *flex groups*	October 7
Mrs. Silvers 1st Grade	Task 3—With Mrs. Dixon, help set up a system or series of systems for packaging and using multiple kinds of materials and equipment for the school's spelling program	October 14
Mrs. Dixon 5th Grade	Task 3—Cited above (Same as Mrs. Silvers' task)	October 14
Mr. Boyd 3rd Grade	Task 4—Determine best way to adapt the school's current spelling curriculum to *flex grouping* plans	October 21

After several weeks of holding such conferences, the teacher is ready for "special instruction," regrouping students according to the types of errors with which they are having the most problems.

5. Students' spelling errors made throughout the week (in spelling and in writing throughout the curriculum) are recorded on a microcomputer. Six students are the "recorders" and have assigned to them four or five students for whom they are responsible for recording a list of misspelled words submitted to them by their group members. The teacher has a system for grouping the errors on the computer and forming special lessons to help students with common problems.

These five procedures are brought to the flex-grouping committee meetings. Members of the committee decide that each of them will try out procedures one and three together to see how easy it is to administer the two systems as well as to see how meaningful the results are. One teacher has a computer in her room and agrees to try out the fifth procedure instead of procedure number two. A nine-week trial period is set, but the teachers agree to meet at least three times during the nine-week period to discuss how well their tryouts are going and to make adjustments as needed.

At the same time that teachers on the team are trying out strategies coming out of Mr. Carlson's task, other strategies are being tried out. The procedures decided upon by the committee setting up a system for flex grouping would go through the similar process of studying what can be done about tracking student progress (Task 2), packaging/using multiple materials for spelling instruction (Task 3), and adapting the school's spelling curriculum to flex grouping (Task 4). Decisions would also be made about evaluating strategies that evolved from the other three tasks. While the simultaneous trying out/evaluating of different systems might appear to be cumbersome, it should be remembered that several, somewhat different systems will eventually be operating at the same time. A part of the success of the development/evaluation of setting up flex groups would be how well different strategies can be made to operate together.

When the trial period is completed and last-minute adjustments made, teachers on a small committee might evaluate what they have decided/developed in any number of ways. One way is to have two or more teachers from within the school but not on the committee to hear the recommendations of the committee prior to the total faculty being presented with a recommended plan. The "hearing committee" should be made up of at least one teacher from the primary grades and one from the upper-elementary school grades. The committee would present its recommendations, show examples of what strategies have been developed, and discuss how the strategies have been "debugged" during tryouts.

Another approach would be to have someone from outside the school but within the school system, such as a supervisor, be on the team to hear the overall plans presented. Some adjustments might be made at this time, but hopefully these would be modest.

When a system for implementing a goal is believed to be operational and a larger group of teachers begin to use it, a period of time is designated as a "schoolwide tryout" period. It might be a semester, two six-week periods, or in some cases a month. Whatever the agreed-upon period, teachers should set a time as well as some criteria for doing an evaluation of the system. Some suggested criteria, phrased as questions to be asked, follow:

1. Is the overall system (in this case, setting up flex groups) streamlined and functional?

2. In what way is the new system an improvement of the regular system (in this case, mostly large-group teaching of the same lessons in spelling) now in place?

3. How can we prove that the recommended system is better than any other proposal the committee might have made?

4. In what ways will we determine that spelling performance of students improves after the system is in operation for a reasonable time?

5. In what ways does the proposed system fit the overall language arts program in our school?

In order to answer these questions, it will be necessary for teachers in a school to be specific about what they expect. For example, in criterion four, it will be necessary for the teachers to decide what kind of improvement they expect in spelling. While it would be easy to say that improved performance on standardized tests in spelling would be the criterion, it is hoped that no school system would depend on such a criterion alone as the way to determine if performance by the general student body of the school has improved. Some notation should be made of the transfer value of spelling. Do students spell better in the content fields now than before flex groups were implemented? Are students more interested in spelling where flex groups have been implemented than before? Do students appear to be better at analyzing their own spelling papers than prior to flex grouping? These are some questions that might be influenced by the new grouping system and teachers should be alert to the possible influence that flex groups have in these areas. It would be naive to believe that one could trace improvement in these areas to one variable, but some general influence might be detected. Teachers, in talking to students, can determine if the new flexible-grouping scheme is liked by them, how they feel the plan is helping (or hurting) them, and so on.

Evaluation of the systems for student-involved corrective teaching would continue to be made. Modifications of the program would be made, where needed. In fact, the systems put in place might look quite differently three years after being fully implemented. Making changes is what being a professional is all about. Teachers in a school, through reading of professional journals and books, through attending professional meetings, and through creating, on their own, systems and procedures for teaching the language arts, can vastly improve what now goes on in language arts.

Author Index

Subject Index

Phonics (as part of decoding), 344–345
Presentation of spelling words
  context (indirect) approach, 94
  direct (list) approach, 94
Prescriptive programs, 8
Primary-Secondary Education Act, 234
Processes (definition of), 3
Programmed instructional materials, 61–62
Progress checklists (for listening), 256
Project teaching
  in British primary schools, 44
  and flex groups, 45
  in the language arts, 44
  and webbing, 45
Pronunciation
  definition of, 303–304
  errors, 305
Proofreading of
  handwriting, 211
  spelling, 114
Province of British Columbia, 223

Rating scales (for oral language), 307
Reading
  as active process, 321–322
  behaviors, 321
  effects on writing, 146, 323–324
  generalizations, 350
  groups (problems with), 36
  interest in, 350
  levels and how to find them, 353–356
  relationships with writing, 145–146, 323–324
  and writing instruction, 323–324
  and writing processes, 145
Research practices (for corrective teaching)
  in handwriting, 187–191
  in listening, 235–239
  in oral communication, 274–278
  in reading, 318–324
  in spelling, 90–97
  in writing, 138–148
Rinsland List for spelling, 107, 113
Role playing (in listening), 252

Schema in reading comprehension, 333
Scott, Foresman and Company, 262n
Seatwork, 59
Self-analysis in handwriting, 211
Self-competition in schools, 79
Self/assessment, evaluative strategies, 114–122
Sentence combining
  definition of, 140
  with microcomputers, 171
  transformations in, 140
Sentence writing (modeling of), 57
Sharing, 296
Show-and-Tell, 296
Signal words/phrases
  in critical reading, 342
  in detecting sequence, 260
  in listening, 255
Single concept cards, 331
Skills
  definition of, 3
  learning of, 4
Slant (in handwriting), 220–221

Small-group discussions
  assessment of participation in, 287–291
  brainstorming, 288–290
  bull/buzz groups, 287
  facilitation of, 275–276
  forms to use, 291–295
  task groups, 291
  tips for conducting, 284–286
  roles of participants, 291–292
Small-group instruction 21
Small Group Teaching (SGT)
  as cooperative learning strategy, 42
  for handwriting instruction, 210
The Snowy Day, 261–262
Speaking instruction (neglect in school), 273
Special-needs instruction, 36–38
Speech speed/thought speed differential, 238–239, 255–256
Spelling curriculum
  for base groups, 104–105
  for corrective teaching, 99–103
Spelling errors
  analysis of, 109
  in a corrective program, 378
  follow-up of, 122
  reminder cards, 114–115
  tracking of, 109–111, 120–122
  types of, 109–111
Spelling generalizations
  controversy in teaching, 94
  deductive teaching of, 95
  guidelines for teaching, 94–95
  inductive teaching of, 95
  and reading generalizations, 350
Spelling levels, 106–108
Spelling patterns
  activities for teaching, 118–119
  contrastive activities, 122–123
  transformations in, 118
Spelling tests
  for finding grade levels, 106–108
  importance of, 95–96
Spelling textbooks/workbooks
  adapting to corrective teaching, 99
  misuse of, 99
Spelling word lists, 108
Sperry Corporation, 234
SQ3R study skills approach, 344
Standardized tests
  kinds of, 73
  major characteristics of, 72
  in reading, 330
Standards
  in critical reading, 341
  in teaching (in general), 81
Stanford Reading Diagnostic Test, 73, 330
Stanford Spelling Project, 92, 97
Starter lines (in writing), 152
Story frames (for writing), 167–168, 333–334
Story grammars, 145
Story maps, 333
Storytelling, 261
Strange Little River, 251
Students in corrective programs
  as active, involved learners, 78
  as daily users of language, 83